MATHEMATICAL PROGRAMMING
Optimization models for business
and management decision-making

MATHEMATICAL PROGRAMMING

Optimization models for business and management decision-making

Mik Wisniewski
Principal Lecturer in Quantitative Methods
Leeds Polytechnic

Tony Dacre
Senior Lecturer in Information Systems
Leeds Polytechnic

McGRAW-HILL BOOK COMPANY

London · New York · St Louis · San Francisco · Auckland · Bogotá · Caracas · Hamburg
Lisbon · Madrid · Mexico · Milan · Montreal · New Delhi · Panama · Paris · San Juan
São Paulo · Singapore · Sydney · Tokyo · Toronto

Published by
McGRAW-HILL Book Company (UK) Limited
Shoppenhangers Road, Maidenhead, Berkshire, SL6 2QL, England
Telephone 0628 23432
Fax 0628 35895

British Library Cataloguing in Publication Data
Wisniewski, Mik
  Mathematical programming: optimization models for
  business and management decision-making.
  1. Management. Decision making. Mathematical models
  I. Title II. Dacre, Tony
  658.4'033
  ISBN 0–07–707223–5

Library of Congress Cataloging-in-Publication Data
Wisniewski, Mik.
  Mathematical programming: optimization models for
  business and management decision-making/Mik
  Wisniewski, Tony Dacre.
  p.   cm.
  ISBN 0–07–707223–5
  1. Decision-making—Mathematical models.
  2. Mathematical optimization.
  I. Dacre, Tony.
  II. Title.
  HD30.23.W565   1990
  658.4'033—dc20   89-13664

Copyright © 1990 McGraw-Hill Book Company (UK) Limited. All rights reserved. No part of this publication may be reproduced, stored in a retrieval system, or transmitted, in any form or by any means, electronic, mechanical, photocopying, recording, or otherwise, without the prior permission of McGraw-Hill Book Company (UK) Limited.

12345 RC 93210

Typeset by Wyvern Typesetting Ltd, Bristol
Printed by Clays Ltd, St Ives plc

Dedicated to our wives and families who have had to put up with our absence (both physical and mental) whilst writing this book

To

Cherrie, Marcus and Rebecca

Hazel (who threatened dire consequences if she didn't appear in the dedication of the next book)

MW and AND

CONTENTS

Preface xi

1 Introduction 1
   1-1 The focus of the text 2
   1-2 Contents of the text 4
   1-3 The general approach adopted in the text 5
   1-4 The management science process 7
   1-5 The use of models in decision-making 11
   1-6 Mathematical prerequisites 14
   1-7 Summary 14

Part A Transportation and assignment 15

2 The transportation model 17
   2-1 The business problem 17
   2-2 Formulating the basic transportation model 18
   2-3 Finding an initial feasible solution 22
   2-4 Testing for an improved solution: the stepping stone method 24
   2-5 Testing for an improved solution: the modified distribution method 31
   2-6 Summary 38
       Student exercises 38

3 Extensions to the transportation model 43
   3-1 Unbalanced transportation problems 43
   3-2 Maximization problems 50
   3-3 Prohibited and priority routes 53
   3-4 Sensitivity analysis 58
   3-5 Degeneracy 67

	3-6 Transportation in practice	70
	Student exercises	71

4 The assignment model — 72
- 4-1 The business problem — 72
- 4-2 Formulating the basic assignment model — 73
- 4-3 The solution program: the Hungarian method — 74
- 4-4 Extensions to the basic model — 80
- 4-5 Sensitivity analysis — 85
- 4-6 Assignment models in practice — 86
- Student exercises — 87

Part B Linear programming — 89

5 Linear programming: problem formulation and the graphical solution method — 91
- 5-1 The business problem — 92
- 5-2 Problem formulation — 93
- 5-3 The graphical solution — 96
- 5-4 Extensions to the graphical method — 104
- 5-5 Summary — 111
- Student exercises — 113

6 Linear programming applications — 114
- 6-1 The process of problem formulation — 114
- 6-2 Resource allocation/product mix problems — 116
- 6-3 Production scheduling — 116
- 6-4 Labour scheduling — 119
- 6-5 Blending/diet/feed-mix problems — 122
- 6-6 Marketing and media-mix applications — 124
- 6-7 Financial analysis — 128
- 6-8 Data envelopment analysis — 130
- 6-9 Summary — 133
- Student exercises — 133

7 The Simplex method — 138
- 7-1 Simplex formulation — 139
- 7-2 The initial tableau — 141
- 7-3 The solution program — 143
- 7-4 Dealing with other types of constraint — 150
- 7-5 Minimization problems — 160
- 7-6 Summary — 167
- Student exercises — 167

8 Sensitivity analysis — 168
- 8-1 Changes in constraints: maximization problems — 169
- 8-2 Minimization problems — 178
- 8-3 Summary of the interpretation of changes in binding constraints — 183
- 8-4 Changes in the objective function: basic variables — 183
- 8-5 Summary of sensitivity analysis — 189
- 8-6 Sensitivity analysis: an example — 190
- 8-7 Conclusion — 192
- Student exercises — 192

9 Extensions to linear programming — 194
- 9-1 The dual — 194
- 9-2 The dual formulation — 197
- 9-3 The relationship between the primal and dual problems — 200
- 9-4 The dual and computational efficiency — 203
- 9-5 Special problems — 204
- 9-6 Assumptions of the basic LP model — 213
- 9-7 Summary — 219
- Student exercises — 219

Part C Further mathematical programming models — 221

10 Integer linear programming — 223
- 10-1 LP and ILP: the gulf between — 224
- 10-2 Binary decision variables — 226
- 10-3 Specification of variable types — 227
- 10-4 A further use for binary variables — 228
- 10-5 Conditional logic in decision models — 231
- 10-6 Threshold constraints — 232
- 10-7 Adjustable constraints — 233
- 10-8 Fixed-charge problems — 235
- 10-9 Combinations of fixed charges — 238
- 10-10 Common relationships in ILP — 240
- 10-11 Non-linear objective functions — 243
- 10-12 Summary — 246
- Student exercises — 246

11 Solution methods for integer linear programming — 249
- 11-1 A branch and bound method — 250
- 11-2 A cutting plane method — 258
- 11-3 An enumeration method — 267
- 11-4 Computational experience — 275
- 11-5 Summary — 277
- Student exercises — 277

12 Goal programming — 280
- 12-1 Soft constraints — 281
- 12-2 Constructing goal programs — 282
- 12-3 Graphical solution — 285
- 12-4 Goals with unlimited targets — 287
- 12-5 A Simplex method for goal programming — 288
- 12-6 Summary — 291
- Student exercises — 292

13 Non-linear programming — 294
- 13-1 Non-linear objective functions and constraints — 294
- 13-2 A review of differential calculus — 299
- 13-3 Lagrange multipliers — 306
- 13-4 The Kuhn–Tucker conditions — 308
- 13-5 Quadratic programming — 312
- 13-6 Linear approximations of non-linear functions — 315
- 13-7 Summary — 321
- Student exercises — 322

14 Dynamic programming — 323
- 14-1 A shortest-route problem — 324
- 14-2 Characteristics of the dynamic programming approach — 329
- 14-3 Knapsack problems — 330
- 14-4 The curse of dimensionality — 334
- 14-5 A problem in order scheduling — 335
- 14-6 The mathematics of dynamic programming — 338
- 14-7 A problem in reliability — 343
- 14-8 A stochastic planning problem — 346
- 14-9 Summary — 350
- Student exercises — 351

Appendix — 354

Bibliography — 356

Index — 361

PREFACE

Over the past few decades there has developed an active and increasing awareness of the role that mathematics and statistics can play in assisting the decision-maker in a business organization. Over the last ten years or so the revolution that has occurred in computing technology has meant that powerful computing facilities are available—literally—on the desk of any decision-maker who wants them. The impact that the advent of such cost-effective technology has had upon quantitative business analysis should not be underestimated. The day-to-day use of such techniques by the decision-maker has proliferated beyond most, if not all, expectations.

One area of quantitative analysis where this impact has been particularly noticeable is that of mathematical programming: those mathematical models that are concerned with finding the 'best' solution to a problem involving alternative and competing uses of limited resources. It is readily apparent that this type of problem is typically one that concerns the decision-maker in every organization. Both as a result of this technological revolution, and as a result of developing management education and training, the interest in these types of mathematical models continues to grow. It is this developing awareness amongst management of the potential usefulness of such mathematical programming models in the decision-making process that has prompted us to write this book.

We are aware that there are a number of books already available in this area, but these generally tend, in our view, to be aimed either at the management science specialist (who has a level of mathematical ability far beyond most managers) or at the reader who is simply trying to get the flavour of the topic without being able to put the techniques into practice. As a result such texts tend either to be too mathematically oriented or far too simplistic in their approach.

As a result we feel that far too often a gap exists between the quantitative specialist and the decision-maker: between the provider of such information and the user of such information. Management science specialists may develop and apply models that are technically 'perfect', but which fail to provide usable information to the decision-maker. Equally, the decision-maker may not have the knowledge or ability to assess the reliability and usefulness of the information that such models generate.

This text is aimed specifically at managers (both practising and potential) who wish to develop their practical expertise in mathematical programming without getting lost in the supporting mathematics. The text introduces in turn the major models and gradually develops an understanding of their structure and their solution process without losing sight of the prime use of such models: the provision of potentially useful management information. As a result the business decision-maker (and the business student) will be able to develop a critical awareness of the role that such models can play in the organization. As such the text is suitable for students across a wide range of subjects: accounting, business administration, economics, finance, management, business studies, and the like, and will be appropriate both for those who are being introduced to the techniques for the first time and for those who are investigating them in more depth and detail.

To assist in this, the text is accompanied by a set of IBM PC (and compatible) programs that will allow the reader both to follow easily the relevant calculations (without having to resort to manual arithmetic) and to experiment with the models introduced so as to assess the way they function and the information they can generate.

At the same time the text will also be useful to the management science specialist who wishes to develop an understanding of the role of such models in the business world and from the perspective of the decision-maker. Information generated by such models must be capable of being used by management if it is to be useful and worth while.

It is our belief that after reading this book both groups will have a better understanding of the practical role such models have to play in the decision-making process.

Mik Wisniewski
Tony Dacre

1
INTRODUCTION

This text has a dual focus. The first is an interest in a particular type of mathematical model—the mathematical programming model—whilst the second is an interest in the potential and actual application of such models to business problems. This two-fold interest is reflected both in the content of the text and in the way the material is introduced and discussed. The text is primarily concerned with how such models can be applied and used in the management decision-making process—an interest, in other words, in the *application* of such models rather than in their *theory*. However, an appreciation of the mathematical logic underpinning these models is essential if the decision-maker is to be in a position to evaluate the reliability of the information generated. We introduce relevant mathematical theory where it is necessary to support an adequate understanding of the relevance of a model to business decision-making.

It is evident that the major role of a manager in any type of business organization relates to decision-making and to problem solving. The key to effective decision-making lies with information. Adequate and accurate information is required by the manager and, equally important, such information must be assessed and used in the most appropriate way to help in the decision-making process. Increasingly such decisions have to be taken in situations which are both complex and dynamic. Equally, with the ever-increasing pace of technological change—particularly in the area of computing technology—the manager is faced with increasing pressure to access more information than ever and to process, use and interpret this information in a rational and systematic way. Partly as a consequence of such pressures, the last few decades have seen a rapid expansion of the application of scientific methods and techniques to the area of management decision-making. Such methods and techniques are generally referred to as *management science* or *operational research*. The manager today is expected not only to apply such techniques to a wide range of business problems but, at the same time, to be able to assess and use the information that such techniques provide.

This text aims to introduce a particular group of such management science techniques and at the same time provide an adequate appreciation and understanding of the information such techniques provide and the areas of business activity where they can play a useful role. The authors recognize that, typically, the manager is largely disinterested in the mechanics of the solution process of such techniques and to some extent this is reflected in the approach adopted in the text. The focus at each stage is firmly on a conceptual understanding of the processes and calculations involved whilst at the same time providing an adequate theoretical and technical understanding of the technique. In short, the text aims to enable the manager to apply such techniques to a business problem, to determine the technique solution and to assess the implications and usefulness of the information contained in the solution.

1-1 THE FOCUS OF THE TEXT

The text focuses on a particular group of management science models, referred to collectively as *mathematical programming*. Typically many business problems involve, in some way, the allocation of scarce resources: the manager will have at his or her disposal a limited supply of some, if not all, resources and must decide how best to use these resources. The resources referred to, of course, may be extremely varied: manpower, raw materials, finance, floorspace, machinery, vehicles and so on. More formally, we can say that such problems will revolve around the attainment of some declared objective in the face of some defined set of constraints. The manager's problem then becomes one of trying to decide how best to achieve this objective within the existing limits of the problem. In their crudest form, mathematical programming techniques are concerned with determining the 'best' decision in situations where a range of alternative decisions are available to the manager. Typical business problems that follow this structure would include the following:

- A firm trying to decide on the combination of output that will maximize profit. The firm will face certain restrictions, or constraints, in that it will have a limited supply of certain resources such as manpower, raw materials, floorspace, capital and so on. In some way the objective has to be attained within the existing constraints.
- A hospital trying to keep its costs to a minimum whilst providing an efficient and proper catering service to its patients. It will typically face certain restrictions such as having to satisfy the varied dietary requirements of the patients, the uncertainty that will exist as to the exact number of patients requiring meals at any one time, the extent of available catering equipment and catering staff and so on.
- A transport company that has to supply customers in different parts of the country with goods from factories and warehouses also located across the country. Typically, the company will wish to provide an adequate service whilst at the same time keeping distribution costs to a minimum.
- An airline company has a number of cabin staff available who have to be assigned to a variety of international routes. The staff have a variety of skills between them and the company must somehow determine how best to allocate its staff to the routes available.
- A food manufacturer that has signed a contract with one of its major customers for a

bulk order for one of its food products. The quality of the product is strictly controlled in terms of the mix of ingredients that can be used. In some way, the manufacturer has to determine how to produce the required quantity of the product at minimum cost whilst at the same time meeting the quality requirements.
- A financial adviser who is trying to put together an investment portfolio for one of her clients. The client has a fixed sum of money available for investment and has detailed requirements in terms of the overall return required, the balance between generating income and growth, the risk element that will be acceptable and so on. The adviser has to determine the best investment portfolio under the available restrictions.
- The manager of a large production firm who is faced with trying to determine an appropriate production schedule for the next six months. There is an inbuilt conflict in the organization in that economies of scale suggest production should be undertaken in as large a batch as possible. Stockholding costs, on the other hand, make such a policy unattractive as large batches of production remain as stocks—incurring a variety of costs—for a considerable period. The manager somehow has to balance these conflicting pressures.
- A large multinational organization that is trying to determine in which part of Western Europe it should locate its new factory. It will face certain constraints—in the form of available finance, labour supply, government grants available and so on—and will be seeking to optimize the return on its investment.

It is clear that, from a business viewpoint, these problems have little in common except for the fact that they all involve selecting the optimum decision from the alternatives available. From the viewpoint of management science, however, all these problems—and a considerable array of related business activities—are identical in that all can be investigated using the techniques of mathematical programming.

Mathematical programming models are a special type of *optimizing* model and they follow a common structure. A mathematical programming application generally consists of three elements all expressed, unsurprisingly, in mathematical terms. First, an *objective function* which details the objective, or target, to be attained. Typically this will involve attempting to maximize or minimize some variable like profit or income declared in a mathematical expression. Second, a set of *constraints* representing the limitations imposed on the structure of the problem under investigation. Frequently, such structural constraints relate to available supplies of scarce resources and their rate of use. Thus, we may have only a limited supply of finance or time or manpower. Third, a set of *constraints* defining the general nature and range of the problem variables. Typically, we may set predetermined limits on the values of the variables that are acceptable. We may specify, for example, that variables must take non-negative values as these may be the only values sensible in the context of the problem. The application of a mathematical programming model falls also into three clearly defined parts. First, *problem formulation*. We must take the existing management problem and translate it into a format suitable for solution by the appropriate mathematical programming technique. This may sound far easier than it actually is in practice. Typically, considerable problems are encountered at the formulation stage (and these problems can generally be resolved only through adequate practice and the development of experience). On the one hand, it is necessary to 'mould' the problem to fit the model (so that we can then use the model to generate potentially useful management information). Yet, at the same time, we must ensure that we are retaining the key elements of the original problem—that is, that we are not manipulating the problem to fit the model. To do so may generate a solution that has little relevance to the original business problem.

The second part of the model application concerns the *solution*. Once we have developed the appropriate solution method, supported by the relevant mathematics, this stage becomes straightforward. It is also the solution stage that reveals why such techniques are referred to as 'programming' techniques: the solution methods revolve around a sequence of logical, step-by-step calculations (literally a calculation program). The third stage relates to *interpretation*. This is, arguably, the most important. It is generally necessary to examine the solution to the mathematical model we have developed and to 'translate' this solution back into the original business context. It is at this stage that the analyst must have the skills appropriate to understand both the mathematical principles of the model and the underlying business context. It is the development of this dual emphasis that this text seeks to encourage in the student.

Over the last few years a variety of such mathematical programming models have been devised to apply to a wide range of typical business problems and to generate an appropriate solution. Such techniques are, arguably, one of the quantitative areas that offer most potential for the business decision-maker. At the same time such techniques are also amongst the most complex in mathematical terms. This text aims to ensure that the decision-maker is able both to use and understand such techniques.

1-2 CONTENTS OF THE TEXT

In order to try and achieve this objective the text takes a deliberate approach in terms of both its content and its presentation. In terms of content the text is subdivided into a number of different parts with each part introducing and explaining a specific type of mathematical programming model, as follows.

Part A introduces the models relating to transportation and assignment problems where typically we wish to optimize the distribution of some item between sources and destinations, or we wish to optimize the allocation of resources to tasks.

Part B introduces the major model used in mathematical programming, that of linear programming. This is the classical mathematical programming technique and relates to the identification of an optimum value for some stated objective, subject to a series of constraints that apply to the problem. As the name suggests, the technique is concerned with situations where all relationships between variables can be expressed in a linear form.

Part C introduces a number of more advanced mathematical programming models. Chapters 10 and 11 cover *integer programming*, which is primarily concerned with those situations where certain aspects of the problem under investigation may relate to discrete outcomes—certain variables may take only discrete or integer values. Chapter 12 introduces the area of *goal programming* which relates to those business areas where the decision-maker may adopt a multiple criteria approach to setting objectives: there may be a number of desirable goals not just a single objective and the technique assesses the effect of such multiple objectives on the available, alternative solutions. Chapter 13 introduces *non-linear programming*, which extends the mathematical programming analysis to areas where non-linear relationships exist between variables. Finally, Chapter 14 introduces *dynamic programming*, which attempts to solve a problem by reducing a complex problem into a set of simpler subproblems. Analysis can then be undertaken into the sequence of interrelated management decisions. Dynamic programming is concerned with trying to optimize the total outcome of such a decision sequence over a given time period.

It is worth noting at this stage that all of these models are historically quite recent. The first formal method of efficiently solving a linear programming model was detailed in 1947 by Dantzig. The development work of Kuhn and Tucker in 1951 generated an active interest in non-linear programming, whilst integer programming had to wait until 1958 before an analysis method for solution was suggested by Gomory. Bellman provided a solution approach to dynamic programming problems in 1957. It should not be thought, however, that these models and their solution methods are static. Over the past 40 years or so considerable attention has been devoted to refining and developing these models and that process continues today with management science and operational research journals publishing the latest theoretical and applied developments. Neither should it be thought that because of their relatively recent origin such models have a limited appeal. A recent survey by Kathawala (*Journal of Operational Research*, 1988, Vol. 39, No. 11) of companies in the United States revealed that over 60 per cent of respondents indicated that they made use of linear programming techniques (with only 5 per cent of respondents actually unfamiliar with the technique). Mathematical programming models have a considerable amount to offer the business decision-maker, as the text will reveal.

1-3 THE GENERAL APPROACH ADOPTED IN THE TEXT

Within each section of the text the structure adopted is as follows. First, a typical business problem is introduced and both the nature and extent of the problem are investigated in terms of the decisions that must be taken and the factors that limit the alternative decisions available. Second, we develop a primarily conceptual understanding of the solution method that can be adopted within the context of the problem. Third, we introduce the appropriate mathematical underpinning to the technique under investigation. Wherever possible the mathematical theory is kept to a minimum and the mathematics introduced is directly related to the conceptual context of the problem. Using such a mathematical approach, however, allows us to develop the general solution method for such a technique without being unduly distracted by the mathematical theory. Finally, we step back from the technical detail of the solution method for the technique under investigation and assess the wider management implications of the model in practical terms. That is, we examine the underlying assumptions of the mathematics of the technique and we investigate the strengths and weaknesses of the technique as a source of management information. At the end of this process not only should you be able to 'solve' a problem using the technique in question but you should also be able to assess the suitability of the technique to a variety of business applications and be able to assess the usefulness (or otherwise) of the information thrown up by the technique.

The International Monitor Company

In order to facilitate such a conceptual and business-context approach we shall be setting the developments of the various techniques introduced firmly into a specific business context. We shall assume, throughout the text, that we are working for a particular company and that we are investigating a variety of problem areas faced by the company and seeking to resolve such problems. The company itself is called the *International Monitor Company* (IMC). The company was founded some 15 years ago by two partners who set out to exploit a perceived gap in part of the electronics market. At the time, the partners produced monitors for specialized medical equipment. Since then, with the rapid advances in the electronics industry, the company has switched direction and is now primarily engaged in the manufacture of a variety of monitors for personal computers produced by the computer industry. Some of the monitors are sold under the company's own name. Others are sold to computer manufacturers to be sold as part of the complete personal computer package.

The company has expanded considerably—along with the rest of the computer industry—over the last few years. It now employs several thousand people at a variety of locations across the country. Some of its activities relate directly to production, some to technical research and others to general management and administration. Like many companies in a similar position IMC has grown and has largely been managed by the two partners on an *ad-hoc* basis. An increasing number of management problems are now becoming apparent in a variety of the company's activities and senior management are now investigating how these problems may be resolved. In line with the general approach adopted in the text, we shall be introducing a specific problem currently faced by IMC's management in each section of the text and seeking to solve the problem through the application of a suitable mathematical programming technique. We shall also be assessing the usefulness of each technique from the management—as opposed to the mathematical—perspective. The authors appreciate that not all managers using this text will face the same problems as IMC's management. However, we feel that the problems introduced will be sufficiently applicable to virtually all types of business organization whatever the type of industry they belong to, whether they are large or small, whether they are profit-oriented or in the public service sector and so on. This perspective will be enhanced through the use of a variety of additional illustrations and exercises at the end of each chapter.

Student activities and exercises

Given the clear focus of the text on the practical applications of mathematical programming techniques to business and decision-making, each chapter of the text will include both a series of student activities and one of student exercises. The student activities occur throughout the chapter itself and are intended to illustrate a particular point or detail in the exposition of the technique at that stage. As the name suggests, the clear purpose of these activities is for you to complete the task set before proceeding further. Each activity is intended to highlight a specific part of the exposition of the technique or to focus attention on a specific issue that is about to be investigated. It is therefore in your interest to complete each activity before proceeding further.

At the end of each chapter you will find a series of student exercises. These exercises have a number of purposes. First, they allow the student to review and practise the techniques introduced in that chapter. Second, they provide an opportunity both to consolidate the development of the technique to date and to consider further developments that could be usefully investigated. Typically, many of these further developments will be introduced in the next chapter. Finally, such exercises allow you to apply the technique to a wider variety of business problems than is possible in the chapter itself. It is imperative, therefore, that you undertake these exercises as a matter of course before proceeding further in the text. Not to do so will lead not only to a less than adequate understanding of the techniques covered to that stage but also—because of the sequential nature of much of the mathematics—to an inability to understand subsequent techniques and discussion.

Computer software

As an aid to such exercises we have developed a set of PC-based computer programs related to the techniques introduced in the text. Full details of the software are given in Appendix 1. If you do not have the opportunity to access such software as part of your studies of mathematical programming you will not find yourself unduly disadvantaged. However, there are considerable benefits in using the software package as an integrated part of the study of these techniques. Briefly, the software will allow you to use a particular technique without having to resort to the tedious manual calculations frequently necessary. This will enable you to focus on the more important aspects of the technique—the general solution method and assessing the information that the solution provides—rather than on the detailed arithmetic. Many of the student exercises are fully compatible with the software and a separate disk containing these exercises as data files is available directly from us. Additionally, any application of these models to a real-world business problem necessitates the use of computer facilities and this software will help familiarize you with the requirements of such commercial computer packages.

1-4 THE MANAGEMENT SCIENCE PROCESS

So far, our discussion has concentrated on the types of mathematical programming models that will be introduced and examined. It is important to realize, however, that the use of such models is only part of the decision-making process. The models themselves, and the information they generate, must be placed firmly in the appropriate decision-making context. Without an adequate understanding of the full decision-making process, the model itself becomes the centre of attention and not the problem under investigation. We can represent the management decision-making process—involving the use of management science techniques—as a series of interrelated stages. Whilst this text is not primarily concerned with such a management science methodology (the references in the Bibliography provide details of texts that do have such an interest) it will be useful to discuss this briefly so as to place the techniques we shall be introducing explicitly in the decision-making structure. The stages can be summarized as follows:

Stage 1: recognition that a problem exists This may seem an obvious first stage in any management decision-making, but in practice its timing may be critical. Some system must exist for monitoring key aspects of business activity. At some time (hopefully sooner rather than later) it will become apparent that a decision will be required either to resolve an existing problem or to forestall a predicted problem. We must also be able to distinguish between the symptoms of a problem and its causes.

Stage 2: explicit problem formulation Once it becomes apparent that a problem exists—and a solution is required—the problem must be explicitly formulated in terms of the following:

- The perceived boundaries or limits to the problem.
- The objectives of the investigation.
- The defined roles of those involved in the investigation.
- Which variables making up the problem are within the control of the decision-maker and which are not.

Without such a clear exposition of the problem to be investigated the exercise is likely to be unproductive in terms of generating useful management information.

Stage 3: model construction This is obviously one of the areas of prime interest in this text but it must be remembered that it is only possible to begin this stage after completion of Stage 2. Not until we have a clear idea of the problem we are investigating and what is required from the investigation can we attempt to determine what an appropriate model might be. (A more detailed discussion of models and model construction appears in Section 1-5.) The selection of a suitable type of model and a formulation of that model appropriate to the problem under investigation requires a combination of both mathematical and managerial skills.

Stage 4: data collection This is a stage generally taken for granted in any academic exposition of technique applications. Textbooks conveniently assume that the data required by a model is available in exactly the right form and detail. In practice, this is frequently not the case. The collection of suitable data will generally provide considerable difficulties for the analyst. As we shall see, the techniques of mathematical programming are particularly 'data hungry'. They require a considerable amount of data and that data must be available in a particularly explicit form. The techniques themselves are useless without such data. The business analyst trying to apply such models to a management problem must fully understand these data requirements not only to be able to apply the model but, more importantly, to be able to assess the usefulness of the model's output.

Stage 5: model solution By and large, this is the easiest stage of the whole process. Solution of the specified model—particularly in the context of mathematical programming—is generally straightforward, particularly when using computer-based solution methods.

Stage 6: model validation and interpretation Whilst the previous stage may be straightforward, the mathematical solution obtained may not actually be appropriate for the problem under investigation. We may find, for example, that the model generates 'nonsense' results for some variable, perhaps because of an inappropriate formulation of the original model. It is necessary, therefore, to *validate* the solution to ensure that the 'answer' to the problem generated actually makes sense in the problem context. Frequently at this stage it will be necessary to return to Stage 3, if an alternative model specification is called for, or Stage 4, if alternative or additional data is required. Because of the complexity of the mathematical programming models, such an iterative process is usual. We may find, for example, that the initial model solution represents a situation that may not be acceptable to management and the model to be solved must be amended accordingly. Even if the model solution proves acceptable, in the sense of being validated, it will frequently need to be interpreted. As we shall see, the output generated by mathematical programming models tends to be both complex and (predictably) mathematical. Such results must then be interpreted into the original business context of the problem: if you like, the solution must be 'translated' into a form the decision-maker can usefully understand.

Stage 7: decision-making Once the solution information has been obtained and assessed it will need to be acted upon. After all, the whole purpose of the model from our perspective is to provide information to assist the decision-maker. It should not be assumed, however, that the information generated from such models will be the only set available. Frequently, this information will relate to only one aspect of the problem under investigation or will be used to supplement information about the problem available from other sources. The decision-maker will need to incorporate all such information sources (including those that are qualitative or judgemental) before reaching a decision. Naturally, this presupposes that the decision-maker is able to accurately assess the usefulness of the quantitative information generated by such techniques.

Stage 8: monitoring the decision and the original problem This actually returns us to the first stage. It is essential that some sort of monitoring system is established both to allow us to gauge the effectiveness of the decision taken and to ensure that the original problem 'disappears'. Only in this way are we able to recognize when a new problem becomes evident and assess the suitability of the mathematical programming technique for the business organization.

A number of comments should be made at this stage. It is apparent that the stages we have detailed are, in themselves, an oversimplification. In the real world the distinction between many of these stages will be unclear (or non-existent). This does not necessarily negate the usefulness of trying to picture the overall process, however. Equally, it is important to realize that the whole group of stages detailed must be seen as a coherent and cohesive set. It will be necessary in practice to jump between stages, to return to previous stages and to repeat the cycle several times before a satisfactory outcome is achieved. A final point relates to Stage 7. The decision-maker will be receiving information (that may or may not be) relevant to the problem from a variety of sources. Some of these—as with our models—will be largely quantitative whilst others will be largely qualitative (based on experience, judgement, hunches, etc.). The decision-maker's task is to reconcile such sets of information, to assess their relevance and their use and, finally, to make a decision. It is evident that this will be possible only given an adequate understanding of the quantitative techniques used. The decision-maker will not be in a position to evaluate such information adequately solely on the basis of the support provided by a management science and operational research specialist (who, typically, will not have the decision-maker's view of the whole problem). It is perhaps unsurprising that the last few years have seen an explosion of interest in such techniques by management (and management education) in general.

The approach we have detailed can be conveniently summarized diagrammatically as in Fig. 1-1. The links between the various stages of the decision-making process and the necessity for a recursive and cyclical approach are evident. When trying to apply a management science technique to a business problem we must anticipate having to return to earlier stages of the process to amend what we have already done. Thus, for example, we may reach the stage of model validation and interpretation but realize from the results of the analysis that the results are inadequate or inappropriate in some way and we must return to an earlier stage in the process. This stage could be that relating to data collection if we feel additional data will resolve the problems, or to model construction if a different type of mathematical programming model may be more suitable, or even to the problem formulation stage if it becomes apparent that the problem as defined cannot be resolved. It is also clear that the model solution stage—finding the 'answer'—is but a single step in the whole process. It is, unfortunately, a stage that can attract an undue share of both the analyst's and the decision-maker's attention to the detriment of other aspects of the process. It is of little use to management simply to find 'the answer' to some problem if the model used to generate this solution is inappropriate in some way in the context of

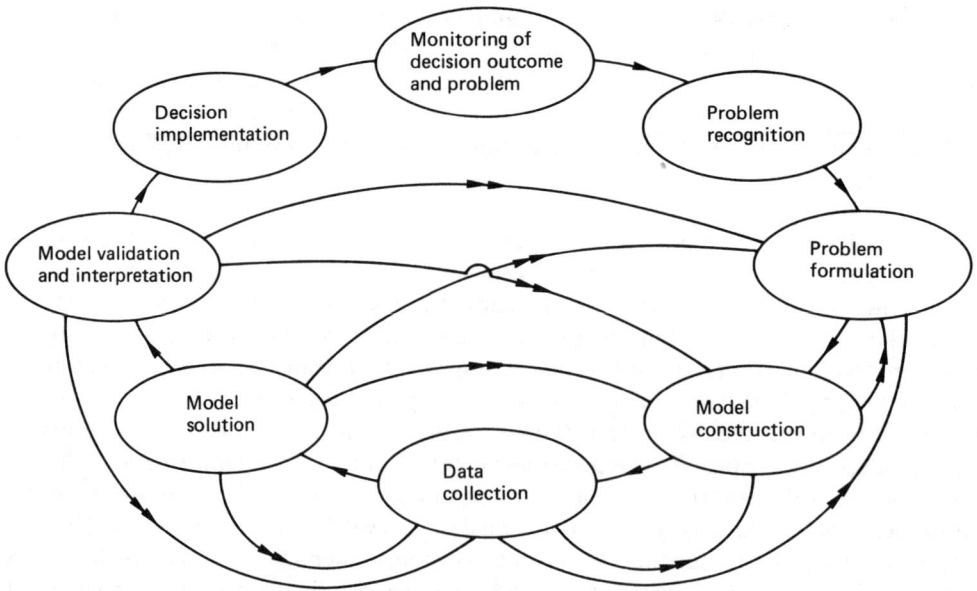

Figure 1-1 Methodology

the business problem, if the data collected and used is inadequate or inappropriate or if the model used is so complex that the decision-maker cannot evaluate its reliability and appropriateness for the problem under investigation.

1-5 THE USE OF MODELS IN DECISION-MAKING

Thus far we have been using the word 'model' in a fairly loose way without attempting a clear definition. As we have seen from Fig. 1-1, models have an essential part to play in many management decisions, and as we have already stated, one particular group of models—those relating to mathematical programming—are the focus of this text. It will be useful at this stage to review what is meant by a model and to examine the alternative forms of models that are available in the management science areas as a whole so that we can place the mathematical programming models we shall be developing firmly in the overall context of models used in decision-making. In its most basic form a model can be viewed as a simplified representation of reality. That is, a model is used to allow us to view the essential elements of a more complex, real-world situation. A model is not intended to mimic every aspect and feature of the situation under investigation. Rather, we develop and use a model to focus attention on what we regard as the key elements of the problem. Thus every model is, to a lesser or greater extent, based on a set of restrictive assumptions. How accurate the model is as a representation of the real world will depend not only on the underlying mathematics but also on the validity of the assumptions behind the model. It is all too easy to forget such assumptions when assessing the usefulness of a model solution. Although there are probably as many different methods of classifying models as there are management scientists, one such classification which is pertinent to this text is shown in Fig. 1-2.

Before examining the diagram in detail it will be worth while reviewing why we have introduced it at all. The important point is that the models we shall be investigating in this text are only some of those that are available to the management science analyst. It is important to remember this when considering the application of a particular model to some business problem. To reiterate an earlier point, the model that we consider appropriate for the business problem is a means to an end. We typically have little interest in the model itself but concern ourselves rather with the management information it may provide. This is a key factor in determining our choice of model from the considerable array available.

The broadest distinction that can be made is between *physical* and *abstract* models. Physical models, as the name suggests, are literally physical representations of some problem, perhaps a scale model of a building or a new aircraft and so on. Abstract models, on the other hand (sometimes referred to as logical or mental models), are constructed with symbols and logic rather than as a physical entity. Abstract models, for our purposes, can be further subdivided into those that are primarily *mathematical* and those that are not. Such mathematical models can be further subdivided into three broad groups. First there are the *descriptive* models. Broadly, such a model attempts to accurately describe some situation but without suggesting any potential decision or course of action. Such models are frequently useful in allowing us to observe the behaviour of some mathematical business system. A typical example might be the simple supply and demand model

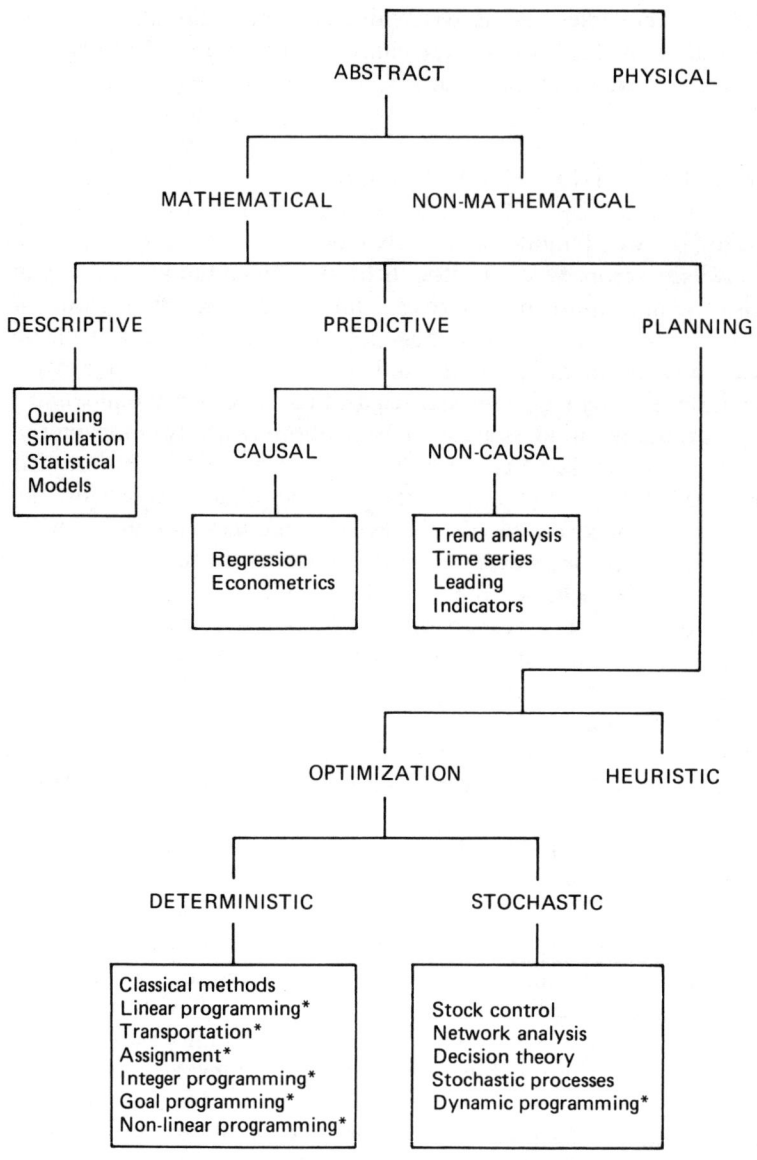

Figure 1-2 A model classification (models asterisked are covered in this text)

frequently encountered in economics. Such a model allows us to determine economic behaviour as parts of the model change. Examples of such descriptive models in the management science area include queuing, simulation and a whole array of statistical models.

Second there are the *predictive* or forecasting models. Typically, these may be built upon some descriptive model but in addition to simply observing behaviour attempt to predict such behaviour should certain aspects of the model alter. Again, as a generalization such predictive models may be classed as either *causal* or *non-causal* models. Causal models, such as those based around regression techniques or econometrics, attempt to determine the causes of change in some variable or set of variables. Literally, such models attempt to determine the factors generating a particular forecast. Non-causal models, on the other hand, are merely concerned with predicting the future movement of some variable with little regard as to what may be causing that variable to behave in a particular manner. Such non-causal methods typically involve a variety of forms of trend analysis, time series analysis or methods of leading indicators.

Third there are the *planning* or normative models. Such a model attempts to suggest some desirable course (or alternative courses) of action which implies that such a model must have built into it some set of goals or objectives. Again, as part of our overall classification we may subdivide such planning models into two broad types, the *heuristic* and the *optimization*. Heuristic models are those that attempt to identify approximate or satisfactory solutions as opposed to optimal solutions. It may be the case that a problem is so complex or so indeterminate that it may not be possible to determine *the* optimal solution or indeed to recognize whether a solution is optimal or not. Under such conditions we may apply intuitive or empirical 'rules' to determine what appears to be a suitable solution. Such an approach is, of course, diametrically the opposite of the other broad group of planning models—those concerned with optimization.

It is already clear that certain types of optimization model are the focus of this text. An optimization model is concerned with identifying the 'best' solution to the stated problem. Again, there are two subgroups of optimization models. The first of these consists of those that are *deterministic*. Such models are based on the assumption that all data pertaining to the problem, and all relationships specified in the problem, can be treated as certain and known. With the exception of dynamic programming, all the mathematical programming models we shall be examining fall into this subgroup (although there are other types of deterministic optimization models that are not of the mathematical programming type). *Stochastic* models, on the other hand, allow for both relationships and data to be treated as uncertain to a greater or lesser extent, typically through the use of probability. Dynamic programming, as we shall see, attempts to incorporate such uncertainty into a mathematical programming framework.

It may seem, at this stage, that a deterministic model, based as it is on the assumption of certainty, would be unduly restrictive in terms of trying to model a business problem where most factors will be uncertain. However, as we shall see as we develop these models, many real-world problems are sufficiently stable over a given period to be treated as deterministic. Also, one important feature of all the deterministic mathematical programming models is that they allow uncertainty to be introduced once an initial optimal solution has been obtained. Through the use of what is known as *sensitivity analysis* we can readily incorporate a degree of uncertainty into the problem and assess its effect on the existing solution. In short, we can use such models to answer the typical 'what if?' questions that most decision-makers will raise.

1-6 MATHEMATICAL PREREQUISITES

Although the text builds up much of the mathematics that we shall require as we develop the models it is assumed that you will start the text with a number of basic mathematical skills. In particular, you should be familiar with:

- The difference between linear and non-linear relationships;
- basic algebraic notation;
- linear graphs;
- the use of simultaneous-equation methods.

Additionally, you will require a pocket calculator to follow the step-by-step calculations and ideally should have access to an IBM-compatible PC to use the accompanying software package.

1-7 SUMMARY

In this introductory chapter we have tried to provide an overview as to how, and why, the mathematical programming models that are the basis of this text will be presented and discussed. We have stated clearly that our interest in this particular group of models is as a source of potentially useful management information and not as a set of mathematical techniques *per se*. As such, we have tried to show that the use of such models—and the information they generate—must be seen as part of the overall management decision-making process and as a means of enabling the manager to make better decisions. Such quantitative models will not provide a decision for management, merely information on which rationally to base such a decision. Equally, we must not forget that information generated by such quantitative models is only part of the information that will be available. It must be interpreted, assessed and evaluated alongside other relevant information. The manager's task is to perform such an activity and we hope that this text will provide the skills and knowledge necessary to perform such a task adequately.

PART A

TRANSPORTATION AND ASSIGNMENT

This part introduces two related mathematical programming models. The *transportation* model was originally developed to deal with problems that involved the transportation of some item from a number of locations to a number of destinations. Typically, applications of this model seek to minimize either the distance travelled in fulfilling the delivery schedule or to minimize the costs of transporting the item. Since its initial development, however, the model has been increasingly applied to problems that are not of this traditional 'transport' type. Assigning sales staff to regional areas, scheduling meals distribution in hospitals, and stock control scheduling are all areas where the transportation model has been successfully adapted and applied. The second model, the *assignment* model, is often regarded as a special form of the basic transportation model. Typically it involves problems where we have to allocate a number of resources (often personnel, machines or equipment of some kind) to a variety of tasks. The model is usually concerned with finding the allocation which will optimize efficiency.

These two models are the first to be introduced in the text because—in terms of both logic and mathematics—they are the simplest to develop and understand. At the same time they also introduce many of the basic ideas and concepts that we shall later require for the more mathematically complex models.

Chapter 2 introduces the basic transportation model and examines both its formulation and solution.

Chapter 3 extends the basic transportation model to consider additional aspects of typical business applications.

Chapter 4 introduces the assignment model and its solution process.

2
THE TRANSPORTATION MODEL

The transportation model was first introduced in what is now seen as its standard form in 1941 by F. L. Hitchcock and further developed in 1949 by T. C. Koopmans. At its most basic the model centres around a common business problem—that of the distribution, allocation or transportation of some item. The problem for the decision-maker arises in that there are a number of supply locations (referred to as *origins*) and a number of demand locations (referred to as *destinations*). Each origin will have available a certain supply of the good and each destination will require a certain quantity of the good to satisfy its own demand. Given that we can quantify in some way the cost of shipping the good from each possible origin to each possible destination we then require a schedule such that the good is transported to the various destinations from the various origins at the minimum possible cost. This chapter will follow the standard process outlined in Chapter 1. First, we shall introduce the business problem we wish to try and solve. Second, we shall develop a solution method both in conceptual and mathematical terms. Third, we shall examine the management implications of the model.

2-1 THE BUSINESS PROBLEM

IMC are currently investigating their production scheduling for one of their PC monitors. The monitor is currently produced at three different factories located in different parts of the country: in Northtown, Midtown and Southtown. Because of the system of nationwide dealerships that IMC operates, production from each of the factories is shipped to one of four distribution depots, which are located in different parts of the country: Depots A, B, C and D. Sales demand for the product occurring in one particular part of the country is then met from the nearest distribution depot. Let us denote the three factories (the origins) by N, M and S and the four distribution depots (the destinations) by A, B, C and D. It is clear that a number of possible distribution patterns are available (in fact there are a

Table 2-1 Transportation costs: £ per unit shipped

	Depot A	Depot B	Depot C	Depot D
Northtown	20	11	12	13
Midtown	11	10	13	15
Southtown	9	12	15	20

total of 12 possible routes—3 × 4), but it is far from clear as to which factory should supply a particular depot. Let us further assume that, on a weekly basis, the production schedules of the three factories are known to be as follows:

Weekly production
Northtown   400 units
Midtown   700 units
Southtown   500 units

and let us further assume that sales forecasts have identified the maximum demand that each distribution depot will have for this item. These are:

Weekly demand
Depot A   200 units
Depot B   400 units
Depot C   500 units
Depot D   500 units

Note that—conveniently!—the number of units to be supplied (1600 per week) exactly matches the amount demanded by the four depots. This is an example of a *balanced* transportation problem where supply and demand are equal. We shall see later the effect of introducing *unbalanced* problems where supply and demand do not match. In order to be able to proceed, we require information on the costs of using each origin–destination route. Assume again that these costs (shown in Table 2-1) have been quantified in terms of the cost of shipping one unit from each origin to each destination. So, for example, to ship one unit from the Northtown factory to Depot A costs £20, whilst to supply the same depot from the Southtown factory costs £9. We now have all the information we require in order to be able to proceed with the model.

2-2 FORMULATING THE BASIC TRANSPORTATION MODEL

It is clear that we have a simple objective. We wish to supply the depots with the quantities of the product they require at minimum transport costs for the company as a whole. Our objective then is to *minimize* total costs. At the same time we face a number of restrictions in terms of how we can achieve this. Simply, there are constraints that we face in terms of the available supply and the current levels of demand. Whatever we do must satisfy these constraints. This dichotomy of a desired objective to be attained in the face of a set of restricting factors typifies all the mathematical programming models we shall be looking at. Let us examine the structure of Table 2-2. This table shows the cost per route, the units

Table 2-2 Transportation table: cost, demand and supply structure

Origins	Destinations				Origin capacity
	Depot A	Depot B	Depot C	Depot D	
Northtown	20	11	12	13	400
Midtown	11	10	13	15	700
Southtown	9	12	15	20	500
Destination requirement	200	400	500	500	1600

available at each of the 3 factories and the units required by each of the 4 depots. It is clear that we require a solution to our problem that determines the quantity of the product that will be shipped on each of the possible 12 routes. In other words, the quantities shipped per route become the variables (and are currently unknown). We shall use the following notation:

c: the per-unit cost of shipping an item from a specific origin to a specific destination.
q: the number of units shipped on a particular route.
x: a particular cell in the cost–quantity table, that is a route between a specific origin and a specific destination.

Further, for convenience, we shall use a subscript notation with the three variables in order to determine which particular origin–destination combination we are referring to. Thus x_{23} will refer to row 2 column 3 of the cost table (relating here to the route between Midtown and Depot C). In general we shall use the convention that the first subscript (referred to as i) relates to the rows and the second subscript (referred to as j) relates to the columns. We can now express the problem in simple mathematical terms.

$$\text{Minimize} \quad 20q_{11} + 11q_{12} + 12q_{13} + 13q_{14}$$
$$+ 11q_{21} + 10q_{22} + 13q_{23} + 15q_{24}$$
$$+ 9q_{31} + 12q_{32} + 15q_{33} + 20q_{34} \quad (2\text{-}1)$$

$$\text{subject to} \quad q_{11} + q_{12} + q_{13} + q_{14} = 400 \quad (2\text{-}2)$$
$$q_{21} + q_{22} + q_{23} + q_{24} = 700 \quad (2\text{-}3)$$
$$q_{31} + q_{32} + q_{33} + q_{34} = 500 \quad (2\text{-}4)$$
$$q_{11} + q_{21} + q_{31} = 200 \quad (2\text{-}5)$$
$$q_{12} + q_{22} + q_{32} = 400 \quad (2\text{-}6)$$

$$q_{13} + q_{23} + q_{33} = 500 \tag{2-7}$$

$$q_{14} + q_{24} + q_{34} = 500 \tag{2-8}$$

$$q_{ij} \geq 0 \tag{2-9}$$

We shall encounter this type of notation in all the mathematical programming models, so it is worth while ensuring that the formulation is clearly understood. First of all we have an objective function, Eq. (2-1). In this example our objective is to minimize the total transport cost for the routes used by the company. This total cost function consists simply of the shipping cost for each possible route (c) multiplied by the number of units of the product (q) that is shipped via that route. In order to achieve such an objective we are limited in terms of what we can and cannot do—we face a series of *constraints*. The first three constraints (Eqs (2-2)–(2-4)) refer to the supply availability of the product at each of the three factories. Equation 2-2, for example ($q_{21} + q_{22} + q_{23} + q_{24} = 700$), indicates that the quantities shipped from the Midtown factory must match the available supply. (Note that this is an implied requirement of the problem given that we know total demand for this item is exactly matched by total supply. In other words, all three factories must ship all their available production.)

Student activity
Explain to what the constraints Eqs (2-5) to (2-8) and Eq. (2-9) relate.

It is clear that the next four constraints relate to the demand requirements of the 4 depots. The amounts shipped to each depot from the 3 factories must total to the exact amount the depot requires. The final constraint, Eq. (2-9) ($q_{ij} \geq 0$), does not appear explicitly in the original problem but you will appreciate its necessity. We are insisting with the inclusion of this constraint that the variables in the model—the quantities to be shipped on each route—must take non-negative values. In the context of the problem negative quantities are nonsense. Again, this implicit constraint is typical of mathematical programming models in general. Having developed the formulation of the basic problem we face, we must now consider how we can proceed. In fact, the solution method we adopt is the same (allowing for differing technical approaches) for virtually all the mathematical programming models that we shall be examining and can be summarized into a number of stages, as follows.

Stage 1: formulate the problem into a standard notation This is the stage we have just completed.

Stage 2: obtain an initial, feasible solution We next require a solution which satisfies the restrictions imposed on the problem. In technical terms we require a solution that is feasible, given the constraints we face.

Stage 3: determine whether the current feasible solution is optimal We next need to be able to determine whether, in some way, the current feasible solution can be improved. If the answer is 'no' then this solution represents the optimum for the given problem and the solution program stops. If the answer is 'yes' then we proceed to Stage 4.

Stage 4: improve the current solution if it is not optimal Obviously, if the current solution is not optimal then we need to improve it. We can then return to Stage 3 and again check for optimality. This process can be repeated until we do obtain an optimal solution (or until we realize that there is no optimal solution for the problem, which is an important point to remember when we come to apply such models in the real world).

Obviously there will be differences in the technical aspects of these stages for each type of mathematical model but the basic process will be as outlined above. There are also a number of features of the transportation model that we shall be encountering in the other forms of mathematical programming model in the text. One is that the solution process (referred to as the program) is *iterative*. We have a simple cycle of stages and this cycle repeats itself until we reach an optimal solution. Each iteration of the program represents a step towards this optimal solution. Second, it is clear that we appear to face an immediate problem in trying to reach a solution in terms of the number of variables as opposed to the number of constraint equations we face. In mathematics, to find a unique solution for a set of variables we require one independent equation for each variable. If we have fewer equations than variables (as is frequently the case in mathematical programming) then the only way to proceed to a solution is to set some of the variables to zero and to solve for the unique solution to the remainder. Such a solution is referred to as a *basic* solution (or as a *basis*). Non-zero variables are referred to as *basic variables* whilst those that have been set to zero are known as *non-basic variables*. (Of course, the whole point of the mathematical program for a particular model is to determine which variables should be basic and which non-basic at each iteration.)

In general, if we have n variables and m independent constraints then we require $(n - m)$ of the variables to be set to zero (to be non-basic), with the remaining variables generally taking non-zero values (to be basic). You may have noticed that we have carefully used the term 'independent constraint'. What does 'independent' mean? To illustrate suppose we had two constraints which stated that:

$$x_1 + x_2 = 100$$

$$5x_1 + 5x_2 = 500$$

It is clear that the two constraints are the same: they are not independent of each other given that one is a multiple of the other. We could not, therefore, find unique values for both x_1 and x_2 even though we have two constraints. (If you are unclear about this point you should attempt to find unique values for both x variables in these equations.) In our transportation formulation we have a total of 12 variables ($n = 12$) and 7 constraints ($m = 7$). However, one of these constraints is redundant to the problem. Because of the necessity for row and column totals to balance we could in fact remove the last constraint (or indeed any one of the constraints) and still find the solution to the problem, given that if the other 6 constraints are satisfied then the last constraint must be also because of the requirement of goods shipped to total to 1600. So, in fact we have only 6 independent constraints and we will therefore require a total of (12 − 6) variables to be non-basic, i.e. to be set to zero in order to solve for the remainder. In general, for a transportation problem this implies that we require $(n - m - 1)$ basic variables in the solution. Such a solution is said to be a basic, feasible solution.

Occasionally, we may find that one of the basic variables in fact takes a zero value in the current solution. This implies that fewer than $(n - m - 1)$ variables take non-zero values in the solution and the solution is said to be *degenerate*. We shall see later why this causes difficulties and how these can be resolved.

2-3 FINDING AN INITIAL FEASIBLE SOLUTION

Our first task, therefore, is to identify an initial solution for the model that is at least feasible—i.e., that satisfies all the constraints that have been imposed. In general, it is largely irrelevant as to how 'good' this initial feasible solution is in terms of the objective function. The iterative mathematical program that is applied to this initial solution will lead us to the optimal solution. Naturally, we may be able to apply a little logic within the context of the problem to identify one initial solution that may give a better initial value for the objective function than another, but in the end this is immaterial to the solution we finally obtain. This brings us to an important feature of this text.

As we have already stated, our interest is primarily in the practical application of these models to business problems. We take it for granted that in the real world the applications of these models would be computer-based and not manually calculated. For this reason we shall not, as a matter of course, necessarily be looking at those solution methods that are technically most efficient (i.e. those that are most efficient in terms of the mathematical calculations involved). The search for solution techniques to mathematical programming models that are ever more efficient we leave to computer programmers and to management scientists who take an active interest in such developments. In the end, from the business user's viewpoint, the solution technique itself is largely irrelevant given that in all cases the data being inputted into the model and the information being extracted from the model will be the same.

Equally, we shall not necessarily introduce all the different variants that exist of the basic solution program. Many of these variants have their roots in the (now historical) necessity for speeding up the manual calculation process. Given modern computing technology, such variations in the solution process hold little interest for us. There are a number of methods available for establishing an initial feasible solution to a transportation problem and we shall examine the most obvious: the *least-cost* method.

> *Student activity*
> Consider the transportation table shown as Table 2-2. What route would you suggest is used first? What quantity of the product would you transport using this route?

The least-cost method

The most logical approach at this stage—given our desire for minimum cost—would be to determine the least-cost cell in the transportation table and to allocate the maximum quantity to that particular route. We would then seek the second lowest-cost cell, allocate the maximum possible quantity to that route and so on until all the production output had been allocated. Consider Table 2-2. The lowest-cost cell is x_{31}, with a cost per unit shipped

Table 2-3 Transportation table: using Route x_{31}

Origins	Destinations Depot A	Depot B	Depot C	Depot D	Origin capacity
Northtown	20 0	11	12	13	400
Midtown	11 0	10	13	15	700
Southtown	9 200	12	15	20	500
Destination requirement	200	400	500	500	1600

of £9. This cell refers to units shipped from the Southtown factory to Depot A. Whilst the factory could supply up to 500 units the depot actually only requires 200. So, the maximum amount to be shipped on this route will be 200 units. This then fulfils the requirements of Depot A and accordingly cells x_{11} and x_{22} (showing respectively the quantities to be shipped to Depot A from the other two factories) can be set to zero. The new transportation table is shown in Table 2-3.

The route that we are using—x_{31}—is referred to as an *occupied* cell and the two routes not being used as *empty* cells. We can now proceed to complete the rest of the table in the same way: selecting the next-lowest-cost cell and allocating the maximum quantity to this route and continuing this process until all depots demands have been satisfied.

Student activity
Complete the rest of the route allocations in this way. Calculate the total cost of using this combination of routes.

The sequence of allocation of quantities to lowest-cost routes is: x_{22}, x_{13}, x_{23}, x_{24} and x_{34}, which produces Table 2-4. Note that we have a basic, feasible solution with 6 $(n - m - 1)$ non-zero variables. The least-cost method does not always provide a non-degenerate basic solution, however, as we shall see later. Using this route allocation the total cost of shipping the total number of units from the three factories to the four depots is:

$$20q_{11} + 11q_{12} + 12q_{13} + 13q_{14}$$
$$+ 11q_{21} + 10q_{22} + 13q_{23} + 15q_{24}$$
$$+ 9q_{31} + 12q_{32} + 15q_{33} + 20q_{34} \quad (2\text{-}1)$$
$$= 12(400) + 10(400) + 13(100) + 15(200) + 9(200) + 20(300)$$
$$= £20\,900$$

which is, therefore, the value of the objective function after the first iteration. We can also

Table 2-4 Transportation table: initial feasible solution—least-cost method

Origins	Destinations				Origin capacity
	Depot A	Depot B	Depot C	Depot D	
Northtown	20 0	11 0	12 400	13 0	400
Midtown	11 0	10 400	13 100	15 200	700
Southtown	9 200	12 0	15 0	20 300	500
Destination requirement	200	400	500	500	1600

confirm from the original model specification that this solution is indeed feasible. Looking at both the row and column totals we see that summing the cells across rows and down columns generates the matching total number of units shipped. So, we have established an initial feasible solution. The next step in the program is to try to determine whether the current solution can be improved. In other words, is the current solution optimal?

Student activity
Looking at the current solution, is there any indication that the current solution could be improved?

There is no obvious answer to this but, using simple logic, we might suspect that improvements are possible given that the current solution does not utilize 3 out of the 6 available low-cost routes (cells x_{21}, x_{12} and x_{32}) whilst the highest-cost route (x_{34}) is being used. It is apparent, however, that we require some rigorous method of checking for optimality.

2-4 TESTING FOR AN IMPROVED SOLUTION: THE STEPPING STONE METHOD

We shall be considering two alternative approaches for testing whether an improved solution is possible. The first is known as the *stepping stone* method. As we have already seen there may be an improved solution available in the problem that can be achieved by switching an empty route for a currently occupied route. That is, to utilize a route that is currently not being used instead of one that is. It would obviously be sensible to do this only if the new route led to a decrease in the total transportation costs (given our objective is to minimize these costs). Effectively, this is what the stepping stone method does. The method examines each empty cell in turn and determines the effect on the objective function if this particular route were to be used instead of an existing one. If we find that the use of such an empty cell leads to a decrease in the objective function value then this implies an improved solution is available. If our examination of all the currently empty cells reveals that a decrease in the objective function is not possible then we know we have found the optimum route allocation. (You will appreciate that, in terms of the previous discussion, if we introduce a new route then it must be at the expense of an existing route in order to retain a basic feasible solution.) In the terminology associated with mathematical programming we will evaluate the consequence of bringing a currently non-basic variable into the solution.

Let us return to Table 2-4. We currently have a total of 6 unused routes. The stepping stone method requires us to examine each unused route in turn. Let us look first of all at Route x_{14}—that between Northtown and Depot D—with a per-unit cost of £13. It is clear that we could only use this route if we reduce the quantity shipped via another route, given that the row and column totals requirements are currently being satisfied by the initial solution. Let us trace the effects of using route x_{14} by assuming we ship one unit via this route. The quantity shipped via Route x_{13} would then have to be reduced by one unit, given that the total available from Northtown is fixed at 400. But reducing the quantity in this cell by one will now mean that this column total is no longer 500 but rather 499. Accordingly, having reduced the quantity in cell x_{13}, we must increase the quantity in another cell in this column. The other two cells in this column are x_{23} and x_{33}. Route x_{33} is currently unused and because we are already trying to assess the effect of introducing another unused cell—x_{14}—we cannot use this cell to balance the column total but instead must use x_{23}, which will therefore have its quantity increased by one unit. In turn, this produces an imbalance in this row—row 2—so we must make the necessary adjustment to some non-zero cell in this row. Given that we also still have an imbalance in column 4 (because we decided to use cell x_{14}), it is sensible to adjust cell x_{24} in row 2, as this will not only balance row 2 but also column 4. Like many aspects of mathematical programming, this process is far more difficult to describe verbally than it is to perform arithmetically. The corresponding adjustments are shown in Table 2-5. As can be seen, these four cells have been adjusted by one unit. We now need to determine the effect of using this (currently unused) route on the objective function.

Table 2-5 Transportation table: using Route x_{14}

Origins	Destinations				Origin capacity
	Depot A	Depot B	Depot C	Depot D	
Northtown	20 0	11 0	12 399	13 1	400
Midtown	11 0	10 400	13 101	15 199	700
Southtown	9 200	12 0	15 0	20 300	500
Destination requirement	200	400	500	500	1600

26 TRANSPORTATION AND ASSIGNMENT

Student activity
Calculate the new value for the objective function. Would you recommend that this currently unused route be used?

From the objective function we can quantify the new total transportation cost as £20 899—a saving of £1. So, it appears that we can improve the current solution by using Route x_{14}. Before choosing to incorporate this route into the solution, however, we need to evaluate *all* the currently unused routes in the table in exactly the same way: to quantify the effect each unused route would have on the objective function if such a route were to be used. Before we do so it is worth while, at this stage, considering the process we have applied to cell x_{14}.

In the examination of the currently unused route we have traced out a closed path through a series of other, currently used routes in the table, stepping from one current route to another until we return to the unused route under investigation. (You may well appreciate how this method earned its name. If we envisage the current occupied cells as stones lying just above the surface of a pond then we can step from one stone to another to get to where we wish to go. Other unused cells can be viewed as stones just below the surface of the pond and hence cannot be used. Not all management scientists are noted for their sense of realism!) The tracing of such a route in this way has allowed us to amend the quantities to be shipped via each route so as to keep the row and column totals in balance as they must be to provide a feasible solution. This route is easily seen in Table 2-6, where the 'stones' tracing the route are shown.

The effect on the objective function of using this sequence of stepping stones can also easily be evaluated. Given the necessity for keeping row and column totals in balance, we made a sequence of adjustments to quantities in the form, $+ - + -$, and we can readily quantify the effect of these changes on the objective function, rather than calculate the new objective function value using all the quantities in the table. The changes are shown in Table 2-7.

What we now need to do is to perform this same sequence of activities for every

Table 2-6 Transportation table: the path using Route x_{14}

		Destinations			
Origins	Depot A	Depot B	Depot C	Depot D	Origin capacity
Northtown	20	11	12	13	
Midtown	11	10	13	15	
Southtown	9	12	15	20	
Destination requirement					

Table 2-7 Changes to quantities and costs using Route x_{14}

	Route x_{14}	Route x_{13}	Route x_{23}	Route x_{24}
Change in quantity	+1 unit	−1 unit	+1 unit	−1 unit
Change in costs	+£13	−£12	+£13	−£15

Net change in costs = £(+13 − 12 + 13 − 15) = −£1

Table 2-8 Changes in quantities and costs using Route x_{12}

Cell	Quantity change	Cost change
x_{12}	+1	+11
x_{22}	−1	−10
x_{23}	+1	+13
x_{13}	−1	−12
Net change in costs	0	+2

currently unused cell in the table: trace a new route using currently used cells and then calculate the net change in costs of using this new route to ship one unit of the good.

Student activity
Using this method, determine whether Route x_{12} would lead to an improved solution.

Using cell x_{12} we can trace an appropriate path and determine the associated costs, as in Table 2-8. In the case of cell x_{12}, using this route in a new solution will actually lead to an *increase* in total costs and not to a decrease as we would require. Similar calculations can be undertaken for all the other unused cells. Two points need to be made, however, before we do this. The first is that in order to draw a closed path we may have to undertake considerable movement around the table—the path in a large table may be quite complex. The second point is that it is permissible to 'jump over' occupied cells that are not needed to trace a direct path. Effectively, we can ignore a cell if it is not at the 'corner point' of the path.

Student activity
Trace the paths and assess the effect on total costs for all the other currently unused routes.

Taking all the unused routes in turn we have:

Cell x_{11}:
Path: x_{11} x_{31} x_{34} x_{24} x_{23} x_{13}
Cost: +20 −9 +20 −15 +13 −12 = +£17

28 TRANSPORTATION AND ASSIGNMENT

Cell x_{21}:
Path: $x_{21}\ x_{31}\ x_{34}\ x_{24}$
Cost: $+11\ -9\ +20\ -15$ $\quad = +£7$

Cell x_{32}:
Path: $x_{32}\ x_{34}\ x_{24}\ x_{22}$
Cost: $+12\ -20\ +15\ -10$ $\quad = -£3$

Cell x_{33}:
Path: $x_{33}\ x_{34}\ x_{24}\ x_{23}$
Cost: $+15\ -20\ +15\ -13$ $\quad = -£3$

Table 2-9 summarizes these results. We see that there are three routes that are currently unused, which, if brought into the solution, would lead to a reduction in the total transport costs—x_{14}, x_{32}, x_{33}. Given that our objective is to minimize these costs, our preference, since we assess only one new route at a time, would be to use either Route x_{32} or Route x_{33}, since both lead to the largest per-unit cost saving. We can, however, go one stage further than this and rationally choose between these two. Given that both offer the same potential for savings per unit it would appear sensible to examine the *total* quantities that could be shipped on each of these new routes and thereby quantify the total cost savings of the two options. Let us examine x_{32} first. This route involves the following steps:

adding units to cell x_{32} and cell x_{24};
subtracting units from cell x_{34} and cell x_{22}.

Given that part of the problem formulation is that no variable can take a negative value (Eq. 2-9), then we can only reduce the quantities in cells x_{34} and x_{22} until they reach zero. This will occur first when we have reduced x_{34} by 300 units. The four cells will then have associated quantities of:

$$x_{32}\quad 300\ (=\ \ \ 0+300)$$
$$x_{34}\quad\ \ \ 0\ (=300-300)$$
$$x_{24}\quad 500\ (=200+300)$$
$$x_{22}\quad 100\ (=400-300)$$

Table 2-9 Changes in costs using all unused routes

Empty cell	Net change in costs
x_{11}	$+£17$
x_{12}	$+£2$
x_{14}	$-£1$
x_{21}	$+£7$
x_{32}	$-£3$
x_{33}	$-£3$

Given that this transfer of units shipped will reduce total costs by £3 per unit, the total cost saving of using the new route x_{32} will be £900 (£3 × 300 units).

Student activity
Calculate the total cost saving if we use Route x_{33} instead. Which of the two new routes should we choose?

The equivalent calculations show that using Route x_{33} would allow us to transfer only 100 units at a total cost saving of £300. At this stage, therefore, the preferred new route is x_{32}.

Student activity
Calculate the new transportation table using the new route and the associated total cost.

The new table is readily calculated and is shown as Table 2-10. The cost of the new solution is £20 000 (£900 lower than the initial solution). The solution program now repeats itself.

1. For each empty cell we trace a path through the table using current routes.
2. For each path we determine the net effect on total cost.
3. Any negative net change indicates an improved solution. We then compute the new basic feasible solution.
4. If there is no empty cell with a negative net change we have reached the optimal solution and the program stops.

You should be able to appreciate that it is necessary to repeat the whole program because a number of the stepping stone paths will now have altered because of the new route allocations.

Table 2-10 Transportation table: the new solution using x_{32}

Origins	Destinations				Origin capacity
	Depot A	Depot B	Depot C	Depot D	
Northtown	20 0	11 0	12 400	13 0	400
Midtown	11 0	10 100	13 100	15 500	700
Southtown	9 200	12 300	15 0	20 0	500
Destination requirement	200	400	500	500	1600

30 TRANSPORTATION AND ASSIGNMENT

Student activity
Determine whether an improved solution is possible for the route allocation shown in Table 2-10.

The evaluation of the net change for each empty cell in Table 2-10 is shown in Table 2-11. From this we see that there is only one currently unused route that will lead to a further reduction in total costs: x_{14}. From Table 2-10 we see that the maximum possible reallocation along this path is 400 units, which will therefore lead to a total cost reduction of £400. We now proceed as before to calculate the table for the new route allocations (i.e. the new basic feasible solution). Before doing so, however, it is worth pointing out that we did not in fact need to calculate the net cost for Route x_{34}, given that this was the route that we removed from the previous basis in order to reduce costs. Note also that we have one currently unused cell—x_{33}—which has neither a positive nor a negative net change. This indicates that the use of this route will leave total cost unchanged. We have, therefore, an alternative route allocation solution to that shown in Table 2-10. The issue of alternative solutions is one to which we shall return in the next chapter. Table 2-12 shows the new basis with an associated total cost of £19 600 (£400 lower than the last solution). Again, the program proceeds as before, searching for an improved basic solution.

Table 2-11 Net change for empty cells

Empty cell	Path	Cost coefficients	Net change
x_{11}	$x_{11} - x_{31} + x_{32} - x_{22} + x_{23} - x_{13}$	$20 - 9 + 12 - 10 + 13 - 12$	+ £14
x_{12}	$x_{12} - x_{22} + x_{23} - x_{13}$	$11 - 10 + 13 - 12$	+ £2
x_{14}	$x_{14} - x_{13} + x_{23} - x_{24}$	$13 - 12 + 13 - 15$	− £1
x_{21}	$x_{21} - x_{31} + x_{32} - x_{22}$	$11 - 9 + 12 - 10$	+ £4
x_{33}	$x_{33} - x_{23} + x_{22} - x_{32}$	$15 - 13 + 10 - 12$	£0
x_{34}	$x_{34} - x_{24} + x_{22} - x_{32}$	$20 - 15 + 10 - 12$	+ £3

Table 2-12 Transportation table: the new solution using x_{32}

Origins	Destinations				Origin capacity
	Depot A	Depot B	Depot C	Depot D	
Northtown	20 0	11 0	12 0	13 400	400
Midtown	11 0	10 100	13 500	15 100	700
Southtown	9 200	12 300	15 0	20 0	500
Destination requirement	200	400	500	500	1600

Student activity
Determine whether any improvement in Table 2-12 is possible.

Again, the paths and associated costs for the non-basic variables are shown in Table 2-13. As we see, there are now no empty cells with a negative net change figure. No further reductions in cost can be achieved by reallocating routes, so we conclude that the route allocations shown in Table 2-12 are optimal. We have, therefore, found the cost-minimizing solution, with units of the goods shipped across the routes shown in Table 2-12 and at a total cost of £19 600.

Table 2-13 Paths and costs for non-basic variables

Empty cell	Path	Cost coefficients	Net change
x_{11}	$x_{11} - x_{31} + x_{32} - x_{22} + x_{24} - x_{14}$	$20 - 9 + 12 - 10 + 15 - 13$	$+£15$
x_{12}	$x_{12} - x_{22} + x_{24} - x_{14}$	$11 - 10 + 15 - 13$	$+£3$
x_{13}	$x_{13} - x_{23} + x_{24} - x_{14}$	$12 - 13 + 15 - 13$	$+£1$
x_{21}	$x_{21} - x_{31} + x_{32} - x_{22}$	$11 - 9 + 12 - 10$	$+£4$
x_{33}	$x_{33} - x_{23} + x_{22} - x_{32}$	$15 - 13 + 10 - 12$	$£0$
x_{34}	$x_{34} - x_{24} + x_{22} - x_{32}$	$20 - 15 + 10 - 12$	$+£3$

2-5 TESTING FOR AN IMPROVED SOLUTION: THE MODIFIED DISTRIBUTION METHOD

Whilst the stepping stone method is simple in its logic, the arithmetic involved in the need to establish a path for each non-basic variable makes the method both tedious and time-consuming for all but the smallest problem. An alternative solution method exists which we shall examine. This is the *modified distribution method* (referred to as the *MODI* method for short). In addition to providing an alternative solution program the method also introduces a number of important principles, which we shall develop throughout the text. You will remember that in the stepping stone method we identified a suitable path for a currently empty cell and then calculated the net change in the objective function of shipping one unit over this new route. This net change can be regarded as an *improvement index*—a figure showing by how much per unit the objective function will 'improve' if we use this route. As we saw for this minimization problem, a negative improvement index indicates an improved route allocation, whilst a positive index indicates a new route that will not reduce total transport costs. The MODI method calculates the equivalent improvement index at each iteration of the program but in a different—and arithmetically easier—way. Before we look at the arithmetic method it will be worth while discussing the logic of what we are about to do. Let us return to Table 2-4, which showed the initial feasible solution to the problem (using the least-cost method). The table is duplicated on page 32.

Each occupied cell actually involves two separate cost considerations. Let us examine cell x_{13}. The obvious cost involved in using this route is the per-unit shipping cost of £12. However, by utilizing this particular route we are implicitly 'saving' the cost of shipping

32 TRANSPORTATION AND ASSIGNMENT

Table 2-4 Transportation table: initial feasible solution—least-cost method

Origins	Depot A	Depot B	Depot C	Depot D	Origin capacity
Northtown	20 0	11 0	12 400	13 0	400
Midtown	11 0	10 400	13 100	15 200	700
Southtown	9 200	12 0	15 0	20 300	500
Destination requirement	200	400	500	500	1600

these units by the other available routes (given that if we did not utilize this route we would have to use others to find a feasible solution). In the example of cell x_{13}, if we did not supply Depot C from Northtown we would have to supply from the Midtown and/or Southtown factories at the appropriate cost per unit. We shall denote this cost saving as u. Similarly, if we did not utilize Route x_{13} then the output from the Northtown factory would have to be redirected to one of the other 3 depots. We shall denote this cost as v. Because of the tabular format of our problem it becomes necessary to distinguish between the u's and v's associated with each route. To do this we use subscript notation to denote the row and column combinations. So, for the route under examination—x_{13}—the total cost 'savings' will be given by $u_1 + v_3$. These 'savings' can be regarded as a type of *opportunity cost*. They are not a cost or saving in the strict financial sense but they do indicate the opportunity or sacrifice costs inherent in using a particular route in the table. They reflect the cost of *not* using this route. (We shall see as we develop further models that mathematical programming makes considerable use of the opportunity cost concept.) It would now be logical to compare these cost savings with the actual cost of using the route. The actual shipping cost of using this route is £12 per unit. Consider IMC's reaction should we find that $(u_1 + v_3) > 12$. Logically, if the cost savings from using this route were greater than the actual shipping costs then we would decide to ship an unlimited quantity of units via this route. But, because of our initial problem formulation, there are finite limits on both the available supply and the required demand. In consequence, therefore, we would specify that the cost savings should be no greater than the actual shipping cost, or:

$$u_1 + v_3 \leq 12 \quad \text{for the Northtown–Depot C route}$$

This expression places an upper limit on the cost savings that can be achieved. However, it is also evident that should the cost savings of using this route be less than the actual shipping costs then there would be no point using the route. In other words, the quantity to be shipped via this route would be zero when:

$$u_1 + v_3 < 12$$

Table 2-14 Costs for occupied cells

Occupied cell	Opportunity cost
x_{13}	$u_1 + v_3 = 12$
x_{22}	$u_2 + v_2 = 10$
x_{23}	$u_2 + v_3 = 13$
x_{24}	$u_2 + v_4 = 15$
x_{31}	$u_3 + v_1 = 9$
x_{34}	$u_3 + v_4 = 20$

This implies, therefore, that this particular route would be used only when the cost savings equal the actual cost of shipping a unit via this route:

$$u_1 + v_3 = 12$$

We can repeat this logic for all currently occupied cells in Table 2-4. The appropriate relationships are shown in Table 2-14. This gives a system of 6 equations and 7 unknowns where the unknowns are the opportunity costs of not using a particular route. Because there are more unknowns than equations it is impossible to find a unique solution. However, given that our interest is in comparing *relative* costs we can overcome this difficulty by setting one of the unknowns arbitrarily to zero. In practice, it is irrelevant as to which variable is treated in this way, so for convenience we shall always set u_1 to zero. With $u_1 = 0$ it now becomes possible to find the value of v_3 (= 12) and with v_3 known we can proceed to find the appropriate value for u_2 and then for the other variables in the set.

Student activity
Determine the appropriate values for all the u and v variables given above, with $u_1 = 0$.

The corresponding values are derived as:

$$u_1 = 0 \quad v_1 = 3$$
$$u_2 = 1 \quad v_2 = 9$$
$$u_3 = 6 \quad v_3 = 12$$
$$ \quad v_4 = 14$$

We can introduce these cost savings into the transportation tableau shown in Table 2-15. Let us now denote a new variable—an improvement index—such that:

$$I_{ij} = c_{ij} - u_i - v_j$$

that is, the index for any cell is simply the difference between the actual per-unit shipping cost and the cost 'savings' (the opportunity costs of not using that route). We can now proceed to calculate such an index for all cells in the table, both occupied and empty.

Student activity
Calculate the improvement indices for all the currently occupied cells in Table 2-9.

Table 2-15 Transportation table: initial feasible solution—least-cost method showing u and v cost savings

Origins	Destinations				Origin capacity	u_i
	Depot A	Depot B	Depot C	Depot D		
Northtown	20 0	11 0	12 400	13 0	400	0
Midtown	11 0	10 400	13 100	15 200	700	1
Southtown	9 200	12 0	15 0	20 300	500	6
Destination requirement	200	400	500	500	1600	
v_j	3	9	12	14		

Table 2-16 Improvement indices for occupied cells

Cell	c	u	v	Index
x_{13}	12	0	12	0
x_{22}	10	1	9	0
x_{23}	13	1	12	0
x_{24}	15	1	14	0
x_{31}	9	3	6	0
x_{34}	20	6	14	0

For each of the currently occupied cells the index is calculated as shown in Table 2-16. So, for each of the current basic variables the improvement index is zero. The logic of this is apparent. The index shows the net change of total costs by changing to a specific route. But given that all these routes are currently used, no further improvement in the objective function value is possible. It is more instructive, however, to perform the same arithmetic on the non-basic variables in the current solution.

Student activity

Calculate the improvement index for each empty cell in Table 2-15. Compare these indices with those obtained for Table 2-4 using the stepping stone method.

The improvement index for each non-basic variable is shown in Table 2-17. It can be seen that we obtain exactly the same values for the improvement indices as we do using the stepping stone method and, logically, the same interpretation can be given to these indices. Thus, if we examine cell x_{33} we conclude that if we were to use this (currently unused) route then total transport costs would fall by £3 per unit shipped. The advantage

Table 2-17 Improvement indices for non-basic variables

Cell	c	u	v	Index
x_{11}	20	0	3	17
x_{12}	11	0	9	2
x_{14}	13	0	14	−1
x_{21}	11	1	3	7
x_{32}	12	6	9	−3
x_{33}	15	6	12	−3

of the MODI approach is that it is not necessary to identify a path through the table for each and every empty cell. It is only necessary to calculate the improvement index and, having decided on the new route to be included, determine the appropriate path through the distribution network. In this example we have (as before) two routes with the same index value of -3 and, as with the stepping stone method, we would next determine which of these routes leads to the largest absolute change in total costs (here we already know it will be cell x_{32}). We now proceed to incorporate this new route into the solution as we did before. To summarize the MODI approach:

Stage 1 For the current solution calculate an appropriate set of u and v values for the basic variables.

Stage 2 For each empty cell calculate the improvement index using the formula $(c_{ij} - u_i - v_j)$.

Stage 3 Identify the cell with the largest negative index. This is the cell to be introduced into the solution.

Stage 4 For this chosen cell determine the appropriate path through the transportation network and the maximum quantity that can be reallocated.

Stage 5 Update the transportation table.

Stage 6 Repeat from Stage 1 until no empty cell shows a negative improvement index. This is the optimal solution.

It may seem at this stage that the MODI method is unduly clumsy and offers little advantage over the stepping stone method. In fact, the determination of the required u and v values can usually be achieved through visual inspection of the current tableau and proves quicker than the tracing of paths through the table as is required by the stepping stone method. In addition, the MODI method offers considerable potential for more detailed analysis of the final solution to a transportation problem (and indeed leads into methods that are applicable to the other forms of mathematical programming). This is an aspect of the MODI method that we shall investigate in Chapter 3. Returning to our

36 TRANSPORTATION AND ASSIGNMENT

Table 2-18 Transportation table: the new solution using x_{32}

Origins	Depot A	Depot B	Depot C	Depot D	Origin capacity	u
Northtown	20 / 0	11 / 0	12 / 400	13 / 0	400	
Midtown	11 / 0	10 / 100	13 / 100	15 / 500	700	
Southtown	9 / 200	12 / 300	15 / 0	20 / 0	500	
Destination requirement	200	400	500	500	1600	
v						

example, we would now have a new solution using Route x_{32} and the corresponding table is as shown in Table 2-18.

Because the basic solution changes it is now necessary to recompute the u and v coefficients in the table. Again, we follow the same procedure (but this time we can determine the appropriate values directly from visual inspection of the table). We arbitrarily set the first u value to zero, and we can then determine what the other u and v values must be, given that for any occupied cell we require $c_{ij} = u_i + v_j$.

Student activity

Complete the u and v values in Table 2-18 and the appropriate improvement indices.

Table 2-19 shows the completed values. The calculations for the improvement indices are shown in Table 2-20. Again, we obtain the same values as we did using the stepping stone method and we confirm that the use of Route x_{14} will lead to a further improvement in the current solution. We can now trace the path of this new route $(x_{14} x_{13} x_{23} x_{24})$ and determine the maximum quantity that can be reallocated (400). The new table can then be constructed.

Student activity

Construct the new transportation table. Calculate the appropriate u and v values and determine whether any further improvement in the objective function is possible.

Table 2-21 shows the new basic solution and the new set of improvement indices is given in Table 2-22. These confirm that we have found the optimal solution, given that no further route reallocation will lead to a reduction in total costs. It can be seen that the

Table 2-19 Transportation table: the new solution using x_{32}

Origins	Destinations				Origin capacity	u
	Depot A	Depot B	Depot C	Depot D		
Northtown	20 0	11 0	12 400	13 0	400	0
Midtown	11 0	10 100	13 100	15 500	700	1
Southtown	9 200	12 300	15 0	20 0	500	3
Destination requirement	200	400	500	500	1600	
v	6	9	12	14		

Table 2-20 Calculations for improvement indices

Cell	c	u	v	Index
x_{11}	20	0	6	14
x_{12}	11	0	9	2
x_{14}	13	0	14	−1
x_{21}	11	1	6	4
x_{33}	15	3	12	0
x_{34}	20	3	14	3

Table 2-21 Transportation table: the new solution using x_{14}

Origins	Destinations				Origin capacity	u
	Depot A	Depot B	Depot C	Depot D		
Northtown	20 0	11 0	12 0	13 400	400	0
Midtown	11 0	10 100	13 500	15 100	700	2
Southtown	9 200	12 300	15 0	20 0	500	4
Destination requirement	200	400	500	500	1600	
v	5	8	11	13		

38 TRANSPORTATION AND ASSIGNMENT

Table 2-22 Improvement indices for the new solution

Cell	c	u	v	Index
x_{11}	20	0	5	15
x_{12}	11	0	8	3
x_{13}	12	0	11	1
x_{21}	11	5	2	4
x_{33}	15	4	11	0
x_{34}	20	4	13	3

MODI method produces the same optimal solution as the stepping stone method which we used earlier.

2-6 SUMMARY

This chapter has introduced the first of the mathematical programming models that we are examining. In problems of the transportation type we typically wish to ship fixed quantities of some item from a number of origins to a number of destinations (although, as the end-of-chapter exercises illustrate, the model can be applied to a surprisingly different number of business problems). Although the basic model is logically simple to develop and to solve it introduces important general features of mathematical programming that are common to all the models we shall be considering. We have seen that the formulation of a transportation problem revolves around the use of a simple table which incorporates both the objective function and the constraints imposed on the problem. Two alternative (but in some ways complimentary) solution methods were presented: the stepping stone method and the MODI method. The stepping stone method requires us, at each stage, to determine the new path that would be required should we use a new cell in the solution and to determine the effect (based on opportunity costs) on the objective function of using this route. The MODI method calculates an improvement index for each unused route to determine whether any further improvement in the objective function value is possible.

In the next chapter we shall examine some of the extensions that can readily be made to the basic transportation model and see how the solution methods are able to deal with such extensions.

STUDENT EXERCISES

You are recommended to solve (at least one of) these problems manually to ensure you understand the mechanics of the solution process.

2-1 The senior management team of the local regional health authority are reviewing their current policy on the supply of blood and plasma to the area's hospitals. At the moment all blood and plasma collected is sent to 1 of 3 central storage and processing depots (A, B and C). At the depot the blood is analysed, labelled and checked for suitability for different categories of patients. On a daily basis the 3 major hospitals in the authority's area (X, Y and Z) are supplied with a regular, fixed quantity of blood each day. The supply is in line with the planned number

Table 2-23

Units of blood/plasma available		Units of blood/plasma required	
Depot A	2500	Hospital X	2000
B	2100	Y	2500
C	1500	Z	1600

Table 2-24

	Hospital		
	X	Y	Z
Depot A	10	12	24
B	19	11	20
C	12	15	22

of operations and transfusions due to take place at that hospital. Emergency supplies are allocated separately. The current status of demand and supply is shown in Table 2-23. The authority has calculated the time that it takes to deliver a supply from each depot to each hospital (time is a critical factor given the required storage conditions). This is expressed in minutes per unit (Table 2-24).

Required:

(a) Formulate this problem using the standard mathematical notation.
(b) Determine the optimal solution to this problem (you may wish to use both solution methods to familiarize yourself with the two alternatives).
(c) From a management perspective do you think we have chosen the correct objective? What others could you suggest?
(d) Explain why, for Hospital Z, the minimum-time route is not used.
(e) The problem is currently formulated as a balanced transportation problem. In what ways do you think an unbalanced problem could arise in this context? How would you try and resolve such an imbalance given the solution programs available?

2-2 A large local authority is reviewing its waste disposal policies in the light of the current environmental debate; 4 waste disposal sites are currently operating of which 2 are landfill sites and 2 are incinerators. The 4 sites handle domestic waste collected from 4 geographical areas managed by the local authority. Denote the areas as A, B, C, D and the 4 sites as L1, L2, I1, I2. The local authority has calculated the transport cost (£ per tonne) of each area using each site as shown in Table 2-25. In addition the authority has also determined the maximum capacity of each site in terms of the quantity of waste it can handle on a monthly basis and the likely amount of waste generated by each area. These are as shown in Table 2-26. As well as quantifying transport costs the

Table 2-25 Transport costs: £ per tonne

	L1	L2	I1	I2
A	12	15	12	18
B	11	10	11	12
C	12	9	8	11
D	11	8	5	10

40 TRANSPORTATION AND ASSIGNMENT

Table 2-26

Depot	Maximum waste processed (tonnes)	Area	Waste supplied (tonnes)
L1	6 000	A	11 000
L2	15 000	B	7 000
I1	5 000	C	5 000
I2	4 000	D	8 000

authority has also analysed the operating costs of each of the 4 sites. On an annual basis these are £360 000, £720 000, £216 000 and £192 000 for the 4 sites respectively.

Required:

(a) If the authority wishes to minimize total transport costs formulate this problem mathematically.
(b) Using the MODI method determine the optimal solution.
(c) What other factors might you wish to consider before implementing the solution found?
(d) Draft a report to management explaining why Site A is required to process the highest-cost waste available.
(e) Management now wish to determine the optimum solution if operating costs are included in the problem. Incorporate these costs (*hint*: calculate a monthly cost per tonne per site) into the problem and re-solve. Compare your solution with that in part (b) and comment upon the solution.
(f) Because of environmental pressure Site L1 cannot take waste from Area A. Determine how you could incorporate such a factor into the problem and—if you can—determine the new solution.

2-3 Following severe traffic disruption over the last few winters a review is currently under way into the policy of salting and gritting the major roads in the area. At present there are 4 depots where—for purposes of security, access and maintenance—gritting vehicles are based. There are also 3 (geographically different) sites where the grit–salt mixture used on the roads is stored. Currently, on receiving an adverse weather prediction the gritting vehicles are directed to one of the three sites (A, B, C) to be loaded with grit–salt. At the moment this operates as a very hit-and-miss affair with the gritting supervisor trying to ensure on an *ad-hoc* basis that not too many vehicles are sent to load up at one particular site—and thereby causing queuing problems and delays—and that, equally, particular sites do not exhaust their supply of grit–salt and cause stock control difficulties. You have been asked to try to determine a more rational policy of allocating vehicles from each depot to a particular site to load up with grit-salt.

Analysis undertaken over the past few winters has revealed that the 4 depots require an average quantity of grit-salt each week over the winter period:

Depot 1	200 tonnes
2	75 tonnes
3	125 tonnes
4	200 tonnes

whilst because of size and space limitations the 3 sites where grit-salt is stored have maximum weekly storage capacities of 200 tonnes, 250 tonnes and 150 tonnes respectively for Sites A, B and C. At this stage in the analysis it is considered that a suitable objective would be to seek to minimize total distance covered by the vehicles between depots and sites and the mileage figures shown in Table 2-27 are appropriate.

Required:

(a) Discuss whether you feel the objective set is the most appropriate. What others could you suggest?
(b) Determine the optimal solution to this problem using the MODI method.
(c) One alternative objective function suggested has been to work out a cost per route calculated by multiplying the distance values shown in Table 2-27 by a fixed cost per mile. Comment upon this suggestion in terms of how you think it will affect the optimal solution.

Table 2-27 Distance between sites and depots: miles

Site	Depot 1	2	3	4
A	1.2	2.1	1.2	2.3
B	3.8	5.4	5.2	4.3
C	3.9	4.4	3.2	4.1

(d) Your solution should indicate one cell's improvement index equal to zero. How do you interpret this and what use do you think this information might be to management?

(e) Because of an inter-union dispute certain site–depot combinations cannot be used. Discuss how this might be incorporated into the problem.

(f) How useful do you think the model is in this context to management? What other factors might management wish to consider before acting upon the solution suggested in (b)?

2-4 The police department in a large city is currently undergoing reorganization and redeployment. This has been made necessary because of major changes in underlying social and economic conditions: demographic changes, employment patterns, slum clearance, etc. The department has 4 stations in the city centre area each of which maintains a small team of officers whose task is to respond to calls from the public requesting emergency assistance. Details of the staff available are shown in Table 2-28. For administration and budgeting purposes the city has been divided into 3 zones: A, B and C. The department is currently trying to determine how to allocate officers from a particular station to a specific zone so that emergency calls are automatically routed to the correct police station. Analysis into the likely number of calls per shift has revealed the following:

Zone	Average no. of calls
A	14
B	20
C	11

Table 2-28

Station	Officers available per 4 hour shift
1	10
2	15
3	8
4	12

The police commissioner feels that, at the moment, the best policy will be to allocate officers from a station to a particular zone so as to minimize the likely response time—i.e. the time taken for the call to be routed to the appropriate station, details taken, an officer informed and travel time to the scene. Details of likely response times are shown in Table 2-29.

Required:

(a) Determine how many officers from each station should be allocated to each zone.
(b) Comment upon the criteria used to determine such a solution.
(c) Given that much of the data relates to averages and is hence variable to some degree, comment upon the

Table 2-29

	Zone		
	A	B	C
Station			
1	6	8	9
2	5	5	5
3	7	6	8
4	8	9	9

effect such variation might be expected to have on the optimal solution. How could such variability be dealt with in this technique?

3
EXTENSIONS TO THE TRANSPORTATION MODEL

In this chapter we consider a number of logical extensions to the basic transportation model which are necessary both to allow it to deal with more complex problems and to make it more realistic in terms of its application to business. The model in the previous chapter was one which we referred to as a *balanced* model, since the total quantity available from origins and the total quantity required by destinations were the same. It is apparent that in the real world such a convenient match between supply and demand is at best not certain and in general unlikely. Situations where supply exceeds demand or demand exceeds supply are common and we need to adapt the basic model to deal with such situations. Additionally, not all transportation problems will have an objective function which requires minimizing: we may well encounter problems where the *maximization* of an objective function is more appropriate. Transportation problems also occur where certain routes may be prohibited for a variety of reasons, or alternatively there may be a requirement that some routes *must* be used no matter what the cost. Methods for dealing with such restrictions are introduced in this chapter. We also examine in detail the optimal solution to the transportation problem to consider how we can assess the effect that changes in the structure of the original problem might have on the optimal solution. This is an important area in mathematical programming known as *sensitivity analysis* and will be expanded as we introduce other programming models. Finally, we consider the problem of *degeneracy* in transportation, which relates to problems where there are fewer than $(n + m - 1)$ basic variables in the solution.

3-1 UNBALANCED TRANSPORTATION PROBLEMS

We return to the transportation problem we were examining in the previous chapter. The demand for the item and the supply available were exactly equal. Let us now assume that the Southtown factory is, for some reason, forced to reduce its output from 500 to 350

44 TRANSPORTATION AND ASSIGNMENT

units, a reduction of 150 units. This may be caused by an industrial dispute that affects production, a shortage of some key resource or indeed may be a planned management decision. We now face an *unbalanced* problem where demand exceeds supply. In other situations we may well face the reverse: supply may exceed demand. Both types of unbalanced problem are dealt with in the same way and we now turn to investigate how the solution program we developed in the last chapter can deal with such an imbalance. Initially, we might consider that the previous optimal solution—shown in Table 2-12—would form the basis for resolving the difficulty. We might argue that as the shortage is caused by the Southtown plant then we should, in some way, distribute the shortage across the depots supplied by Southtown. We might suggest, for example, that as Depots A and B are supplied by Southtown then these depots should have their supply reduced by, say, 75 units each. Whilst this approach may appear logical it will not necessarily lead us to the new optimal solution. Such an approach ignores the opportunity costs inherent in the problem. Given that at least one depot must be supplied with less than it actually requires we should attempt to determine the effect such shortfalls will have on costs. The way we deal with such unbalanced problems is straightforward: we introduce a *dummy* row (or a dummy column if supply exceeds demand), which will represent the unsatisfied demand.

Unbalanced problems: demand exceeds supply

The general structure of a transportation table which includes such a dummy row is shown in Table 3-1. The table shows the dummy row representing that demand that cannot be satisfied from the existing 3 factories with excess demand equal to 150 units. We can now treat the dummy row in exactly the same way as any other. Each cell represents a potential transportation route, although such routes are symbolic rather than physical since each cell in this row actually represents unsatisfied demand at one of the 4 depots. We now allocate costs to these cells and then, using the least-cost method, determine an initial feasible

Table 3-1 Transportation table: a dummy row

Origins	Destinations				Origin capacity
	Depot A	Depot B	Depot C	Depot D	
Northtown					400
Midtown					700
Southtown					350
Dummy origin					150
Destination requirement	200	400	500	500	1600

Table 3-2 Transportation table: dummy row cost coefficients

Origins	Destinations				Origin capacity
	Depot A	Depot B	Depot C	Depot D	
Northtown	20	11	12	13	400
Midtown	11	10	13	15	700
Southtown	9	12	15	20	350
Dummy origin	0	0	0	0	150
Destination requirement	200	400	500	500	1600

solution. Using either the stepping stone or the MODI method we can then proceed in the usual way to determine whether an improved solution exists. It would be logical to assign each cell in the dummy row a zero-cost coefficient, since transportation of excess demand does not actually take place and no transport cost as such will be incurred by using such a 'route'. The table then becomes Table 3-2.

We can now proceed to establish an initial feasible solution using the least-cost method. It is apparent that the first allocation will be to one of the cells in the dummy row. It will not, in general, matter which of the 4 cells we choose (given that our solution program will eventually determine the new optimal allocation). However, let us arbitrarily choose to use cell x_{41}; that is, the shortfall in supply will be imposed on Depot A. We also decide that we shall use the MODI program for finding the optimum solution.

Student activity
Determine the tableau for the initial feasible solution. Calculate the appropriate u and v values for the MODI method.

The allocation of quantities to cells in least-cost order would be: $x_{41}, x_{31}, x_{22}, x_{13}, x_{23}$, x_{24}, x_{34} and the solution has an associated total transport cost of £19 550. The appropriate u and v values are also shown in Table 3-3. (Note that u_4 takes a negative value. This has no specific significance given that the absolute value of the coefficients for u and v are arbitrary—remember that we use them to calculate *relative* improvement indices.) Using these values we can then determine the improvement indices for each of the unused cells, as shown in Table 3-4.

Using the criteria developed in the last chapter, Route x_{44} is the new route to be added to the solution, given that it will have the largest effect on reducing total transport costs. The corresponding path will be: $x_{44}, x_{34}, x_{31}, x_{41}$, with a maximum quantity reallocated of 150 units. The logic of this reallocation is apparent. Initially, we decide on an arbitrary

Table 3-3 Transportation table: initial feasible solution

Origins	Destinations				Origin capacity	u
	Depot A	Depot B	Depot C	Depot D		
Northtown	20 0	11 0	12 400	13 0	400	0
Midtown	11 0	10 400	13 100	15 200	700	1
Southtown	9 50	12 0	15 0	20 300	350	6
Dummy origin	0 150	0 0	0 0	0 0	150	-3
Destination requirement	200	400	500	500	1600	
v	3	9	12	14		

Table 3-4 Improvement indices for unused cells

Cell	c	u	v	Index
x_{11}	20	0	3	17
x_{12}	11	0	9	2
x_{14}	13	0	14	-1
x_{21}	11	1	3	7
x_{32}	12	6	9	-3
x_{33}	15	6	12	-3
x_{42}	0	-3	9	-6
x_{43}	0	-3	12	-9
x_{44}	0	-3	14	-11

basis that Depot A was to bear the full brunt of the supply shortfall and would be supplied with 150 units less than it required. At this next stage (which is not necessarily the optimal) total transport costs will be reduced if we transfer the shortfall instead to Depot D. You may also have noticed that the improvement indices calculated above are (allowing for the new dummy row cells) identical to those we calculated for the original problem in Table 2-15 in Chapter 2. Adding the dummy row has not altered the relative opportunity costs of the other routes (which is what the u and v values measure).

Student activity
Calculate the new tableau incorporating Route x_{44} and determine the new u and v values, together with the improvement indices.

Table 3-5 Transportation table: first iteration

Origins	Destinations				Origin capacity	u
	Depot A	Depot B	Depot C	Depot D		
Northtown	20 0	11 0	12 400	13 0	400	0
Midtown	11 0	10 400	13 100	15 200	700	1
Southtown	9 200	12 0	15 0	20 150	350	6
Dummy origin	0 0	0 0	0 0	0 150	150	−14
Destination requirement	200	400	500	500	1600	
v	3	9	12	14		

Table 3-6 Improvement indices for non-basic variables

Cell	c	u	v	Index
x_{11}	20	0	3	17
x_{12}	11	0	9	2
x_{14}	13	0	14	−1
x_{21}	11	1	3	7
x_{32}	12	6	9	−3
x_{33}	15	6	12	−3
x_{41}	0	−14	3	11
x_{42}	0	−14	9	5
x_{43}	0	−14	12	2

The new table and associated u and v values are shown in Table 3-5 with an associated cost of £17 900 (a reduction of £1650 from the last iteration, = £11 × 150 units). Again, we can repeat the MODI process and calculate the improvement indices for the non-basic variables (Table 3-6).

We confirm that these indices are the same as those used at the equivalent solution stage in Chapter 2. You should appreciate that what the solution program has done at this stage is to allocate the supply shortfall to the depot with the lowest opportunity cost—the depot where the consequences of *not* supplying the full quantity demanded will be lowest. The rest of the solution program will now be identical to that in the last chapter (allowing for the extra row in the table).

Student activity
Complete the rest of the program and determine the optimal solution to this problem.

The optimal solution is shown in Table 3-7 and again the improvement indices are readily calculated (Table 3-8). These confirm that no further improvement in the current route allocation is possible and that the optimal transport costs are £17 100. The new optimal solution has resulted in Depot D having unsatisfied demand of 150 units. It is also apparent that there has been a reallocation of routes used and quantities shipped to balance the rest of the table. Depot C, for example, is now supplied from Midtown as well as from Northtown, whereas in the original problem its sole supplier was the Northtown

Table 3-7 Transportation table: third iteration

Origins	Destinations				Origin capacity	u
	Depot A	Depot B	Depot C	Depot D		
Northtown	20 / 0	11 / 0	12 / 50	13 / 350	400	0
Midtown	11 / 0	10 / 250	13 / 450	15 / 0	700	1
Southtown	9 / 200	12 / 150	15 / 0	20 / 0	350	3
Dummy origin	0 / 0	0 / 0	0 / 0	0 / 150	150	−13
Destination requirement	200	400	500	500	1600	
v	6	9	12	13		

Table 3-8 Improvement indices—optimal solution

Cell	c	u	v	Index
x_{11}	20	0	6	14
x_{12}	11	0	9	2
x_{21}	11	1	6	4
x_{24}	15	1	13	1
x_{33}	15	3	12	0
x_{34}	20	3	13	4
x_{41}	0	−13	6	7
x_{42}	0	−13	9	4
x_{43}	0	−13	12	1

factory. It is evident that a simple inspection approach to this problem would have been unlikely to find the new optimal solution, as we have been able to do using the dummy-row approach.

Unbalanced problems: supply exceeds demand

The previous section examined the solution program when demand exceeded supply. For situations where the supply exceeds demand we can again amend the basic solution process through the use of a dummy column rather than a dummy row. To illustrate, assume that the Southtown factory has been able to expand production to 750 units. Demand from the 4 depots remains the same so there will be excess supply to the amount of 250 units. The structure of the transportation table would then be as shown in Table 3-9, where the dummy column represents those units *not* shipped to depots. In effect, such a column would represent the addition to stock levels caused by surplus production. The process of determining the new optimal solution remains exactly the same as before. We could allocate costs of zero to each of the cells in the dummy column, again on the grounds that units that are not shipped from the factories have a zero transport cost. Whilst this is perfectly acceptable, it will be informative to extend the basic problem. Given that any units appearing in this column are added to stocks at a particular factory, we could use an appropriate stockholding cost in the problem instead. Assume, for example, that stockholding costs had been quantified as shown in Table 3-10 so that, for example, to hold one

Table 3-9 Transportation table: a dummy column

Origins	Destinations				Dummy dest'n	Origin capacity
	Depot A	Depot B	Depot C	Depot D		
Northtown						400
Midtown						700
Southtown						750
Destination requirement	200	400	500	500	250	1850

Table 3-10 Stockholding costs

	Cost of holding 1 unit of stock
Northtown	£2
Midtown	£4
Southtown	£3

unit of the product in stock at Northtown costs £2 but £4 at Midtown. Naturally, the use of such stockholding costs does not affect the way in which we determine an optimal solution but does allow us to develop a more realistic model and illustrates the flexibility of the basic transportation model and the ease with which we can incorporate additional aspects of a real-world business problem into the model. The solution of this model is left to you as an end-of-chapter exercise.

3-2 MAXIMIZATION PROBLEMS

So far we have examined problems that are concerned with minimizing the objective function. There is nothing in principle to prevent us formulating, and then solving, a transportation problem that instead involves *maximizing* an objective function. To illustrate this, and the amendments necessary to the solution program, let us return to the problem formulated in Table 3-1. There we had a shortfall of supply and were able to determine how best to allocate this shortfall in order to minimize the relevant transport costs. We could equally have formulated a different objective function. It would have been just as realistic to try to determine the new optimal solution by looking not at transport costs but at the effect on company profitability of allocating the shortfall to each of 4 depots. Assume, for example, that the 4 depots are able to earn the unit profit on sales shown in Table 3-11. It would now be sensible to assess the impact of the reduction in supply in terms of its effect on profit rather than its effect on costs. Given that we know we cannot satisfy all of existing demand, where should we prioritize? We can reformulate the problem so that each cell in the table now has a net profit coefficient associated with it—the difference between the unit profit on sales at a particular depot and the transport costs involved in supplying that unit to the depot. We would then have a transportation table as in Table 3-12.

So, for example, the net profit earned on a unit sold by Depot D and supplied from the factory at Southtown will be £21 (£41 less the transport cost of £20). It should be apparent that the profit coefficients for the dummy row will remain at zero: such routes contribute nothing to profit. The objective function for the problem is now as follows:

$$\begin{aligned}\text{Maximize} \quad & 25q_{11} + 29q_{12} + 32q_{13} + 28q_{14} \\ & + 34q_{21} + 30q_{22} + 31q_{23} + 26q_{24} \\ & + 34q_{31} + 28q_{32} + 29q_{33} + 21q_{34} \\ & + 0q_{41} + 0q_{42} + 0q_{43} + 0q_{44} \end{aligned} \quad (3\text{-}1)$$

Table 3-11 Unit profit on sales

	Profit per unit sold
Depot A	£45
Depot B	£40
Depot C	£44
Depot D	£41

Table 3-12 Transportation table: net profit coefficients

	Destinations				
Origins	Depot A	Depot B	Depot C	Depot D	Origin capacity
Northtown	25	29	32	28	400
Midtown	34	30	31	26	700
Southtown	34	28	29	21	350
Dummy origin	0	0	0	0	150
Destination requirement	200	400	500	500	1600

whilst the constraints (relating to totals available and totals required) will remain the same. The solution program that we apply to a maximization problem remains more or less the same, although there are certain critical changes required. Let us first examine how we would determine an initial feasible solution. Previously, with a minimization problem we identified such a solution by choosing routes on a least-cost basis. Given that our objective is now maximization, it is sensible to reverse this process: to allocate routes to those cells that will contribute most to the objective function.

Student activity
Determine an initial feasible solution for this problem and calculate the associated profit. Use x_{31} as the first allocation. Consider how we would apply both the stepping stone and MODI methods to determine an optimal solution to such a problem.

The route allocations will be: $x_{31}, x_{13}, x_{23}, x_{22}, x_{24}, x_{34}, x_{44}$, and the solution shown in Table 3-13 generates a total profit of £43 050. The mathematical program for identifying whether an improved solution exists is also readily modified.

The stepping stone method

If we were using the stepping stone method to search for an improved solution we would proceed much as before. For each empty cell we would trace a suitable path through the table, locating as corner stones currently occupied cells. We would then evaluate the effect on the objective function of using this route. Rather than looking for a route that had a *negative* coefficient associated with it (as in minimization problems), we would instead

Table 3-13 Transportation table: an initial feasible solution

Origins	Destinations				Origin capacity
	Depot A	Depot B	Depot C	Depot D	
Northtown	25 0	29 0	32 400	28 0	400
Midtown	34 0	30 400	31 100	26 200	700
Southtown	34 200	28 0	29 0	21 150	350
Dummy origin	0 0	0 0	0 0	0 150	150
Destination requirement	200	400	500	500	1600

seek to identify a route which had a *positive* coefficient. To illustrate, let us examine two of the empty cells: x_{21} and x_{14}. For x_{21} we can trace a suitable path as:

$$x_{21} - x_{31} + x_{34} - x_{24}$$

and the effect on the objective function will be:

$$+34 - 34 + 21 - 26 = -£5$$

That is, if we were to use this new route then the objective function would be reduced by £5 per unit shipped, which is clearly inadvisable given the objective function. Conversely, for Route x_{14} we have:

$$x_{14} - x_{13} + x_{23} - x_{24}$$

and with the effect on profit as:

$$28 - 32 + 31 - 26 = +£1$$

In this case the use of this (currently unused) route will be to increase profit by £1 for each unit shipped via this route, which is in accord with our objective. In a similar vein we could evaluate all the other currently empty cells in exactly the same way and choose the cell with the highest positive coefficient to introduce into the next solution.

The MODI method

The same logic naturally applies to the MODI method. Table 3-14 shows the initial feasible solution and the associated u and v values for the table. Using these u and v values we can now evaluate the opportunity cost of each currently unused cell. Again, if we examine cell x_{21} and x_{14} we have Table 3-15, confirming that cell x_{14} will increase profits at this stage of the solution. Again, it is left as an end-of-chapter exercise to complete the solution to this

Table 3-14 Transportation table: initial solution: MODI method

Origins	Destinations				Origin capacity	u
	Depot A	Depot B	Depot C	Depot D		
Northtown	25 0	29 0	32 400	28 0	400	0
Midtown	34 0	30 400	31 100	26 200	700	−1
Southtown	34 200	28 0	29 0	21 150	350	−6
Dummy origin	0 0	0 0	0 0	0 150	150	−27
Destination requirement	200	400	500	500	1600	
v	40	31	32	27		

Table 3-15 Improvement indices

Cell	Profit	u	v	Improvement index
x_{21}	34	−1	40	−5
x_{14}	28	0	27	1

problem using the MODI method. Maximization problems, therefore, are easily solved using virtually the same mathematical program as for a minimization problem.

3-3 PROHIBITED AND PRIORITY ROUTES

So far we have assumed that all the routes in a transportation table are available for use in both the solution program and the optimal solution. In practice this may not always be the case. For a variety of reasons it may be that one (or more) routes in the table are *prohibited*: they cannot be used. Reasons for this may be several: it may not be physically possible to use a particular route (there may be roadworks for example); there may be legal reasons for not using a route (if certain routes involve the crossing of state or national boundaries); there may be an industrial dispute preventing the use of a particular origin–destination route, and so on. Similarly, there may be certain routes in a problem that we wish to take *priority*—routes that must be used no matter what is the effect on the objective function. There may be some contractual obligation to supply a particular customer, there

Prohibited routes

Let us return to the example illustrated in Table 3-2, which is reproduced here. You will remember that we faced an initial problem where output of the Southtown factory had been reduced by 150 units and we had to determine which of the 4 depots should have their supplies reduced. The new optimal solution we determined allocated the shortfall to Depot D (the solution being shown in Table 3-9). However, let us now assume that Depot D must *not* have its supplies affected. That is, Route x_{44} is prohibited: it cannot be used in any solution. (This may occur, for example, because Depot D has a contract to supply a major customer with 500 units and the company does not wish to jeopardize the contract.) One simple way to incorporate this into the problem is physically to cross out this cell in the table so that it cannot be used in any subsequent calculations. We can then proceed to find the optimal solution (using either the stepping stone or the MODI method) but without using this route at any stage. Whilst this is perfectly acceptable for those problems where we are calculating a solution manually, it will not do for the typical computer package. There is no way we can instruct such a package to 'cross out' one or more routes in the problem—at least not directly. We can, however, achieve the same effect in an indirect way by amending the associated cost coefficient. We can replace this cost with what is known as a *penalty* cost. In this example, we could assign any large number as the penalty cost (say £1000) to this cell. Because of our desire to minimize the total transport costs such a penalty value will effectively prevent the solution program from ever considering the use of this particular route in the solution. The penalty value we use can be any arbitrarily large number (often referred to as 'M'; hence 'the big M method'). The initial solution to the problem and the corresponding table is shown as Table 3-16.

Table 3-2 Transportation table: cost coefficients and supply/demand constraints

Origins	Destinations				Origin capacity
	Depot A	Depot B	Depot C	Depot D	
Northtown	20	11	12	13	400
Midtown	11	10	13	15	700
Southtown	9	12	15	20	350
Dummy origin	0	0	0	0	150
Destination requirement	200	400	500	500	1600

Table 3-16 Transportation table: initial feasible solution—prohibited route

Origins	Destinations Depot A	Depot B	Depot C	Depot D	Origin capacity	u
Northtown	20 / 0	11 / 0	12 / 400	13 / 0	400	0
Midtown	11 / 0	10 / 400	13 / 100	15 / 200	700	1
Southtown	9 / 50	12 / 0	15 / 0	20 / 300	350	6
Dummy origin	0 / 150	0 / 0	0 / 0	1000 / 0	150	−3
Destination requirement	200	400	500	500	1600	
v	3	9	12	14		

The effect of the penalty value on the x_{44} cell is now apparent. If we examine this cell in terms of its u and v values we have:

$$x_{44} \quad 1000 - (-3) - 14 = £989$$

and it is apparent, in the context of all the other cells' cost coefficients, that this empty cell will never be utilized in a solution—its improvement index takes too high a value. The optimal solution for this problem is readily found by use of the MODI method (you may wish to confirm the solution and the use of the penalty value at each iteration yourself).

As we already know from our earlier analysis, the optimal solution without the prohibited route uses cell x_{44}. Now that this is no longer available there are considerable changes in the route allocations used in the optimal solution. Total transport costs for the solution shown in Table 3-17 are £17 350. These compare with the total costs of £17 100 for the original problem. Management can see that by prohibiting the x_{44} route (i.e. by not allowing unsatisfied demand in Depot D) costs increase by £250. This actually leads to an important point about the use of prohibited and priority routes in transportation. It is generally advantageous to solve a problem that involves such restrictions in two ways: first of all with the restriction in place (as we have in Table 3-17) and then again with the restriction removed. Comparison of the two results provides management with direct information about the effect of such a restriction on the objective function value. In other words, management are able to quantify the cost of a specific management decision in terms of prohibiting this route. From Table 3-17 we can also confirm that the optimal solution with the prohibited route results in higher costs. If we examine the u and v values for the prohibited route we see that $-(u-v) = -2$, indicating that if the penalty value was

Table 3-17 Transportation table: optimal solution—prohibited route

Origins	Depot A	Depot B	Depot C	Depot D	Origin capacity	u
Northtown	20 / 0	11 / 0	12 / 0	13 / 400	400	0
Midtown	11 / 0	10 / 250	13 / 350	15 / 100	700	2
Southtown	9 / 200	12 / 150	15 / 0	20 / 0	350	4
Dummy origin	0 / 0	0 / 0	0 / 150	1000 / 0	150	−11
Destination requirement	200	400	500	500	1600	
v	5	8	11	13		

set to zero (i.e. we allow this route to be used if at all appropriate) then the use of this cell would result in a lower value for the objective function at the next iteration.

So, prohibited routes can be readily incorporated into the transportation method. Whilst the above example involved a minimization problem, prohibited routes are also easily incorporated into maximization problems. In such a case the penalty value would be assigned some arbitrarily large *negative* number, given that we will be searching for cells with the highest positive coefficients to maximize the objective function value.

Priority routes

Just as management may seek to impose restrictions on routes that cannot be used, so they may seek to impose restrictions on routes that must be used. For a particular route—x_{ij}—then the restriction may take one of three forms:

1. $x_{ij} = k$
2. $x_{ij} \geq k$
3. $x_{ij} \leq k$

Option 1 implies that the quantity to be shipped via a certain route (ij) must match some defined figure (k). We may specify, for example, in relation to the problem examined in Table 3-2 that the Northtown factory must supply Depot A with exactly 100 units. This is easily dealt with. Before we determine an initial feasible solution we would meet this requirement by allocating 100 units to this route. We would then reduce the total available for shipping via row i ($= 1$ in this example) by 100 also, and correspondingly reduce the

Table 3-18 Transportation table: priority Route x_{11}

Origins	Destinations				Origin capacity
	Depot A	Depot B	Depot C	Depot D	
Northtown	1000	11	12	13	300
Midtown	11	10	13	15	700
Southtown	9	12	15	20	350
Dummy origin	0	0	0	0	150
Destination requirement	100	400	500	500	1500

total demand from destination j by 100 units. Naturally, the grand total of units to be shipped would also be reduced by a corresponding 100 units. This route would then be treated as a prohibited route in order to prevent any further allocation to this cell. The initial table for this problem would then be as shown in Table 3-18.

Row i, column j and the grand total have all been reduced by amount k ($= 100$). The solution program can then proceed as before to find the new optimal solution. Naturally, when the new optimal solution is obtained it must be remembered that 100 units are also being shipped by the priority route and the value for the objective function adjusted accordingly. Option 2 can be treated in an equivalent manner. Assume this time that the requirement was for a minimum of 100 units to be shipped via route x_{11}. That is:

$$x_{11} \geq 100$$

Following a similar logic, we would first allocate the minimum quantity of 100 units to this route. We would then reduce the corresponding row and column totals and the grand total also. However, we would not then proceed to declare this route a prohibited one as we did before. According to the constraint this route can be used to ship *more than* the minimum (should the cost coefficient warrant this), so we would leave the route in the table as a viable alternative. Whether more than 100 units would be shipped via this route would, of course, depend on that cell's improvement index. Again, when the final solution had been found we would need to remember to add back in the quantity shipped via this priority route. The final option—that of $x_{ij} \leq k$—is not one we can deal with at this level. The mathematical complexities involved in incorporating this type of constraint into the transportation program are, from our perspective, not justified. This does not mean, however, that we cannot deal with this type of problem. As we shall see in Part B—when we introduce the more powerful linear programming model—we can readily apply a different mathematical program to transportation problems involving this type of restriction.

3-4 SENSITIVITY ANALYSIS

We next turn to examine the area generally known as *sensitivity analysis* (or as *post-optimality analysis*). This is an area of considerable importance to all the mathematical programming models we shall be examining and it is worth while ensuring that the basic principles are fully appreciated. Virtually all of the models we shall be introducing—including the transportation model—are concerned with determining the optimal solution to some problem. From a management viewpoint, however, whilst such an optimal solution may be useful it will generally not be sufficient by itself. Typically, management will want to know not only what to do at present to optimize some objective but also how further improvements in the objective could be achieved by changing the parameters, or structure, surrounding the problem. Additionally, management will need to consider—and plan for—possible changes in the structure of the problem for which we have found an optimal solution. Questions that may arise to which management will require an adequate and prompt answer would be along the lines of:

- What should we do if the Southtown–Depot C route becomes cheaper?
- What should we do if demand from Depot D increases?
- What should we do if supply from Northtown changes?

Information generated from the optimal solution to allow management to respond to these '*what if*' questions is what sensitivity analysis attempts to provide. Clearly, we could introduce such 'what if' scenarios into our model formulation, reformulate the model from the beginning and then solve the amended problem for the new optimal solution. Realistically, however, this will not always be a viable option. Whilst the problems we have examined have been small (in terms of the number of possible routes) real-world applications may well encompass several thousand possible routes and even with the use of appropriate computer packages the solution of a new problem every time such a 'what if' question arises is not something to be undertaken lightly. Sensitivity analysis, however, aims to avoid the necessity for returning to a reformulation of the original problem. The whole purpose of such analysis (as indicated by its alternative title of *post-optimality* analysis) is to answer such questions directly from the information available in the current final solution. In the area of transportation models this effectively means from the optimal transportation table itself. We shall examine how this is to be achieved and explore three such areas of sensitivity analysis.

Multiple optimal solutions

It is not unusual in transportation problems to find that there may be more than one optimal solution to a given problem. This typically arises because of the large number of routes available in the problem and because many of these routes will have the same cost (or equivalent) coefficient. We have already seen that such an alternative optimal solution will exist whenever:

$$c_{ij} - u_i - v_j = 0$$

The implication of such an index value is that the use of such a route will leave the value of the objective function unchanged. Let us examine Table 3-17, which we found to be the optimal solution to the excess demand problem we examined earlier. If we examine Route x_{33} with an improvement index of 0 ($= 15 - 4 - 11$) then we see that this route could be used in the solution without any change in the objective function value. In this case it would replace Route x_{32}. The existence of such alternative optimal routes is not just a matter of passing arithmetic interest. The availability of such routes provides management with extremely useful information. We now know that—should the current optimal routing become unavailable for any reason—an alternative exists that will not involve the company in any additional transport costs. Such flexibility is likely to be highly prized by management since they are now in a position to respond to changes in the problem environment quickly and efficiently (and, arguably as important) without the need for a total recomputation of the new problem solution.

Changes in the objective function coefficients

We next turn our attention to changes in the objective function coefficients. Staying with the problem illustrated in Table 3-17, it is not unreasonable to suppose that the per-unit cost coefficients used to determine the current solution will be subject both to uncertainty and to future change: uncertainty because in business few figures can be quantified with precision, future change because the environment in which business operates is not a stable one. If we examine, say, the Midtown–Depot A route we see this has a per-unit cost of £11. It would be reasonable to assume that this figure was likely to be some sort of average cost and as such liable to variation (i.e. uncertainty). Similarly, over time it would also be reasonable to assume such a cost would be liable to change, as transport expenses rise, labour costs increase, vehicle repair costs escalate and so on. In terms of sensitivity analysis we may wish to examine the effect a change in *one* of the objective function coefficients will have on the current optimal solution. We see from Table 3-17 that the Midtown–Depot A route is currently unused. By how much would we have to reduce the per-unit transport costs in order to make this route part of the optimal solution? Similarly, the Southtown–Depot A route is currently optimal. But suppose its per-unit cost was to rise to, say, £12. Would this route still be used in the optimal solution? To examine such issues we must distinguish between those variables that are *non-basic* (not currently in the optimal solution) and those which are *basic*.

Non-basic variables Let us return to Route x_{21} with a current cost of £11 per unit shipped. We see from Table 3-17 that the corresponding u and v values are 2 and 5 respectively, and using the MODI method we confirm that this route is currently suboptimal given that its improvement index is:

$$c_{ij} - u_i - v_j > 0$$
$$11 - 2 - 5 = 4 > 0$$

It is apparent that as long as this improvement index is greater than or equal to ($\geqslant$) 0 then this route will remain suboptimal. We can rewrite the above expression to make this explicit:

$$c_{21} \geqslant u_2 + v_1 \geqslant 7$$

60 TRANSPORTATION AND ASSIGNMENT

In other words, as long as the per-unit cost of this route is at least £7 then it will not be used in the optimal solution. The per-unit cost on this route must be reduced by at least £4 from its current value of £11 if we wish to use this route without incurring higher total transport costs for the company. The usefulness of this information should not be underestimated. We know from the optimal solution that a given route is not being used because its relative costs are too high. Management can now evaluate, for any such route, the cost savings that have to be achieved before the route can be used. Either as an efficiency measure or as a means of determining the viability of the existence of a route we can use such sensitivity analysis in the decision-making process.

Student activity
Calculate by how much the per-unit cost of each other unused route would have to change before it would be included in the optimal solution.

Note that the calculation for Route x_{33} gives:

$$c_{33} \geq u_3 + v_3 \geq 15$$

This implies that this route will not be used as long as its per-unit cost is £15 or more, which is actually the same as the current per-unit cost. In other words, as we are already aware, this route would provide an alternative optimal solution.

Basic variables For basic variables sensitivity analysis is not quite as simple. The additional complication arises that, should the cost coefficient of a basic variable change, this will have the effect of changing the corresponding values for u and v in the final table. This will then require a reassessment of the non-basic variable improvement indices also. We shall illustrate with reference to Route x_{31}. Let us assume that the per-unit cost of this route changes to some amount, C. Given that for a basic variable:

$$c_{ij} - u_i - v_j = 0$$

we then have

$$C - u_3 - v_1 = 0$$

and either u_3 or v_1 must change to ensure this index remains at zero. The new u and v values are shown in Table 3-19. (Note that we have chosen to alter v_1 rather than u_3. It would make no difference to our conclusions if we had left v_1 unchanged and altered u_3 instead.) Before proceeding you should confirm through your own calculations that the u and v values shown are appropriate for the table structure as shown in Table 3-19.

It is evident that this existing optimal route will remain optimal only if it is not replaced by a currently non-basic variable. So, if we examine the non-basic variables and determine (as we have just done in the previous section) by how much their cost coefficient has to change in order for them to become basic then we can assess the implications of the change in the cost coefficient of the basic variable, x_{31}. Some simple calculations will clarify this. Let us examine Route x_{11}, currently non-basic. For it to remain non-basic we must have:

Table 3-19 Transportation table: change in a basic variable's coefficient

Origins	Destinations Depot A	Depot B	Depot C	Depot D	Origin capacity	u
Northtown	20 0	11 0	12 0	13 400	400	0
Midtown	11 0	10 250	13 350	15 100	700	2
Southtown	C 200	12 150	15 0	20 0	350	4
Dummy origin	0 0	0 0	0 150	1000 0	150	-11
Destination requirement	200	400	500	500	1600	
v	$C-4$	8	11	13		

or
$$c_{11} - u_1 - v_1 \geq 0$$
$$20 - 0 - (C-4) \geq 0$$
$$24 - C \geq 0$$
$$24 \geq C \quad \text{or} \quad C \leq 24$$

In other words, as long as C, the cost of transporting a unit over the x_{31} route, does not increase to more than £24 then Route x_{31} will not be replaced by Route x_{11}. If the per-unit cost of using Route x_{31} were to rise to more than £24 it would be cheaper to use Route x_{11}.

Student activity
Calculate the improvement index for x_{11} if $C = 24$ and again if $C = 25$. What conclusion do you come to about the viability of using Route x_{11}?

However, we cannot examine x_{11} in isolation. If the per-unit cost of x_{31} increases then other currently non-basic routes may be eligible to enter the solution also. Similar calculations must be undertaken for all the other empty cells in the table and in the same way we can assess the maximum possible value for C before any particular empty cell becomes basic (and replaces cell x_{31}).

Student activity
Perform the equivalent calculations for the other non-basic variables in Table 3-19 and assess the implications of your calculations.

The appropriate calculations are:

x_{11}		$24 - C \geq 0$	or $C \leq 24$
x_{12}	$11 - 0 - 8 \geq 0$	$3 \geq 0$	
x_{13}	$12 - 0 - 11 \geq 0$	$1 \geq 0$	
x_{21}	$11 - 2 - C + 4 \geq 0$	$13 - C \geq 0$	or $C \leq 13$
x_{33}	$15 - 4 - 11 \geq 0$	$0 \geq 0$	
x_{34}	$20 - 4 - 13 \geq 0$	$3 \geq 0$	
x_{41}	$0 + 11 - C + 4 \geq 0$	$15 - C \geq 0$	or $C \leq 15$
x_{42}	$0 + 11 - 8 \geq 0$	$3 \geq 0$	
x_{44}	$1000 + 11 - 13 \geq 0$	$998 \geq 0$	

First of all, note that 3 of the cells involve C whilst the rest do not. Reference back to Table 3-19 reveals the reason for this. Those cells not involving C are those whose improvement index does not use the x_{31} cell. In other words, a change in the cost coefficient of the x_{31} cell will not affect whether or not these unused routes enter the basic solution. Simply, the stepping stone paths for these cells do not use x_{31}. Of more interest, however, are those cells which do involve C in their improvement index. These are x_{11}, x_{21} and x_{41}, which, potentially, could replace the basic Route x_{31} should that cell's cost rise too far. As we have already seen for cell x_{11}, the critical value for C is £24. Should the per-unit cost of Route x_{31} rise above £24 then it would be replaced in the optimum solution by Route x_{11}. The same interpretation can be given to the improvement indices for cells x_{21} and x_{41}. For cell x_{21} the critical value for C is £13 and £15 for x_{41}. Let us now return to the original question we posed: how much can the per-unit cost of Route x_{31} rise before the optimal solution changes? It is now evident that the *smallest* of these recalculated improvement indices indicates the *maximum* increase in the cost coefficient for x_{31} before it becomes non-basic. Should the cost of Route x_{31} rise above £13 this route becomes uneconomic compared with the alternative of Route x_{21}, and x_{21} will replace x_{31} in the solution.

It is evident that we could repeat these calculations for each currently used route in the optimal solution. Using sensitivity analysis in this way, therefore, allows management to quantify the maximum change in unit costs for a particular route that can be allowed before such a cost change forces that route out of use in the current solution. Management know, therefore, the extent of control they must enforce on these routes in terms of controlling escalating costs. Moreover, management are also able to predict what the exact effect will be on the optimal solution should such a cost change.

Changes in the constraints

Just as we can undertake sensitivity analysis on parts of the objective function to assess the effect of changes on the optimal solution, so we can assess the equivalent impact of changing *one* of the constraints in the problem. Remember that each constraint in the transportation problem relates to the available supply of or to the required demand for the product. By allowing one such constraint to change we are therefore assessing the effect of a change in one of the underlying supply–demand conditions. On reflection, there are potentially a considerable number of possible combinations of such changes that could occur. We shall focus on four such possible changes and we shall illustrate sensitivity analysis by reference to the problem we were examining in Chapter 2. The final solution to this problem is shown in Table 3-20 (Table 2-21).

Table 3-20 Transportation table: optimal solution: supply–demand sensitivity

	Destinations					
Origins	Depot A	Depot B	Depot C	Depot D	Origin capacity	u
Northtown	20 0	11 0	12 0	13 400	400	0
Midtown	11 0	10 100	13 500	15 100	700	2
Southtown	9 200	12 300	15 0	20 0	500	4
Destination requirement	200	400	500	500	1600	
v	5	8	11	13		

Increase in the demand from Destination j The first constraint change we shall consider is where the demand from a particular destination increases. From our analysis earlier in this chapter we know that this increase will lead to excess demand and will therefore require a dummy row. Let us assume that Depot B now requires 1 extra unit (we will find that sensitivity analysis in any mathematical programming model typically involves assessing such marginal changes in one aspect of the problem formulation). Naturally, given that now total demand exceeds total supply 1 depot must have unsatisfied demand of 1 unit. The question arises: which depot should it be? We cannot necessarily assume that it should be Depot B (where the excess demand originates). Rather, we would need to consider (as we did in Section 3-1) the opportunity costs involved in not supplying each depot. As we have seen, this is effectively what the v coefficients in the final table show. We adopt a simple rule to assess the impact of such an increase in demand. We allocate the shortfall to the depot which has the *highest v* coefficient—here Depot D with a coefficient of 13. Given that one depot must do without part of its demand, this coefficient indicates that it is preferable (in opportunity cost terms) for it to be Depot D. So, Depot D will now be supplied with only 499 (of its required 500) units, thereby releasing 1 unit which can be supplied to Depot B (which has extra demand). To identify the precise effects on the solution we follow a similar process to the stepping stone method. We trace a path between Depot D (which is having its demand reduced) and Depot B (which is having its demand increased). Unlike the stepping stone method, however, this path will be a *'dead-end'* path. We will not require it to create a closed loop but simply link Depots D and B. The new table we require is shown as Table 3-21.

To trace an appropriate 'dead-end' path we must allocate 1 unit to cell x_{44}—Depot D—and at the same time reduce one of this column's used cells. If we reduce cell x_{24} we can then increase the allocation to cell x_{22} to balance row 2 at 700. This also has the effect of bringing column 2 into balance with its new total of 401. The new solution, therefore, will be as in Table 3-22.

Table 3-21 Transportation table: dead-end path for Depots B and D

<table>
<tr><th rowspan="2">Origins</th><th colspan="4">Destinations</th><th rowspan="2">Origin capacity</th></tr>
<tr><th>Depot A</th><th>Depot B</th><th>Depot C</th><th>Depot D</th></tr>
<tr><td>Northtown</td><td>20</td><td>11</td><td>12</td><td>13
400</td><td>400</td></tr>
<tr><td>Midtown</td><td>11</td><td>10
100</td><td>13
500</td><td>15
100</td><td>700</td></tr>
<tr><td>Southtown</td><td>9
200</td><td>12
300</td><td>15</td><td>20</td><td>350</td></tr>
<tr><td>Dummy origin</td><td>0</td><td>0</td><td>0</td><td>0</td><td>1</td></tr>
<tr><td>Destination requirement</td><td>200</td><td>401</td><td>500</td><td>500</td><td>1601</td></tr>
</table>

Table 3-22 Transportation table: new solution

<table>
<tr><th rowspan="2">Origins</th><th colspan="4">Destinations</th><th rowspan="2">Origin capacity</th></tr>
<tr><th>Depot A</th><th>Depot B</th><th>Depot C</th><th>Depot D</th></tr>
<tr><td>Northtown</td><td>20</td><td>11</td><td>12</td><td>13
400</td><td>400</td></tr>
<tr><td>Midtown</td><td>11</td><td>10
101</td><td>13
500</td><td>15
99</td><td>700</td></tr>
<tr><td>Southtown</td><td>9
200</td><td>12
300</td><td>15</td><td>20</td><td>350</td></tr>
<tr><td>Dummy origin</td><td>0</td><td>0</td><td>0</td><td>0
1</td><td>1</td></tr>
<tr><td>Destination requirement</td><td>200</td><td>401</td><td>500</td><td>500</td><td>1601</td></tr>
</table>

The dead-end path linking Depot D to Depot B is therefore given by:

$$+ x_{44} - x_{24} + x_{22}$$

and the effect on total cost will be:

$$+ 0 - 15 + 10 = -£5$$

The same result, however, can be calculated in an easier way. The net effect on the objective function will be given by:

$$v_i - v_j$$

where v_i is the destination generating the excess demand and v_j is the destination with the highest v coefficient.

Here, we have:

$$v_i - v_j = 8 - 13 = -5$$

Similarly, the dead-end path allows us to determine the maximum increase in demand from Depot B that can be dealt with in this way. We see from the dead-end route that the maximum reallocation (before a basic cell becomes non-basic) is 100—the current allocation of cell x_{24}, which is reduced as we reallocate from Depot D to Depot B. So, some simple calculations allow us to predict the effect of such excess demand on both the optimum route allocation and the objective function.

Decrease in the demand from Destination j In a similar vein we can assess the effect that a decrease in one destination's demand will have. The same logic applies as before. We now face excess supply and a dummy column will be required. The sensitivity rule this time is amended to the following:

1. Allocate the excess supply to the origin with the highest u coefficient.
2. Trace a suitable dead-end path from this dummy column cell to the destination whose demand has fallen.
3. Calculate the effect on the objective function by:

$$-(v_i + u_j)$$

where v_i is the v coefficient for the destination reducing its demand and
u_j is the u coefficient associated with the origin which has been allocated the excess supply.
4. The dead-end path can be used to determine the maximum demand reduction that can be catered for in this way.

Student activity
Assume that Depot C reduces its demand. Perform the appropriate sensitivity analysis on the optimal solution shown in Table 3-20 and determine the new solution.

We would first allocate the excess supply to the Southtown factory as this has the highest u coefficient at 4. Given that the table would now have a fifth (dummy) column, we can trace a dead-end path as:

$$x_{35} - x_{32} + x_{22} - x_{23}$$

The effect on the objective function is given by:

$$-(v_i + u_j) = -(11 + 4) = -£15$$

This can also be confirmed from the dead-end route as:

$$0 - 12 + 10 - 13 = -15$$

Similarly, the maximum reallocation that can be accommodated in this way is 300 units (the maximum reduction in Route x_{32}).

Increase in the supply from Origin i The equivalent calculations when faced with an increase in the supply of a particular origin are as follows:

1. Allocate the excess supply to the origin with the highest u coefficient.
2. Trace a suitable dead-end path from this dummy column cell to the origin whose supply has increased.
3. The effect on the objective function is given by:

$$u_i - u_j$$

where u_i is the u coefficient for the origin increasing its supply, and
u_j is the u coefficient associated with the origin which has been allocated the excess supply.

4. The dead-end path can be traced to determine the maximum supply increase that can be catered for in this way.

Student activity
Assume that the Northtown factory increases its supply. Carry out the appropriate sensitivity analysis using Table 3-20 and determine the new optimal solution.

Again, we would allocate the excess supply to the Southtown factory as it has the highest u coefficient. An appropriate dead-end path would be:

$$x_{35} - x_{32} + x_{22} - x_{24} + x_{14}$$

and the net effect on the objective function given by:

$$u_i - u_j \quad \text{where} \quad 0 - 4 = -£4$$

Again, this can readily be confirmed from the dead-end path traced out. The maximum reallocation that can take place is 100 units (from cell x_{24}).

Decrease in the supply from Origin i Finally, we examine the effect of a decrease in the supply. Again, the rules become apparent:

1. Allocate the excess demand to the destination with the highest v coefficient.
2. Trace a suitable dead-end path from the dummy demand cell to the origin decreasing its supply.
3. The effect on the objective function is given by:

$$-(u_i + v_j)$$

where u_i is the u coefficient associated with the origin decreasing its supply, and
v_j is the v coefficient associated with the destination now with unsatisfied demand.

4. Again, the maximum change in allocation can be determined from the dead-end path.

Student activity
Assume the Midtown factory reduces its supply. Perform the appropriate sensitivity analysis using Table 3-20 and determine the new optimal solution.

Depot 4 is allocated the excess demand and the dead-end path will be:

$$x_{44} - x_{24}$$

with an associated net effect on the objective function of $-(13+2) = -£15$. The maximum change that could occur is 100 units.

It can be seen, therefore, that sensitivity analysis is readily undertaken both on the objective function and on the constraints in the problem. You may have noticed that we have been careful to introduce and assess only one such change at a time. The reason for this is evident. We are seeking to determine the effect on the current optimal solution of a change in one part of the original problem formulation. Should more than one aspect of the original problem formulation alter then we would not be able to distinguish the cause–effect pattern on the optimal solution. Simply, we could not determine which change in the problem was associated with which change in the solution. We can, therefore, assess the effect of only one change in the problem at any one time. Should two or more aspects of the problem change simultaneously then we would have to recompute the new solution from the new formulation. Nevertheless, the importance of sensitivity analysis should not be underestimated. It is an extremely powerful way of countering some of the rigid assumptions underpinning transportation models (and other mathematical programming models also) and enabling the model to more realistically represent a real-world problem. At the same time, such sensitivity analysis provides management with extremely useful information. In this example we could use the results of the analysis in a number of ways. Management could now set cost targets for the routes not currently used in the solution. Management are also able to use the results of sensitivity analysis as a means of contingency planning. They are able to predict their decisions should the circumstances surrounding the problem change in the future. Naturally, in practice such sensitivity analysis as we have illustrated in this chapter would be undertaken via computer-based methods. Typically, a transportation model software would include such sensitivity analysis as a standard part of its output.

3-5 DEGENERACY

The last topic that we examine is that of *degeneracy*. A solution to a transportation problem is said to be degenerate if the number of occupied cells is less than $(n + m - 1)$. This problem can occur either at the intermediate stages of the solution program or in the optimal table. We shall examine the problem and see how it can be resolved. It has to be said, however, that the problem is not a particularly severe one. Computer software will typically have methods built into it to resolve the difficulties caused by degeneracy and, in practical terms, the user may never be aware of the problem. However, it is as well to understand the processes involved. Consider the problem shown by Table 3-23.

You will be aware that the problem is a familiar one. It is the original transportation model that we examined and solved. What will be less familiar to you is the solution shown in the table. A careful check will indicate that the solution given is feasible in that all rows and columns balance as required. Further perusal of the table, however, will also reveal that the solution shown is not basic in that there are only 5 occupied cells, whereas a basic

Table 3-23 Transportation table: degeneracy

Origins	Destinations				Origin capacity
	Depot A	Depot B	Depot C	Depot D	
Northtown	20 200	11 200	12 0	13 0	400
Midtown	11 0	10 200	13 500	15 0	700
Southtown	9 0	12 0	15 0	20 500	500
Destination requirement	200	400	500	500	1600

solution should have 6 ($n + m - 1 = 4 + 3 - 1$). This solution is said to be *degenerate*. You may also realize why a degenerate solution is problematical. It becomes apparent that neither the stepping stone method nor the MODI method can be used with this table to generate the next iteration. For the stepping stone method it is impossible to trace out closed paths for certain of the empty cells: $x_{14}, x_{24}, x_{31}, x_{32}, x_{33}$. Without such paths we cannot evaluate whether an improved solution is possible. Similarly, with the MODI method we cannot establish a unique set of u and v coefficients. (Try it and see. You will be unable to determine a coefficient for u_3 and for v_4.) Whilst such a degenerate solution has occurred at an intermediate stage in the solution program in this example (we know this simply because we have previously determined the optimal solution) it can equally well occur in the optimal table in some problems. Fortunately, there is a simple method available for resolving the difficulties caused in both cases.

The problem typically arises in that the allocation to a particular cell may fulfil the row and column requirements simultaneously. The general method of resolving the difficulty is to add some *artificial* allocation to a currently empty cell in order to create the closed paths necessary for either the stepping stone or the MODI method to function. Such an artificial allocation (we shall denote it with the symbol α) does not actually take a specific numerical value as such but is simply assumed to take a value greater than zero (i.e. to be basic) but sufficiently small so as to not affect the objective function value or the row and column totals. If you wish you can visualize α as an infinitesimally small, positive number. The cell in which the α allocation is to be made must be one that does not form a path with any of the currently occupied cells. In the case of Table 3-23 we could allocate α to any of the cells for which we could not calculate an improvement index, or find a closed path: $x_{14}, x_{24}, x_{31}, x_{32}, x_{33}$. In general, it will not matter which we use. If we decide to use x_{31}, for example, on the grounds that we are then using the least-cost cell then we would have a table such as Table 3-24.

Given that cell x_{41} is now technically occupied (even though we have not actually allocated a real quantity to this route), we are able to determine closed paths for the empty cells or calculate improvement indices and to use either of the two solution programs to

Table 3-24 Transportation table: artificial allocation

Origins	Destinations				Origin capacity
	Depot A	Depot B	Depot C	Depot D	
Northtown	20 200	11 200	12 0	13 0	400
Midtown	11 0	10 200	13 500	15 0	700
Southtown	9 α	12 0	15 0	20 500	500
Destination requirement	200	400	500	500	1600

Table 3-25 Transportation table: degeneracy: first iteration

Origins	Destinations				Origin capacity
	Depot A	Depot B	Depot C	Depot D	
Northtown	20 0	11 200	12 0	13 200	400
Midtown	11 0	10 200	13 500	15 0	700
Southtown	9 $\alpha + 200$	12 0	15 0	20 300	500
Destination requirement	200	400	500	500	1600

proceed. You should confirm for yourself that all the empty routes can now have a path traced out. If we were to do this we would find that cell x_{14} would enter the solution at the next stage in terms of having the maximum effect on reducing total costs. The table for the next stage in the program would then be as shown in Table 3-25.

Given that α is an artificial quantity that is infinitesimally small it can now be dropped from the table, leaving $x_{41} = 200$ and still leaving a basic, feasible solution. In other words, this solution is no longer degenerate and we can now proceed as before to find the optimal solution. Degeneracy, therefore, is a problem easily resolved in the transportation program.

3-6 TRANSPORTATION IN PRACTICE

Whilst the problems we have used in the past two chapters to illustrate the principles of the transportation model have been relatively simplistic (deliberately so to allow us to focus on the key aspects of the model without the distraction of complex formulations), they are also sufficiently realistic to demonstrate the potential of the model in the real world. Additionally, as the end-of-chapter exercises show, the model is by no means restricted in its application to traditional transportation-type problems. Nevertheless, it should not be assumed that the transportation model is without its difficulties when trying to apply it to business problems. These are apparent if we summarize the key characteristics required of the transportation problem as follows:

- There is a fixed—and known—number of origins and destinations.
- There is a known supply for each origin.
- There is a known demand for each destination.
- Each origin–destination route has a known and constant contribution to the objective.
- There is a clear, single and quantified objective to be achieved.

Whilst such characteristics are typical of many business situations—particularly those relating to operational or day-to-day decision-making—it is also clear that such characteristics may well have a restrictive effect on the areas where transportation can be applied. To some extent, however, some of these restrictive assumptions can be overcome through the use of sensitivity analysis whereby we are able to quantify the effects of relaxing some of these assumptions and provide management with information about the effects on the solution, should these assumptions be incorrect or inappropriate in some way. For example, we can quantify the effect of changing the supply–demand requirements of a particular origin or destination. We can equally, through the use of dummy rows or columns allow for varying numbers of origins and destinations. Similarly, sensitivity analysis will enable us to assess the effect of each parameter in the objective function on the current solution so that we can, to some extent, allow for variation in these parameters.

There are aspects to some of these assumptions, however (particularly the last two), that are restrictive. Implied in the fourth assumption is that the relationships dealt with in the transportation problem are *linear* in form. This is an aspect of many of the models introduced in this text to which we shall return in Part B when we examine linear programming. Suffice it to say at this stage that the basic transportation model will not cope with non-linear relationships as might exist, for example, in terms of returns to scale. Returning to earlier examples, we assumed a constant (i.e. linear) per-unit transport cost. It may be more realistic under some circumstances to assume that there may be economies of scale. Transporting, say, 100 units over a particular route may cost £1000 (i.e. £10 per unit). Transporting 200 units over the same route will not necessarily cost £2000. Quantity discounts may apply, for example, if we transport more than a certain quantity over a certain route. We may equally be able to utilize larger and more efficient (i.e. cheaper) vehicles to transport larger quantities and so on. However, as we shall see later in the text, we may be able to modify other types of mathematical programs to deal with those problems where the transportation model is less appropriate. It is also appropriate to

EXTENSIONS TO THE TRANSPORTATION MODEL 71

conclude that such limiting assumptions have not prevented the extensive use of the basic transportation model in business.

STUDENT EXERCISES

3-1 Complete the solution to the excess supply problem illustrated in Table 3-10 using zero-cost coefficients for the dummy column. Carry out a full sensitivity analysis on this solution.

3-2 Complete the solution to the excess supply problem illustrated in Table 3-10 using the stock cost coefficients for the dummy column. Which set of objective function coefficients do you feel is most appropriate?

3-3 Assume that Table 3-10 represents the monthly pattern of supply and demand. For month 1 demand from the 4 depots is as shown. In month 2 demand at each of the depots is expected to increase by 10 per cent and by a further 10 per cent in month 3. Using stock costs for the objective function determine the optimal solution for each of these months and comment upon the supply–demand situation and current stock levels at the end of this period. What advice would you give management based on this solution?

As a follow-up exercise undertake a complete sensitivity analysis on the current optimal solution. Comment on the usefulness of such an analysis in a real-world context.

3-4 Return to the problem illustrated in Table 3-12. Find an initial solution using Route x_{21}. The solution will be degenerate. Find the optimal solution from this degenerate position.

3-5 For the problem illustrated in Table 3-14 find the optimal solution.

3-6 Solve the problem shown in Table 3-17. Assess the effect of insisting on this priority route and advise management on a suitable course of action.

3-7 Amend the problem shown in Table 3-17 so that Route x_{11} must have at least 100 units transported. Assess the effect of this restriction. How could such information be used?

3-8 Return to Table 3-22. Attempt to use both the stepping stone method and the MODI method to establish the next solution table.

3-9 Return to the problem shown in Exercise 2-1. From the current optimal solution perform a sensitivity analysis on each of the currently unused routes. Comment on how such information could be used by management in the context of the problem set.

3-10 Return to the problem shown in Exercise 2-2(f) where one of the routes available is prohibited. Solve this problem and assess the effect such a prohibition has on the objective function and the optimal solution.

3-11 Return to Exercise 2-3(e). Assume that the route combinations of A1 and C3 can no longer be used. Determine the new optimal solution.

3-12 Return to the problem described in Exercise 2-3. Each site now intends increasing the quantity of salt–grit it holds by 20 per cent in order to provide a buffer stock in case of severe weather. Reformulate and resolve the problem.

4

THE ASSIGNMENT MODEL

The past two chapters have examined problems that involve the transportation of an item from some origin to some destination and the solution algorithm involved the allocation of origins to destinations (via the use of appropriate routes). An associated but rather more specialized problem relates to the assignment of *resources* to specific *activities*. Typically, we may have a given number of tasks that have to be assigned to a given (and equal) number of workers, or a number of machines to produce certain items, a number of vehicles to be assigned to certain routes, and so on. The *assignment* model is concerned with determining an optimal solution to such problems: assigning available resources to the available tasks. Unlike the transportation model, assignment problems require a one-to-one matching: in the case of workers-to-tasks assignments we would require one worker to be assigned to one task. In this chapter we shall examine the basic assignment model and its solution. The solution program we shall use is known by a number of names: the Hungarian method, the opportunity cost method, König's method. As before we shall illustrate the model and its solution program with a typical business problem.

4-1 THE BUSINESS PROBLEM

As we saw in the previous chapters, IMC have 3 factories that manufacture 1 of their products. Not surprisingly, given the high-tech nature of the firm's business, the production process is technically complex. The company have a policy of regular preventative maintenance of their production facilities at each factory. On a Sunday, when all factories are closed for production, special maintenance crews inspect and overhaul the production and assembly equipment in each factory in preparation for the coming week's output. Because this work can take all day (depending on the faults found in the production equipment) the company has found it necessary to establish 3 separate maintenance teams. The problem the company faces is: which maintenance crew should be assigned to

Table 4-1 Maintenance team costs (£00)

Team	Factory		
	Northtown	Midtown	Southtown
A	11	10	9
B	6	8	10
C	10	13	15

which factory? As with every business decision there are costs involved. Each maintenance team comprises a mixture of individuals with different skills, on different pay grades, with different levels of experience, and so on. Let us assume that the company have been able to quantify the cost of assigning each maintenance team to each factory as shown in Table 4-1.

The table shows the weekly cost (measured in £00) of assigning a particular team to a particular factory to complete the maintenance schedule. Thus, for example, if Team A is assigned to Northtown then the weekly cost will be £1100. We can view this cost as an aggregate of a variety of costs incurred in such an assignment: wage costs for the team members (which could comprise normal and overtime payments), travel costs, equipment costs, and so on. It is apparent, in the context of the problem, that each team can only be assigned to one factory, given that the maintenance schedule could take all day to complete. Equally, each factory requires only one team to be assigned to it to complete the required task. We require, therefore, a one-to-one assignment of teams to factories or, in general, of resources to tasks that is optimal in terms of some declared objective.

4-2 FORMULATING THE BASIC ASSIGNMENT MODEL

As with the transportation model we can express the problem in simple mathematical terms. Using a similar notation we shall denote i as referring to the teams (or resources) and j as referring to the factories (or tasks). Therefore, c_{ij} will refer to the cost of assigning a particular resource (i) to a particular task (j). We can also define a further variable, x, such that:

$x_{ij} = 1$ if resource i is assigned to task j

$x_{ij} = 0$ otherwise

The problem formulation then becomes one of minimizing the total costs subject to the constraints that each team (resource) is assigned to 1 factory (task) and that each factory has 1 team assigned to it. The mathematical formulation then becomes:

$$\text{Minimize} \quad c_{11}x_{11} + c_{12}x_{12} + c_{13}x_{13}$$
$$c_{21}x_{21} + c_{22}x_{22} + c_{23}x_{23}$$
$$c_{31}x_{31} + c_{32}x_{32} + c_{33}x_{33} \quad (4\text{-}1)$$
$$\text{subject to} \quad x_{11} + x_{12} + x_{13} = 1 \quad (4\text{-}2)$$

$$x_{21} + x_{22} + x_{23} = 1 \qquad (4\text{-}3)$$

$$x_{31} + x_{32} + x_{33} = 1 \qquad (4\text{-}4)$$

$$x_{11} + x_{21} + x_{31} = 1 \qquad (4\text{-}5)$$

$$x_{12} + x_{22} + x_{32} = 1 \qquad (4\text{-}6)$$

$$x_{13} + x_{23} + x_{33} = 1 \qquad (4\text{-}7)$$

$$\text{All } x_{ij} = 0 \text{ or } 1 \qquad (4\text{-}8)$$

The first 3 constraints require that each team be assigned to 1, and only 1, task. The next 3 constraints require each factory to have 1 and only 1 team assigned to it. It is clear that the assignment problem we face follows a similar structure to the transportation problems we have examined thus far. In fact, we could apply the transportation algorithm to the assignment problem to find the optimal solution. However, for large assignment problems the transportation method is technically inefficient and you will realize that all the solutions generated by the transportation method will be degenerate with the attendant difficulties of resolving this problem. Accordingly, a more efficient, but specialized solution algorithm has been developed, the *Hungarian method* (generally regarded as having been named after the two Hungarian mathematicians who originally suggested methods for solving this type of problem).

4-3 THE SOLUTION PROGRAM: THE HUNGARIAN METHOD

In order to determine the solution we follow a fixed sequence of stages, the first of which is to determine a suitable cost table. This is shown in Table 4-2.

In general we should be able to construct such a table (or its equivalent) for any assignment problem. The rows refer to the resources we have available and the columns to the tasks that must be completed. It is evident that in this problem there are a total of 6 ($3! = 3 \times 2 \times 1$) possible assignments that could be made. Each of these will have an associated cost and we seek the assignment that minimizes this total cost figure. In the small problem that we are investigating we could actually quantify the cost of each of these 6 assignments and then simply choose the smallest. For larger problems, however, it is equally apparent that such an approach is not cost effective. A problem involving, say, 10

Table 4-2 Maintenance team costs (£00)

Team	Factory		
	Northtown	Midtown	Southtown
A	11	10	9
B	6	8	10
C	10	13	15

resources and 10 tasks (which would be considered a small problem by many businesses) would have 10! (= 3 628 800) possible assignments. The Hungarian method uses the concept of opportunity costs to determine the optimal solution. Let us investigate the concept further.

> *Student activity*
> Using the least-cost approach developed for transportation models determine an initial, feasible solution for this problem.

Using the least-cost approach we would first assign Team B to the Northtown factory. We would then assign Team A to the Southtown factory. This would leave Team C to be assigned to the Midtown factory. Total costs of such an assignment will be £2800 per week (£900 + £600 + £1300). However, on reflection it is apparent that such an approach may not be the most appropriate. Northtown is the least-cost assignment for both Team B and Team C. Similarly, whilst Team C has been assigned to Midtown, both Team A and B could service this factory at a lower weekly cost. It is clear that, as with transportation problems, we must look at the opportunity costs involved in assigning a particular team to a particular factory, and use these to determine the optimum solution. In short, we shall seek to minimize these opportunity costs.

Calculating the opportunity costs

There are, in fact, two sets of opportunity costs involved in Table 4-2. There is the opportunity cost of assigning a resource to a task (here, a team to a factory) and there is also the opportunity cost of assigning factories to teams. This distinction may seem little more than semantic argument, but let us examine Table 4-2 in more detail. For Team A the minimum-cost assignment is to Southtown, at a cost of £900. Should we decide *not* to assign Team A to Southtown then we will incur higher costs: an extra £200 if this team is assigned to Northtown and £100 if assigned to Midtown. Effectively, these represent the opportunity costs of misassigning Team A. Similarly, if we look at Northtown we see its optimum assignment is Team B, at a cost of £600. If we decide *not* to use this assignment then the opportunity costs will be an extra £500 if we assign Team A and £400 if we assign Team C to the Northtown factory. Accordingly, it is these joint opportunity costs that we must evaluate in order to determine the optimal assignment allocation. To do this we require an opportunity cost table (rather than a real cost table such as we already have in Table 4-2). The Hungarian solution method is based on two properties of the opportunity cost table that we shall develop. First, a constant may be added or subtracted to any row or column in the original cost table without affecting the relative values of the variables (this is similar to the concept used in the MODI method for transportation problems, where we evaluated the improvement index for a cell in terms of its relative opportunity costs). Second, as long as the cost table contains only non-negative values then the optimal solution has a total cost which is also non-negative and can be found using the Hungarian method. The opportunity cost table we require is readily constructed. We perform two steps: first, we calculate the opportunity costs involved in misassigning the resources (teams). This is achieved by subtracting the minimum-cost assignment in each row from all cost cells in that row. Second, we repeat this process but now using the columns: we

76 TRANSPORTATION AND ASSIGNMENT

subtract the least-cost entry in each column from all cells in that column. This will provide the opportunity costs of misassigning the tasks (factories).

Student activity
Perform step 1 on Table 4-2. Subtract the minimum-cost assignment in each row from all cells in that row.

It can be seen that the minimum-cost assignment of resources to tasks means Team A to Southtown, Team B to Northtown and Team C to Northtown. All three assignments have zero opportunity costs. (Of course, this also shows that this assignment pattern is infeasible since we cannot allocate both Team B and Team C to Northtown.) However, Table 4-3 shows only the opportunity costs associated with assigning resources to tasks. We also need to incorporate the equivalent opportunity costs of assigning tasks to resources.

Student activity
Perform step 2. Subtract the lowest opportunity cost assignment in each column in Table 4-3 from all cells in that column.

Table 4-3 Resource opportunity costs (£00)

Team	Factory		
	Northtown	Midtown	Southtown
A	2	1	0
B	0	2	4
C	0	3	5

Testing for optimality

Using the opportunity cost table, we can now apply a simple test to determine whether we can derive the optimal assignment solution. If we can assign each resource to a particular task such that all resources are assigned and all tasks completed *and* so that each such assignment has a zero opportunity cost then we have found an optimal assignment solution. This sounds far more complicated than it is. Let us illustrate with Table 4-4. In the table there are 4 zero opportunity cost assignments, so at first it may appear that an optimal solution has been found, given that we only require 3 assignments and we have 4 zero opportunity costs. Unfortunately, not all these zero-cost assignments can be utilized *simultaneously*. Of the zero-cost assignments, 2 involve Team A (at Midtown and Southtown) but obviously within the formulation of the problem Team A can only be assigned to 1 of these tasks. Whichever of these we assign to Team A, it will then require either Team B or Team C to be assigned to the remaining factory at an opportunity cost

THE ASSIGNMENT MODEL

Table 4-4 Resource and task opportunity costs (£00)

Team	Factory		
	Northtown	Midtown	Southtown
A	2	0	0
B	0	1	4
C	0	2	5

Table 4-5 Resource and task opportunity costs (£00)

Team	Factory		
	Northtown	Midtown	Southtown
A	--2--	--0--	--0--
B	0	1	4
C	0	2	5

greater than zero. Similarly, 2 of the zero opportunity costs involve Northtown (with Teams B and C). Again, only 1 assignment is required, which will leave 1 team to cover a task, again, with an opportunity cost greater than zero. So, although we appear to have sufficient zero-cost assignments, in effect we do not have an optimal solution. We can reveal the same conclusion through the use of a simple test. We can determine the *minimum* number of vertical and horizontal lines that must be drawn through the opportunity cost table to cover all zero-cost entries. If the minimum number of lines is less than the number of resources (or tasks) then an optimal solution has not yet been determined. The appropriate lines are shown in Table 4-5.

Thus, in order to cover all the zero-cost cells in the table we require 2 lines, drawn as shown. Given that there are 3 resources (and tasks) the number of lines is less than the number of resources, and therefore the table does not represent an optimal assignment allocation. To determine such an optimal solution we must revise the opportunity cost table.

Revising the opportunity cost table

It is clear that a solution whereby each resource is assigned to its minimum opportunity cost task simply does not exist. Therefore, we must somehow assign a resource to a task so as to minimize the associated opportunity costs involved in the complete set of assignments. The lines drawn in Table 4-5 represent those resource–task assignments with a zero opportunity cost. The remaining assignments (of which there are 4: B–Midtown, B–

Table 4-6 Revised opportunity costs (£00)

Team	Factory		
	Northtown	Midtown	Southtown
A	2	−1	0
B	0	0	4
C	0	1	5

Table 4-7 Completed revised opportunity costs (£00)

Team	Factory		
	Northtown	Midtown	Southtown
A	3	0	0
B	0	0	3
C	0	1	4

Southtown, C–Midtown, C–Southtown) all have positive opportunity costs. Given that we seek to minimize these costs it appears sensible to examine the assignment of Team B to Midtown as this has the lowest opportunity cost at £100. This assignment is logically the one we investigate at this stage, given that we now know we cannot assign all resources to the required tasks without incurring some opportunity cost. Since we are dealing in opportunity costs in order to select appropriate assignments, we must transform the actual opportunity cost of Team B–Midtown of £100 to an artificial opportunity cost of £0. Remembering that adding (or subtracting) a constant will not affect the relative values, we can subtract £100 from the Midtown column in Table 4-5. The result of this is shown in Table 4-6.

However, this process of adjusting Team B–Midtown to £0 has created a problem. We now have a negative opportunity cost for Team A–Midtown. Such a value makes no sense: Team A cannot be assigned to Midtown with a negative opportunity cost (which would imply there was actually a benefit to be achieved from this particular assignment). Accordingly, we must adjust row 1 so that this negative opportunity cost returns to a zero value. We can achieve this by adding 1 to each cell in row 1. However, this will now cause the Team A–Southtown opportunity cost to take a value of +1 (whereas we know the actual opportunity cost is zero). Accordingly, we must adjust column 3 by subtracting 1 from each cell. Table 4-7 summarizes the results of these row–column manipulations.

This process may seem unduly complex, but in fact simplifies to a basic program. In revising the opportunity cost figures we take the following steps:

1. Identify the cell with the lowest non-zero opportunity cost (here cell x_{22} at 1).

2. Subtract this value from all cells in the table not covered by the lines drawn earlier.
3. Add this value to those cells at the intersection of the lines drawn earlier.

Here we have subtracted 1 from cells x_{22}, x_{23}, x_{32}, x_{33}. We have added 1 to cell x_{11} which is at the intersection of the lines drawn in Table 4-5. Using the revised opportunity cost table we again check to see whether an optimal solution exists. Again, we draw the minimum number of lines to cover the zero-cost cells in the table.

Student activity
Determine the appropriate lines for Table 4-7 and confirm whether or not we have an optimal solution.

The appropriate lines are shown in Table 4-8. Notice, that as is often the case with assignment problems, there are different combinations of lines that we could have drawn to the same effect. It is generally unimportant as to which set of lines is actually drawn as long as they are the minimum number required. Here, we have 3 lines to cover all the zero-cost cells. Given that we also have 3 resources (and tasks) then, according to our decision rule, this means that we have an optimal solution to the assignment problem. From Table 4-8 we can determine what the optimal assignments are and from the original cost table (shown in Table 4-2) we can quantify the total cost of such assignments. From Table 4-8 we see that the only zero opportunity cost assignment for Team C is Northtown. Similarly, the only zero opportunity cost assignment to Southtown is Team A. This leaves Team B assigned to Midtown (also with a revised opportunity cost of zero). Total cost of this assignment will be £2700 (£1000 + £900 + £800). This is the assignment schedule which minimizes the total costs. Note also that such an optimal assignment solution does not actually use the minimum-cost assignment (Team B to Northtown). This is readily explained through the opportunity cost approach we have adopted.

Determining the minimum number of lines

It is not always apparent in larger-scale problems how we should draw lines through the zero-cost cells in the table so as to use the minimum number. If, in fact, the number of lines drawn is not the minimum we will not be able to assign a resource to a task with zero cost. However, the following approach is often useful as a general method. We choose a row or

Table 4-8 Completed revised opportunity costs (£00)

Team	Factory		
	Northtown	Midtown	Southtown
A	3	0	0
B	0	0	3
C	0	1	4

column which contains only a single zero-cost coefficient (say, row 3 in Table 4-8). We then draw a line through the *column* containing this coefficient (or through the appropriate row if we had chosen a column with a single zero coefficient). We repeat this process by choosing another row or column with only a single zero coefficient until all such coefficients are covered (note that we do not count a zero coefficient in a row/column that is already covered by a line). So, in Table 4-8 we draw a line through column 1 (as row 3 has a single zero-cost coefficient in cell x_{11}). We next choose column 3 as having a single zero-cost coefficient (x_{13}) and draw a line through row 1. This leaves only 1 uncovered zero coefficient (x_{22}) which can be covered either with a line through row 2 or column 2. This process will normally determine the minimum number of lines required.

Summary of the Hungarian method

We can summarize the Hungarian method into a number of convenient stages:

Step 1 Determine a suitable cost table for the problem.

Step 2 Subtract the smallest coefficient in each row from all other coefficients in that row.

Step 3 Subtract the smallest coefficient in each column from each other cell in that column. The resulting table is the opportunity cost table.

Step 4 Determine the minimum number of lines required to cover all the zero-cost cells.

Step 5 If the minimum number of lines is the same as the number of resources or tasks go to Step 7.

Step 6 Determine the revised opportunity cost table. Identify the smallest non-zero cell. Subtract this opportunity cost coefficient from all uncovered cells and add the coefficient to those cells at the intersection of the lines drawn.
   Return to Step 4.

Step 7 This table represents the optimal assignment solution. Identify the individual assignments through the zero-cost coefficients in the table. Determine the total cost of these assignments through the original cost table derived in Step 1.

4-4 EXTENSIONS TO THE BASIC MODEL

As with transportation, the basic assignment model is somewhat restrictive in its approach but can be readily extended to cover more realistic situations. We shall examine four such extensions to the basic model: multiple optima, unequal assignments, prohibited and priority routes and maximization problems.

Table 4-9 Illustrative revised opportunity costs (£00)

Resources	Tasks			
	W	X	Y	Z
A	0	10	12	15
B	23	0	14	0
C	15	0	12	0
D	0	13	0	20

Multiple optima

Again, as in the transportation model, multiple optima are not infrequent in assignment problems and indicate alternative assignments that will leave the optimal value of the objective function unaltered. Such alternatives are evident from the final opportunity cost table. Assume, for the purpose of illustration that we have Table 4-9, which represents the final, revised opportunity costs for some problem (we have simply generalized into resources and tasks here). You should confirm for yourself that the table does, in fact, represent an optimal set of assignments.

The assignments would be as follows. We would first assign Resource A to Task W (as this is the only zero opportunity cost of Resource A). We would next assign Resource D to Task Y (as this again is the only remaining zero-cost assignment for Resource D). This leaves us with 2 resources (B and C) and 2 tasks (X and Z). It is clear from Table 4-9 that either of the 2 remaining resources could be assigned to either of the 2 tasks at zero opportunity cost. In fact, we have 2 alternative optimal solutions for the problem. As we have seen before, such alternatives are potentially extremely useful to management. We know that, at no extra cost, there are 2 methods of fulfilling the required set of assignments. This provides management with some flexibility in their decisions.

Unequal assignments

We have conveniently assumed so far that the number of resources available exactly matches the number of tasks to be completed. Frequently this will not be the case. We may have more resources than required to complete a given set of tasks and part of the solution will require us to determine which resource(s) will not be required. Similarly, we may face more tasks than can be completed with the available resources and we seek to determine which task must remain uncompleted. We can deal with such unequal assignments through the use of *dummy* rows or columns (exactly as we did in the transportation model). Assume, by way of illustration that we had 4 repair–maintenance teams rather than 3. Given that we have only 3 factories (tasks), 1 of the repair crews will not be utilized. Assume the cost patterns shown in Table 4-10.

Given that the Hungarian method requires a balance between resources and tasks we must introduce a dummy task into the problem. Such a dummy task (represented as a

Table 4-10 Maintenance team costs (£00)

Team	Factory		
	Northtown	Midtown	Southtown
A	11	10	9
B	6	8	10
C	10	13	15
D	8	12	13

Table 4-11 Maintenance team costs (£00): dummy column

Team	Factory			
	Northtown	Midtown	Southtown	Dummy
A	11	10	9	0
B	6	8	10	0
C	10	13	15	0
D	8	12	13	0

column) will require cost coefficients. Using the same logic as we did when dealing with dummy rows/columns in the transportation model, we can assign zero costs to this column to derive a cost table as in Table 4-11.

Applying the Hungarian method to the problem (which is set as an exercise at the end of the chapter) the optimal solution table can be found as shown below at a total cost of £2500 and the optimal set of assignments as:

Team A assigned to Southtown,
Team B assigned to Midtown,
Team C not assigned,
Team D assigned to Northtown.

The use of dummy rows can be incorporated in exactly the same way if we face a problem where we have more tasks than resources. The dummy row would, in this case, represent a task that could not be completed because of the shortage of resources. It is also worth noting that in larger-scale assignment problems there may well be a need for more than one dummy row or column. If we had, say, 5 repair teams then we would need 2 dummy columns (as only one resource can be assigned to each task). This will not affect the solution method.

Prohibited and priority assignments

Equally, there will be applications of the assignment model where we wish to incorporate either priority or prohibited assignments: assignments which must be made no matter what the cost, and assignments which must not be made regardless of the effect on cost. Priority routes are easily dealt with, given the structure of the assignment model. If we insist on a particular resource–task assignment being made then the appropriate row and column representing the resource and task are simply removed from the opportunity cost table and the remaining assignments are then determined through the normal Hungarian method. Prohibited routes are dealt with through the use of penalty costs, as was the case in the transportation model. To illustrate this let us return to the problem shown in Table 4-11. Assume that we have a prohibited assignment: Team A cannot be assigned to Southtown. As we already know, this is part of the current optimal solution but we can incorporate this additional restriction into the problem and still use the Hungarian method for solution. We allocate this prohibited assignment an arbitrary, high-penalty cost (as with transportation the number used is irrelevant as long as it is sufficiently high). If we use a penalty value of £1000 then the cost table becomes as shown in Table 4-12.

We can now derive the opportunity cost table in the same way as before and use the Hungarian method to determine the new optimal solution. Again, this is left as an end-of-chapter exercise. The optimal assignments are now:

Team A assigned to Midtown,
Team B assigned to Southtown,
Team C not assigned,
Team D assigned to Northtown,

with a total cost of £2800 (£300 higher than the original optimal). As with transportation, it is usually worth while finding the optimal solution both with and without the prohibited routes in order to be able to quantify the effect such prohibitions have on the value of the objective function.

Table 4-12 Maintenance team costs (£00): prohibited route

Team	Factory			
	Northtown	Midtown	Southtown	Dummy
A	11	10	1000	0
B	6	8	10	0
C	10	13	15	0
D	8	12	13	0

Table 4-13 Potential weekly sales (£00)

Staff	Sales areas			
	North	Central	South	West
JG	12	15	11	13
ADH	12	13	10	14
WSK	15	13	12	15
PL	17	17	13	19

Maximization problems

So far we have examined only minimization problems. The maximizing of some objective may be equally appropriate in some cases. Given that the Hungarian method is essentially concerned with minimizing the relevant opportunity costs we must transform the objective function in a maximization problem. Let us assume that IMC is reviewing its sales and marketing strategy. It has divided the country into 4 sales regions and has 4 sales staff available. The task of each member of the sales team is to sell as many of the company's products to the various retail outlets in the assigned region as possible. Naturally, the skills and talents of the sales staff vary as does the composition of customers amongst the various sales areas. We have been able to quantify the potential monthly sales figures that could be achieved by assigning each member of the sales team to each of the sales areas. The 4 sales areas—North, Central, South and West—and the 4 sales staff, denoted by their initials, are shown in Table 4-13.

In this case we would be seeking the assignment of sales staff to areas so as to maximize the potential weekly sales. We follow a similar process as before: we derive the opportunity costs implied in the potential sales figures. As before, we first derive the opportunity costs per row and then per column. The difference this time is that when deriving the opportunity costs per row we subtract each cell's coefficient from the *largest* row coefficient. The logic of this is evident. The largest coefficient in a row (for example, £1500 for the JG row) shows the maximum potential sales for that member of the sales team. Allocating this member of the sales team to any other sales area will lead to a reduction in potential sales and will therefore incur an opportunity cost. Once we have derived the opportunity costs in terms of the rows then we proceed to apply the Hungarian method exactly as before, given that we wish to minimize the opportunity costs of misassigning staff and sales areas. That is, we find the opportunity costs in terms of the columns (subtracting the smallest coefficient in a column from all other cells in that column), we determine the minimum number of lines required to cover the zero-cost cells and we check for optimality. The derived opportunity costs for this problem are given in Table 4-14 and, again, it is left as an end-of-chapter exercise to confirm that the optimal assignment is given by:

Table 4-14 Derived opportunity costs (£00)

Staff	Sales areas			
	North	Central	South	West
JG	3	0	1	3
ADH	1	0	0	0
WSK	0	2	0	1
PL	1	1	2	0

JG to Central,
ADH to South,
WSK to North,
PL to West.

Prohibited routes in maximization problems It should be noted that, in a maximization problem, prohibited routes can be dealt with in the same way as for a minimization problem. The only difference that occurs is that the penalty value to be used must be a prohibitively large *negative* value in order to prevent that assignment from entering into the solution. Once the opportunity costs are evaluated then the negative penalty value will be transformed into a positive penalty opportunity cost and the solution program will proceed on the same lines as before.

4-5 SENSITIVITY ANALYSIS

Unlike a transportation problem, an assignment problem contains little in the way of sensitivity analysis that can be usefully undertaken on the optimal solution table. Because of the solution method and the $0-1$ structure of the assignment problem, the simplest approach to sensitivity analysis is generally to recompute the new solution to an amended problem from the beginning. The only potentially worthwhile area relates to the initial objective function coefficients. We may be able, for simpler assignment problems, to assess the change in such an objective function coefficient for a currently unused assignment. Let us illustrate by returning to the original problem examined in Section 4-3. The final solution to this problem was shown in Table 4-7 (duplicated overleaf).

The optimal assignments were found to be: Team A–Southtown, Team B–Midtown and Team C–Northtown. Given that the table shows the opportunity costs involved in other possible assignments, we can perform some simple sensitivity analysis. Let us examine the Team C–Midtown assignment. This has an opportunity cost of £100, implying that to use this assignment will increase the objective function by this amount. Equally, it implies that if we reduce the original costs of this assignment then the opportunity costs of this cell will fall to zero and the assignment could form part of the optimal solution. (Whether it actually does so will depend on the combination of other zero-cost cells in the

Table 4-7 Completed revised opportunity costs (£00)

Team	Factory		
	Northtown	Midtown	Southtown
A	3	0	0
B	0	0	3
C	0	1	4

Table 4-15 Optimal table for the revised problem (£00)

Team	Factory		
	Northtown	Midtown	Southtown
A	3	0	0
B	0	0	3
C	0	0	4

table.) From Table 4-1 we see that the actual cost of this assignment is £1300. If we were able to reduce these costs to £1200, therefore, this assignment's opportunity costs would fall to zero and this assignment could form part of the optimal solution. The final table based on the amended cost of £1200 for this cell is shown in Table 4-15.

It is clear that this assignment now has a zero opportunity cost and could form part of the optimal assignment structure (in fact in this example it gives rise to an alternative optimal to the original solution). We could equally well perform the same analysis on the other non-zero opportunity costs in the optimal table. Apart from this, however, there is little further sensitivity analysis that we can usefully perform, although given the relatively simple solution program for assignment problems recalculating the solution for a change in one of the problem parameters is not an unduly onerous task.

4-6 ASSIGNMENT MODELS IN PRACTICE

Despite its apparent limitations the assignment model has been applied to a considerably diverse range of business applications. One of the appealing features of the model to the decision-maker is its simplicity in terms of the solution program and the fact that a manager can relate the solution process (in terms of opportunity costs) to his or her own judgemental decision-making approach. Typically, most managers would approach an assignment problem in exactly the same way as we have with the Hungarian method. The decision-maker will be concerned with determining assignments with a view to minimizing the opportunity costs even if they have never heard of either opportunity costs or the assignment algorithm. On the negative side, however, the model does require precise data on the objective function coefficients to be used. The costs of each assignment (or profits, output or whatever the units used for the objective function) must be known with certainty. It is arguable whether, in practice, business organizations would have such information. Whereas with transportation we could ameliorate the restrictive effects of such data requirements through the use of sensitivity analysis, with assignment models such analysis is far more limited and cumbersome. Nevertheless, the applications of the assignment model in modern business decision-making should not be overlooked. It offers considerable potential to the decision-maker, albeit in specialized areas of activity.

STUDENT EXERCISES

4-1 Confirm that Table 4-9 is optimal.
4-2 Confirm the solution shown for the problem given in Table 4-11.
4-3 Confirm the solution shown for the problem given in Table 4-12.
4-4 Confirm the solution shown for the problem given in Table 4-13.
4-5 A commercial software development business employs a team of 4 programmers. The firm is currently negotiating with 5 customers with regard to developing a separate custom-written computer package for each customer. The firm has estimated the time it would take each programmer to produce each package. These estimates are shown in Table 4-16. Determine which programmer should be assigned to which package.

Interpret the results of your final solution fully, evaluating any additional information provided by the solution.

Table 4-16 Estimated time taken to complete each package (working days)

Programmer	Package				
	1	2	3	4	5
A	15	26	8	23	18
B	10	20	4	21	16
C	11	19	7	20	16
D	14	23	7	21	17

4-6 The firm's boss has decided that Programmer A in Exercise 4-5 must be assigned to Package 4. Determine the effect this will have on the current optimal solution.
4-7 The firm has now decided that assigning programmers on the basis of estimated time may not be the most appropriate method. Instead the firm wishes to assign programmers on the basis of the relative profitability of each assignment pairing. At present the 4 programmers are paid at the rate of £20, £23, £25 and £30 per working day respectively. The firm expects to be paid £750, £1000, £500, £750, £600 upon completion of each of the 5 programs. Determine the new assignment solution.
4-8 The firm is still insisting that Programmer A be assigned to Package 4. Assess the impact this will have.

PART B

LINEAR PROGRAMMING

This part of the text focuses upon the principal model used in mathematical programming: that of linear programming (LP), which has become the workhorse of the mathematical programming stable. Originally LP was developed to investigate the problem of resource allocation, which is at the heart of most, if not all, business decisions. Much of economic and business analysis is concerned with decision-making, where the decisions to be taken relate to finding the best possible use of an organization's limited resources. All organizations must, from time to time, take decisions relating to issues such as:

- how many people should be employed,
- what quantities of output should be produced,
- where capital should be invested,
- which areas of activity should expand or contract,

and so on. Such decisions bring problems because the decision-maker normally has available only a limited amount of most—if not all—resources and must decide on some rational basis how these resources can be utilized most effectively. Linear programming is a mathematical technique concerned with optimizing some desired objective under such conditions of limited resources. Since its inception, however, applications of LP have become extremely diverse, ranging from financial organizations investigating portfolio and cash flow management, through production departments and marketing organizations and to problems of waste disposal and pollution control. The technique has found favour both in the capitalist organizations in the USA and the state planning agencies in the USSR and in a wide range of organizations in between. Applications are common at both the level of micro-economic analysis and at the macro-economic level. In the real world, linear programming is carried out via computer-based analysis. The basic concepts underpinning the technique, however, can best be illustrated and understood using a graphical approach and Chapter 5 introduces both the basic LP problem and the graphical method of solution. Chapter 6 looks in detail at a range of typical applications of LP in business and investigates the formulation of such problems so that they can be solved using LP techniques. The solution method is investigated further in Chapter 7, with the Simplex method introduced as the general solution program. Chapter 8 introduces the techniques of post-optimality analysis where we investigate the detailed assessment of the optimal solution and the managerial implications of that solution. Finally, we extend the basic LP model in Chapter 9 and also review the practical applications of LP in business decision-making.

5
LINEAR PROGRAMMING: PROBLEM FORMULATION AND THE GRAPHICAL SOLUTION METHOD

In this chapter we shall examine the structure of the basic linear programming model and its formulation and we shall introduce the graphical method as a means of finding an optimal solution to such a problem. LP is the first of our models that is decidedly mathematical (and this is one of the reasons it was not the first to be introduced in the text). Typically, LP problems have two common features: they involve some declared *objective* which we seek to maximize or minimize and they involve a set of *constraints* which limit the ways in which we can attain this objective. The formulation of a business problem into a form suitable for solution via the LP method is the first stage of the process. We require a mathematical expression showing the objective function and a set of mathematical expressions showing the constraints, or limits, on how we can optimize this declared objective. This formulation stage of a business problem is almost an art form in its own right, requiring not only a familiarity with the technique itself but also familiarity with the business problem under investigation. It is an aspect of LP which can be developed only through adequate practice (for which there is no real substitute) and is an aspect of the technique to which we return in detail in the next chapter. Fortunately, the actual solution of LP problems is more straightforward. In practice, such solutions are computer-generated and typically involve a technique known as the Simplex method (or one of its many variants). To begin with, however, we shall examine a more mundane solution process: the graphical method. The graphical method is particularly useful as an introduction to the solution of this type of problem as it facilitates an understanding of the basic concepts behind the technique. Such an understanding is essential before we introduce a more mathematical solution process. We will develop one application of the technique to illustrate its main features. This application, like many in real life, will be centred around a production problem. Typically, the use of LP revolves around three successive stages:

1. problem formulation;
2. problem solution;
3. solution interpretation.

We shall examine each stage in turn.

5-1 THE BUSINESS PROBLEM

As we have seen, IMC manufactures a variety of computing and computing-related equipment. One such product is a monitor for use with business computer systems and IMC currently has plans to produce two models of the same monitor: Model A which is the basic, low-price monochrome monitor and Model B which is a more sophisticated and expensive colour graphics monitor. The company is not actually involved in manufacture directly but rather buys the various component parts which are required for the two models from outside suppliers. The components are then assembled by IMC to produce Model A and Model B and each unit produced is then thoroughly inspected for quality and performance. IMC then sells the two models under its own brand name. There are, therefore, two basic stages to the production process within the firm—the assembly of the components and the inspection of the final product. Information about the resources required to produce the two models has been obtained from both the production department and the accounts department. Model A requires 28 hours of labour to assemble from component parts, while Model B requires 42 hours. After assembly each computer is then tested in the inspection department to ensure it is working satisfactorily. Because of the technical complexity of the product—and the firm's desire to maintain good quality control—the inspection test is time-consuming, with Model A requiring 12 hours of inspection although Model B requires only 6 hours as more care and time is taken in the assembly stage. At present the company employs 400 people in the assembly department, each working a 7 hour day; 100 people are presently employed in the inspection department but they work an 8 hour day. The company presently operates a 6 day working week. Current wage rates are £4 per hour in assembly and £3 per hour in inspection. The accounts department has calculated that in terms of the components and parts Model A costs £71 and Model B £113 to produce. Currently the two models sell for £259 and £349 respectively. An additional aspect of the problem the firm faces is that each model requires a particular component—a microchip that forms part of the monitor's memory. The supplier of these chips can provide no more than 600 in any one working week.

It is clear that the production manager faces a simple decision problem: *how many units of Model A and B should be produced weekly?* At this stage, even with such a simplified problem, there is no obvious means of determining the decisions that obviously must be taken in terms of the optimal mix of production. Clearly, before we can attempt to identify a solution to the problem we must identify what the company is trying to achieve—in other words, what is the company's *objective*? At this stage we assume the company's objective is profit maximization—a rational assumption given the commercial nature of the company. So, effectively, we need to determine the level of production that will maximize profit. A quick review of the circumstances the company faces indicates that, on a weekly basis, there are 3 factors that will restrict the level of production—and hence profit—the company can achieve. The following limitations will *constrain* the company's decisions:

- the available labour supply in the assembly department,
- the available labour supply in the inspection department, and
- the available labour supply of microchip components.

Having identified the general nature of the company's objective and the constraints it faces, we can now represent the problem facing the company by using some simple mathematical notation.

5-2 PROBLEM FORMULATION

To derive a mathematical formulation of this business problem we must examine both the company's objective and the constraints imposed on the decisions it has to take.

Formulating the objective function

We can tabulate the information we have in order to determine the nature of the profit function that the company faces; this is done in Table 5-1. The table summarizes the key financial data pertaining to the two products. The revenue achieved per unit is shown, together with the per-unit cost, which can be calculated from the component costs, the labour costs involved in assembly and the labour costs involved in inspection. The profit contribution can be derived as £40 per unit of the Model A monitor and £50 per unit of Model B. If we denote the units of Model A that are produced as A and the units of Model B as B then our firm's profit function can be expressed as:

$$\text{Profit} = 40A + 50B \tag{5-1}$$

So if the firm were to decide to produce, say, 100 units of A and 50 units of B then profit can be calculated as:

$$\text{Profit} = 40(100) + 50(50) = 4000 + 2500 = £6500$$

Similarly, if the production levels were 200 of A and 400 of B then profit should be

Table 5-1 The firm's revenue, costs and profit

	Model A	Model B
Revenue (per unit)	£259	£349
Total costs comprising: (a) components (b) assembly (hours needed ×£4) (c) inspection (hours needed ×£3)	£219 (£71) (£112) (£36)	£299 (£113) (£168) (£18)
Profit (revenue − costs)	£40	£50

£28 000. Equation (5-1), therefore, allows us to quantify the profit achieved from any combination of production of A and B. At this stage it may appear obvious as to what the firm ought to do. Given that the firm receives £50 profit per unit of B produced and only £40 per unit of A, it appears that the firm ought to produce as many units of B as possible in order to maximize profit. However, the profit function we have identified is concerned only with one part of the problem. We also need to examine the resource requirements of the two models as well as their profit contributions. There would be little point in the firm producing a unit of B at a profit of £50 if we found out later that the same resources could have been used to produce, say, 2 units of A at a profit of £80. Accordingly, we must also formulate the constraints relevant to the problem.

Formulating the constraints

In the same way as we developed a concise mathematical expression for profit, we can also formulate expressions relating to the three constraints in terms of production of A and B. To summarize the relevant production information we have Table 5-2. The table simply shows the relationships between the available resources and the rates of use of these resources. Reading down the first column of data we see that a unit of Model A will require 28 hours of assembly time, 12 hours of inspection time and 1 of the microchip components. Similarly, per unit of B we require 42 hours of assembly, 6 hours of inspection and, again, 1 microchip. Under 'Requirements per unit produced' we effectively have the demand for each of our limited resources. For example, if we decide to produce 100 units of A and 50 units of B then the total demand for assembly hours will be:

$$28(100) + 42(50) = 4800 \text{ hours per week}$$

Under 'Total available', on the other hand, we have the available supply. For the assembly department we have a labour supply of 400 workers each of whom works 7 hours a day for 6 days each week. On a weekly basis, therefore, the firm has a total of 16 800 hours of assembly time available for producing the two models. Obviously, the constraint the company faces is that the demand for this resource—generated by producing A and B—must not exceed the available supply. This is the equivalent of saying:

Table 5-2 Production data

	Requirements per unit produced		Total available
	Model A	Model B	
Assembly	28 hours	42 hours	16 800 hours $(400 \times 7 \times 6)$
Inspection	12 hours	6 hours	4 800 hours $(100 \times 8 \times 6)$
Microchip components	1 chip	1 chip	600 chips

Demand ≤ supply

or, in the case of the assembly department,

$$28A + 42B \leq 16\,800 \tag{5-2}$$

Similarly, for the other two constraints we have:

$$12A + 6B \leq 4800 \tag{5-3}$$

$$1A + 1B \leq 600 \tag{5-4}$$

indicating that we have a maximum of 4800 hours available each week in the inspection department, and a total of 600 microchips available per week. To summarize, our LP problem can now be expressed as:

$$\begin{align*}
\text{Maximize} \quad & 40A + 50B \\
\text{subject to:} \quad & 28A + 42B \leq 16\,800 \\
& 12A + 6B \leq 4\,800 \\
& 1A + 1B \leq 600 \\
& A, B \geq 0
\end{align*} \tag{5-5}$$

The last constraint plays no formal part in our solution but simply indicates that economically—as opposed to mathematically—the values for A and B can never be negative. Negative levels of production obviously have no meaning in our problem and indeed negative values for variables in an LP problem are in general unacceptable.

Formulating other types of constraint

So far in our illustrative problem, all the constraints have been of the less than or equal to type ($\leq$). Other constraints may take the form of either greater than or equal to ($\geq$) or exactly equal to ($=$) and are easily incorporated in the LP formulation. For example, IMC may have a contractual agreement to supply, say, a minimum of 100 units of Model A to a retailer each week. This would require an additional constraint such that:

$$A \geq 100$$

Minimization problems

Similarly, we have assumed that IMC wishes to maximize profit. Whilst this may be sensible in terms of this problem there will be other applications involving minimization—in terms say of costs. Assume, for example, that IMC have a contract to supply a total of 450 units of the two products to a major customer. The contract is a fixed-price one: IMC have negotiated a fixed price for the product they supply. Management would now be interested in fulfilling the contract at minimum cost. If we refer back to Table 5-1 a suitable objective function would now be:

$$\text{Minimize} \quad 219A + 299B \tag{5-6}$$

subject to the constraints we faced for the maximization problem and the additional restriction that:

$$1A + 1B \geq 450 \tag{5-7}$$

Summary of the formulation stage

The simple illustrative problem we have introduced summarizes the key features of the formulation stage of LP. First of all, we require a single objective that we regard as desirable—here maximum profit. Second, we identify relevant *decision variables*—here the quantities of the two products that we must decide to produce. Third, we quantify the impact each decision variable has on the declared objective. Fourth, we must then determine the factors that limit the values that these decision variables can take: we must determine the constraints to the problem in other words. Lastly, we must quantify the relationship between each decision variable and each constraint. Only when the formulation stage is complete can we proceed to search for a solution.

5-3 THE GRAPHICAL SOLUTION

Although we have been able to develop a precise mathematical formulation of the problem we are investigating there is, as yet, no obvious method of finding a solution to our problem. One basic—and easily understood—method of solution is to present the information in the problem visually in the form of a graph. Whilst such a method is restricted to the simplest of LP problems it will enable us to identify the following:

- all those combinations of production of Model A and Model B that are possible, given the constraints we face, and
- the unique combination of production of Model A and Model B that maximizes our objective function, profit,

and it will also allow us to develop a conceptual understanding of the LP solution process. Initially, we shall develop a graph showing the three constraints the firm faces. The graph will indicate the entire range of possible solutions to our problem, in terms of the available resources. That is, the graph will show all the different production levels that are possible with the existing resources. We shall then introduce the objective function onto the graph to identify which of the many possible solutions represents the optimum allocation of available resources, in terms of the declared objective of profit maximization.

Graphing the constraints

It is important to realize at this stage that all our constraints—and the objective function—are *linear* in form. Graphically, this means that each constraint can be represented by an appropriate straight line and, in order to graph this line, we will require a minimum of two pairs of coordinates for A and B. If we examine our first constraint relating to the assembly department we have:

$$28A + 42B \leq 16\,800$$

The constraint implies that our limited resource—assembly hours available—has two alternative and competing uses. The available hours may be used to produce A *or* to produce B, *or* to produce some combination of the two. Simply, the more of one product

LINEAR PROGRAMMING: PROBLEM FORMULATION AND THE GRAPHICAL SOLUTION METHOD

we wish to produce then the fewer assembly hours will remain for production of the other product. Let us assume, arbitrarily, that we decide to produce *zero* output of B, i.e. $B = 0$. This means that all of our available labour in the assembly department can be allocated to production of the other model. As each unit of A requires 28 hours of labour we can easily calculate how many units of A can be produced:

$$\text{Units of A produced} = \frac{16\,800}{28} = 600 \text{ units}$$

In terms of this one constraint this value of 600 units represents the maximum possible production of A when all of this particular resource—assembly time—is allocated to the production of this particular model. Similarly, we can calculate the maximum possible production of B if we allocate all available assembly hours to its production:

$$\text{Units of B produced} = \frac{16\,800}{42} = 400 \text{ units}$$

Accordingly, we have two sets of coordinates for this constraint:

1. $A = 600, B = 0$
2. $A = 0, B = 400$

which allows us to draw the linear constraint, shown in Fig. 5-1.

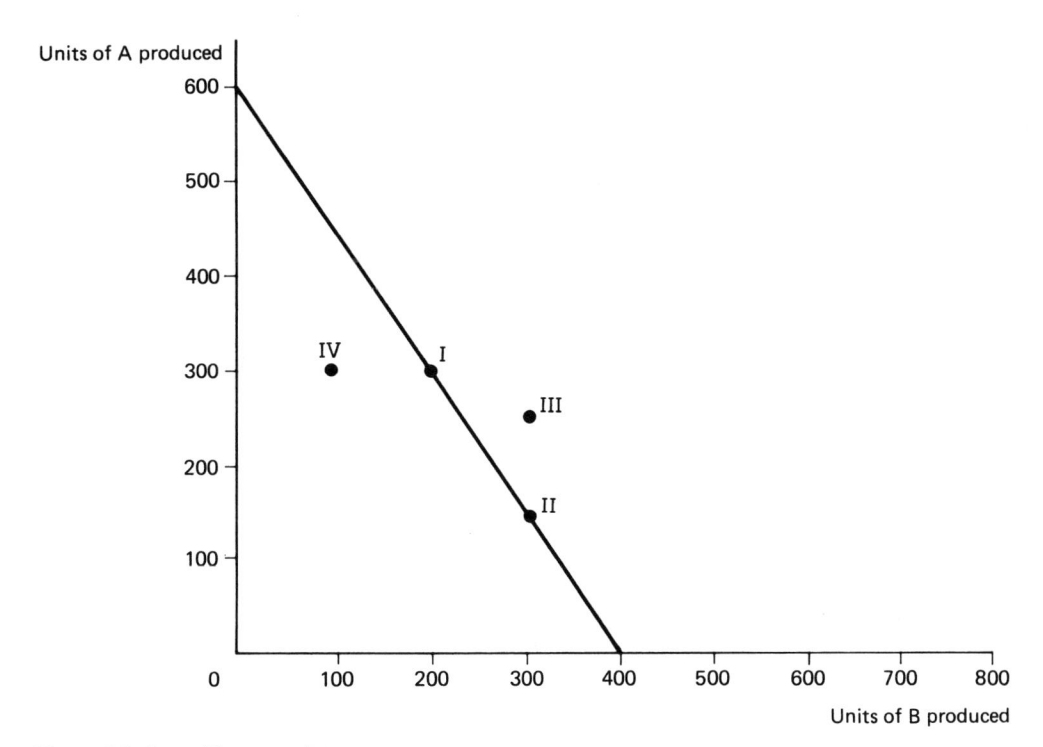

Figure 5-1 Assembly constraint

This line effectively shows both the production possibilities and the competing demand for this particular resource. The straight line itself indicates all the combinations of A and B which require exactly 16 800 assembly hours and the potential trade-off between production of A and production of B in the context of this resource. As we can see from Fig. 5-1, the more we wish to produce of one particular model then the less we are able to produce of the other. For example, point I, which occurs on the line we have identified, represents $A = 300$, $B = 200$. This combination of production of Models A and B will require:

$$28(300) + 42(200) = 8400 + 8400 = 16\,800 \text{ hours}$$

Similarly, point II, which also falls on the line, represents $A = 150$, $B = 300$ and again this requires exactly 16 800 hours. Point III, on the other hand, and any other point to the *right* of this constraint line, represents a combination of A and B that requires more assembly hours than are available. Point III represents $A = 250$, $B = 300$:

$$28(250) + 42(300) = 7000 + 12\,600 = 19\,600 \text{ hours}$$

This area to the right of the line, therefore, represents *infeasible* combinations of A and B for this constraint, that is, those combinations of A and B which cannot be produced with our current resources. Quite simply, there are certain production levels—and combinations of production—for which we do not have the resources. Similarly, point IV, and any other point to the *left* of the constraint line represents a combination of A and B that requires fewer assembly hours than are available. Point IV represents $A = 300$, $B = 100$:

$$28(300) + 42(100) = 8400 + 4200 = 12\,600 \text{ hours}$$

and this area represents *feasible* combinations of A and B for this constraint. That is, those levels of production—and those combinations of production of the two models—for which we do have sufficient resources. Indeed, at point IV we actually have more resources than we require. To summarize, the graphical representation of the constraint divides the graph into three distinct areas:

1. an area where $28A + 42B > 16\,800$

   which is infeasible, as it represents over-utilization of the available resource. The infeasible area is usually delineated with hatch lines on the graph.

2. an area where $28A + 42B < 16\,800$

   which is feasible, but represents under-utilization of the resource. That is, we can produce such a combination of the two products but we will be left with spare, unused resources.

3. the line where $28A + 42B = 16\,800$

   which is also feasible and represents full utilization, that is, demand for the resource arising from these production levels will match exactly the available supply of the resource.

Figure 5-2 shows this distinction. Note that the requirement in our original formula-

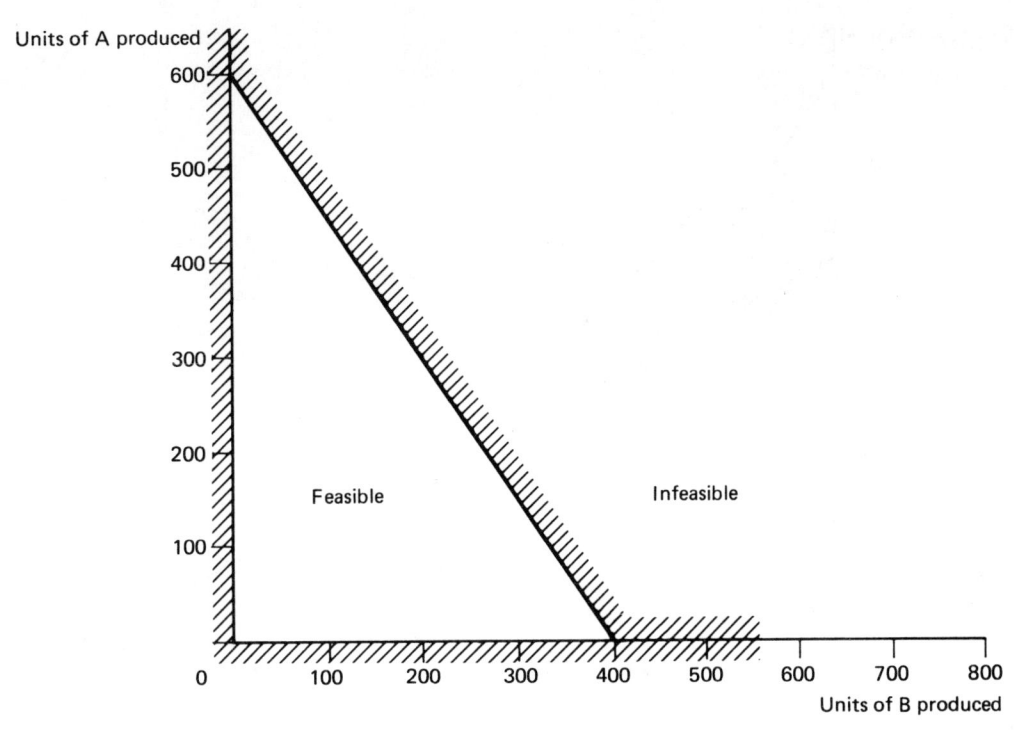

LINEAR PROGRAMMING: PROBLEM FORMULATION AND THE GRAPHICAL SOLUTION METHOD 99

Figure 5-2 Assembly constraint: feasible and infeasible areas

tion that both A and B must be non-negative implies that our feasible area—in this case—is bounded by the vertical and horizontal axes on the graph.

Student activity
You should confirm that you understand the method involved by calculating the equivalent coordinates for constraints 2 and 3, and drawing a suitable graph showing all three constraints.

The appropriate coordinates for constraint Eq. (5-3) and Eq. (5-4) are:

1. Constraint Eq. (5-3), inspection time:
   (a) $A = 400$, $B = 0$
   (b) $A = 0$, $B = 800$

2. Constraint Eq. (5-4), component availability:
   (a) $A = 600$, $B = 0$
   (b) $A = 0$, $B = 600$

These two additional constraints are shown in Fig. 5-3, together with the assembly constraint, and have been labelled A (assembly), I (inspection) and M (microchip) to help identification. The feasible and infeasible areas for each constraint can readily be

100 LINEAR PROGRAMMING

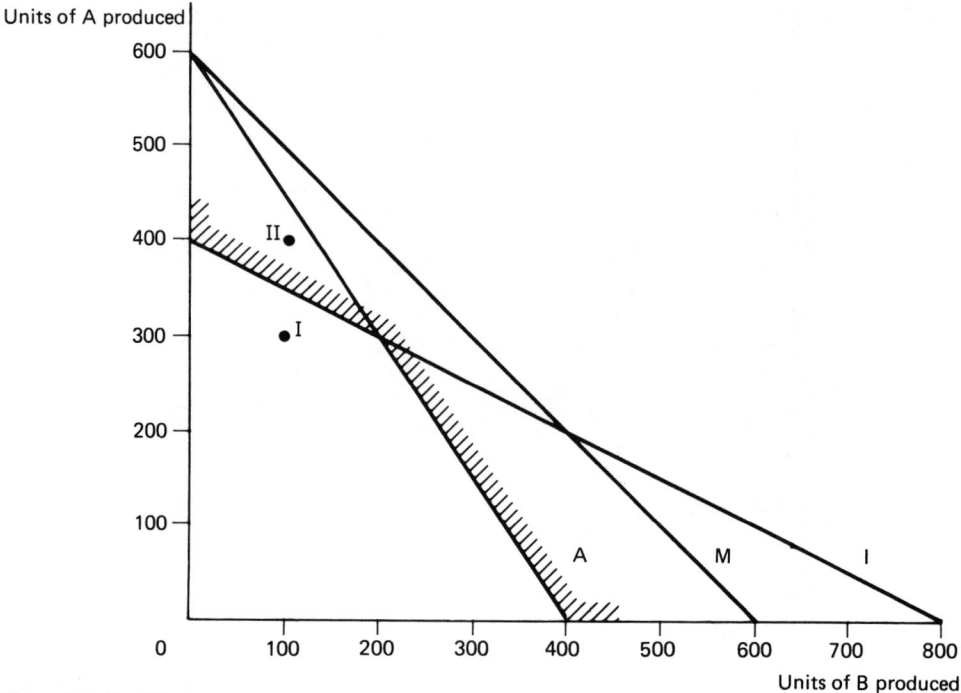

Figure 5-3 Feasible area

identified. More importantly, the area which is feasible for all three constraints *simultaneously* can be identified. This area runs from the origin, along the A axis to 400, down the inspection constraint line until its intersection with the assembly constraint, down to 400 on the B axis and then back to the origin.

To illustrate this let us examine point I in Fig. 5-3. We see this shows a combination of 300 units of Model A and 100 units of Model B. This is feasible for all three of our constraints as we can confirm directly from the constraint expressions:

assembly: $28(300) + 42(100) = 12\,600$ hours
which is less than the 16 800 hours available;

inspection: $12(300) + 6(100) = 4200$ hours
which is less than the 4800 hours available;

microchips: $1(300) + 1(100) = 400$
which is less than the 600 microchips available.

Point II, on the other hand, represents B at 100 units but A at 400. From Fig. 5-3 this production combination can be seen to be feasible for the assembly constraint (A) and the microchip constraint (M) but *not* for the inspection constraint (I). Again, this can be verified directly from the constraints:

assembly: $28(400) + 42(100) = 15\,400$ hours
which is less than the 16 800 hours available;

inspection: 12(400) + 6(100) = 5400 hours
which exceeds the 4800 hours available;

microchips: 1(400) + 1(100) = 500
which is less than the 600 microchips available.

So, the feasible area shows all combinations of A and B that are feasible to all three constraints simultaneously. Any combination outside this area may satisfy one, or two, but not all three constraints.

Student activity
Determine from Fig. 5-3 which of the following production combinations are feasible. Confirm the feasibility using the constraint expressions.

1. $A = 500, B = 50$
2. $A = 350, B = 150$
3. $A = 150, B = 300$

Graphing the objective function

So, Fig. 5-3 allows us to identify those combinations of A and B that are feasible and those that are not, given our existing constraints. Whilst this is an improvement on our original problem we still do not know which of our many feasible combinations of A and B will achieve our objective of profit maximization. To resolve this we now need to introduce the objective function into our analysis and onto our graph. Again, the objective function is linear in form, but unlike our constraints—which faced some maximum resource supply—the objective function is not related to a fixed, constant value. We could relate the A and B coefficients in the assembly constraint, for example, to the maximum resources available—16 800 hours. For the objective function, however, we have only the A and B coefficients and not a fixed constant. However, let us choose some arbitrary profit figure, say £10 000, and try and identify the key features of the profit function. The function allows us to calculate the combinations of A and B that generate this particular profit level. For example, if B is set to 0 then we must produce 250 units of Model A to attain this profit level:

$$\text{Profit} = £10\,000$$

$$B = 0 \text{ units}$$

so, to give £10 000 profit,

$$A = \frac{\text{Profit}}{\text{Profit per unit of Model A}} = \frac{10\,000}{40} = 250 \text{ units}$$

Similarly, if $A = 0$ then B will have to be 200 units to generate the same profit of £10 000. Visually, this is shown on Fig. 5-4. This line shows all combinations of A and B that will produce the same profit, £10 000, and is known as an *iso-profit* line—that is, a line showing equal profit anywhere along its length. Any combination of A and B that occurs on this iso-profit line generates a profit of £10 000 and, presumably, the firm will be completely

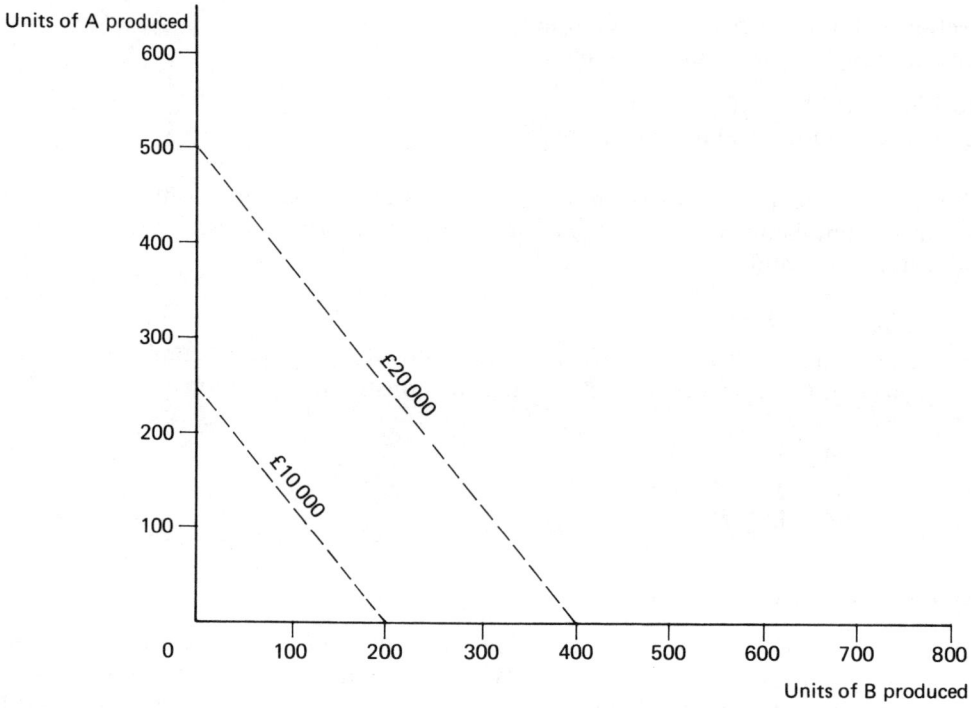

Figure 5-4 Objective function

indifferent as to where on a particular profit line it is. Similarly, we could draw the iso-profit line representing £20 000 profit. The appropriate coordinates will be:

1. $A = 500, B = 0$
2. $A = 0, B = 400$

This is also shown on Fig. 5-4. Obviously, we could draw any number of such iso-profit lines. The important points to note are:

1. All would be parallel, i.e. have the same slope. The slope is given by the relationship of A's profit to that of B. This obviously stays the same no matter what we produce.
2. The further away the iso-profit line is from the origin the higher the profit represented.
3. The firm will be interested only in which profit line it can attain, not where on a particular profit line it happens to be.

Identifying the solution

We can now proceed to determine the optimal solution to our problem. In terms of our objective function we are interested in achieving as high a level of profit as possible. Returning to our constraints in Fig. 5-3 we see that some of the many possible iso-profit lines will lie totally outside the feasible area, representing profit levels which are not attainable given our fixed resources. Other iso-profit lines will, however, fall within the feasible area, either in total or in part.

Student activity
Draw the two iso-profit lines for £10 000 and £20 000 on the graph that you drew in an earlier Student Activity. Comment on the feasible solutions for each profit line.

You will see that the iso-profit line of £10 000 falls entirely within the feasible area. So any combination of A and B which generates a profit of £10 000 will be feasible in terms of the available resources. The iso-profit line for £20 000, which in terms of our objective is preferable, falls only partly within the feasible area. This indicates that some production levels of A and B which generate this particular profit are feasible whilst others are not. We are searching for the highest iso-profit line that also coincides with some part of the feasible area. It is apparent that as our iso-profit line increases—i.e. moves upwards and to the right, away from the origin—less and less of the line falls within the feasible area. Eventually, in our efforts to reach a higher profit line, there will come a stage where we reach point I on Fig. 5-5 (which shows both our iso-profit lines and the outline of the feasible area).

Point I represents the optimal solution to the problem. Although most of the combinations of A and B that generate this particular profit of £22 000 lie outside the feasible area and therefore require more resources than we have available there remains

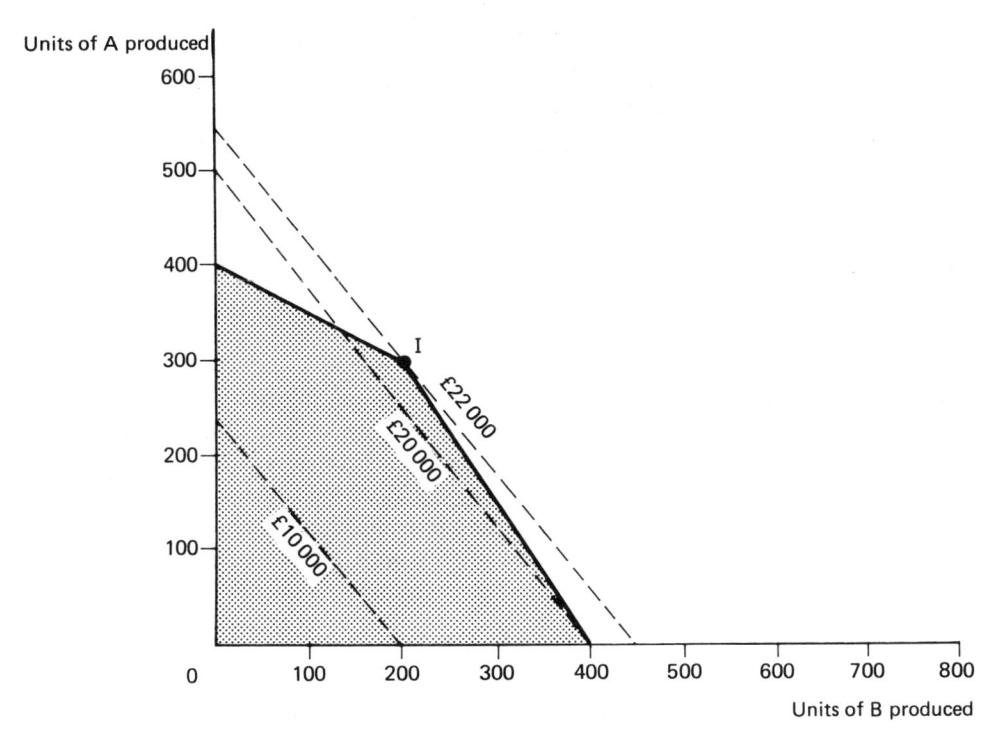

Figure 5-5 Feasible area and iso-profit lines: optimal solution

one point—a single combination of A and B—that occurs on the boundary of our feasible area and, therefore, can be produced with the available resources. From Fig. 5-5 this point can be seen to represent:

$$A = 300$$
$$B = 200$$

which is, therefore, our profit-maximizing combination of the two products. Profit at this output combination will be:

$$\text{Profit} = 40(300) + 50(200) = £22\,000$$

The next higher iso-profit line—£22 001—would have left the feasible area altogether. This means that, although this profit level is preferable, it can be attained only with a combination of A and B that is infeasible given our current levels of resources. Similarly, other combinations of A and B which are feasible will generate an iso-profit line lower than £22 000, which obviously would not be consistent with our objective. At this stage, therefore, the optimum solution can be found by superimposing the objective function onto the graph showing the feasible area. Any objective function line will suffice because we simply need to identify from the slope of the line which corner point of the feasible area will represent the optimum solution.

Summary of the graphical procedure

Let us summarize the graphical procedure we have developed thus far:

1. Produce a graph showing all constraints in the problem.
2. Identify clearly the feasible area and its boundary.
3. Choose a specific, arbitrary value for the objective function and, using this, plot the objective function on the graph.
4. Move the objective line outward and away from the origin but parallel to the initial objective function line.
5. Identify the point on the boundary of the feasible area that the objective function encounters *last* as it moves outward.
6. This feasible point is the optimum solution.

As a general point it is worth while noting that the optimal solution to an LP problem will normally occur at one of the corner—or extreme—points of the feasible area. This makes the task of identifying the appropriate optimal solution somewhat easier. Having drawn the graph it is simply a question of identifying visually which corner point represents the optimum given the slope of the objective function line, i.e. which corner point the objective function line will encounter last as it moves outward from the feasible area.

5-4 EXTENSIONS TO THE GRAPHICAL METHOD

Whilst the graphical method provides the optimal solution to the defined problem it is unlikely that this by itself will satisfy management. As we have seen with the transportation and assignment models, additional, and potentially useful, management information can often be derived from the optimal solution via the use of sensitivity analysis. Such analysis exists in its most refined and advanced form in the LP model, and whilst some aspects must be deferred until Chapter 8 we can usefully commence the analysis now.

Binding and non-binding constraints

In Fig. 5-5 we derived the profit-maximizing combination of A and B production to be $A = 300$ and $B = 200$. This is the combination that will generate the highest possible profit within the limitations imposed by our three constraints. If we return to the constraints we can confirm that our optimal solution does in fact satisfy these limitations. We had:

$$28A + 42B \leq 16\,800 \quad (5\text{-}2)$$

$$12A + 6B \leq 4\,800 \quad (5\text{-}3)$$

$$1A + 1B \leq 600 \quad (5\text{-}4)$$

Constraint Eq. (5-2), relating to assembly time, indicates that initially we have 16 800 assembly hours available. Our solution requires:

$$28(300) + 42(200) \text{ hours} = 8400 + 8400 = 16\,800 \text{ hours}$$

That is, this particular resource is fully utilized at our optimal point. The demand for this resource, generated by producing 300 units of Model A and 200 units of Model B, is matched exactly by the available supply. Returning to Fig. 5-3, we can also confirm this visually as the optimal point occurs on the line of this constraint. We saw earlier that a combination of A and B that occurs on the constraint line itself requires all of the resources available. Similarly, constraint Eq. (5-3) indicates that we have 4800 inspection hours available. Our solution requires:

$$12(300) + 6(200) = 3600 + 1200 = 4800 \text{ hours}$$

Again, this resource is fully utilized, as we can confirm from Fig. 5-3 where the optimum combination again occurs on this constraint line. Obviously these two constraints are effectively preventing profit from increasing further by limiting production. We have seen that we would prefer the objective function (representing profit) to be pushed as far outward from the origin as possible, but that this will be limited by the available resources—that is, by the feasible area. We have identified that these two constraints will stop the objective function from moving further outward as, at the optimum position, all of the available resources in the assembly and inspection departments are fully used to generate this combination of A and B and the associated profit of £22 000. Accordingly, these constraints are known as *binding* constraints. A binding constraint is one that is preventing the objective function from taking an improved value, and represents full utilization of a particular resource. The third resource, however, Eq. (5-4), relating to the available supply of microchips, is not fully utilized, as can be seen from the graph, where the optimum point is below the constraint line. To verify we have:

$$300 + 200 = 500 \text{ units}$$

i.e. 500 components are required whereas 600 are available. This third constraint is *non-*

binding. It is not, at our optimal point, having a directly restrictive effect on production and profit. In the context of this one constraint we could still expand production—and hence profit—beyond our current position. It is the binding constraints that prevent us from doing this, however. Obviously, in management terms, the distinction between binding and non-binding constraints is crucial. A binding constraint represents a resource that is fully utilized at the optimum point. Production—and hence profit—cannot be increased further, as the resource represented by a binding constraint has been exhausted. A binding constraint implies that the acquisition of additional resources will lead directly to an improved value for the objective function. In our example additional supplies of scarce resources will generate more profit, as they will allow increased production of Model A and/or Model B. A non-binding constraint, on the other hand, implies unused resources. At the optimum production levels there will be spare, unused resources relating to a non-binding constraint as here, with 100 unused microchips. The management implications of identifying binding constraints is an important aspect of the technique, to which we shall return later in this section.

Simultaneous equations solution

As is probably apparent, one of the drawbacks of using the graphical method of solution is the inaccuracy inherent in a graph. In our problem the solution is (conveniently!) easy to read from the two scales, as the optimum production levels are in terms of whole units. In other situations this is unlikely to be the case and we may have difficulty reading a precise value from the graph for the two variables in the problem. We can overcome this by verifying the graphical solution using simultaneous equations. This will also have the effect of providing additional information about the solution that may be useful to the decision-maker. Having identified the two binding constraints, we can transform the original inequalities into strict equalities (equations) as we know that at our optimum point the two sides of the constraints will be equal (i.e. supply will equal demand). Thus, the first binding constraint can be expressed in equation form as:

$$28A + 42B = 16\,800 \tag{5-8}$$

and the second binding constraint as:

$$12A + 6B = 4800 \tag{5-9}$$

We know from the graph that the solution occurs at the intersection of these two—binding—constraints. In fact, this will always be the case. That is, a solution will need to satisfy all the binding constraints simultaneously. Accordingly, we can solve for A and B using normal simultaneous equation solution methods. This will confirm the solution previously obtained from the graph and is a useful check on the accuracy of the graphical solution. There are a variety of techniques available for solving sets of simultaneous equations. We shall use one of the more straightforward methods. To determine the solution we perform the following calculations:

1. We multiply Eq. (5-8) by 12 to give:

$$336A + 504B = 201\,600$$

2. We multiply Eq. (5-9) by 28 to give:

$$336A + 168B = 134\,400$$

3. We subtract the two equations (the order of subtraction is immaterial):

$$\begin{array}{r} 336A + 504B = 201\,600 \\ -336A - 168B \;\; -134\,400 \\ \hline 336B = \;\; 67\,200 \end{array}$$

and solving for B this gives $B = 200$. Substituting $B = 200$ back into either of the two original equations we confirm that $A = 300$. Once we have identified the binding constraints from the graph, therefore, we can find the precise values for our variables using this solution method, which is far more accurate and reliable than simply reading values from the scales on the graph.

Simple sensitivity analysis

More importantly, however, the use of simultaneous equations allows us to develop an additional part of our analysis. We said previously that binding constraints indicate resources that are fully utilized at the current solution. In other words, binding constraints represent scarce resources. The implication behind such a constraint is that an increase in the supply of one of these resources will lead, other things being equal, to an increase in production and therefore in profit. Simultaneous equations allow us to quantify these effects precisely. It is often the case in business and economics that we are trying to assess the effects of changes in resource allocations. We may be considering expanding the workforce, buying additional resources, raising more finance, and so on. To illustrate how we can provide information about such a decision let us assume that we can, somehow, acquire one extra hour of assembly time. We know that this is a binding constraint, and therefore the resources the constraint represents are currently fully utilized. The implication is that if we acquire an extra unit of this resource it becomes possible to increase production and thereby increase profit. Our two binding constraints will now be:

$$28A + 42B = 16\,801 \quad (5\text{-}10)$$

$$12A + \;\;6B = \;\;4\,800 \quad (5\text{-}3)$$

Student activity
Using simultaneous equations, determine the new solution and interpret the changes that have occurred.

Solving these two equations now gives:

$$A = 299.9821$$

$$B = 200.0358$$

and at these new production levels we can use the objective function to calculate that profit will now be £22 001.07. As a result of this one extra unit of assembly time, therefore,

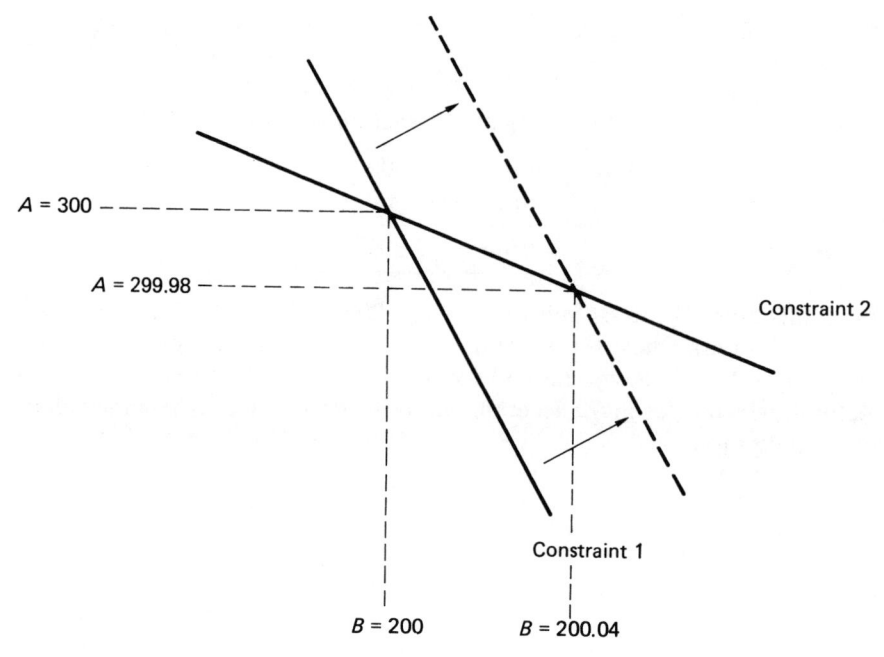

Figure 5-6 Change in constraint 1

optimum production of Model A will decrease by 0.0179 units while production of Model B increases by 0.0358, with an associated increase in profit of £1.07. It is important to realize that these figures represent *marginal* changes in our solution arising from a marginal change in one of our binding resources. Whilst such precise changes cannot be identified on a graph, the general principle of this change in constraint 1 is shown on Fig. 5-6, with the extra unit of assembly time pushing this constraint line outward. This will change the feasible area slightly and so will enable the objective function to move further away from the origin. The same marginal analysis can be carried out on the inspection constraint. If we now return to the original problem and assume that one extra hour of inspection time becomes available then we have:

$$28A + 42B = 16\,800 \tag{5-2}$$

$$12A + 6B = 4\,801 \tag{5-11}$$

Student activity
Determine the effect this extra hour will have on the optimal solution.

Solving gives:

$$A = 300.125$$
$$B = 199.9167$$
$$\text{Profit} = £22\,000.83$$

Here an extra unit of inspection time will lead to increased production of Model A and a decreased production of Model B, with an associated increase in profit of £0.83. We now have not only an optimal solution, but information on the effect of obtaining more of the two scarce resources. In effect, the two marginal profit changes we have calculated:

£1.07 for an additional hour of assembly time
£0.83 for additional hour of inspection time

represent the *scarcity value*—often referred to as the *opportunity cost*—of these resources. Effectively, such opportunity costs measure the value to the firm of additional scarce resources. They show the profit we forgo by *not* acquiring more of these scarce resources. It is important to realize that these figures represent the increase in profit, i.e. after the normal costs of obtaining these extra resources have been deducted. Effectively, this allows the organization to determine the prices it is willing to pay for such scarce resources. In the case of assembly hours this would be anything up to:

$$£4.00 + £1.07 = £5.07$$
$$\text{normal cost} \quad \text{opportunity cost}$$

and for inspection time:

$$£3.00 + £0.83 = £3.83$$

Taking the figure for assembly hours of £5.07, this indicates the maximum price IMC would be willing to pay to acquire additional assembly time. The figure comprises the normal labour cost of £4.00 per hour and the opportunity cost of £1.07. If the firm can acquire additional assembly hours at a cost of less than £5.07 then total profits will increase. At a cost of more than £5.07 the extra profit generated would not be sufficient to cover the extra costs incurred. A similar logic can be applied to inspection time. Obviously, these opportunity costs can also be used by management to prioritize the acquisition of additional resources. Other things being equal, additional assembly time is more valuable than additional inspection time and given a choice the company would be advised to seek additional time in the assembly department rather than in the inspection department, as this will lead to higher additional profit.

Student activity
Calculate the opportunity cost for the third constraint if an extra microchip is acquired. Why is it zero?

Such opportunity costs arise because resources for the two binding constraints are fully utilized at the optimal position—that is, they are scarce. A resource that is not scarce at the current optimum, as with the microchip constraint, has a zero opportunity cost. We already have surplus supplies of this particular resource. Increasing the supply further, say to 601 units, will not allow us to produce extra units of Models A and B and will therefore have a zero effect on profit—the objective function. One further point relating to the opportunity costs of the binding constraints needs to be made at this stage. As we increase the supply of a particular resource—say, assembly time—the relevant constraint line moves outward from the origin, changing the optimal combination of A and B. As we can

110 LINEAR PROGRAMMING

see from Fig. 5-3, there will eventually come a point where resources which are currently under-utilized—the microchip component—will all be required to make full use of the additional supply of assembly time. As can be seen from the graph, constraint line A will move outward and away from the origin (as we acquire additional assembly time) until all three constraint lines intersect. Technically, at this point, a non-binding constraint becomes binding and we will have reached the maximum worthwhile increase in assembly hours. At this point in this particular problem all constraints will be binding and an increase in profit can no longer be achieved by an increase in just this one scarce resource. We have, as yet, no method of calculating precisely when this point will be reached. This method will be discussed after the Simplex procedure has been introduced in Chapter 7.

Incorporating other types of constraint

As we saw earlier, other types of constraint are easily included in the formulation of a problem and are just as easily incorporated into our graphical solution. Attention should be paid, however, to the feasible/infeasible areas represented in such a problem, as they tend to be more detailed and complex than the simple introductory problem we have examined so far. For example, assume we face additional constraints such that:

$$A \geq 100 \qquad (5\text{-}12)$$

$$A + B \geq 450 \qquad (5\text{-}7)$$

which relate to the restrictions discussed earlier. IMC have a contract to supply at least 100

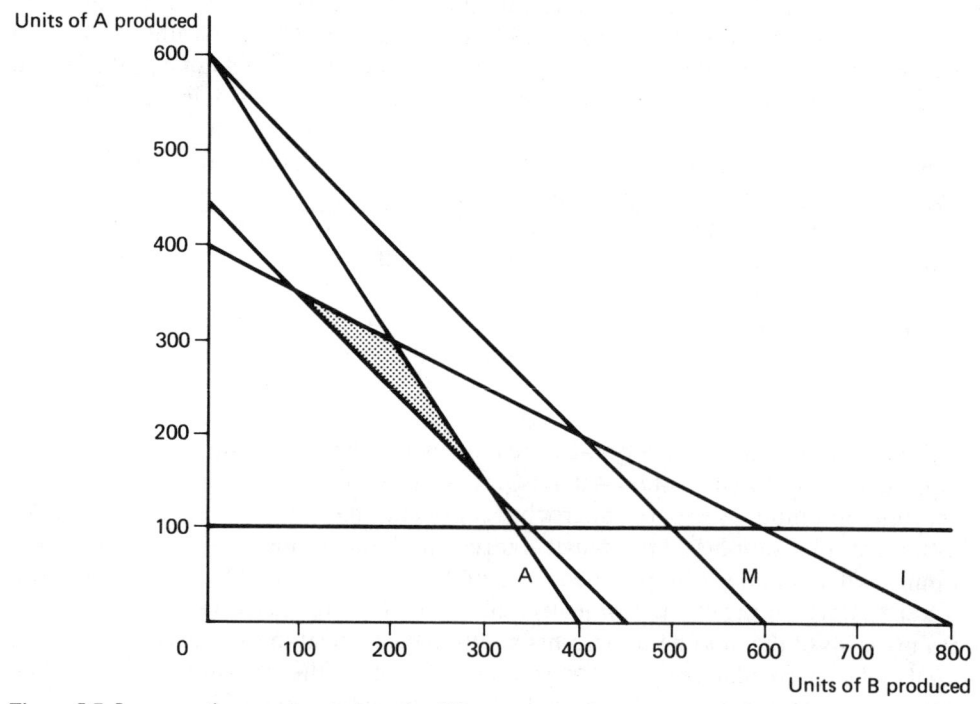

Figure 5-7 Incorporating new constraints: feasible area

units of Model A and a total output of 450 units. Figure 5-7 shows these constraints (together with the existing three production constraints), together with the new feasible area.

Minimization problems

We have assumed in our example that the firm wishes to maximize profit. Problems involving minimization—in terms say of costs—are equally common. The only amendment required to our solution method is to note that the objective function should now be as *close* to the origin as the feasible area allows, and not as far away as possible under maximization. In a minimization context we are interested in keeping the value of the objective function as low as possible. Otherwise, solution and interpretation of these problems are indentical. To illustrate let us review the problem:

$$\text{Minimize} \quad 219A + 299B \quad (5\text{-}6)$$
$$\text{subject to:} \quad 28A + 42B \leq 16\,800 \quad (5\text{-}2)$$
$$12A + 6B \leq 4\,800 \quad (5\text{-}3)$$
$$1A + 1B \leq 600 \quad (5\text{-}4)$$
$$1A \geq 100 \quad (5\text{-}12)$$
$$1A + 1B \geq 450 \quad (5\text{-}7)$$

We have a cost minimization problem with constraints representing the production limits we face, together with minimum requirements for production of Model A of 100 units and combined production of both Model A and Model B of 450 units. The feasible area is that already shown in Fig. 5-7. Given that the objective is now to keep costs to a minimum, we require the objective function line to be as close to the origin as possible. By superimposing a suitable objective function line on the graph we can readily determine the appropriate optimal solution.

Figure 5-8 shows the outline of the feasible area and an iso-cost line for the problem. Given the desire to have this line as close to the origin as possible, it is evident that the optimal solution will occur at point I, with $A = 350$ and $B = 100$. This will be the corner point of the feasible area that the iso-cost line intercepts *last* as it moves towards the origin.

5-5 SUMMARY

The simple problem we have used to illustrate the basic structure of the LP model and the graphical solution method illustrates the main features of most LP applications. The problem also illustrates the implicit key assumptions of the model:

1. We must be able to quantify an objective. Here we wish to maximize profit. In other applications we may wish to consider
    - maximizing revenue,
    - minimizing costs,

112 LINEAR PROGRAMMING

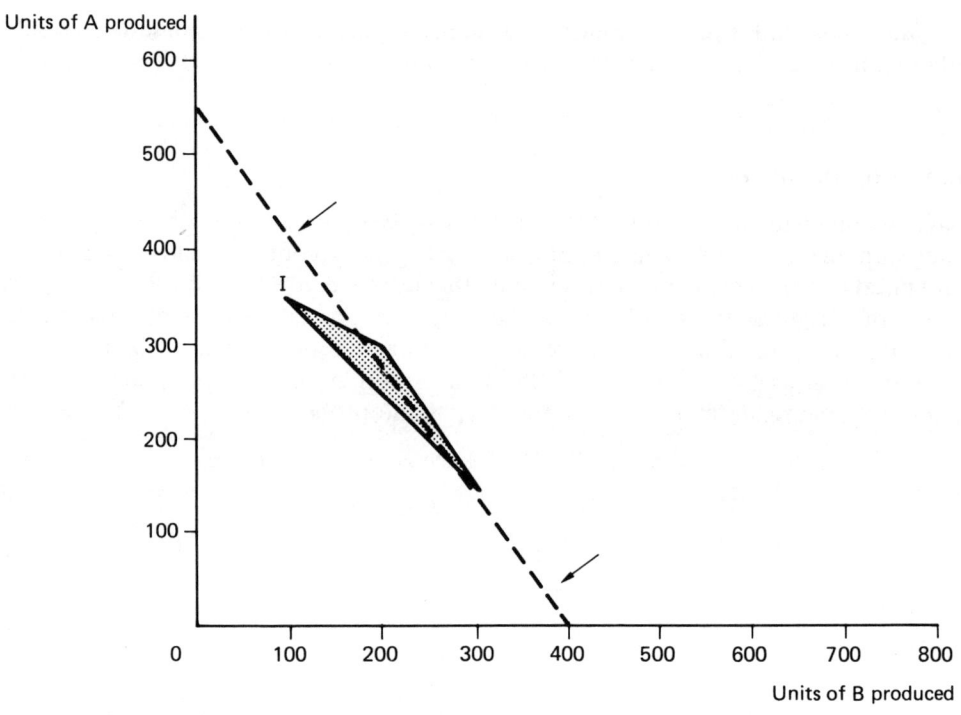

Figure 5-8 Outline of feasible area and iso-cost line

- maximizing production,
- minimizing inflation, etc.

Although this sounds simple, there will be many areas where there may be a number of objectives that the decision-maker may wish to take into account, not simply one. We may also face a situation where we may not be able to quantify the objective the organization has chosen.

2. The concept of optimization must be applicable to the problem under examination. In order to be able to use the technique we are about to develop we must assume that the decision-maker wishes to optimize some desired objective. However, the concept of 'optimization', although useful in theoretical decision-making, is not always appropriate. In many organizations management may be more interested in attaining a reasonable or 'satisficing' solution to the current problem rather than an ideal and optimum solution.
3. Relevant resources must be in limited supply and we must be able to quantify the rate of use of these resources. If relevant resources were not in limited supply then there would be few problems for the decision-maker. It is precisely because some critical resources are constrained that we must resolve their allocation and use in a rational way.
4. There must be alternative courses of action available between which we must choose. The limited resources that we have available must—in some way—have competing and alternative uses. The problem we face is deciding between competing uses for the fixed resources at our disposal.
5. All the appropriate relationships can be expressed in a linear form. This precludes such

possibilities as economies of scale or diminishing returns to scale, which will generally be non-linear.

It is important that the decision-maker is aware of the assumptions under which the LP model is formulated and solved if the information generated by the solution program is to be evaluated properly. We shall return to discuss these assumptions and their implications for decision-making in more detail later on in the text. It should not be assumed, however, that such factors will necessarily hinder the application of LP to business problems. As we shall see in the next chapter, the range of potential and actual applications of the model is staggering in its diversity.

STUDENT EXERCISES

5-1 For the problem shown in Fig. 5-7 determine the optimal solution from the graph.
Confirm the solution using simultaneous equations and distinguish between the binding and non-binding constraints.

5-2 For the problem shown in Fig. 5-7 assume the objective function is:

$$\text{Minimize} \quad 219A + 299B$$

(a) Find the optimal solution to this problem.
(b) Confirm your solution using simultaneous equations.
(c) Distinguish between the binding and non-binding constraints.
(d) Calculate the opportunity costs for the binding constraints and interpret these in the context of the business problem.

5-3 Return to the original problem introduced in Chapter 5 (Eqs (5-1) to (5-5)). IMC now decide that a suitable objective will be to maximize revenue rather than profit.
(a) Formulate the new objective function.
(b) Determine the new optimal solution.
(c) Undertake sensitivity analysis on the optimal solution and interpret the results in the context of the business problem.

5-4 To the problem in Exercise 5-3 add a further constraint which requires production of Model A to be at least 325 units.
(a) Repeat the analysis you have undertaken.
(b) Using the cost minimization objective function from Exercise 5-2 determine the new optimal solution and undertake appropriate sensitivity analysis.

5-5 A company publishing textbooks is planning its production of the next book scheduled to be printed. The book will be published in both paperback and hardback format. The paperback sells for £10 per copy and costs £5 to produce and market. The hardback sells for £20 and costs £17. Market research has indicated that total sales of the book are unlikely to exceed 10 000 copies. Of these at least 4000 are expected to be in paperback format with at least 2000 in hardback. On the other hand, the company does not expect to sell more than 4000 hardback copies. In addition, there are potential problems involved in producing the paperback edition. The printing equipment is needed for other paperback books and is available for printing this book for a period of only 5000 hours. Each paperback takes 40 minutes to produce.
(a) Formulate this problem assuming the company wishes to maximize profit.
(b) Solve this problem. Identify the binding and non-binding constraints and undertake appropriate sensitivity analysis. Interpret the results of this analysis in the context of the problem.
(c) The company now decides it wishes to maximize revenue from sales. Reformulate the problem and repeat stages (a) and (b). Compute the profit the company would earn.
(d) The production manager is strongly arguing that production should be determined by costs. Reformulate the problem in terms of cost minimization and repeat parts (a) and (b). Compute the profit the company would earn.
(e) Which of the three alternative objective functions do you think is most appropriate?

6
LINEAR PROGRAMMING APPLICATIONS

In the previous chapter the technique of linear programming was introduced in the context of a simple production problem and a method of determining the solution to such a simple problem provided. In subsequent chapters we shall examine a more rigorous and general-purpose solution method and discuss the wealth of management information that can be obtained from the application of the technique. Before doing so, however, it will be worth while examining a variety of typical applications of LP. This will serve two purposes. The first is that it will provide an overview of the tremendous diversity of business applications to which the technique has been applied. The second is that it will provide an insight into the process of problem formulation. In the previous chapter it was apparent that an LP problem typically falls into three parts: problem formulation, solution and interpretation. As we shall see the solution of an LP problem is generally straightforward (even when a suitable computer package is not used) and the interpretation of that solution is equally straightforward to someone who is adequately familiar with the technique. Both these stages, however, are totally dependent upon the correct and appropriate formulation of the problem. This chapter focuses upon a number of detailed examples of typical business formulations.

6-1 THE PROCESS OF PROBLEM FORMULATION

The process of formulating an LP application requires the practitioner to be able to 'translate' the business problem under investigation into a form suitable for solution by the technique. Over the years such formulation has developed almost into an art form and it is only fair to point out that it is this stage that will provide most difficulty in virtually every LP application. The methods of solution and interpretation are, fortunately, fairly similar no matter what the problem. The formulation, however, is likely to be almost unique to the problem under consideration. Fortunately, many problems do fall into general application categories that provide some guidance to the practitioner on the basic formulation approach to be adopted. It is also worth while pointing out that there is no magic formula that can be provided to the student to ease the burden of this process. The development of appropriate LP formulation skills comes only with time and practice and the more examples and case studies you are able to access the quicker these skills will be developed. This can, however, be facilitated by adopting a logical process when attempting to formulate a problem. Naturally, like all such processes, it will not conform exactly to every problem that is examined but it does provide a useful general framework and is detailed below:

1. Provide a detailed verbal description of the problem under consideration, ensuring that related information is unambiguous and sufficiently precise. It is essential that we have a clear and adequate understanding of the problem under investigation before we seek to apply the technique itself.
2. Determine the overall objective that appears to be relevant. It will usually (but not always) be clear whether the objective relates to some maximization or minimization, to cost or profit, and so on. An adequate understanding of the overall objective can be of considerable assistance in unravelling other aspects of the problem.
3. Determine the factors (constraints) that appear to restrict in some way the attainment of the objective identified in the previous stage. These stages together will provide a detailed verbal exposition of the complete problem under investigation. The next step is to put the verbal description into a suitable mathematical framework.
4. Define the decision variables that are relevant to the problem and, as is often important, ensure that their units of measurement are explicitly stated. Failure to do so may well lead to difficulty in formulating appropriate constraints and in interpreting the solution results.
5. Using these decision variables, formulate an objective function. It is clear that this function should incorporate all the decision variables. If it does not it signifies either a lack of information or an incorrect choice of decision variables.
6. For each of the restrictions identified in step 3 formulate a suitable mathematical constraint. Again, each constraint must include at least some of the decision variables and, again, the units of measurement of each constraint should be explicit.
7. Lastly, check the entire formulation to ensure linearity of all variables and constraints.

It should not be concluded, on the basis of this schematic process, that problem formulation will be as simple and straightforward as this. It will typically involve considerable backtracking (the methodology structure discussed in Chapter 1 is clearly most appropriate to this process). You may consider initially that you have identified the appropriate decision variables but are then unable to formulate a particular constraint involving these variables. This failure suggests a full reconsideration of the problem is necessary. Equally you may complete the formulation only to find that there is no apparent solution to the problem as formulated. Typically this may imply an incorrect formulation. It is equally important—once an optimal solution has been found—to 'translate' the solution back into the original—verbal—problem to ensure that the mathematical solution is appropriate for the original problem. A frequent mistake made by many students is to produce a formulation (often lacking some critical constraint) to solve the problem and then simply to assume that because they have a solution then their formulation must be correct. Only if the mathematical solution can be tied in with the original problem are we in a position to assume that our problem formulation is the correct one. To illustrate this process and to provide examples of some of the more common areas of LP applications to business problems we shall now turn to look at a number of problems and their formulation in detail. These problems have been categorized in terms of their general area of applicability but it must be stressed that the divisions between such categories are extremely arbitrary and serve only as a general guide. In the real world practical applications of the technique will not fall neatly into one particular category, although it is frequently useful to undertake such categorization to help focus upon an appropriate overall structure to the formulation. Equally in this chapter, our interest does not lie in the solution of such problems, only in their formulation. We shall, however, be using all these problems as the basis for future exercises.

6-2 RESOURCE ALLOCATION/PRODUCT MIX PROBLEMS

We have already introduced and examined in detail one application that falls into this general category (the IMC problem in the previous chapter) and there is little need to examine its key features in detail here. This is, however, one of the classic areas of LP applications. Given that in most business organizations at least some resources will be in short supply and that such resources face competing demands then LP is an obvious method of determining an optimum allocation of such scarce resources. Typically such problems involve a range of available resources each of which is available in only limited quantities. Demand for these resources typically arises from the production of items, and the solution to the problem provides the 'ideal' product mix in the sense that it optimizes the use of the available resources in the context of some defined objective—typically expressed in terms of profit, of revenue or of cost. Such problem formulations—as illustrated with the IMC case in the last chapter—typically involve decision variables that relate to the quantities of product items to be produced and constraints detailing the limited resources available and their rate of use in the production process.

6-3 PRODUCTION SCHEDULING

A related area of application is that of *production scheduling*. It is not usually sufficient for an organization to determine an optimal product mix for a single moment in time. Production takes place over a defined period and decisions are required in terms of scheduling production levels during this period. For example, an organization may want to establish weekly production levels over the next month. Whilst a simple product-mix approach may help in determining an optimal solution for any given week, it is unlikely to produce an optimal solution for the entire period of one month given that, on a weekly basis, demand for the products may change, resource allocations may differ and priorities may alter from week to week. It becomes necessary, therefore, to establish an optimal solution for the entire period and not simply for part of the period.

Consider the following problem. The production manager of a large brewery faces the

Table 6-1 Resource availability for the next 4 week cycle

	Labour	Barley
Week 1	2 000 hours	30 000 kg
Week 2	1 500	30 000
Week 3	2 500	40 000
Week 4	3 000	30 000

Table 6-2 Estimated production costs

	Production costs per barrel
Week 1	£13.00
2	£15.50
3	£15.00
4	£16.00

problem of determining the production of lager over a 4 week cycle. That is, production must be planned and scheduled over a 4 week period. The start of the planning process is the forecast of lager production that will be required 4 weeks hence for delivery to supermarkets, pubs, clubs and other customers. Once the production target has been determined the manager must determine how much lager should be produced in each week over the next 4 week cycle. Because of the variety of products produced by the brewery such planning is critical in terms of determining resource availability. In addition to lager the brewery produces a variety of other alcoholic and low-alcohol drinks all of which require the same production facilities as the lager product. In particular two such resources are critical—labour availability and the Austrian barley used in the brewing process. Both these resources are also required by other products that the brewery makes. Each barrel of lager produced requires 0.8 hours of labour and 10 kg of barley. Over the next 4 week cycle the availability of the two resources is projected to be as detailed in Table 6-1.

Production costs also vary over the 4 week cycle partly because of overtime arrangements with other product lines. Costs per barrel for the next 4 weeks are estimated to be as given in Table 6-2.

An additional problem arises in that, because of limited transport facilities, the barrels of lager are only shipped out from the brewery at the end of each production cycle. Accordingly, stockholding costs are incurred for any production that takes place in the first 3 weeks. Such costs are estimated at 90 pence per barrel per week. The brewery has forecast demand for the next cycle to be 10 000 barrels. We have, therefore, a clear verbal exposition of the problem. Let us proceed to determine a suitable formulation. Our objective here is clearly to organize weekly production of lager over this 4 week cycle at the lowest possible cost. It is also clear that we face a number of restrictions as we try to achieve this. There is a limit on the weekly availability of labour and on the weekly availability of barley. There is also a third restriction in terms of the total demand over the planning

Table 6-3 Costs

Decision variable	Production cost	Storage cost	Total cost
X_1	£13.00	£2.70	£15.70
X_2	£15.50	£1.80	£17.30
X_3	£15.00	£0.90	£15.90
X_4	£16.00	—	£16.00

cycle. The next step is to choose the decision variables. Clearly, at the end of the analysis, we will require to know the quantities of lager to be produced in each of the 4 weeks of the next cycle and it appears sensible to choose decision variables that relate to the quantity of lager produced in each week. Thus we shall have X_1, X_2, X_3 and X_4 relating to output (measured in barrels) in each of the 4 weeks respectively. The next step is to determine a suitable objective function. We are seeking a cost minimization function and costs comprise two elements: there is a direct production cost per barrel and a weekly storage cost per barrel. We can summarize the relevant costs as in Table 6-3. The objective function now becomes:

$$\text{Minimize} \quad 15.7X_1 + 17.3X_2 + 15.9X_3 + 16X_4 \qquad (6\text{-}1)$$

It is worth noting that, as with many applications, simplifying assumptions are frequently required. Here, in terms of storage costs, we assume that such costs are incurred from the end of each week in which production takes place. If this were a real business application we should naturally wish to be more precise, although the overall structure of the problem formulation would remain the same. We next require a constraint for each restriction we face in the problem. Taking the weekly labour restrictions first of all we have:

$$0.8X_1 \leq 2000 \qquad (6\text{-}2)$$
$$0.8X_2 \leq 1500 \qquad (6\text{-}3)$$
$$0.8X_3 \leq 2500 \qquad (6\text{-}4)$$
$$0.8X_4 \leq 3000 \qquad (6\text{-}5)$$

where each constraint relates that week's production (X_i) to that week's available supply of labour. We have a similar set of constraints relating to barley:

$$10X_1 \leq 30\,000 \qquad (6\text{-}6)$$
$$10X_2 \leq 30\,000 \qquad (6\text{-}7)$$
$$10X_3 \leq 40\,000 \qquad (6\text{-}8)$$
$$10X_4 \leq 30\,000 \qquad (6\text{-}9)$$

Finally, we have the overall production target of 10 000 barrels. Again, there is some potential ambiguity here. It is not clear whether this represents an exact production restriction or a minimum restriction (with surplus production being stockpiled to meet excess demand). We shall assume that this figure represents an exact production target and the constraint is then:

$$1X_1 + 1X_2 + 1X_3 + 1X_4 = 10\,000 \qquad (6\text{-}10)$$

The full problem formulation is then given as:

$$\text{Minimize} \quad 15.7X_1 + 17.3X_2 + 15.9X_3 + 16X_4$$

$$\begin{aligned}
\text{subject to:} \quad 0.8X_1 &\leq 2\,000 \\
0.8X_2 &\leq 1\,500 \\
0.8X_3 &\leq 2\,500 \\
0.8X_4 &\leq 3\,000 \\
10X_1 &\leq 30\,000 \\
10X_2 &\leq 30\,000 \\
10X_3 &\leq 40\,000 \\
10X_4 &\leq 30\,000 \\
1X_1 + 1X_2 + 1X_3 + 1X_4 &= 10\,000 \\
X_1, X_2, X_3, X_4 &\geq 0
\end{aligned}$$

A quick visual inspection also confirms that all aspects of the formulation are indeed linear. In addition to variants on this basic approach (relating not only to production over time but also to production for stockholding purposes, production to match with labour supply, and so on) there is another broad group of applications that fall into this general category of production scheduling. The previous application examined the scheduling decision from the viewpoint of time. What may be equally relevant in some applications is to determine a suitable production schedule in the context of a 'produce or buy' decision. Typically, an organization may be able to produce some item in house or may consider subcontracting some or all of the production to an outside organization. The decision then becomes one of optimizing total production in terms of scheduling between in-house production or outside production subject to a variety of constraints typically involving time, resources and finance. An example of this will be found in the end-of-chapter exercises.

6-4 LABOUR SCHEDULING

A similar scheduling approach is often required with problems relating to labour requirements and labour availability. The problem frequently involves assigning a variety of staff to a variety of tasks. Unlike the assignment problems that we examined in Chapter 4, such decisions are often made more complex by a time perspective. Let us examine the following problem. The consortium behind the Channel Tunnel project that will link the UK to France are keen to ensure that they can keep the rail link running efficiently with an adequate repair and maintenance programme. As part of the initial evaluation the

Table 6-4 Staff requirements per shift period

Time	Minimum no. of staff required per shift
00.01–04.00	30
04.01–08.00	120
08.01–12.00	150
12.01–16.00	80
16.01–20.00	150
20.01–24.00	50

consortium have attempted to evaluate an appropriate policy in terms of establishing a repair and maintenance team that would be available for emergency repairs round the clock. From an engineering viewpoint it has been estimated that over a 24 hour period the minimum requirements in terms of trained technical repair staff will be as shown in Table 6-4.

The pattern reflects the expected peaks in passenger traffic in the morning and late afternoon. Agreements with the UK and French trades unions require that staff work a continuous 8 hour shift and must come on duty at the start of 1 of the 6 periods. So, for example, a minimum of 80 staff must be on call for the 4 hour period between 12.01 and 16.00. Some of these 80 staff may have started at 08.01 whilst others will have started at 12.01. Pay rates are currently £30 per 8 hour shift. Additionally, staff who are on duty on any of the 3 periods between 20.01 and 08.00 receive a bonus payment for unsocial hours, currently £7.50 for each 4 hour period that occurs during these unsocial hours. Our objective here is clearly to provide an adequate cover of staff during particular shifts whilst keeping costs to a minimum. It is also clear that the unsocial hours payment will have considerable bearing on our solution. The only restrictions that are applicable in the problem relate to the minimum number of staff that must be available at any given time. We must be a little cautious about our choice of decision variables. Our initial choice might relate to variables that show the number of staff on duty at 1 of the 6 periods. If we were to formulate our problem in this way, however, we would encounter difficulty with the constraints and the objective function. It can be seen why this would happen. Let us examine 1 of the periods in question, say, from 20.01–24.00. A given number of staff will be on duty during this period but these staff will fall into 2 groups. There will be those who started work at 16.01 and for whom this period is the second part of their 8 hour shift. There will also be those who have just come on duty and who will continue to work until 04.00. Accordingly, it is more appropriate to choose decision variables that show the number of staff starting work in a given period. We shall, therefore, have variables X_1 to X_6 representing the number of staff starting work in each of the 6 4-hour periods. The objective function itself will be made up of two elements: the normal pay of £30 plus any payment for unsocial hours worked. This latter payment could be zero, for 1 period or for 2. We can summarize the relevant data as in Table 6-5.

Accordingly, the objective function is:

$$\text{Minimize} \quad 45X_1 + 37.5X_2 + 30X_3 + 30X_4 + 37.5X_5 + 45X_6 \qquad (6\text{-}11)$$

Table 6-5 Staff costs per shift

Time started	Normal pay	Number of unsocial periods worked	Bonus	Total
00.01–04.00	£30.00	2	£15.00	£45.00
04.01–08.00	30.00	1	7.50	37.50
08.01–12.00	30.00	0	0	30.00
12.01–16.00	30.00	0	0	30.00
16.01–20.00	30.00	1	7.50	37.50
20.01–24.00	30.00	2	15.00	45.00

Equally, the constraints relate to the number of staff who must be available during each period. The verbal description of the problem indicates that these staff numbers are the minimum required, hence our constraints will take the form $\geq$. It is clear on reflection, however, that we could equally write these constraints as strict equations ($=$), given that any staff over this minimum will incur a cost and that we are seeking to minimize such costs. We must be cautious in using such an approach, however, as there is no guarantee that a feasible solution is possible with such strict constraints. Using the form $\geq$ allows the solution program to indicate whether the minimum number of staff will actually be sufficient. Denoting X_1 as the staff who start at 00.01 we then have:

$$X_1 + X_6 \geq 30 \qquad (6\text{-}12)$$

that is, staff available for work during this time will comprise those who started at 00.01 (X_1) and those who started at the earlier period of 20.01 (X_6). Similarly, for the other constraints we have:

$$X_1 + X_2 \geq 120 \qquad (6\text{-}13)$$
$$X_2 + X_3 \geq 150 \qquad (6\text{-}14)$$
$$X_3 + X_4 \geq 80 \qquad (6\text{-}15)$$
$$X_4 + X_5 \geq 150 \qquad (6\text{-}16)$$
$$X_5 + X_6 \geq 50 \qquad (6\text{-}17)$$

giving a complete formulation as:

$$\text{Minimize} \quad 45X_1 + 37.5X_2 + 30X_3 + 30X_4 + 37.5X_5 + 45X_6$$

$$\begin{aligned}
\text{subject to:} \quad X_1 + X_6 &\geq 30 \\
X_1 + X_2 &\geq 120 \\
X_2 + X_3 &\geq 150 \\
X_3 + X_4 &\geq 80 \\
X_4 + X_5 &\geq 150 \\
X_5 + X_6 &\geq 50 \\
X_1, X_2, X_3, X_4, X_5, X_6 &\geq 0
\end{aligned}$$

Note again that the formulation is linear and note also that each decision variable appears in two of the constraints—given that each variable relates to staff coming on duty during each 4 hour period and that staff work for 2 periods in succession. Typical variations on this general category of problem include allocating resources to product lines, allocating machine time to products, allocating personnel to tasks and allocating sales staff to sales areas or to sales lines.

6-5 BLENDING/DIET/FEED-MIX PROBLEMS

A large category of LP applications fall into the area generally known as *blending*. Typically such problems revolve around the requirement to mix together a variety of ingredients in order to produce some final product in such a way that the final product meets certain specified criteria. Applications of blending problems range from the oil industry where crude oils have to be blended with other ingredients to make a variety of petrols and related fuels, through the chemical industry producing drugs, medicines, fertilizers, etc., to the food industry where different foodstuffs have to be mixed together to produce some food item or a balanced meal. Let us examine the following scenario. Over the past few years there has been an increasing trend away from meat and meat derivatives towards vegetarian foodstuffs. A large national chain of burger bars has recently decided to cash in on this trend and—on an experimental basis—offers a vegetarian alternative to the standard hamburger: the Big Mik veggieburger. The Big Mik comes in two alternative sizes: standard and large. Both are made with the same ingredients but whereas the standard veggieburger has a net uncooked weight of 150 g the large has an equivalent weight of 200 g. The two principal ingredients are a soybean mix and a vegetable mix, with a third component being breadcrumbs and seasoning. All ingredients are required to be fresh at the start of each working day. A standard veggieburger requires 100 g of soybean mix and 30 g of vegetable mix with the remainder of the net weight comprising crumbs and seasoning. For the large burger the corresponding ingredients are 150 g of soybean and 30 g of vegetable mix. Market research estimates that, on a daily basis, at least 30 standard and 25 large veggieburgers can be sold. At the moment the burger bar makes up 10 kg of soybean mix each day, 4 kg of vegetable mix and 1.5 kg of crumbs–seasoning. In addition, the veggieburgers are served with a fresh wholemeal roll and the bakery supplying these can provide only 100 each day. The two burgers cost £0.50 and £0.60 respectively to produce and cook whilst the roll costs £0.05. The two burgers sell for £1.10 and £1.50 respectively.

It is clear that the problem centres around the mixing or blending of the various ingredients in order to produce the two alternative products. The decision variables are clearly the quantities of the two types of veggieburger that can be produced each day. Equally, the restrictions arising in the problem relate to the fixed supply of the three types of ingredient available: soybeans, vegetable mix and the breadcrumbs–seasoning mix. In addition, however, there are other restrictions. Clearly, we must limit production in line with the available supply of wholemeal rolls and we must also ensure that production is sufficient to meet anticipated daily demand. The one aspect that is not clear is the objective to be pursued. Given the information available we could clearly formulate the problem in terms of three different objectives: profit, cost and revenue. Again, this illustrates a feature of many LP applications: that fundamentally the same problem can be solved with a variety of objective functions. In the real world we would need at this stage to seek clarification from the decision-maker as to the most appropriate objective (the importance of the methodology outlined in Chapter 1 again becomes evident here). In this case we shall assume the firm is interested in profit maximization. If we denote X_1 as the quantity of the standard veggieburger to be produced and X_2 as the quantity of the large then the objective function will be:

$$(1.10 - 0.50 - 0.05)X_1 + (1.50 - 0.60 - 0.05)X_2$$

or

$$0.55X_1 + 0.85X_2 \qquad (6\text{-}18)$$

Similarly, the constraints relating to the availability of the three basic ingredients to be blended will be:

$$100X_1 + 150X_2 \leq 10\,000 \quad \text{(soybean mix)} \qquad (6\text{-}19)$$

$$30X_1 + 30X_2 \leq 4\,000 \quad \text{(vegetable mix)} \qquad (6\text{-}20)$$

$$20X_1 + 20X_2 \leq 1\,500 \quad \text{(crumbs/seasoning)} \qquad (6\text{-}21)$$

Note that we have expressed these three constraints in terms of grams. We could just as well have formulated in terms of kilograms (i.e. dividing all the parameters through by 1000). Naturally, this will not affect our solution but only the way we interpret the information relating to these constraints. The remaining constraints are given by:

$$X_1 + X_2 \leq 100 \qquad (6\text{-}22)$$

$$X_1 \geq 30 \qquad (6\text{-}23)$$

$$X_2 \geq 25 \qquad (6\text{-}24)$$

Again, it is worth noting that we have specified the rolls constraint as an inequality ($\leq$) rather than as a strict equality ($=$). This appears sensible given that potentially we could have surplus, unused rolls. Should the number of rolls available be more than is required then this will become evident at the solution stage. Had we formulated the problem with this constraint as a strict equality then it is possible that we would have found we had no feasible solution. That is, we would have had insufficient ingredients to allow us to produce 100 burgers and use all the available rolls. The complete formulation, therefore, is:

$$\begin{aligned}
\text{Maximize} \quad & 0.55X_1 + 0.85X_2 \\
\text{subject to:} \quad & 100X_1 + 150X_2 \leq 10\,000 \\
& 30X_1 + 30X_2 \leq 4\,000 \\
& 20X_1 + 20X_2 \leq 1\,500 \\
& X_1 + X_2 \leq 100 \\
& X_1 \geq 30 \\
& X_2 \geq 25 \\
& X_1, X_2 \geq 0
\end{aligned}$$

6-6 MARKETING AND MEDIA-MIX APPLICATIONS

Applications of LP to the areas of marketing and media selection have become increasingly common, particularly in the United States. Media selection problems typically relate to problems where a fixed advertising budget can be used to purchase advertising across a range of different media—TV, radio, newspaper adverts, and so on—with each alternative media selection offering different degrees of advertising exposure at different costs. Marketing problems typically relate to determining the optimum allocation of sales staff and advertising effort to achieve sales (frequently measured as profit contribution) arising from such activities. Consider an advertising agency that has been commissioned to produce a nationwide advertising campaign on behalf of one of its clients. It is seeking to ascertain what the most cost-effective advertising campaign would be, particularly in the context of which advertising media to use. As a preliminary exercise the agency has decided to undertake market research to determine which types of media its client's customers (both actual and potential) favour. It has decided to undertake a consumer survey to collect such data. The structure of the survey is as follows. Three types of consumer (categorized by socio-economic group) will be surveyed: skilled manual employees, professional employees and the retired. The intended initial sample size will be between 800 and 1000 consumers and each consumer will be surveyed either in a face-to-face interview or by a telephone interview. Because of the nature of the required sample some of these interviews will take place during the day but others will take place during the evening. There is some flexibility in the mixture of socio-economic types selected for the sample. At least one-quarter of the total sample must be skilled manual and at least one-quarter must be professional. There is no explicit restriction on the number of retired to be included. Similarly, the agency needs to ensure that a mixture of interview methods and times is achieved in order to obtain a suitably representative sample. Accordingly, at least 20 per cent of the sample must be included in each of the four different types of interview (day–face to face, day–phone, evening–face to face, evening–phone). Finally, the agency wants to ensure that a sufficient number of the working population are included in the sample and has decided that the number of customers surveyed in the evening must be at least as large as the number surveyed during the day. Interview costs have also been calculated depending on whether the interview is undertaken during the day or evening and whether it is a personal or a telephone interview. A personal interview during the day will cost the agency £4 per person, but £8 during the evening. Telephone interviews are less expensive and cost £3.50 regardless of the time undertaken.

This is obviously quite a complex problem and does not fit neatly into the general format of the other problems we have examined thus far. The overall objective, however, is clear. The agency must undertake the survey at minimum cost but whilst meeting the various restrictions on the composition of the sample that have been detailed. What is less clear are the decision variables we must use in the formulation. It will help to produce an overall structure of the final sample selected.

Table 6-6 shows the different sample groups (the three socio-economic groups) and the four different interview times–type combinations. The table helps considerably because it is now evident that our total sample will be made up of 12 subsets and it is these which will form the decision variables. If we denote these as $X_1, X_2, \ldots X_{12}$, they will relate to the 12 subsets shown in the table, moving along each row in turn. Each decision

Table 6-6 Overall sample structure

Socio-economic group	Interview time			
	Day		Evening	
	Personal	Phone	Personal	Phone
Skilled manual				
Professional				
Retired				

variable will indicate the number of people surveyed who fall into that particular category. For example, X_{10} will be the number of retired people interviewed by phone during the day. Given the information on interview costs we can now formulate an appropriate objective function:

$$\text{Minimize} \quad \begin{aligned} & 4X_1 + 3.5X_2 + 8X_3 + 3.5X_4 \\ & + 4X_5 + 3.5X_6 + 8X_7 + 3.5X_8 \\ & + 4X_9 + 3.5X_{10} + 8X_{11} + 3.5X_{12} \end{aligned} \quad (6\text{-}25)$$

This approach is quite common in more complex LP problems: using decision variables that are subsets of the main variables identified in the problem. Such subset variables allow for complex formulation because, as we shall see, they facilitate constraints that are based around interrelationships between the subset variables. If we now turn to our restrictions we see that the first relates to the required sample size, which must be between 800 and 1000. It is evident that our total sample will be made up of $X_1 + X_2 + \ldots + X_{12}$, so the two constraints are easily formulated.

$$X_1 + X_2 + X_3 + X_4 + X_5 + X_6 + X_7 + X_8 + X_9 + X_{10} + X_{11} + X_{12} \geq 800 \quad (6\text{-}26)$$

and

$$X_1 + X_2 + X_3 + X_4 + X_5 + X_6 + X_7 + X_8 + X_9 + X_{10} + X_{11} + X_{12} \leq 1000 \quad (6\text{-}27)$$

We next examine the restrictions in terms of the composition of the total sample. At least a quarter of the total sample must be made up of skilled manual and at least a further quarter of professional. From Table 6-6 we see that the total number of consumers included in the sample from the skilled manual group will be:

$$X_1 + X_2 + X_3 + X_4$$

The immediate problem we face is that the total sample size is unknown (until we actually derive the optimal solution). We could adopt the approach of setting limits to the size of this group. Given that the total sample must be between 800 and 1000 it follows that $(X_1 + X_2 + X_3 + X_4)$ must be between 200 and 250 to satisfy this restriction. We could formulate two constraints as we have just done for the total sample size. However, there is an alternative approach that is worth illustrating, given that it will require only one constraint in the formulation rather than two. We know that the total sample size (currently undetermined) is given by $(X_1 + X_2 + \ldots + X_{12})$, so we can express this restriction as:

$$X_1 + X_2 + X_3 + X_4 \geq 0.25(X_1 + X_2 + X_3 + X_4 + X_5 + X_6 \\ + X_7 + X_8 + X_9 + X_{10} + X_{11} + X_{12})$$

and collecting the decision variables together on the left-hand side of the expression gives:

$$X_1 + X_2 + X_3 + X_4 \\ - 0.25(X_1 + X_2 + X_3 + X_4 + X_5 + X_6 + X_7 + X_8 + X_9 + X_{10} + X_{11} + X_{12}) \geq 0$$

and collecting terms together to simplify gives:

$$0.75X_1 + 0.75X_2 + 0.75X_3 + 0.75X_4 \\ - 0.25X_5 - 0.25X_6 - 0.25X_7 - 0.25X_8 \\ - 0.25X_9 - 0.25X_{10} - 0.25X_{11} - 0.25X_{12} \geq 0 \qquad (6\text{-}28)$$

This is quite a common 'trick' in LP formulations and is generally applicable whenever some group of variables is restricted in terms of a total that itself is unknown until the final solution to the problem is obtained. The main problem with this approach is that it produces a constraint that is difficult to relate directly to the problem and can prove difficult to interpret and evaluate once the final solution has been obtained. It offers the advantages, however, that it formulates the restrictions in terms of one constraint rather than two (and the fewer constraints we have then the easier the solution and subsequent interpretation become) and that it allows future modification of the problem quite readily. Assume, for example, that the agency now decided it required between 1500 and 2000 people to be surveyed. This constraint will remain unaltered as the total sample is expressed not as a specific value but as the aggregate of all the subset values. The constraint relating to the restriction on the proportion of professionals to be included follows the same logic and is given by:

$$X_5 + X_6 + X_7 + X_8 \geq 0.25(X_1 + X_2 + X_3 + X_4 + X_5 + X_6 \\ + X_7 + X_8 + X_9 + X_{10} + X_{11} + X_{12})$$

which in turn simplifies to:

$$-0.25X_1 - 0.25X_2 - 0.25X_3 - 0.25X_4 \\ + 0.75X_5 + 0.75X_6 + 0.75X_7 + 0.75X_8 \\ - 0.25X_9 - 0.25X_{10} - 0.25X_{11} - 0.25X_{12} \geq 0 \qquad (6\text{-}29)$$

Equally, the restrictions relating to the fact that at least 20 per cent of the total sample must come from each of the four interviewing methods can be formulated in much the same way. If we examine personal interviews conducted during the day these will comprise $X_1 + X_5 + X_9$ and the appropriate constraint will be:

$$X_1 + X_5 + X_9 \geq 0.2(X_1 + X_2 + X_3 + X_4 + X_5 + X_6 + X_7 + X_8 + X_9 + X_{10} + X_{11} + X_{12})$$

giving:

$$0.8X_1 - 0.2X_2 - 0.2X_3 - 0.2X_4 \\ + 0.8X_5 - 0.2X_6 - 0.2X_7 - 0.2X_8 \\ + 0.8X_9 - 0.2X_{10} - 0.2X_{11} - 0.2X_{12} \geq 0 \qquad (6\text{-}30)$$

The other three constraints will be:

$$-0.2X_1 + 0.8X_2 - 0.2X_3 - 0.2X_4 - 0.2X_5 + 0.8X_6$$
$$-0.2X_7 - 0.2X_8 - 0.2X_9 + 0.8X_{10} - 0.2X_{11} - 0.2X_{12} \geq 0 \quad (6\text{-}31)$$

$$-0.2X_1 - 0.2X_2 + 0.8X_3 - 0.2X_4 - 0.2X_5 - 0.2X_6$$
$$+0.8X_7 - 0.2X_8 - 0.2X_9 - 0.2X_{10} + 0.8X_{11} - 0.2X_{12} \geq 0 \quad (6\text{-}32)$$

$$-0.2X_1 - 0.2X_2 - 0.2X_3 + 0.8X_4 - 0.2X_5 - 0.2X_6$$
$$-0.2X_7 + 0.8X_8 - 0.2X_9 - 0.2X_{10} - 0.2X_{11} + 0.8X_{12} \geq 0 \quad (6\text{-}33)$$

Finally, we have the restriction relating to the evening selected sample being at least as great as that selected during the day. This can be expressed:

$$X_3 + X_4 + X_7 + X_8 + X_{11} + X_{12} \geq X_1 + X_2 + X_5 + X_6 + X_9 + X_{10}$$

and again collecting terms and reordering gives:

$$-X_1 - X_2 + X_3 + X_4 - X_5 - X_6 + X_7 + X_8 - X_9 - X_{10} + X_{11} + X_{12} \geq 0 \quad (6\text{-}34)$$

The full formulation, therefore, is given by:

Minimize $\quad 4X_1 + 3.5X_2 + 8X_3 + 3.5X_4 + 4X_5 + 3.5X_6$
$\quad\quad\quad\quad\quad + 8X_7 + 3.5X_8 + 4X_9 + 3.5X_{10} + 8X_{11} + 3.5X_{12}$

subject to:

$$X_1 + X_2 + X_3 + X_4 + X_5 + X_6 + X_7 + X_8 + X_9 + X_{10} + X_{11} + X_{12} \geq 800$$

$$X_1 + X_2 + X_3 + X_4 + X_5 + X_6 + X_7 + X_8 + X_9 + X_{10} + X_{11} + X_{12} \leq 1000$$

$$0.75X_1 + 0.75X_2 + 0.75X_3 + 0.75X_4 - 0.25X_5 - 0.25X_6$$
$$-0.25X_7 - 0.25X_8 - 0.25X_9 - 0.25X_{10} - 0.25X_{11} - 0.25X_{12} \geq 0$$

$$-0.25X_1 - 0.25X_2 - 0.25X_3 - 0.25X_4 + 0.75X_5 + 0.75X_6$$
$$+0.75X_7 + 0.75X_8 - 0.25X_9 - 0.25X_{10} - 0.25X_{11} - 0.25X_{12} \geq 0$$

$$0.8X_1 - 0.2X_2 - 0.2X_3 - 0.2X_4 + 0.8X_5 - 0.2X_6$$
$$-0.2X_7 - 0.2X_8 + 0.8X_9 - 0.2X_{10} - 0.2X_{11} - 0.2X_{12} \geq 0$$

$$-0.2X_1 + 0.8X_2 - 0.2X_3 - 0.2X_4 - 0.2X_5 + 0.8X_6$$
$$-0.2X_7 - 0.2X_8 - 0.2X_9 + 0.8X_{10} - 0.2X_{11} - 0.2X_{12} \geq 0$$

$$-0.2X_1 - 0.2X_2 + 0.8X_3 - 0.2X_4 - 0.2X_5 - 0.2X_6$$
$$+0.8X_7 - 0.2X_8 - 0.2X_9 - 0.2X_{10} + 0.8X_{11} - 0.2X_{12} \geq 0$$

$$-0.2X_1 - 0.2X_2 - 0.2X_3 + 0.8X_4 - 0.2X_5 - 0.2X_6$$
$$-0.2X_7 + 0.8X_8 - 0.2X_9 - 0.2X_{10} - 0.2X_{11} + 0.8X_{12} \geq 0$$

$$-X_1 - X_2 + X_3 + X_4 - X_5 - X_6 + X_7 + X_8 - X_9 - X_{10} + X_{11} + X_{12} \geq 0$$

$$X_1, X_2, X_3, X_4, X_5, X_6, X_7, X_8, X_9, X_{10}, X_{11}, X_{12} \geq 0$$

This problem illustrates particularly well how flexible LP is as a technique, allowing complex restrictions to be built into the model quite easily.

6-7 FINANCIAL ANALYSIS

The area of financial analysis is a popular one for applications of LP. This is perhaps hardly surprising given that LP is concerned primarily with the optimal allocation of scarce resources and that most financial decision-making is concerned with the same issue. Typically, such financial applications concern themselves with some aspect of portfolio selection (where alternative investments are available), with capital budgeting (trying to determine which project to support financially) or with a financial-mix problem (trying to determine the optimal means of financing activities).

Let us consider the following problem. One of the major high street banks has a branch in a large university town. In the current economic climate the bank has found that it faces considerable demand for its finance from students (who wish to use the money borrowed for a variety of purposes). The loan budget for the next accounting period has been set by the bank's head office at £1.5 million. The branch currently categorizes three types of student loan: a general-purpose loan which may be either secured or unsecured and a loan for the purpose of purchasing a car. At present, students are charged a rate of interest of 5 per cent p.a. on secured general loans, 8 per cent p.a. on unsecured general loans and 9 per cent on car loans. The branch has a policy such that no more than 10 per cent of the total budget should go to unsecured loans and no more than 25 per cent to car loans, whilst at least 60 per cent should be general loans of either type. The branch also has a policy that funds which are not loaned out can be invested in the short-term money market and currently attract a rate of interest of 7.5 per cent p.a. However, the amount invested in this way at any one time must not be more than 20 per cent of the total. Additionally, the branch is keen to ensure its loan structure is not unduly risky. Each of the four uses of funds has been allocated a risk value by the branch manager (although these are seen to be highly subjective): 1, 4, 3, 1 respectively for secured loans, unsecured loans, car loans and money market investment with a higher figure indicating a greater degree of risk in terms of defaulting. The branch wishes to ensure that, on average, the risk factor for the whole loans–investment portfolio is no more than 1.75.

The overall objective in the problem is to determine a suitable spread in terms of the use of the total funds available. Our decision variables will relate to the four altenative uses of the funds available and will show the amount allocated to each of the four possible uses. The objective function will then be:

$$\text{Maximize} \quad 0.05X_1 + 0.08X_2 + 0.09X_3 + 0.075X_4 \qquad (6\text{-}35)$$

where the resulting value of the objective function will indicate the monetary return on the total funds allocated. The first restriction we face relates to the supply of available funds.

$$X_1 + X_2 + X_3 + X_4 \leqslant 1500 \qquad (6\text{-}36)$$

where we have chosen to measure all monetary units in £000s to help keep the resulting arithmetic manageable. It is clear that for most of the remaining restrictions we face a situation similar to that found in the previous section, where we related one or more decision variables to the total and where the total took an unspecified numerical value. We are required to ensure that no more than 10 per cent of total funds are allocated to unsecured, general loans, X_2. This implies that:

$$X_2 \leqslant 0.1(X_1 + X_2 + X_3 + X_4)$$

It should be apparent that we cannot necessarily assume that all the available funds will be utilized (i.e. all the available £1.5 million), hence it would be potentially incorrect to formulate a constraint such that $X_2 \leq £1500$. However, it is worth noting the approach that is sometimes taken once the optimal solution has been determined. We saw in the last section that one problem with this type of constraint formulation is that it makes subsequent interpretation difficult. Once we know the optimal solution, and hence the total amount of funds required, we could then reformulate this constraint using the actual total funds figure and re-solve. Naturally, this will not affect the solution itself but may make subsequent evaluation of binding constraints in particular much easier. However, for the present we can obtain this constraint in a suitable format as:

$$-0.1X_1 + 0.9X_2 - 0.1X_3 - 0.1X_4 \leq 0 \tag{6-37}$$

In a similar way we can derive the other constraint formulations as:

$$-0.25X_1 - 0.25X_2 + 0.75X_3 - 0.25X_4 \leq 0 \quad \text{(car loans)} \tag{6-38}$$

$$0.4X_1 + 0.4X_2 - 0.6X_3 - 0.6X_4 \geq 0 \quad \text{(general loans)} \tag{6-39}$$

$$-0.2X_1 - 0.2X_2 - 0.2X_3 + 0.8X_4 \leq 0 \quad \text{(short-term investment)} \tag{6-40}$$

The remaining restriction relates to the average risk factor. Given the risk weightings, we can derive an expression showing the weighted risk factor as a proportion of the total funds allocated. Given that $(1X_1 + 4X_2 + 3X_3 + 1X_4)$ will be the total risk weightings and that $(X_1 + X_2 + X_3 + X_4)$ is the total use of funds, then

$$\frac{(X_1 + 4X_2 + 3X_3 + 1X_4)}{(X_1 + X_2 + X_3 + X_4)}$$

will be the average risk factor for any given level of funds allocation. Whilst we know that this average must be no more than 1.75, it appears that we have a problem as the ratio expression derived is clearly non-linear. However, we can rearrange the current expressions into a more convenient (and linear) format:

$$\frac{(1X_1 + 4X_2 + 3X_3 + 1X_4)}{(X_1 + X_2 + X_3 + X_4)} \leq 1.75$$

$$(1X_1 + 4X_2 + 3X_3 + 1X_4) \leq 1.75(X_1 + X_2 + X_3 + X_4)$$

giving:

$$-0.75X_1 + 2.25X_2 + 1.25X_3 - 0.75X_4 \leq 0 \tag{6-41}$$

The complete formulation to the problem is, therefore, given as:

Maximize $\quad 0.05X_1 + 0.08X_2 + 0.09X_3 + 0.075X_4$

subject to:
$$X_1 + X_2 + X_3 + X_4 \leq 1500$$
$$-0.1X_1 + 0.9X_2 - 0.1X_3 - 0.1X_4 \leq 0$$
$$-0.25X_1 - 0.25X_2 + 0.75X_3 - 0.25X_4 \leq 0$$
$$0.4X_1 + 0.4X_2 - 0.6X_3 - 0.6X_4 \geq 0$$
$$-0.2X_1 - 0.2X_2 - 0.2X_3 + 0.8X_4 \leq 0$$

$$-0.75X_1 + 2.25X_2 + 1.25X_3 - 0.75X_4 \leq 0$$
$$X_1, X_2, X_3, X_4 \geq 0$$

6-8 DATA ENVELOPMENT ANALYSIS

Finally in this chapter we turn to an area of application that amply illustrates the ever-increasing range of business problems to which LP has been applied. Data envelopment analysis (DEA) is, even by management science standards, a relatively new area, and, in the space available and at the level we have currently achieved, it is impossible to do more than provide a thumbnail sketch of this application area. DEA, however, does indicate that LP is not a static technique in terms of the areas to which it is applied. New areas of application are constantly being developed. Let us consider the information shown in Table 6-7.

The data relates to 5 retail stores that form part of a larger national group. The stores are located in different parts of the country and, as can be seen, have different characteristics in terms of size, number of staff employed, profitability, and so on. Naturally, one aspect of management interest is likely to be in relative performance—what we can refer to as comparative efficiency. How is an individual store performing in comparison with the other stores in the data set? Whilst there are a number of different ways we could approach such an investigation into efficiency the one we shall explore utilizes features of the basic LP model. We can actually view the information in the table as a set of inputs and a set of outputs. Although it may appear artificial at first, we can regard the operating cost as an input: we are providing resources (measured in financial terms) to each store. Similarly, we can regard the other variables as outputs: they arise as the consequence of the input. A financial input allows a store to function and to sell its product, to employ staff, to acquire sales floorspace and to give rise to a profit. We could accordingly determine an efficiency measure such that:

$$\text{Efficiency} = \frac{\text{outputs}}{\text{inputs}} \leq 1$$

An organization with an efficiency rating of 1 would be using its inputs to generate outputs in the optimal manner—that is, operating at maximum efficiency. A figure less than 1 implies suboptimal efficiency. In our case, however, we have a problem given that

Table 6-7 Data for 5 retail outlets

	Operating cost (£000)	Total sales (£000)	No. of staff	Floorspace available (000 sq.ft.)	Operating profit (£000)
Store 1	258	271	14	14.6	23.5
Store 2	160	195	12	7.5	14
Store 3	263	302	15	16.3	23
Store 4	144	133	8	10.2	11
Store 5	213	264	12	12.5	21

we have both inputs and outputs for 5 separate stores to consider. One approach is to determine a single measure of efficiency by adapting the expression to:

$$\text{Efficiency} = \frac{\text{weighted total of outputs}}{\text{weighted total of inputs}} \leq 1$$

which aggregates the inputs and outputs. Like any measure of average, however, this lends itself to the criticism that when the items making up the totals are dissimilar then the weighted average itself must be suspect. In our case we clearly have considerable disparities between the 5 stores. To resolve this difficulty one approach that has been adopted is that each organization in the data set should adopt the set of weights most favourable to its own input–output combination. In Table 6-7 this implies that we could calculate a measure of efficiency using, say, weights appropriate to Store 1 (which will obviously be the best weights possible for this particular store). Using these weights we can then proceed to calculate a suitable measure of efficiency for each store in the data set. The results (varying between 0 and 1) will then allow a comparison of the relative efficiency of Store 1 (whose weights were used) with other stores. Should other stores have a higher efficiency rating than Store 1 (all such ratings calculated using Store 1's weights) then this would indicate a comparatively inefficient performance by Store 1. It would indicate that Store 1—even on the assumption that its weightings were optimal—was not using its inputs to generate maximum outputs: other stores are performing more efficiently. This analysis can then be repeated for each store in the data set in turn—using that store's weights as the optimal and assessing relative efficiency between stores based on that assumption. In general we can specify the measure of efficiency for Store k as:

$$\text{Efficiency of Store } k = \frac{u_1 Y_{1k} + u_2 Y_{2k} + \ldots + u_n Y_{nk}}{v_1 X_1 k + v_2 X_{2k} + \ldots + v_m X_{mk}} \leq 1$$

where u_i denotes the weight given to output i,
Y_{ik} denotes the amount of output i from store k,
v_i denotes the weight given to input i and
X_{ik} denotes the amount of input i to store k.

In our example the situation is simplified because there is deemed to be only one input: operating cost. The efficiency of Store 1 can therefore be expressed as:

$$\frac{271u_1 + 14u_2 + 14.6u_3 + 23.5u_4}{258v_1} \qquad (6\text{-}42)$$

In order to compare this store's efficiency (its input to its outputs) with other stores we can also use these weights to calculate an equivalent efficiency measure for each store in the data set. Because of our original efficiency definition we will require all these ratios to be ≤ 1. It is apparent that the LP formulation will revolve around trying to determine a set of weights for Store 1 that will maximize its own efficiency ratio. Our problem thus becomes:

$$\text{Maximize} \quad \frac{271u_1 + 14u_2 + 14.6u_3 + 23.5u_4}{258v_1} \qquad (6\text{-}43)$$

$$\text{subject to:} \quad \frac{271u_1 + 14u_2 + 14.6u_3 + 23.5u_4}{258v_1} \leq 1 \qquad (6\text{-}44)$$

$$\frac{195u_1 + 12u_2 + 7.5u_3 + 14u_4}{160v_1} \leq 1 \qquad (6\text{-}45)$$

$$\frac{302u_1 + 15u_2 + 16.3u_3 + 23u_4}{263v_1} \leq 1 \qquad (6\text{-}46)$$

$$\frac{133u_1 + 8u_2 + 10.2u_3 + 11u_4}{144v_1} \leq 1 \qquad (6\text{-}47)$$

$$\frac{264u_1 + 12u_2 + 12.5u_3 + 21u_4}{213v_1} \leq 1 \qquad (6\text{-}48)$$

Effectively, we are using the optimal set of weights for Store 1 (the decision variable values we have to determine) to measure the relationship between input and outputs at the other stores in the data set. It is immediately apparent, however, that the constraints and the objective function are non-linear. The constraints are readily amended into a linear format: we multiply through by the denominator and then subtract the right-hand side value from both sides. The objective function poses more of a problem, however. This can be resolved by setting the denominator to some arbitrary value (typically 100 or 1000) and adding a new constraint such that the formulation becomes:

Maximize $\quad 271u_1 + 14u_2 + 14.6u_3 + 23.5u_4 \qquad (6\text{-}49)$

subject to:
$$258v_1 = 100 \qquad (6\text{-}50)$$
$$271u_1 + 14u_2 + 14.6u_3 + 23.5u_4 - 258v_1 \leq 0 \qquad (6\text{-}51)$$
$$195u_1 + 12u_2 + 7.5u_3 + 14u_4 \; - 160v_1 \leq 0 \qquad (6\text{-}52)$$
$$302u_1 + 15u_2 + 16.3u_3 + 23u_4 \; - 263v_1 \leq 0 \qquad (6\text{-}53)$$
$$133u_1 + \; 8u_2 + 10.2u_3 + 11u_4 \; - 144v_1 \leq 0 \qquad (6\text{-}54)$$
$$264u_1 + 12u_2 + 12.5u_3 + 21u_4 \; - 213v_1 \leq 0 \qquad (6\text{-}55)$$
$$u_1, u_2, u_3, u_4 \leq 0$$

The problem can now be solved to determine the optimal weights for the efficiency ratio for Store 1 and this ratio compared with that for all the other stores to help assess relative performance. To illustrate this we shall briefly examine the solution to this problem. A strong word of caution is necessary first, however. The illustrative problem used is meant to be indicative of the way in which DEA can be applied. In practice, for any meaningful results to be achieved, a considerably larger number of stores would need to be included. The following results should accordingly be seen as an illustrative example only. After solution we obtain the following values:

$$u_1 = 0$$
$$u_2 = 2.241\,917$$
$$u_3 = 2.389\,107$$
$$u_4 = 1.228\,157$$
$$v_1 = 0.387\,597$$

and an efficiency ratio for Store 1 of 0.95. If we use these same weights (which are optimal for Store 1) to calculate an equivalent ratio for Store 5 then we obtain a value for the efficiency ratio of 1.0. This implies that, even with the most favourable weights, Store 1 is less efficient than Store 5. The analysis is now readily repeated for each store in the data set with appropriate amendments to the objective function and to the first constraint—thus the formulation is reworked to relate to the appropriate parameters for Store 2, Store 3, and so on. Further analysis is also readily undertaken into the relative importance of each output factor in this efficiency ratio measure.

6-9 SUMMARY

In this chapter we have introduced a variety of applications of LP to typical business and management problems and shown how such problems can be suitably formulated for solution by the technique. As we stressed at the beginning of this chapter, the formulation stage of the technique is the one that creates the major stumbling block, not only for the novice but for the practised business analyst also. We have attempted to illustrate some of the more common difficulties encountered in problem formulation and have suggested ways in which these difficulties can be resolved. There is, however, no adequate substitute for self-practice and investigation of real-life case study material in the development of personal skills to help in the formulation stage. We strongly urge the student to attempt all the end-of-chapter exercises that follow and to reference as much of the case study material as is practical that is detailed in the Bibliography. Only through the student's own efforts will the appropriate skills be developed. It must also be remembered that in the real world the formulation of such business problems will be more difficult. The problem will not, in the beginning, be explicit and unambiguous, data on relationships between variables may be of poor quality or simply not available, management may have an unclear view as to the overall objective of the exercise, and so on. Typically (following the lines of the methodology discussed in Chapter 1), it will be necessary to adopt a cyclical approach to the formulation–solution procedure with repeated backtracking between the various stages.

STUDENT EXERCISES

You are advised to attempt as many of the following questions as possible, not only to practise the formulation of such problems but also because these exercises will form the basis for later ones. Observe also that we have indicated the number of decision variables and constraints that should appear in your formulation as a guide, should you encounter difficulty in determining whether your formulation is appropriate. Note finally that for some problems variants on the formulation are possible.

6-1 A company currently manufactures an electric paint spray aimed at the DIY market. The product has been so successful that for the next few months it appears unlikely that the manufacturing plant will be able to keep up with demand. The firm is unwilling to have excess demand and, if at all possible, would like to ensure that supplies are available in sufficient quantities to meet consumer demand. Accordingly the production manager is negotiating with an outside contractor who is able—for a price—to produce the paint spray under licence. The production manager's dilemma is to determine what quantities should be produced by the company and by the contractor. The paint spray is constructed from 4 basic components: a rigid plastic container which holds the paint, a spray jet system, the electric motor which powers the spray and the casing or body of the spray. Each of these components is manufactured by the company and undergoes a 3-stage process: the item parts are

Table 6-8 Time required per component (minutes per item)

	Container	Jet	Motor	Body	Total time available
Manufacture	3	2	8	1	5000
Assembly	2	1	3	1	3000
Inspection	1	1	1	1	7000

Table 6-9 Cost per item (£)

	Container	Jet	Motor	Body
In house	1.00	1.50	5.00	2.00
Contractor	1.25	3.00	7.50	2.75

manufactured, assembled and then checked before final assembly. In terms of the next production cycle the company estimates it will face a demand for 500 paint sprays per week. Table 6-8 shows the appropriate production requirements.

In addition the firm has calculated the cost of producing each component in house as well as the cost of purchasing from the external contractor. These costs are shown in Table 6-9.

Required:
Formulate this problem to determine the quantity of components that should be produced in house and those that should be purchased.
[8 decision variables and 7 constraints]

The external contractor now indicates that he is willing to continue producing components under licence only if the total production of these generates at least £4000 revenue per week. Reformulate the problem.
[8 decision variables and 8 constraints]

6-2 A financial accountant has the task of advising a client on a suitable mixture of investments. The client is a retired schoolteacher who has some firm views on the mix and type of investments that should be made. The client has expressed an interest in 5 types of stock and the accountant has calculated the expected annual yield for each as shown in Table 6-10. The client wishes that at least 40 per cent of any investment should go into short-term government securities, which can be readily cashed should the need arise. The client also wants as diversified a portfolio as possible with at least 5 per cent of the total investment in each of the 5 types but no more than 25 per cent in any of the first 4. The accountant, however, regards the electronics and property sectors as high-risk and advises that no more than 15 per cent of the total investment should go into any one of these and certainly no more than 25 per cent into both together. The client is unsure at the moment as to how much will be invested.

Required:
Formulate the problem to determine the portfolio that will maximize expected annual yield.
[5 decision variables and 11 constraints]

Table 6-10

Stock type	Expected yield (%)
Electronics	13
Petro-chemicals	9
Property	12.5
Energy	10
Short-term government securities	8

Table 6-11 Production costs (£ per unit)

	Month 1	Month 2	Month 3
C114	30	40	40
H118	70	50	50

Table 6-12

	Required per unit		Availability		
	C114	H118	Month 1	Month 2	Month 3
Labour (h)	0.4	0.5	500	750	500
Steel (kg)	1.2	0.8	1600	1000	750

6-3 An engineering firm has obtained a contract to supply metal castings to a Japanese car manufacturer, component nos C114 and H118. The contract calls for 1500 units of C114 and 1700 units of H118 to be delivered in 3 months' time. The firm is sure, however, that, with other workload commitments and various supply constraints, the order cannot be fulfilled in one production batch. It will be necessary, therefore, to schedule production over each of the next three monthly cycles. In other words, it may be necessary to produce some of each component in month 1, month 2 and month 3. The company is currently trying to determine its optimal production schedule in order to meet the contract. Information obtained on per-unit production costs for each component is shown in Table 6-11.

Production costs vary over the next 3 months because of other contractual obligations. In addition, it is evident that production in months 1 and 2 will need to be stored until a full delivery is made to the customer at the end of month 3 (we make the simplifying assumption that production and stocks appear at the end of each month). The costs have been quantified—in terms of capital tied up in stocks, warehouse costs, insurance, security, etc.—at 20 per cent of the production cost per month. In terms of production there are two key areas where the firm faces problems—in terms of the skilled labour needed to produce the castings and in terms of a specially formulated type of steel needed in the manufacturing process. Details of the available supplies and requirements are given in Table 6-12.

Required:
Formulate the problem so as to determine the quantity of each casting to be produced in each of the next 3 months.
[6 decision variables and 8 constraints]

6-4 The manager of a large unit trust programme is reviewing their current investment portfolio. 5 different investments are currently being considered and the relevant information is given in Table 6-13, where:

- P/E ratio is the current share price/current earnings per share.
- Change in earnings is the average percentage change in earnings per share over the last 10 6-monthly accounting periods.
- Change in share price is the percentage change in share price over the last 6 months.
- Yield is the current dividend as a percentage of current price.

The manager is seeking to determine a suitable portfolio with the following conditions:

- Yield is to be maximized.
- The P/E ratio should be less than 17.
- The percentage change in earnings should be at least 6 per cent on average.

- The percentage change in share price should be at least 7 per cent on average.
- Investment in option E should be no more than 10 per cent of the total investment.
- Investment in option C should be at least 10 per cent of the total investment.
- Investment in options A and B should be no more than 30 per cent of the total investment.

Table 6-13

Investment	P/E ratio	Change in earnings (%)	Change in share price (%)	Yield (%)
A	11.9	5	7.5	10.2
B	11.8	4.6	6.4	7.4
C	22.7	8.7	18.9	11.0
D	13.4	5.2	4.8	7.0
E	15.3	8.6	8.4	12.6

Required:
(a) Formulate the problem so as to maximize yield.
(b) If the fund manager knows that he has a maximum of £5 million available, reformulate the problem.
[5 decision variables and 7 constraints]

6-5 A firm manufactures 3 products—A, B and C—and is trying to ascertain its production and stock schedule for the next 3 week period. The 3 products cost, respectively, £80, £70 and £90 to produce and take 12, 9 and 13 hours of labour time per unit. On a weekly basis there is a maximum of 1000 hours of labour time available. The firm is trying to decide how much of each item it should produce each week. Production must be adequate both to meet expected weekly demand and to meet the stockholding requirements. At the moment the firm has 5 units of each of the 3 items in stock. At the end of week 3 it wants stock levels to increase to 10 units each. In addition expected demand for the 3 products over the next 3 weeks is as shown in Table 6-14. Units produced at the end of 1 weekly period incur stockholding costs for each successive week of 5 per cent of production cost.

Table 6-14

	Product		
	A	B	C
Week 1	10	5	10
2	15	10	12
3	15	15	16

Required:
Formulate this problem so as to determine the optimal production pattern for these 3 items over the next 3 week period. [18 decision variables and 15 constraints]

6-6 A company is test-marketing one of its new products in a particular region and intends undertaking an extensive 1 week advertising campaign to raise consumer awareness about the new product. The firm has an advertising budget of £500 000 and intends using regional TV, regional radio and regional newspaper advertising. An advert on TV will cost £50 000 and is expected to reach 300 000 potential customers. For radio the equivalent figures are £20 000 and 10 000 customers and for newspapers £2000 and 50 000 customers. The combination of adverts on the 3 forms of media is flexible, although the company wants at least 2 adverts on TV, 5 on radio and 10 in newspapers. In addition the number of newspaper adverts must be no more than 2.5 times the number of combined radio and TV adverts.

Required:
Formulate the problem if the company wishes to maximize the number of customers exposed to the advertising campaign. [3 decision variables and 5 constraints]

Table 6-15 Component percentage per grade

Component	Fuel grade			Availability
	A	B	C	
1	15	35	15	10 000 litres
2	20	20	20	20 000
3	35	20	30	15 000
4	30	25	35	30 000

6-7 An oil company produces aviation fuel in 3 different grades (A, B, C) for the different types of aircraft being flown. Each grade is mixed from 4 different components with the precise mixture varying between each grade. Details are given in Table 6-15. The fuel grades sell for 78p, 75p and 70p per litre respectively. Past demand indicates that at least 10 000 litres of each grade of fuel will be required.

Required:
Formulate the problem to determine the quantity of each type of fuel to be produced.
[3 decision variables and 7 constraints]

6-8 Return to Exercise 2-2 (on waste disposal). Reformulate this problem as an LP problem. Do you think there is any advantage in presenting the problem in this way?

6-9 Return to Exercise 4-5 (on the software company). Reformulate this problem as an LP problem.

6-10 A computer company is investigating a suitable stock control problem for one of their high street stores. In addition to selling their computer equipment the store also stocks and sells a range of computer supplies: boxes of floppy disks, PC cleaning kits, boxes of printer paper and anti-glare screens for monitors. Each of these items has been found to contribute to the store's profit at the rate of: £0.40, £2.20, £1.75 and £3.60 per item sold respectively. The company is trying to decide what quantity of each item should be held in stock in order to meet sales on a weekly basis. Additional relevant factors are as follows. The store has 350 cubic feet of storage space available and the 4 items take up respectively 0.5, 0.1, 1.3 and 0.4 cubic feet per unit stocked. The store has determined that, regardless of profitability, at least 200 boxes of disks should be stocked each week and at least 50 boxes of printer paper. It is felt that such items—frequently required by customers—should always be available. However, because of fire regulations the store is allowed to stock no more that 500 boxes of disks and 100 boxes of paper at any one time. Finally, the accounting department has been analysing the cash flow situation in the store. Holding items in stock naturally incurs costs (security, insurance, handling charges, etc.). The accounting department has decided as a matter of cash flow policy that these stock costs should be no more than £75 per week. The 4 items respectively incur stockholding costs of £.06, £0.18, £0.10 and £0.25 per item per week.

You are required to advise on a suitable quantity of stocks to be held.

Required:
(a) Formulate the problem in terms of maximizing the profit earned.
   [4 decision variables and 6 constraints]
(b) Reformulate the problem if the accounting department now decides it wishes to limit stockholding costs to no more than 10 per cent of profit earned each week.

7
THE SIMPLEX METHOD

In Chapter 5 we developed a simple method of finding a solution to an LP problem and began the process of providing additional managerial information relating to the opportunity costs of scarce resources, thereby allowing the organization to prioritize such scarce resources. The graphical solution of an LP problem, however, is particularly limited in that it can deal easily only with problems involving two variables. For this reason—and the fact that we usually require more detailed information than the graphical method can produce—we turn to a more general method of solution. The *Simplex method* is such a solution process and consists of a series of sequential computational steps in an iterative process. Each iteration—or stage—represents a step towards an optimal solution. Such a method is ideally suited for solution by computer but it is important that the user understands the basic concepts behind the solution method, to facilitate interpretation of relevant computer output and to be able to evaluate in terms of its usefulness to decision-making the information generated by the Simplex method. Although the procedural arithmetic of the Simplex method gets somewhat complicated at times it is worth remembering that an adequate grasp of this procedure allows us to incorporate as many constraints and as many variables into our problem as we wish, something not available under the graphical solution. It is also important to remember that an adequate understanding of the principles behind the procedure is essential even if you are unlikely in practice to calculate the solution to an LP problem manually. The information useful to the decision-maker through such a procedure must be extracted from the computer solution and then interpreted and evaluated in the context of the specific problem. You will only be able to do this if your understanding of the technique itself is adequate. To illustrate the principles of the Simplex method we shall return to the production problem facing IMC that we examined in Chapter 5. If you are able to you should use appropriate computer software to duplicate many of the arithmetic stages we shall be introducing in this chapter.

7-1 SIMPLEX FORMULATION

At this stage the Simplex method can best be understood as a process that sequentially solves sets of simultaneous equations at the various corner points of the feasible area and with each solution determines whether any improvement in the objective function is possible. You will remember that earlier in Chapter 5 it was stated that a solution will generally be found at one of the corner points of the feasible area. The Simplex method takes advantage of this. Effectively, in any LP problem there will be a finite number of such corner points. The Simplex algorithm determines the values for the decision variables at such a point and calculates the corresponding value for the objective function. A simple test is then undertaken to determine whether any of the remaining corner points would generate an improved value for the objective function. If not, then the solution program stops, having found the optimal solution. (You will be aware of the strong similarities between the Simplex and the transportation method introduced in Chapter 2.) You will also remember the initial problem formulation from Chapter 5 as:

$$\text{Maximize} \quad 40A + 50B \quad (7\text{-}1)$$
$$\text{subject to:} \quad 28A + 42B \leq 16\,800 \quad (7\text{-}2)$$
$$12A + 6B \leq 4\,800 \quad (7\text{-}3)$$
$$1A + 1B \leq 600 \quad (7\text{-}4)$$
$$A, B \geq 0$$

Because the Simplex method solves sets of equations we must transform our constraint inequalities into equations. We do this by adding a new variable—known as a *slack variable*—to each of the constraints. A slack variable is simply an arithmetic device for transforming this type of inequality constraint into an equation and measures the arithmetic difference between the two sides of a constraint, once the decision variables in the problem, here A and B, take specific values. So, for Eq. (7-2), relating to assembly time, the constraint becomes:

$$28A + 42B + S_1 = 16\,800 \quad (7\text{-}5)$$

where S_1, the slack variable in constraint Eq. (7-5), measures the difference between the two sides of this constraint. Effectively this will be the difference between the number of assembly hours required for any values for A and B and the maximum supply available. So if we were to set A at 100 and B at 100 a total of 7000 assembly hours would be required at this production level. There are a total of 16 800 hours available so S_1 will be 9800 (16 800 − 7000), literally the amount of this resource not utilized at the current output levels.

Student activity
Transform Eq. (7-3) and Eq. (7-4) to include appropriate slack variables.

As with our A and B variables, the slack variables must be non-negative and, as they measure unused resources, will make a zero contribution to profit. That is, in terms of our objective there is no contribution to be achieved from slack variables. Thus our problem becomes:

$$\text{Maximize} \quad 40A + 50B + 0S_1 + 0S_2 + 0S_3 \quad (7\text{-}6)$$
$$\text{subject to:} \quad 28A + 42B + S_1 = 16\,800 \quad (7\text{-}7)$$
$$12A + 6B + S_2 = 4\,800 \quad (7\text{-}8)$$
$$1A + 1B + S_3 = 600 \quad (7\text{-}9)$$
$$A, B \geq 0 \quad (7\text{-}10)$$
$$S_1, S_2, S_3 \geq 0 \quad (7\text{-}11)$$

where S_1, S_2, S_3 are the slack variables introduced to balance the two sides of each constraint and represent any unused resources in each constraint. We shall use the convention that the subscript number relates to the constraint in question. Thus S_1 relates to constraint 1 and S_3 to constraint 3. Again, conventionally, slack variables are implicitly assumed in the objective function rather than explicitly shown as in Eq. (7-6). Normally, the objective function would remain as:

$$40A + 50B$$

with the slack variables making an implicit zero contribution to profit. We should also note that, typically, a computer package will automatically provide such slack variables into the problem formulation. A suitable package will usually require the decision variable coefficients for each constraint and the constraint type ($\leq, \geq, =$) and will then make any necessary adjustments to the formulation for slack variables (and the surplus and artificial variables that we shall shortly be introducing). Effectively, therefore, we now have a set of 3 linear equations with 5 variables and we are searching for an optimal solution that satisfies these equations. You should be aware that when we have a set of simultaneous equations which have more variables (unknowns) than equations then it is impossible to find a unique solution. We require at least as many equations as variables. This will not occur in an LP problem once we add slack variables. The Simplex method revolves around a series of algebraic computations designed to find alternate feasible values for our variable set that satisfy the constraint equations. If we use the objective function then the method evaluates which of the possible alternate solutions represents an optimum. Given that we have more unknowns than equations, the Simplex method can only find a solution by assigning zero values to some of the unknowns and then solving the equations for the rest. In general, with k equations and n variables at least $(n - k)$ variables will need to be assigned zero values in order to allow us to identify a solution. Such a solution is referred to as a *basic* solution (or *basis*) and will relate to a specific corner point of the graphical representation of the problem. Variables assigned zero values are identified as non-basic variables whilst the remaining variables are basic variables. Not all such corner points, however, will represent a feasible solution and the Simplex method will search for solutions that are both basic and feasible until an optimum point is established. This may sound complicated but, as we shall see, reduces to a simple set of arithmetic calculations. The idea of basic variables is similar in principle to that involving used and empty cells in the transportation tables that we examined in Chapters 2 and 3. In our current problem, we have 3 equations and 5 unknowns (A, B, S_1, S_2, S_3). The Simplex method, therefore, will require two of these variables to be set to zero in order to find the unique solution for the remaining variables in the set.

7-2 THE INITIAL TABLEAU

It is conventional, as well as more practical, to present an LP problem in tabular—rather than equation—form. Each tableau will represent a basic (and usually feasible) solution and, as we shall see, allows an easy method of keeping track of the various computational steps undertaken in the Simplex method: which variables are basic and which non-basic and the values these variables take. If we transform the problem into tabular form we have Tableau 7-1.

Tableau 7-1 Initial tableau

	A	B	S_1	S_2	S_3	Value
Objective function	40	50	0	0	0	
Constraint 1	28	42	1	0	0	16 800
Constraint 2	12	6	0	1	0	4 800
Constraint 3	1	1	0	0	1	600

The first row in the tableau represents the objective function equation (Eq. (7-6)), with the remaining rows representing the three constraint equations (Eqs. (7-7) to (7-9)), whilst each column represents the coefficients for a particular variable. So, taking the second row as an example we see that we have our constraint equation, Eq. (7-7)—$28A$, $42B$, $1S_1$ with a value of 16 800. Similarly, the first column allows us to identify how much of each of the three resources a unit of Model A requires—that is, 28 hours of assembly, 12 hours of inspection and 1 microchip. Note that the slack variables—representing unused resources—contribute zero to the objective function. You should ensure that you are satisfied that the tableau and our original formulation are identical before proceeding further. It is also worth pointing out, at this stage, that there are considerable variations in terms of a tabular presentation of a Simplex formulation, although all such tableaux contain the same information. Similarly, computer packages may present such tableaux in slightly different formats from the one shown here. We now need to establish an initial— and feasible—solution. The only way we can proceed is to set 2 of the 5 variables to zero and to solve for the values of the remaining 3 (given that we have only three equations). We could set any of the variables to zero to start the process but we begin by assuming that zero units of Models A and B are produced. Although it is obvious to us that there are more profitable alternatives than this particular combination of A and B, this approach— setting our decision variables to zero initially—has the advantage of requiring no initial analysis to be undertaken. In general, the first LP tableau for any problem will relate to a situation where the decision variables are assigned zero values. So we set $A = 0$ and $B = 0$ and, obviously, profit will equal zero whilst the slack variables must take the following values:

$$28(0) + 42(0) + S_1 = 16\,800 \therefore S_1 = 16\,800$$

$$12(0) + 6(0) + S_2 = 4\,800 \therefore S_2 = 4\,800$$
$$1(0) + 1(0) + S_3 = 600 \therefore S_3 = 600$$

That is, all of our resources are unused. This first basic, feasible solution can be shown in Tableau 7-2. Thus the variables identified in the left-hand column take the value specified in the right-hand column. Note that variables A and B do not appear in this column variable list and, in the Simplex method, automatically take a zero value. That is, A and B are non-basic and therefore equal to zero. Interpretation of the Simplex tableau is from now on standard. We can determine from the variable list which variables form part of the current solution and, by default, which variables do not. Equally, we can readily determine the value that these variables have been assigned in the current solution. Tableau 7-2 represents point I on Fig. 7-1, which is one of the corner points of our feasible area. As we shall see, in evaluating alternate solutions the Simplex method takes advantage of the fact that the optimum solution will, in general, occur at one of the corner

Tableau 7-2 Initial solution

	A	B	S_1	S_2	S_3	Value
PROFIT	40	50	0	0	0	0
S_1	28	42	1	0	0	16 800
S_2	12	6	0	1	0	4 800
S_3	1	1	0	0	1	600

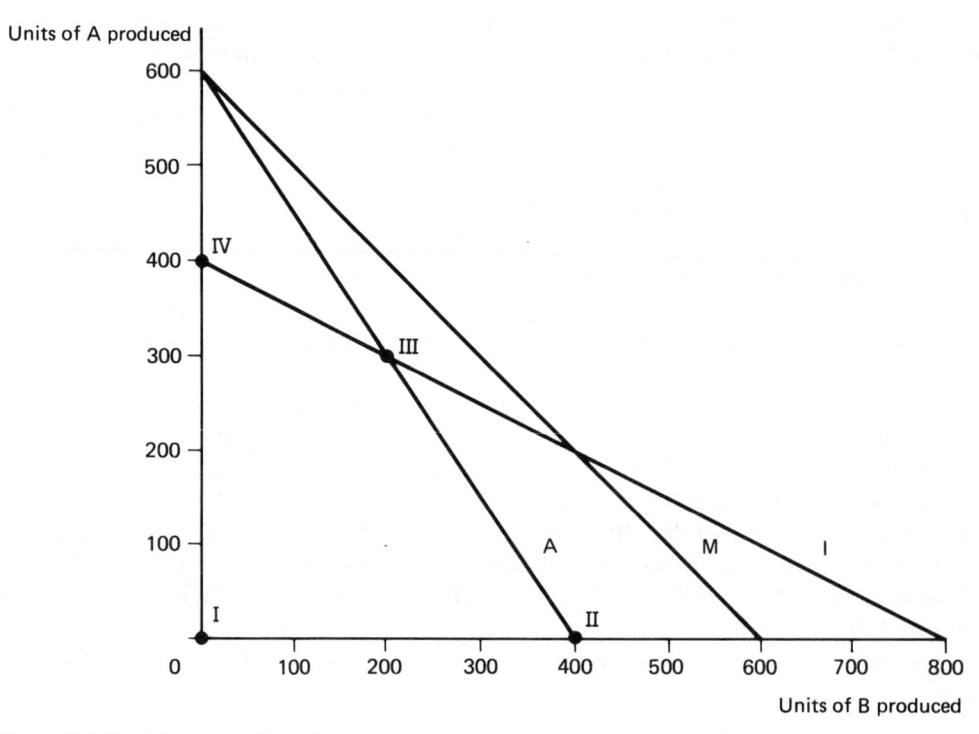

Figure 7-1 Feasible area and solution points

points of the feasible area. This means that each successive tableau, once we have identified a basic solution, will represent a specific corner point of the feasible area. (In fact, this is how the method derives its name, with *Simplex* being a mathematician's term (albeit more rigorously defined) for an n-dimensional area with corners pointing out of the feasible area.) It might be thought that it would be necessary to examine all the corner points of the feasible area in order to identify which represents the optimum. With large problems the number of such corner points could easily run into millions and—even using computer facilities—searching for all these corner points would be extremely tedious. In practice, fortunately, this is not necessary. Instead, the Simplex method identifies in which *direction* from the current corner point we should move in order to improve the value of the objective function. The corner points in all other directions can then be ignored as they will not represent an improved value for the objective function.

Effectively what we have done in Tableau 7-2 is to solve our set of 3 constraint equations. To repeat an earlier point, you should be aware that with 5 unknown variables (A, B, S_1, S_2, S_3) and only 3 equations a unique solution, using simultaneous equations, is impossible. The only way we can solve our equation system is by choosing arbitrary values for 2 of our variables and then finding the values for the other 3 variables that satisfy our equations. Here, we have chosen to set A and B to zero, allowing us to assign unique values to S_1, S_2 and S_3. It can be seen that we shall have to repeat this process at other corner points of the feasible area, that is, setting 2 variables to zero and solving for the remainder.

7-3 THE SOLUTION PROGRAM

From the current feasible solution the Simplex method now determines whether an adjacent corner point represents an improvement in the value of the objective function. In Fig. 7-1 we need to determine whether point II or IV—the two adjacent corner points—represent any improvement in profit. (Note that point III is not adjacent. To reach point III we must first pass through point II or IV.) This is readily determined from the objective function row in Tableau 7-2. The coefficients in this row indicate the effect any non-basic variable (i.e. a variable currently not in our solution and taking a value of zero) would have on the objective function if that variable were given some positive value (i.e. were to enter the basis). As we can see, variables A and B currently take zero values and have coefficients in this row of 40 and 50 respectively. That is, if we choose to produce a unit of A then the objective function will change by £40, and by £50 if we produce a unit of B. These are currently the only non-basic variables that could enter the solution at this stage. It would be sensible at this stage, therefore, given that we wish to maximize profit, to produce B rather than A—that is to move from point I on Fig. 7-1 along the B axis. So B will enter the basis. Our choice is, therefore, determined by the *highest* positive coefficient in the objective function row of Tableau 7-2. We next need to determine how far along this axis we can move in our search for profit—that is, how many units of B we can produce without violating any of our three constraints. From Tableau 7-2, we know that at point I we currently have unused resources for all three constraints (16 800 hours, 4800 hours and 600 components) and from the B column in the tableau we know how many of each of these resources will be required per unit of B produced (42 hours, 6 hours and 1 component, respectively). A simple ratio, therefore, of these currently unused resources to the input requirements per unit of B produced will indicate the maximum production of B relative to each constraint.

$$\frac{\text{Value}}{\text{B coefficient}} = \frac{16\,800}{42} = 400 \text{ units of B}$$

$$= \frac{4800}{6} = 800 \text{ units of B}$$

$$= \frac{600}{1} = 600 \text{ units of B}$$

These ratios represent transformation possibilities—the degree to which we can transform currently available resources into units of B. Under Eq. (7-7) maximum production of B must be limited to 400 units, and to 800 and 600 for Eqs (7-8) and (7-9) respectively. These maxima are determined by the available unused resources under each constraint and the resource requirements per unit of B. Obviously, it is the *smallest* of these positive ratios which will indicate the maximum production of B at this stage. Thus, when we produce 400 units of B resources available under the assembly time constraint will be fully utilized, although some unused resources will still be available under Eqs (7-8) and (7-9).

In terms of our problem, the logic of this stage is readily apparent. From our current position of zero production of A and B—and therefore total non-use of available resources—we have decided to produce B (in preference to A) and have identified that, at this stage, maximum production of B will be set at 400 units. This maximum is determined by the available assembly hours, all of which will be required if we are to attain this particular production level. In terms of the Simplex jargon, we have identified that variable B is set to enter the basis. As we have three constraints we can only have three basic variables. It follows that if B is to become basic then one of the existing basic variables must become non-basic, that is take a zero value. Here it is the S_1 variable (unused assembly hours) that will be forced to leave the basic solution, given that the ratios we have calculated indicate that maximum production of B is limited most by the assembly constraint. Effectively, we will have moved to point II on Fig. 7-1, where constraint Eq. (7-7) is binding and Eqs (7-8) and (7-9) non-binding. We must now, in our Simplex method, transform Tableau 7-2 (which represents point I) to relate to point II. This is done through a series of algebraic manipulations. Extracting row S_1, which relates to the variable that is to become non-basic, from Tableau 7-2 we have:

$$28A + 42B + 1S_1 = 16\,800$$

We know at point II that A and S_1 will both be zero, so we can solve for B by dividing through by 42 to give:

$$\frac{28A}{42} + \frac{42B}{42} + \frac{1S_1}{42} = \frac{16\,800}{42}$$

giving
$$0.6667A + 1B + 0.0238S_1 = 400 \qquad (7\text{-}12)$$

which, as A and S_1 are both non-basic and, therefore, set to zero, gives $B = 400$. Equation (7-12) is simply a general algebraic expression that relates to the assembly constraint. In

Tableau 7-3(a)

	A	B	S_1	S_2	S_3	Value
PROFIT						
B	0.666 67	1	0.023 81	0	0	400
S_2						
S_3						

mathematical terms it is identical to the original constraint, Eq. (7-7), except that we have transformed it to relate to the new basic variable—B—rather than to the previous basic variable—S_1. This new expression relating to B, therefore, replaces the S_1 row in Tableau 7-2 to give Tableau 7-3(a).

However, B not only uses resources from constraint Eq. (7-7) but from constraints Eqs (7-8) and (7-9) also. Accordingly, we must adjust the existing rows S_2 and S_3 in Tableau 7-2 to take the new value of B into account. In other words, by producing 400 units of B we will reduce the unused resources available under the other two constraints, S_2 and S_3, from their current levels of 4800 and 600 respectively and we must now identify in the tableau the new values that S_2 and S_3 will take. As we have seen, row B gives a general expression for the number of units of B produced. Row S_2 in Tableau 7-2 indicates that 6 units of this resource (unused inspection hours) will be required for every unit of B produced. So, effectively, we must reduce S_2—the amount of unused inspection time—by 6 times the units of B produced. Rather than adjusting S_2 by $-(6 \times 400)$, however, we shall adjust S_2 by using the algebraic expression for B (Eq. (7-12) above), giving:

	S_2	12	6	0	1	0	4800
	$-6 \times B$	-4	-6	$-0.142\,86$	0	0	-2400
giving	S_2	8	0	$-0.142\,86$	1	0	2400

This indicates that if we produce 400 units of B then S_2—unused inspection hours—will fall to 2400. We can confirm that this is indeed correct as we initially had 4800 hours available and each unit of B produced requires 6 inspection hours, so total resource requirements at the indicated level of B production will be 2400 hours, leaving 2400 hours unused at this production level.

Student activity
Make the appropriate adjustments to the S_3 row in Tableau 7-2.

A similar calculation can be performed for S_3, where B requires 1 component per unit produced, and again using Eq. (7-12) we have:

	S_3	1	1	0	0	1	600
	$-1 \times B$	$-0.666\,67$	-1	$-0.023\,81$	0	0	-400
giving	S_3	0.333 33	0	$-0.023\,81$	0	1	200

Tableau 7-3(b)

	A	B	S_1	S_2	S_3	Value
PROFIT						
B	0.666 67	1	0.023 81	0	0	400
S_2	8	0	−0.142 86	1	0	2400
S_3	0.333 33	0	−0.023 81	0	1	200

Again, this indicates that with 400 units of B produced, we shall still have 200 unused microchips. Substituting these new rows into Tableau 7-3(a) gives us Tableau 7-3(b). Only our profit row—the objective function—now remains to be amended in the same way. Each unit of B contributes £50 to profit, so using the same arithmetic process as before and using Eq. (7-12) we have:

		PROFIT	40	50	0	0	0	0
		−50 × B	−33.3333	−50	−1.190 48	0	0	−20 000
giving		PROFIT	6.6667	0	−1.190 48	0	0	−20 000

which provides a complete tableau as shown in Tableau 7-3, relating to point II in Fig. 7-1. This tableau is interpreted in the same way as before. Basic variables (those in the first tableau column) take the values indicated, that is:

Tableau 7-3 Second iteration

	A	B	S_1	S_2	S_3	Value
PROFIT	6.666 67	0	−1.190 48	0	0	−20 000
B	0.666 67	1	0.023 81	0	0	400
S_2	8	0	−0.142 86	1	0	2 400
S_3	0.333 33	0	−0.023 81	0	1	200

$$B = 400$$
$$S_2 = 2400$$
$$S_3 = 200$$
$$\text{Profit} = £20\,000$$

whilst non-basic variables (those not in the first tableau column) take a zero value:

$$A = 0$$
$$S_1 = 0$$

Note that in the Simplex method, because of the arithmetic procedure used, the objective function will take a negative value in the tableau, but that this actually shows positive profit, i.e. £20 000. We must remember at each stage to reverse the arithmetic sign preceding the objective function value. Typically, this adjustment will be undertaken automatically by a computer package. Interpretation of the variable values is straightforward:

Production of A =   0 units
Production of B = 400 units

Unused resources: Constraint 1 $S_1 = $ 0
                  Constraint 2 $S_2 = 2400$
                  Constraint 3 $S_3 = $ 200

Profit = £20 000

So, the current position can be summarized by saying that we are producing zero units of Model A and 400 units of Model B to generate a profit of £20 000. This production combination will require all available assembly hours (there will be no slack; that is, this constraint will be binding), 2400 of the available 4800 inspection hours and 400 of the available 600 microchips. These last two constraints, in other words, will be non-binding.

Subsequent iterations

Having completed Tableau 7-3 we must begin the process again. That is, having reached this particular solution—which represents an improvement over our earlier position—can any further increase in the objective function value be achieved? This can be resolved by again looking at the objective function coefficients in Tableau 7-3. It must be stressed at this stage, however, that after the initial tableau the coefficients in all subsequent tableaux are *marginal* coefficients: they indicate the marginal effect of any change and not the total or absolute effect. We shall examine this in more detail. Looking at the Profit row in Tableau 7-3 we see that B now has a zero coefficient, i.e. B can contribute nothing extra to profit as maximum production with existing resources has already been achieved. S_1, not currently in our solution, has a coefficient of −£1.19. That is, if we introduce S_1 into our solution (having just taken it out!) profit will decline by £1.19 for each unit of S_1 we introduce. Effectively, if we insist on having unused assembly hours then production of B must suffer and profit will decline. The only variable still with a positive profit contribution is variable A and the positive coefficient of £6.6667 indicates that, in our next iteration, profit will increase by this amount for each unit of A produced. At first sight this may seem incorrect, as we know from the original objective function that A contributes £40 to profit, not £6.6667. However, this latter figure must, as indicated previously, be interpreted as the marginal profit contribution, not the total. We shall confirm this shortly. As can be seen from point II in Fig. 7-1, the only way we can produce A in our current position is to reduce production of B. This reduction in B is necessary in order to release scarce resources (assembly hours) for A's production. Remember that we are using *all* of the assembly resource to produce B. Given that we need 28 assembly hours to produce each unit of A, the only way to make the resource available for A production is to decrease B production. We are effectively being told by the coefficient of £6.667 that this reduction in B, in order to produce A, will be profitable. The A variable, therefore, is set to enter our solution and accordingly as before one of the existing basic variables must leave the solution. We need to identify which one. Just as the coefficients in the objective function row represent marginal profit, so the other coefficients in the A column now represent marginal resource requirements per unit of A at this stage in our solution. That is, each unit of A will require an extra:

0.666 67 units of B
8   units of S_2 (unused inspection time)
0.333 33 units of S_3 (unused microchips)

These marginal coefficients are readily confirmed. We must sacrifice 0.666 67 units of B for every unit of A we wish to produce. This will release some assembly hours (all currently used for B production) for producing A. The number thus released will be:

0.666 67 (number of assembly hours needed per unit of B)
= 0.666 67 (42)
= 28 hours

So, producing 0.6667 fewer units of B will release *exactly* the number of assembly hours required to produce 1 unit of A (this is confirmed from the original constraint, Eq. (7-2)). Similarly, this reduction in B production will release some of the currently used inspection hours:

0.666 67 (no. of inspection hours needed per unit of B)
= 0.666 67 (6)
= 4 hours

But A requires a total of 12 hours per unit, so an additional (marginal) 8 hours will be needed per 1 unit of A, which is the relevant coefficient in the A column in Tableau 7-3. Similarly, with the microchip components, 0.666 67 (1 component) will be released by the reduction in the number of units of B produced, with an additional 0.333 33 still required, given that each unit of A produced requires 1 microchip. Finally, the marginal profit figure in Tableau 7-3 can also be confirmed:

Change in profit

Gain | *Loss*
1 unit A at £40 per unit | 0.666 67 units B at £50 per unit
= £40 | = 0.666 67 (50) = £33.335

Net gain = £40 − £33.335 = £6.6667

So, we confirm that the tableau now represents the marginal coefficients. Having interpreted the information in our current tableau and decided that production of A is worth while, we must now identify the maximum possible production of A with the available resources. Again, we are looking at the rate of transformation of resources into A production. Currently, B takes a value of 400 units. If we wish to produce A then, as we have seen, this will require 0.666 67 units of B to be sacrificed for every unit of A that we wish to produce. The ratio

$$\frac{400}{0.666\,67} = 600$$

therefore, indicates that, in terms of this particular resource transformation, the maximum possible production of A will be 600 units. At this level we will have transformed (sacrificed) all of the existing B production for production of A. Similarly, for the other two variables in the current solution, S_2 and S_3, the ratio

$$\frac{2400}{8} = 300$$

indicates the maximum production of A in terms of unused inspection time and the ratio

$$\frac{200}{0.333\,33} = 600$$

indicates the maximum production of A in terms of unused microchip availability. As before, it is the *smallest* positive ratio (300, for S_2) which indicates the maximum production of A that is feasible. So, A will enter the basis and S_2 will leave. Again, we now need to transform the existing tableau to relate to the new position. The procedure is exactly as before:

1. we obtain a new row for A by dividing the S_2 row (relating to the variable that is to become non-basic) through by 8 (which is the appropriate coefficient linking S_2 and A);
2. we adjust all other rows in the tableau using the new A row and the appropriate coefficient in the A column.

Student activity
Perform this arithmetic to produce the new tableau and interpret the new solution.

The new tableau, which represents point III in Fig. 7-1, will be as given by Tableau 7-4. Here we now have:

Tableau 7-4 Third iteration

	A	B	S_1	S_2	S_3	Value
PROFIT	0	0	−1.0714	−0.8333	0	−22 000
B	0	1	0.035 7	−0.0833	0	200
A	1	0	−0.017 86	0.125	0	300
S_3	0	0	−0.017 86	−0.0417	1	100

$$A = 300 \quad S_1 = 0$$
$$B = 200 \quad S_2 = 0$$
$$S_3 = 100$$
$$\text{Profit} = £22\,000$$

Interpretation is straightforward: we are producing 300 units of A and 200 units of B to generate £22 000 profit. Constraints 1 and 2 are binding (there is no slack for these two constraints; S_1 and S_2 are both zero) whilst constraint 3 is non-binding, with 100 unused components. The iterative process now begins again. Once more we try to identify whether further improvement in the objective function is possible by examining coefficients in the profit row. All are now either zero or negative. Obviously, with reference to Fig. 7-1, the adjacent corner points are II, which we have just left, or IV. Logically, we can see that a move to point IV would not be profitable as we have already rejected the opportunity of moving to this point when examining the initial tableau. There are no further positive profit contributions to be achieved. In other words, Tableau 7-4 represents our optimum position, confirming our previous graphical solution. The optimum solution, therefore, is to produce 300 units of A and 200 units of B.

Summary of the Simplex method

To summarize the Simplex method as it has been developed thus far:

1. Transform the problem into a suitable form for solution by the Simplex by introducing slack variables into the appropriate inequality constraints.
2. Obtain an initial tableau by setting the decision variables to zero.
3. Identify the variable to enter the basis from the highest positive coefficient in the objective function row. The column relating to this variable is known as the *pivot column*.
4. Identify the variable to leave the basis by calculating the ratios of the values to the coefficients in the pivot column. Select the lowest positive ratio to identify which current basic variable is to become non-basic. The row associated with this variable is known as the *pivot row*.
5. Transform the existing pivot row by dividing through by the *pivot coefficient* (the coefficient common to both the pivot column and the pivot row).
6. Adjust the other rows in the tableau, using the new row calculated in step 5 and the appropriate coefficient from the pivot column.
7. Repeat from step 3 until all entries in the objective function row are zero or negative. This tableau will represent the optimal solution.

The simplex method can therefore be seen to be a general solution program that can easily be expanded to incorporate any number of variables and any number of constraints. The method is based on a series of logical and repetitive stages that involve straightforward—if somewhat tedious—calculations to be performed to generate a tableau of information relating to a basic solution, ensuring that each successive tableau represents an improved value for the objective function.

7-4 DEALING WITH OTHER TYPES OF CONSTRAINT

Our problem so far has involved only one type of constraint, taking the form $\leq$. There are two other forms of constraint that we need to be able to introduce into the Simplex process:

1. constraints representing some minimum restriction, taking the form greater than or equal to, $\geq$; and
2. constraints representing some strict equality, taking the form equal to, $=$.

Constraints taking the form $\geq$

Let us expand the original problem that we have been using up to now, and assume that IMC has a contract to supply a minimum of 100 units of Model A on a weekly basis to a particular customer, that is:

$$A \geq 100 \qquad (7\text{-}13)$$

This constraint has been incorporated into Fig. 7-2, with the new feasible area highlighted. As we can readily see, the optimal solution will remain unchanged for we are

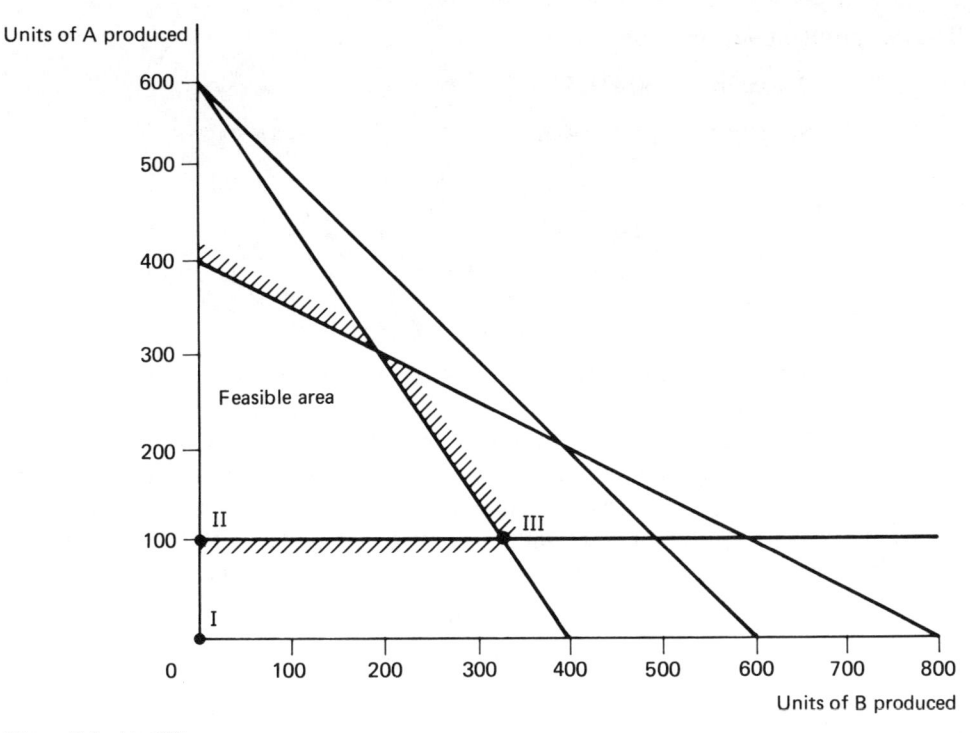

Figure 7-2 $A \geqslant 100$

already supplying more than this minimum quantity of Model A. However, we also need to be able to introduce this type of constraint into the Simplex procedure. As with our other constraints, we need to transform the new constraint into an equation. To do this we do not, as before, add a slack variable to the left-hand side of the expression, but rather a *surplus* variable to the right-hand side.

$$A = 100 + S_4 \qquad (7\text{-}14)$$

with $A, S_4 \geqslant 0$.

Interpretation of this new variable is simple. Under the new constraint A must take a minimum value of 100. To introduce a slack variable into this type of constraint would have no meaning. If you recollect, a slack variable measures the amount by which the left-hand side of the constraint falls short of the right-hand side. Here such an interpretation is meaningless as, by the very nature of this new constraint, the left-hand side cannot be less than the right. However, there is nothing in the constraint to prevent A taking a value over 100. In this case S_4—the surplus variable—would be the amount by which A *exceeds* the minimum requirement, that is, the amount by which the left-hand side of the constraint exceeds the right. Thus, if A were 250, S_4 would have to take a value of 150 to satisfy the equation. If A were to take the absolute minimum value permitted by the constraint then S_4 would obviously take a zero value, with no surplus when A is at the absolute minimum. We can rearrange the equation to have all our variables on the left-hand side:

$$A - S_4 = 100 \qquad (7\text{-}15)$$

and thus our problem becomes:

$$\begin{aligned}
\text{Maximize} \quad & 40A + 50B \\
\text{subject to:} \quad & 28A + 42B + S_1 = 16\,800 \\
& 12B + 6B + S_2 = 4\,800 \\
& 1A + 1B + S_3 = 600 \\
& 1A - S_4 = 100 \\
& A, B, S_1, S_2, S_3, S_4 \geq 0
\end{aligned}$$

As before, as with the slack variables, a surplus variable makes no contribution to the value of the objective function. As previously, we could now put this problem into tabular form. Before we do this, however, let us evaluate the effect of our new constraint on the Simplex procedure. You will remember that we identify an initial basic feasible solution by setting our decision variables—A and B—to zero and solving for the remaining slack variables. However, if we attempt to do that now, having introduced our $\geq$ constraint, we encounter difficulty. If A and B are set to zero then we have, as before:

$$\begin{aligned}
S_1 &= 16\,800 \\
S_2 &= 4\,000 \\
S_3 &= 600
\end{aligned}$$

but now, to satisfy the last constraint, S_4 must take a value of -100:

$$A - S_4 = 100$$
but $$A = 0$$
therefore $$-S_4 = 100$$
$$S_4 = -100$$

which violates our formulation, as we specified that *all* variables must be non-negative. It is easy to see why this problem has arisen. Returning to Fig. 7-2, we see that our attempt at an initial feasible solution ($A, B = 0$) puts us *outside* the boundary of the feasible area at point I. In other words $A, B = 0$ is no longer a feasible solution that we can use to start our Simplex procedure. To resolve this problem, and in order to initiate the Simplex method, we have to introduce yet another type of variable. This new variable—an *artificial variable*—is simply an arithmetic device that allows the Simplex procedure to function with this type of constraint. As we shall see, unlike the other variables, it has no meaning as such in our problem but is simply used by the procedure to allow us to establish a basic solution. We introduce an artificial variable into our last constraint to give:

$$A - S_4 + A_4 = 100 \tag{7-16}$$

We use the standard subscript notation, A_4, to indicate that the artificial variable relates to the fourth constraint. We can now identify an initial basic solution by setting our problem variables—A, B—to zero and any surplus variables—here S_4—to zero also. This allows the slack variables to take the values as specified and A_4 to take a value of 100 to satisfy this last constraint. As before, we now have a 4-equation problem with 7 unknowns (A, B, 3 slack variables, 1 surplus variable and 1 artificial variable), so 3 of the 7 variables must be non-basic—that is, they must take a zero value to allow us to identify the appropriate solution for the remaining variables. Such a solution—and indeed any further iterations which contain an artificial variable as a basic variable—represents only a basic solution and not a feasible one. It is important to realize that this basic solution relates only to the Simplex tableau and not to our problem as such. We cannot interpret A_4 in the context of our original problem. It is simply a mathematical device to allow the method to work. As we shall see, once the artificial variable has performed its task, it will effectively disappear from the problem. It is also worth repeating the point made earlier that, typically, an LP computer package will generate artificial variables as necessary once it is provided with the basic constraints and decision variables. It remains necessary, however, for the user to be able to interpret the various tableaux that will contain such artificial variables. So our new problem is as follows:

$$\text{Maximize} \quad 40A + 50B$$

$$\text{subject to:} \quad 28A + 42B + S_1 = 16\,800$$

$$12A + 6B + S_2 = 4\,800$$

$$1A + 1B + S_3 = 600$$

$$1A - S_4 + A_4 = 100$$

$$A, B, S_1, S_2, S_3, S_4, A_4 \geq 0$$

In order to ensure that the artificial variable is forced out of our tableau as soon as possible, so that we can return to a real, and feasible, solution, several alternative methods are available. By and large, the problem of artificial variables will be resolved within the computer program that is being used to solve the problem, with artificial variables introduced and removed by the program, so that in effect the user need not be concerned with the technical detail of artificial variables at all, except in so far as they will almost inevitably appear somewhere in the computer output. The rest of this section, however, works through an appropriate solution method that is commonly used to illustrate how artificial variables function in the iteration. You may find that the method detailed here differs from that used in whatever computer program you are accessing, although the general approach remains the same. Perhaps the most popular method of eliminating artificial variables is the *method of penalties* (alternatively known as the 'big M' method). You may remember that technically our objective function assigns a zero value to all variables except those relating directly to the original problem—here the decision variables A and B. What we can do is to assign an arbitrarily large negative contribution for any artificial variable that enters our problem. Effectively, this means that the value of the objective function—here profit—will be adversely affected as long as the artificial variable takes any non-zero value. The Simplex procedure will then automatically try to eliminate such a penalizing variable as soon as possible. So we can establish an objective function for the problem

$$\text{Maximize} \quad 40A + 50B - 1000A_4 \qquad (7\text{-}17)$$

where we have assigned an arbitrarily large negative contribution to profit for A_4. As long as this figure far exceeds any other in our objective function the method will work

Tableau 7-5 Initial tableau

	A	B	S_1	S_2	S_3	S_4	A_4	Value
PROFIT	40	50	0	0	0	0	-1000	
S_1	28	42	1	0	0	0	0	16800
S_2	12	6	0	1	0	0	0	4800
S_3	1	1	0	0	1	0	0	600
A_4	1	0	0	0	0	-1	1	100

satisfactorily. (You may remember that exactly the same principle is in operation for prohibited routes in the transportation model.) So the tableau becomes that shown as Tableau 7-5.

In order for the objective function row to incorporate the artificial variable and its associated penalty value we must manipulate the tableau to give a zero coefficient in this row for the A_4 column. This can be done by multiplying the A_4 row by 1000 (the penalty value) and adding the result to the objective function row to give

PROFIT   1040   50   0   0   0   -1000   0   100000

Thus, A_4 takes a value of 100 and profit is $-£100\,000$ (-1000×100). If we had more than one artificial variable in the problem, as is often the case, we would amend the objective function row accordingly by multiplying each A row in turn by its penalty value and adding each result to the objective function row. This new objective function row will then incorporate all the artificial variables to represent the initial basic solution. So, the initial tableau becomes as given in Tableau 7-6, and interpretation of the current solution is straightforward. The decision variables, A and B, do not appear in the variable list and, therefore, take zero values. Accordingly, the slack variables (S_1, S_2, S_3) take their maximum values equal to the maximum available resources. S_4 does not appear in the variable list and also takes a zero value. The artificial variable, A_4, does appear and takes a value of 100 (the minimum requirement for A). Because the artificial variable appears in the solution the value of the objective function takes a positive value (remember that previously profit has been shown as a negative figure in the tableau). We interpret this by saying that, because of the penalty value attached to A_4 (i.e. to not producing the minimum quantity of A) we incur a loss of £100 000. Such a penalty will remain for as long as we are not producing the minimum quantity of A required in the problem formulation. We can now proceed to apply the Simplex procedure as before. The pivot column is column A (as it has the largest positive coefficient) and the pivot row can be identified as usual by calculating the ratios of value to pivot column coefficients. In this case the ratios will be:

Tableau 7-6 Initial solution

	A	B	S_1	S_2	S_3	S_4	A_4	Value
PROFIT	1040	50	0	0	0	-1000	0	100000
S_1	28	42	1	0	0	0	0	16800
S_2	12	6	0	1	0	0	0	4800
S_3	1	1	0	0	1	0	0	600
A_4	1	0	0	0	0	-1	1	100

for S_1 $16\,800/28 = 600$
S_2 $4\,800/12 = 400$
S_3 $600/1 = 600$
A_4 $100/1 = 100$

By selecting the smallest positive ratio we identify the pivot row to be A_4. Effectively, A_4 will leave the solution and A will enter. On reflection, this is an entirely logical choice, as the artificial variable relates directly to the minimum production of Model A that is needed to satisfy the associated constraint. By choosing A to enter the solution the Simplex method is attempting to remove the artificial variable from the basis—and return the tableau to a basic *and* feasible solution—as soon as possible. Notice that because of the penalty value arithmetic we performed earlier to give the Profit row in Tableau 7-5 variable A enters the problem rather than variable B (which has a higher real profit at £50). Because of the penalty value attached to *not* producing A, the Simplex method temporarily ignores the real profit contributions in order to bring the required variable into the solution at an early a stage as possible.

Student activity
Derive the new tableau for the next stage of the problem and interpret the solution shown.

Performing the usual arithmetic transformations (or preferably getting a computer to do it for you as you should be doing at this stage) gives the new tableau shown as Tableau 7-7. Interpretation of our tableau is straightforward:

Tableau 7-7 First iteration

	A	B	S_1	S_2	S_3	S_4	A_4	Value
PROFIT	0	50	0	0	0	40	−1040	−4000
S_1	0	42	1	0	0	28	−28	14000
S_2	0	6	0	1	0	12	−12	3600
S_3	0	1	0	0	1	1	−1	500
A	1	0	0	0	0	−1	1	100

$$S_1 = 14\,000$$
$$S_2 = 3\,600$$
$$S_3 = 500$$
$$A = 100$$
$$B, S_4 \text{ and } A_4 = 0$$
$$\text{Profit} = £4000$$

We are currently producing 100 units of A—the absolute minimum required in the problem—and zero units of B, and generating a profit of £4000. This combination of production requires some—but not all—of the available resources. S_1, S_2 and S_3—measuring the unused resources available under the 3 supply constraints—take the values shown. These are, therefore, non-binding constraints at this stage. S_4, relating to the fourth constraint, takes a zero value. Remember that S_4, a surplus variable, shows the amount by which our solution exceeds the minimum requirement specified by the constraint. Obviously, with $A = 100$ there is no surplus. This constraint, in other words, is binding. A_4 also takes a zero value. It has effectively fulfilled its function by allowing the Simplex method to operate and to provide a solution that is both basic and feasible. We can see from Fig. 7-2 that the new tableau and its solution relate to point II, with the minimum A production constraint being the only binding constraint. This solution is now on the boundary of the feasible area. We can readily recognize this from the tableau. If a tableau contains an artificial variable in its basis then the solution represented is not feasible. If the tableau has removed the artificial variable from the basis then we have returned to a feasible solution. Note from the A_4 column in Tableau 7-7 that this variable has a high, negative objective function coefficient which will prevent A_4 from re-entering the basis. The Simplex procedure now proceeds in exactly the same way as before, searching for an improved basic, feasible solution, although an explanation of the logic behind the next iteration will prove useful at this stage. From the objective function row in Tableau 7-7 we see that there are 2 variables which—by entering the next solution—will make a positive contribution to profit. These are B, with a coefficient of £50, and S_4, with a coefficient of £40. The A coefficient is zero. This is, perhaps, surprising as we can see from Fig. 7-2 that at the current position—point II—a further increase in A production is both feasible and profitable. However, let us return to S_4, with the positive coefficient of £40, S_4, you will remember, measures the surplus A production, over and above the minimum production level required, so that in effect we have two variables in the tableau relating to Model A production. These are A itself and S_4, which shows the production of A that exceeds the minimum requirement set out in constraint 4. So, we know that at this stage profit could be increased either by producing Model B or by producing units of Model A that are surplus to the minimum requirement. However, at this stage the most profitable next step is to produce B, given its higher per-unit profit of £50. B, therefore, will enter the basis and we can as usual calculate the appropriate ratios to determine which current variable must leave.

Student activity
Determine which variable would leave the current solution.

Calculation of the appropriate ratios (the values to the B column coefficients) reveals that the S_1 variable will leave the current basis. That is, production of B will increase to utilize all resources available under the assembly constraint. This will move us to point III in Fig. 7-2 and accordingly we must transform Tableau 7-7 to represent this new solution point.

Student activity
Calculate the new tableau for this point and interpret the solution.

Tableau 7-8 Second iteration

	A	B	S_1	S_2	S_3	S_4	A_4	Value
PROFIT	0	0	−1.1905	0	0	6.67	−1006.67	−20 666.67
B	0.6667	0	0.023 81	0	0	0.6667	−0.6667	333.33
S_2	8	0	−0.142 86	1	0	8	−8	1 600
S_3	0.3333	0	−0.023 81	0	1	0.3333	−0.3333	166.67
A	0.6667	1	0.023 81	0	0	−1	1	100

The new tableau is shown as Tableau 7-8. Interpretation:

$$A = 100 \qquad S_1 = 0$$
$$B = 333.33 \qquad S_2 = 1600$$
$$S_3 = 166.67$$
$$\text{Profit} = £20\,666.67 \qquad S_4 = 0$$
$$A_4 = 0$$

At this current solution we are producing 100 units of A and 333.33 units of B to generate a profit of £20 666.67. Constraints 1 and 4 are binding whilst constraints 2 and 3 are not. If you refer back to Tableau 7-3 (which relates to the original problem without the minimum A constraint) you will see obvious similarities in the coefficients at this stage. The iterative process of the Simplex method continues as before. When you examine the Profit row of Tableau 7-8 you can see that only one non-basic variable still has a positive contribution to make to profit: S_4. You will also realize that this coefficient—at £6.67—is the same as we had at the equivalent stage in Tableau 7-3 before we introduced this new constraint. Given that S_4 relates to production of A which is surplus to the minimum constraint requirement of 100 units, this coefficient confirms that it is profitable to produce more than the minimum required quantity of A. Put another way, it is profitable at this stage to reallocate scarce resources from existing production and into extra units of Model A. The new tableau is easily determined.

Student activity
Determine the new tableau for the problem and interpret the solution.

Tableau 7-9 Third iteration

	A	B	S_1	S_2	S_3	S_4	A_4	Value
PROFIT	0	0	−1.0714	−0.8333	0	0	−1000	−22000
B	0	1	0.03571	−0.0833	0	0	0	200
S_4	0	0	−0.01786	0.125	0	1	−1	200
S_3	0	0	−0.01786	−0.0417	1	0	0	100
A	1	0	−0.01786	0.125	0	0	0	300

The new tableau becomes as shown in Tableau 7-9. The solution—which we confirm is optimal, as there are no further positive coefficients in the objective function row—shows that:

$$A = 300 \qquad S_1 = 0$$
$$B = 200 \qquad S_2 = 0$$
$$S_3 = 100$$
$$S_4 = 200$$
$$A_4 = 0$$
$$\text{Profit} = £22\,000$$

Optimal production of A and B is 300 and 200 units respectively. Constraints 1 and 2 are binding (the corresponding slack variables take a zero value) whilst constraint 3 is non-binding. Note that S_4, the surplus variable, takes a value of 200. Given that the optimal value for A is 300, the value for S_4 indicates we are producing 200 units more than the required minimum. The artificial variable does not appear in the solution, taking a zero value.

The two-phase method Whilst the method of penalties is a logical and easy-to-understand method of dealing with artificial variables it is not necessarily the most efficient in computational terms. A variety of other methods have been developed to speed up the iterative process of the Simplex in dealing with artificial variables. We shall briefly mention one of the most common: the *two-phase-method*. We break the solution program into two phases. The first phase is concerned simply with achieving a feasible solution—with removing all artificial variables from the basis. The second phase then returns to the original criteria for optimization made explicit in the objective function. Effectively, we create a new (artificial) objective function for phase I which, for our example, would be:

$$\text{Minimize} \quad 1A_4$$

which will achieve its minimum value (zero) only when A_4 takes a zero value (i.e. is non-basic). The two-phase method then constructs a tableau using this new objective function and which incorporates the original objective function as a row (so that the iterative arithmetic can be undertaken on the objective function also). At the end of phase I the artificial variable(s) will have been removed (as long as there is indeed a feasible solution to the problem under investigation), and phase II begins when we again return to the original objective function. Tableau 7-10 shows the initial (phase I) tableau for the problem we have just been investigating, with the second row representing the artificial objective function that we now use. We shall see shortly that when we are dealing with mimimization problems (which is what we now have) the pivot column is that which has the largest negative coefficient, here for A. Performing the usual calculations, we would determine that A_4 will leave the basis and, again, we could update the tableau using the method outlined in the earlier sections of this chapter. If we do this we obtain Tableau 7-11, where it can be seen that the basis contains no artificial variable. This will represent

Tableau 7-10 Phase I: initial tableau

	A	B	S_1	S_2	S_3	S_4	A_4	Value
PROFIT	40	50	0	0	0	0	0	0
Art OF	-1	0	0	0	0	1	0	-100
S_1	28	42	1	0	0	0	0	16 800
S_2	12	6	0	1	0	0	0	4 800
S_3	1	1	0	0	1	0	0	600
A_4	1	0	0	0	0	-1	1	100

Tableau 7-11 Phase I: first iteration

	A	B	S_1	S_2	S_3	S_4	A_4	Value
PROFIT	0	50	0	0	0	40	-40	-4 000
Art OF	0	0	0	0	0	0	0	0
S_1	0	42	1	0	0	28	-28	14 000
S_2	0	6	0	1	0	12	-12	3 600
S_3	0	1	0	0	1	1	-1	500
A_4	1	0	0	0	0	-1	1	100

the end of phase I and the start of phase II. To begin phase II we simply remove the artificial OF row from the tableau (and usually remove the artificial variable column also). We can then use the original OF (here for Profit) to assess the next iteration of the Simplex. Again, as with the method of penalties, the arithmetic involved in the two-phase method will generally be undertaken within the computer package you are using.

Constraints taking the form =

Occasionally an LP problem will also involve constraints that are expressed as strict equations requiring an exact balance between the two sides of the expression. This may occur, for example, if the company wishes to meet some contractual obligation *exactly*, with no surplus, or it may want full utilization of a particular resource, with no slack. In such a case we need only to introduce an artificial variable into the constraint, with no slack or surplus variables. For example, suppose the company had 450 cardboard cartons in stock for packing their production before transportation. Management want all these cartons to be used in the next week because a change in advertising has led to a change in the design of carton and therefore new cartons will be used.

So here
$$A + B = 450 \tag{7-18}$$

which in our problem would give:

$$A + B + A_5 = 450 \tag{7-19}$$

with the artificial variable, A_5, introduced to allow us to identify a basic solution (with A and B both zero) and to start the Simplex method. The problem can be solved in the usual way, as detailed in the previous section.

Constraints involving negative RHS values

So far, the constraints we have included in the Simplex tableaux have all involved non-negative values on the right-hand side (RHS) of the constraint expression. Occasionally we encounter constraints which involve a negative RHS and these cannot be included in the Simplex tableau. We shall demonstrate why with a simple illustration. Let us assume that IMC are trying to break into the Japanese market. From the next production batch 10 units of Model A are to be sent to Japan to be tested to ensure they meet appropriate Japanese import regulations. At the same time management have decided that they intend trying to stimulate demand for Model B by restricting the output of Model A. They anticipate that if supplies of Model A are restricted then customers will turn instead to Model B (which you will remember is the higher-priced and higher-profit version). These two factors can be combined into a single constraint:

$$B \geq A - 10 \tag{7-20}$$

That is, production of B must be no less than that of A after the 10 units of A have been shipped for testing. Equation (7-20) can be rewritten into a form suitable for the Simplex as:

$$B - A \geq -10 \tag{7-21}$$

or in the usual format as:

$$-1A + 1B \geq -10 \tag{7-22}$$

At first sight there appears to be no difficulty. We could, as usual, include a suitable surplus variable and a corresponding artificial variable (given that we have a $\geq$ constraint). However, let us examine Eq. (7-22) in more detail. It is apparent that at some stage in the Simplex program we might set $A = 0$. This would then require:

$$1B \geq -10 \tag{7-23}$$

and certain values of B which would satisfy Eq. (7-23) (such as $B = -5$) would violate the fundamental requirement of the formulation that all variables must be non-negative. We would encounter difficulties in the Simplex tableau if we incorporated this type of constraint. Fortunately, using some simple algebraic manipulation, we can transform a constraint with a negative RHS into a form suitable for solution by the Simplex program. Let us return to Eq. (7-21). We can apply a simple rule such that we multiply the constraint through by -1 and change the direction of the inequality. The new constraint (logically the same as the original) will now have a non-negative RHS. For example we know that:

$$10 \geq -5$$

is true. But if we apply our rule we have instead:

$$-10 \leq 5$$

which is also perfectly true. In our problem we have:

$$-1A + 1B \geq -10$$

If we multiply by -1 and change the direction of the inequality to give

$$1A - 1B \leq 10 \tag{7-24}$$

Equation (7-24) is logically identical to Eq. (7-21) but now has an RHS which is non-negative and can be included in the Simplex tableau without further difficulty. Any solution which satisfies Eq. (7-24) implicitly satisfies the original constraint, Eq. (7-21). Note that the same rule can be applied to a constraint taking the form $\leq$. In the case of an equality constraint ($=$) we would simply multiply through by -1. There would be no need to alter the direction of the constraint equality. It is also worth noting that care must be taken when interpreting the tableaux of a problem that was originally formulated with a negative RHS constraint. We must remember to interpret a solution in the context of the original constraint and not the amended form. An example of this is given as an end-of-chapter exercise.

7-5 MINIMIZATION PROBLEMS

We saw for the graphical solution that minimization problems pose no real difficulty, with the only difference from maximization problems being that we require the objective function line to be as close to the origin as possible rather than as far away as possible as is the case with maximization. We will also need to amend the Simplex method. The basic method we have used so far will not work for minimization problems unless we make some appropriate adjustment to the procedure. The difficulty arises because our current solution method chooses, in each iteration, the largest *positive* coefficient in the objective function row to determine the new basic variable whereas, in a minimization problem, we are searching for the *lowest* possible value for the objective function. Accordingly, we will need to amend the rule we use to choose the pivot column at each iteration. In addition, manual solutions of minimization problems tend to be particularly lengthy and tedious because they invariably include a number of constraints of the form $\geq$ or $=$, which, as we have seen, necessitate the introduction of a number of artificial variables. You will realize that this must be the case as, in a minimization problem, we are trying to force the objective function towards the origin and only these types of constraint will provide a feasible area that does not include the origin. Accordingly, minimization problems are more appropriate for computer solution where we can concentrate on the managerial importance of the solution rather than worry about the method of solution.

However, for the sake of completeness one of the methods used for solving Simplex minimization problems (there are again several alternatives) is given here. Once again, you should remember that a computer package may use a slightly different solution approach, although it will generate the identical optimal tableau. (The following problem also usefully illustrates how a number of artificial variables can be introduced into a problem and dealt with through the Simplex method.) Let us examine IMC's production problem from a slightly different perspective to that so far. Let us assume that we have the same production resource constraints as before but with three additional restrictions imposed:

$$A \geq 100 \quad (7\text{-}13)$$

$$B \geq 150 \quad (7\text{-}20)$$

$$A + B = 450 \quad (7\text{-}18)$$

That is, production of A must be at least 100 units (the constraint we examined earlier), production of B must be at least 150 units and the combined production must be exactly equal to 450 units (the number of packing cartons that the company wishes to use up before a new design becomes available). In such a problem a minimization objective becomes more appropriate. If we wish to meet these constraints whilst minimizing production costs then we can use the appropriate unit costs that we originally derived in Table 5-1 and we then have a problem formulation such that:

$$\text{Minimize} \quad 219A + 299B \quad (7\text{-}25)$$

$$\begin{aligned}
\text{subject to:} \quad 28A + 42B &\leq 16\,800 \\
12A + 6B &\leq 4\,800 \\
1A + 1B &\leq 600 \\
1A &\geq 100 \\
1B &\geq 150 \\
1A + 1B &= 450
\end{aligned}$$

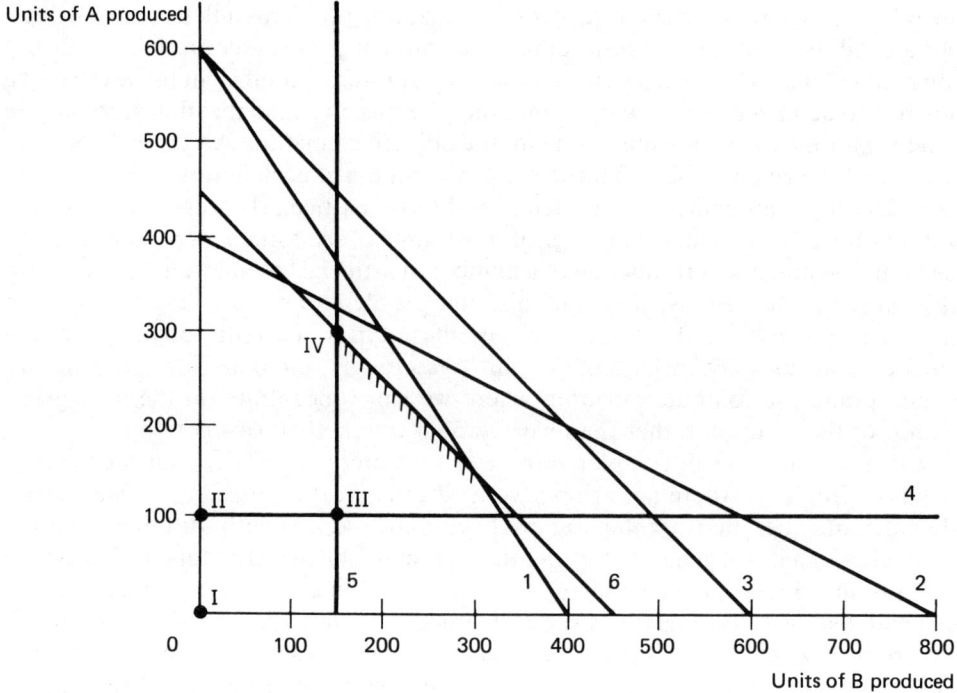

Figure 7-3 Minimization problem

This problem is shown on Fig. 7-3. The feasible area as such cannot be shown as the only feasible solutions occur on the line representing the last constraint. However, the appropriate part of this line is highlighted in Fig. 7-3 to assist identification and the relevant constraints are labelled 1–6. Introducing slack, surplus and artificial variables we then have:

$$28A + 42B + S_1 = 16\,800$$
$$12A + 6B + S_2 = 4\,800$$
$$1A + 1B + S_3 = 600$$
$$1A - S_4 + A_4 = 100$$
$$1B - S_5 + A_5 = 150$$
$$1A + 1B + A_6 = 450$$
$$A, B, S_1, S_2, S_3, S_4, S_5, A_4, A_5, A_6 \geq 0$$

and using the method of penalties the objective function is:

$$\text{Minimize} \quad 219A + 299B + 1000A_4 + 1000A_5 + 1000A_6 \qquad (7\text{-}26)$$

where we attach an arbitrary penalty of £1000 to each of the artificial variables. Here, unlike the maximization problems, the penalty value associated with an artificial variable takes a positive value. Given that we wish to keep the objective function value as low as

Tableau 7-12 Initial tableau

	A	B	S_1	S_2	S_3	S_4	S_5	A_4	A_5	A_6	Value
Cost	219	299	0	0	0	0	0	1000	1000	1000	
	28	42	1	0	0	0	0	0	0	0	16800
	12	6	0	1	0	0	0	0	0	0	4800
	1	1	0	0	1	0	0	0	0	0	600
	1	0	0	0	0	−1	0	1	0	0	100
	0	1	0	0	0	0	−1	0	1	0	150
	1	1	0	0	0	0	0	0	0	1	450

possible, this will ensure that artificial variables—with their high penalty costs—are removed from the basis as soon as possible. In tabular form this gives Tableau 7-12.

As before, the slack and artificial variables would form the initial solution, with A, B and the surplus variables taking zero values. We need, however, to introduce the penalties associated with the artificial variables into the objective function. This is done by using the last 3 rows of the tableau to eliminate the cost coefficients of the artificial variables in the objective function row. Thus, if we multiply row 5 by 1000 (the cost coefficient of A_4), row 6 by 1000 (the cost coefficient of A_5) and row 7 by 1000 (the cost coefficient of A_6) and subtract these from the objective function then we have a new objective function row given as:

Cost = −1781 −1701 0 0 0 1000 1000 0 0 0 −750000

where the value of £750 000 indicates the current penalty cost of having A_4, A_5 and A_6 in our solution at 100, 200 and 450 units respectively. Thus, the initial tableau becomes Tableau 7-13, giving both A and B equal to zero, and the tableau corresponds to point I in Fig. 7-3. In terms of the basic Simplex method, we now proceed in exactly the same way as for a maximization problem except for the first stage. When looking for a variable to enter the solution (i.e. become the pivot column) we look for a variable that will reduce costs most from its currently high penalty position, that is a variable that will lower the value of the objective function most rather than increasing the value as in a maximization problem. So, we choose the variable with the largest *negative* coefficient, the exact reverse of a maximization problem, and the iterative procedure will stop when there are no further negative values in the objective function row. So, looking at the tableau, variable A will enter the solution first and, having chosen the pivot column, we can proceed exactly as before. Logically, variable A enters first because it is the cheapest way of meeting one of the minimum production restrictions, as can be seen from the original objective function

Tableau 7-13 Initial solution

	A	B	S_1	S_2	S_3	S_4	S_5	A_4	A_5	A_6	Value
Cost	−1781	−1701	0	0	0	1000	1000	0	0	0	−750000
S_1	28	42	1	0	0	0	0	0	0	0	16800
S_2	12	6	0	1	0	0	0	0	0	0	4800
S_3	1	1	0	0	1	0	0	0	0	0	600
A_4	1	0	0	0	0	−1	0	1	0	0	100
A_5	0	1	0	0	0	0	−1	0	1	0	150
A_6	1	1	0	0	0	0	0	0	0	1	450

Tableau 7-14 First iteration

	A	B	S_1	S_2	S_3	S_4	S_5	A_4	A_5	A_6	Value
Cost	0	−1701	0	0	0	−781	1000	1781	0	0	−571 900
S_1	0	42	1	0	0	28	0	−28	0	0	14 000
S_2	0	6	0	1	0	12	0	−12	0	0	3 600
S_3	0	1	0	0	1	1	0	−1	0	0	500
A	1	0	0	0	0	−1	0	1	0	0	100
A_5	0	1	0	0	0	0	−1	0	1	0	150
A_6	0	1	0	0	0	0	0	0	0	1	350

showing costs of A and B. Using the same procedure as before (by calculating appropriate ratios), we determine that A_4 becomes the pivot row and the new tableau is Tableau 7-14. The current solution is:

$$A = 100 \quad S_1 = 14\,000 \quad A_4 = 0$$
$$B = 0 \quad S_2 = 3\,600 \quad A_5 = 150$$
$$S_3 = 500 \quad A_6 = 350$$
$$S_4 = 0$$
$$S_5 = 0$$
$$\text{Cost} = £571\,900$$

Tableau 7-14 corresponds to point II in Fig. 7-3. Production of A is 100 (the minimum required) and that of B is zero. The artificial variable associated with the minimum A production, A_4, is zero and has left the basis. The other two artificial variables still remain at this stage, although the value taken by A_6 has decreased by 100 to 350, given that we are now closer to the desired production level of 450 units. The three production constraints are non-binding with spare resources still available. The Simplex program now seeks an improved solution and by examining the objective function coefficients we see that the variable that will reduce costs most at this next stage is B, with the largest negative coefficient of −£1701. Accordingly, B is set to enter the basis and you may wish to confirm through your own calculations that variable A_5 will leave. The new tableau will then be Tableau 7-15. The current solution is:

Tableau 7-15 Second iteration

	A	B	S_1	S_2	S_3	S_4	S_5	A_4	A_5	A_6	Value
Cost	0	0	0	0	0	−781	−701	1781	1701	0	−316 750
S_1	0	0	1	0	0	28	42	−28	−42	0	7 700
S_2	0	0	0	1	0	12	6	−12	−6	0	2 700
S_3	0	0	0	0	1	1	1	−1	−1	0	350
A	1	0	0	0	0	−1	0	1	0	0	100
B	0	1	0	0	0	0	−1	0	1	0	150
A_6	0	0	0	0	0	1	1	−1	−1	1	200

$$A = 100 \quad S_1 = 7700 \quad A_4 = 0$$
$$B = 150 \quad S_2 = 2700 \quad A_5 = 0$$
$$S_3 = 350 \quad A_6 = 200$$
$$S_4 = 0$$
$$S_5 = 0$$
$$\text{Cost} = £316\,750$$

The tableau represents point III in Fig. 7-3, with production of both models at the minimum levels required. It is clear from the current solution that we have still not reached a feasible position, given that A_6 takes a non-zero value. We are still 200 units short of the required production level of 450 units. The three production constraints are still non-binding, although the two minimum production constraints (Eqs (7-13) and (7-20)) are binding, as they currently take zero values. Note also that we still cannot attach a real meaning to the objective function-cost—as it still includes a penalty value for A_6. The next iteration will bring S_4 into the basis and remove A_6 (again you may wish to confirm this from your own calculations). S_4, you will realize, is the variable relating to surplus production of A (that is, surplus to the minimum requirement of 100 units). This is the most cost-effective method of reducing costs further at this stage (again, logically because of the lower total cost per-unit figure for Model A). The new tableau is then as shown by Tableau 7-16. The current solution is:

Tableau 7-16 Third iteration

	A	B	S_1	S_2	S_3	S_4	S_5	A_4	A_5	A_6	Value
Cost	0	0	0	0	0	0	80	1 000	920	781	−110 550
S_1	0	0	1	0	0	0	14	0	−14	−28	2 100
S_2	0	0	0	1	0	0	−6	0	6	−12	300
S_3	0	0	0	0	1	0	0	0	1	−1	150
A	1	0	0	0	0	0	1	0	−1	1	300
B	0	1	0	0	0	0	−1	0	1	0	150
S_4	0	0	0	0	0	1	1	−1	−1	1	200

$$A = 300 \quad S_1 = 2100 \quad A_4 = 0$$
$$B = 150 \quad S_2 = 300 \quad A_5 = 0$$
$$S_3 = 150 \quad A_6 = 0$$
$$S_4 = 200$$
$$S_5 = 0$$
$$\text{Cost} = £110\,550$$

We recognize from Tableau 7-16 that we have reached the optimal solution. No further negative coefficients remain in the objective function row, and all artificial variables have been removed from the basis. The minimum cost combination of output is 300 units of A and 150 units of B with an associated total cost of £110 550. The tableau represents point IV on Fig. 7-3. The binding constraints are Eq. (7-20), relating to the output requirement of 450 units (you will realize that *any* constraint taking the form = must be binding in a feasible solution) and the constraint relating to minimum production of B, Eq. (7-19). We recognize this as a binding constraint as the associated surplus variable, S_5, takes a zero value. All other constraints are non-binding. It can be seen, therefore, that the solution of minimization problems using the Simplex method is readily undertaken. The only change in the program that is required is to choose as the entering variable that variable with the largest negative coefficient in the objective function row and to repeat the program until all coefficients in this row are non-negative. Because of the typical nature of minimization problems such calculations are not normally to be recommended on a manual basis.

Changing the objective function in a minimization problem

The approach taken in dealing with a minimization problem outlined in the previous section is not the only one that can be adopted. It is possible to amend the objective function in a minimization problem so that the basic method of the Simplex program does not need to be amended at all. This approach revolves around changing the minimization objective function to a maximization format. If we return to the previous minimization problem we had an objective function such that:

$$\text{Minimize} \quad 219A + 229B \tag{7-25}$$

$$\begin{aligned}
\text{subject to:} \quad 28A + 42B &\leq 16\,800 \\
12A + 6B &\leq 4\,800 \\
1A + 1B &\leq 600 \\
1A &\geq 100 \\
1B &\geq 150 \\
1A + 1B &= 450
\end{aligned}$$

We can show that this is the equivalent of requiring:

$$\text{Maximize} \quad -219A - 229B \tag{7-26}$$

$$\begin{aligned}
\text{subject to:} \quad 28A + 42B &\leq 16\,800 \\
12A + 6B &\leq 4\,800 \\
1A + 1B &\leq 600 \\
1A &\geq 100 \\
1B &\geq 150 \\
1A + 1B &= 450
\end{aligned}$$

That is, we now have a maximization problem but subject to the same constraints as before. In other words if we multiply the minimization objective function through by -1 then we transform the problem into a standard maximization formulation and we can proceed to solve as we do for any maximization problem. It is left as an end-of-chapter exercise for you to confirm that the new problem formulation involving Eq. (7-26) will generate the same optimal solution as the original problem formulation. It is largely a matter of personal preference (and sometimes determined by the computer software you are using) as to which method of dealing with minimization problems you adopt. The method of transforming the objective function into a maximization problem has the advantage that it leaves the Simplex algorithm unchanged. We can use exactly the same decision rules (about entering and leaving variables) in both minimization and maximization problems. The advantage of leaving the minimization objective function unaltered—and amending the Simplex program slightly—is that the logic of the solution method can be directly related to the business problem. We can readily see (and understand) why variables are selected to enter and leave the various tableaux on the basis of their effect on the objective function. Multiplying through by -1 (particularly for more complex problem formulations) may provide the same optimum solution but this may not be as easy to interpret, particularly for the business decision-maker whose mathematical abilities may be restricted in any case. Throughout the rest of this part we shall deal with minimization problems through the amended Simplex method and not through changing the objective function.

7-6 SUMMARY

The Simplex procedure that we have introduced in this chapter may seem unduly complex when taking into account the different types of constraint and objective functions that we would normally wish to incorporate into our model. In practice, however, the user of the technique need not normally concern herself or himself with the technical problems of solving Simplex iterations manually. Although the arithmetic necessary is not particularly taxing, most users ought, by this stage, to be using an appropriate computer package to determine the solution where it is necessary only to provide details of the constraints and objective function with the package taking care of the details of introducing slack, surplus and artificial variables as appropriate. A thorough understanding of the technique, as detailed in this chapter, is, however, a sound investment on the part of the student for it is only with such an adequate understanding that you will be able to extract full and accurate information from the final tableau. Additionally, it is only with an adequate understanding of this process that we are able to undertake a complete sensitivity analysis of the optimal solution we have found. It is to this topic that we turn in the next chapter.

STUDENT EXERCISES

7-1 Using the problem formulation involving Eqs (7-1) to (7-4), introduce an extra constraint with Eq. (7-19). Solve this problem manually working through the Simplex iterations and confirming your solution at each iteration on the appropriate graph.

7-2 Take the problem formulation as shown with Eq. (7-25) (together with the 6 corresponding constraints) and solve using a computer package.
   Amend the objective function to that shown in Eq. (7-26) and re-solve the problem. Compare your two solutions.

7-3 Assume that IMC are now considering a third type of monitor for their product range, Model C. This model would contribute £45 to profit, would require 40 hours of assembly time, 10 hours of inspection time and 1 microchip per unit produced.
   Formulate the new problem incorporating this added variable and solve for the optimal solution. Interpret the solution obtained.

7-4 For further practice at the Simplex method return to both the illustrative examples used in Chapter 6 and the exercises at the end of that chapter. For each of these problems you are required to:

(a) formulate the problem into a format suitable for the Simplex;
(b) (preferably) using a computer package input and solve each problem;
(c) for the optimal solution obtained return to the original problem formulation and ensure that the optimal values are appropriate for all the constraints specified;
(d) from step (c) determine which constraints are binding and which are not at the optimal solution.

8
SENSITIVITY ANALYSIS

In Chapter 7 we developed the Simplex method as a general program for solving problems involving any number of variables and constraints. Decision-makers are unlikely to be content simply with the information relating to the optimal solution to a particular problem that we have so far been able to provide. It will not be sufficient, in the context of the illustrative problem we have been investigating, simply to provide information on the optimal production combination of the two models. Management will also be interested in any additional information about the problem that can be brought to light. In particular they are likely to raise a number of 'what if' questions in the context of the optimal solution. That is, management will wish to know *what* changes will occur in the optimal solution *if* changes in the structure of the original problem occur:

- What if we expand the labour force in a particular department?
- What if labour costs change?
- What if selling prices change?
- What if Model A becomes more profitable or Model B less so?

And so forth. It is apparent why management will raise such 'what if' questions. Not only will they need to establish what actions they can take that will lead to further profit but they will also wish to undertake forward, or contingency, planning in case key parameters of the problem change unexpectedly in the future. In the context of a real-world problem, which might involve several hundred variables and several thousand constraints, it would be inappropriate (not to say expensive) to have to reformulate the original problem every time a question such as this was raised and then recompute and reinterpret the solution. Fortunately, the final tableau provided by the Simplex method contains all the information we are likely to need to evaluate such changes in the original problem structure. The process of resolving these 'what if' questions in the context of the optimal solution is known as *sensitivity analysis*. In this chapter we shall look at the way in which such analysis can be undertaken both to provide additional information about the optimal solution and to relax some of the more rigid assumptions underpinning LP as a technique. We shall look first of all at changes in the binding constraints in maximization problems. We shall then look at changes in the binding constraints in minimization problems. Our attention will then focus upon changes in the objective function parameters.

An important point to note at this stage is that in terms of sensitivity analysis much depends on the way information is presented on the computer output that you may be using. Different packages provide the same sensitivity information but are presented in different ways. We shall detail such information in the context of the tableaux format that we have developed. You should compare this with the output from whatever computer software you are using and the 'rules' that we shall develop in this chapter will need interpreting in the context of your own computer output. A further point to note is that if your computer program provides the sensitivity information that we shall be calculating then you may notice slight discrepancies in the figures. This may arise because our (manual) calculations involve coefficients only to 2 or 3 decimal places which may cause slight rounding differences.

8-1 CHANGES IN CONSTRAINTS: MAXIMIZATION PROBLEMS

In this section we examine the effect of changes in the right-hand side (RHS) value of binding constraints on the optimal solution to a maximization problem. We shall examine each of the three different types of constraint in turn: $\leqslant, \geqslant, =$. In order to facilitate an understanding of the logic of sensitivity analysis we shall first investigate the standard problem we have used throughout this section. To this problem formulation we shall then add a constraint of the form $\geqslant$ to see how sensitivity analysis can be applied and finally we shall introduce an equality constraint ($=$) and repeat the analysis.

Constraints $\leqslant$

Let us return to the original problem we investigated. The formulation is:

$$\text{Maximize} \quad 40A + 50B \tag{8-1}$$
$$\text{subject to:} \quad 28A + 42B \leqslant 16\,800 \tag{8-2}$$
$$12A + 6B \leqslant 4\,800 \tag{8-3}$$
$$1A + 1B \leqslant 600 \tag{8-4}$$

Tableau 8-1 Optimal solution

	A	B	S_1	S_2	S_3	Value
PROFIT	0	0	−1.07143	−0.83333	0	−22 000
B	0	1	0.03571	−0.08333	0	200
A	1	0	−0.01786	0.125	0	300
S_3	0	0	−0.01786	−0.04167	1	100

The optimal solution is shown in Tableau 8-1. The interpretation of the solution is:

Production of A = 300 units $S_1 = 0$
Production of B = 200 units $S_2 = 0$
             $S_3 = 100$

Profit = £22 000

The assembly constraint (Eq. 8-2) and the inspection constraint (Eq. 8-3) are both binding whilst the microchip constraint (Eq. 8-4) is non-binding and the associated slack variable, S_3, takes a value of 100 units. As we saw in the previous chapter there are no further positive coefficients in the objective function row in our final tableau and this means that no further changes can be made to our solution which will increase the value of the objective function further. There are, however, coefficients in the OF row which take negative values. In Tableau 8.1 these relate to S_1 and S_2, at -1.07 and -0.833 respectively. It is no coincidence that the only variables with negative coefficients in this row relate to the slack variables of the two constraints in our final solution that are binding—assembly and inspection hours. As we have seen previously, and as is confirmed in the final tableau, with S_1 and S_2 both equal to zero the two corresponding resources are fully utilized at the optimal solution. We have also seen previously (in Chapter 5) that we can calculate the opportunity cost associated with such scarce resources using simultaneous equations. This is, in fact, the interpretation we can give to these negative coefficients in the objective function row of the final tableau: they indicate the effect on the objective function of a change in the supply of resources to a particular constraint. (In LP the terms *opportunity cost*, *shadow price* and *dual value* are used interchangeably to refer to these coefficients.) Let us examine the coefficient of -1.07 for the S_1 variable.

In the optimal solution S_1 is a non-basic variable, that is, it takes a value of zero. There are, therefore, no unused assembly hours. The negative coefficient indicates that, if we were to force variable S_1 into the solution, then the value of the objective function would suffer. Here, if we forced S_1 into the basis—that is, if we *insist* on having unused assembly hours—then profit must decrease by £1.07 for each hour of assembly time we insist on not using, given that the only way we can have unused assembly hours is to reduce the production of the two models. This is, not surprisingly, a singularly useless piece of information for the decision-maker. However, an alternative—and, in managerial terms far more useful—interpretation can be applied. In fact, we have encountered this coefficient of -1.07 before in Chapter 5, Section 5-4. There we identified this coefficient as the opportunity cost relating to this binding resource constraint. The opportunity cost was interpreted as the increase in the value of the objective function that would occur if we could obtain an extra unit of this scarce resource over and above the current supply limit. Thus, if we can obtain an additional unit of this resource—an extra hour of assembly time—over and above our current supply of 16 800 hours then the objective function—profit—will increase by £1.07 as a result of the additional production that such extra resources facilitate. Such an opportunity cost allows us to quantify the scarcity value of this particular resource, that is, how much extra we would be prepared to pay to obtain extra supplies of this resource. How will this extra profit be achieved? Previously we had to rely on using simultaneous equations to calculate the effect on the solution of such a marginal change in one of the constraints. The information is now provided within the final tableau itself. The coefficients in the S_1 column indicate the *marginal* effect on the basic variables in the final solution of a *marginal* change in the supply of resources to this particular constraint. (More generally, the coefficients indicate the effect of a change in the right-hand side of the relevant constraint.) Thus, from the tableau, we can identify that an extra assembly hour, over and above the 16 800 hours currently available and fully utilized, will lead to the following effects on the current basic variables:

$$\begin{array}{ll} \text{effect on } B & +0.035\,71 \text{ units of B} \\ \text{effect on } A & -0.017\,86 \text{ units of A} \\ \text{effect on } S_3 & -0.017\,86 \text{ units of } S_1 \end{array}$$

That is, if we obtain an extra hour of assembly time the optimum solution will change such that:

Production of B increases to	200.035 71
Production of A decreases to	299.982 14
The number of unused microchips decreases to	99.982 14

and the net effect on profit will be:

Gain
0.035 71 units of B
0.035 71 × £50 unit profit
= + £1.7855 profit

Loss
0.017 86 units of A
0.017 86 × £40 unit profit
= − £0.7144 profit

Net gain = £1.7855 − £0.7144 = £1.071 profit

which, allowing for arithmetic rounding error, confirms the opportunity cost we have already identified from the tableau. In other words, an extra hour made available in the assembly department will generate an additional profit of £1.07. Effectively, by acquiring extra supplies of a scarce resource we will be pushing the line of this constraint outward, which in turn will allow the objective function, profit, to move further away from the origin by reallocating resources from Model A to Model B. Note that the profit coefficient of −1.07 in the tableau actually indicates an *increase* in profit that will occur if we have additional supplies of this resource available. The negative value—as with the value for profit—arises from the arithmetic procedure in the method.

Student activity
Reformulate the original problem to amend the assembly constraint to:

$$28A + 42B \leqslant 16\,801$$

and solve the amended problem using a computer package. Confirm the changes in the solution that have occurred.

The question still unresolved is: given that additional assembly hours will generate more profit, how much extra of this scarce resource should we acquire? In the context of our problem, for example, the company may be in the position of taking on additional labour in the assembly department. The opportunity cost of £1.07 indicates that it will be profitable to do so, provided the cost of these additional assembly hours is less than £5.07 (the normal labour cost of £4.00 plus the opportunity cost of £1.07). But, obviously, management will want to know whether to take on 1 extra person or 100. Logically, it would appear sensible that if we add 1 hour to assembly and profit increases by £1.07, then an extra 2 hours will add £2.14 to profit, 3 hours £3.21, and so on, with the comparable effect on the values of B, A and S_3. That is, if one extra assembly hour generates an increase in B production of 0.035 71 units then 2 extra assembly hours will lead to 2 times the increase—0.071 42 units—3 extra hours to 3 times the increase, and so on. However, from our perception of the problem, and the previous graphical approach, it is also obvious that this increase in production and profit arising from the acquisition of extra units of this resource cannot continue indefinitely. There must be a finite increase in this resource that is profitable. We can actually determine from the final tableau when this will occur. From the S_1 column coefficients (relating to the assembly constraint) we have seen that production of B increases, A decreases and the number of unused microchips decreases as we expand the assembly department. What we are effectively doing to increase profit is reallocating existing resources—assembly, inspection, microchips—from A to B. Eventually there will come a point when, with the increase of available assembly hours, we will have transferred all of some other resource to B production. Further expansion in assembly would then be pointless as we will not be able to increase B production any further as we will have exhausted either the fixed supply of inspection hours (i.e. A will be zero) or microchips (S_3 will be zero). At this point the constraints that are currently binding and their associated opportunity costs, which we have been using for our analysis, will change. Such a point will represent the maximum worthwhile increase in assembly hours. When will this occur? Again, we can determine this from the information in the tableau. With respect to production of A the acquisition of an extra unit of assembly time makes it worth while to reduce the units of A produced and transfer the resources released—together with the additional assembly hour—to production of B. As we have seen we are reducing A by 0.017 86 for each extra unit of assembly time we can acquire. Production of A is currently 300 units, so a simple calculation allows us to determine the maximum increase in assembly hours that is possible before production of A decreases to zero:

$$\frac{300}{0.017\,86} = 16\,800 \text{ extra assembly hours}$$

So, the maximum increase in assembly hours before production of A reaches zero (and transfer of other fixed resources from A to B ceases) is 16 800 hours. This figure indicates that if we acquire an *extra* 16 800 assembly hours, over and above what we already have, the new optimal solution will be to produce zero units of A. We will then have transferred all the resources currently required to produce 300 units of A to Model B. Similarly, with microchips. We currently have 100 unused microchips. These will be used (i.e. will decrease) at a rate of 0.017 86 units per additional hour of assembly time acquired. The ratio:

$$\frac{100}{0.017\,86} = 5600 \text{ extra assembly hours}$$

gives us the maximum increase in assembly hours before we exhaust the supply of microchips to use in additional B production. So, in our problem, we have calculated the ratios of the current value of a variable divided by its coefficient in the column relating to the constraint we are investigating. It is important to note that we have done this only for the *negative* coefficients, as positive coefficients in the S_1 column, e.g. for B, indicate the value of the variable is increasing rather than decreasing and logically there will be no limit to any such increase. The maximum increase in assembly hours that will be possible, therefore, will be indicated by the smallest of these ratios, here 5600. This will indicate the point where production of B can no longer increase simply by expanding the assembly department as we will have exhausted the fixed supply of some other resource—here microchips. What will the new optimum solution be? This can be determined from the tableau. The maximum worthwhile increase in assembly hours is 5600 hours. Production of B is currently 200 units and each extra assembly hour that we acquire adds 0.035 71 units to B production, so the increase in B is:

$$5600 \times 0.035\,71 = 200 \text{ units extra}$$

Therefore the new level of B is 400 units. Similarly, current A production is 300 units. Each extra hour of assembly time reduces A by 0.017 86 so the decrease in A will be:

$$5600 \times -0.017\,86 = -100 \text{ units}$$

Therefore the new level of A is 200 units. Finally, we currently have 100 unused microchips. Each extra assembly hour reduces this amount by 0.017 86, so the decrease in unused microchips will be:

$$5600 \times -0.017\,86 = -100 \text{ units}$$

So the new level of unused microchips will be 0. Lastly we come to the objective function. Current profit is £22 000. Each extra assembly hour generates an extra £1.07 profit, so the extra profit attained as we increase the supply of assembly time will be:

$$5600 \times 1.071\,43 = £6000 \text{ profit}$$

and the new profit level is £28 000. The new solution, therefore, if assembly is expanded up to its calculated limit, will be:

$$A = 200 \qquad S_1 = 0$$
$$B = 400 \qquad S_2 = 0$$
$$\text{Profit} = £28\,000 \qquad S_3 = 0$$

The optimal tableau, therefore, provides management with information about the effects of expansion of the assembly department. Profit can be increased from its current optimal level by acquiring up to an extra 5600 hours at a cost per labour hour of no more than £5.07 per hour. This information will enable management to employ additional personnel in this department at existing wage rates (or higher) or, perhaps, to offer overtime (with an appropriate bonus of no more than £1.07 per hour) to its existing workforce. At the new optimum, point I, all three constraints will be binding. Any further increase in the supply of assembly hours would not result in any further increase in profit. Let us briefly review what we have accomplished so far. We have identified the opportunity cost, or scarcity value, of one of the resources used in the production process. We have found that assembly hours are in short supply (given that the relevant constraint is binding). The appropriate coefficient from the OF row in the optimal tableau indicates what the effect on the OF value would be if we change the existing (and fully utilized) supply of assembly hours. The remaining coefficients in the appropriate column also allow us to predict the effect on the current optimal solution of changing the RHS of this constraint. Finally, by using these coefficients and the current basic variable values we are able to quantify the maximum change in the RHS of the constraint that could occur before the current optimal solution changes (and some currently basic variable becomes non-basic as some other constraint becomes binding).

Student activity
Using a computer package solve the problem again, but using an assembly constraint where there are 22 400 hours available, i.e. 16 800 + 5600. Then change the constraint to 22 401 and reinterpret the solution in terms of binding and non-binding constraints and their opportunity costs.

Constraints $\geqslant$

A similar sensitivity process can be undertaken on constraints in maximization problems which take the form $\geqslant$. Let us amend our basic problem formulation such that:

$$\text{Maximize} \quad 40A + 50B$$
$$\text{subject to:} \quad 28A + 42B \leqslant 16\,800$$
$$12A + 6B \leqslant 4\,800$$
$$1A + 1B \leqslant 600$$
$$1A \geqslant 325 \qquad (8\text{-}5)$$

The change in the basic problem is that we now have a $\geqslant$ constraint (Eq. (8-5)) which requires A to be at least 325 units. It is apparent that Eq. (8-5) will require a surplus variable (S_4) and an artificial variable (A_4). Using a penalty value of £1000 the optimal tableau for the problem can be derived as Tableau 8-2.

Tableau 8-2 Optimal solution

	A	B	S_1	S_2	S_3	S_4	A_4	Value
PROFIT	0	0	0	−8.33	0	−60	−940	−20 500
S_1	0	0	1	−7	0	−56	56	1400
B	0	1	0	0.166 67	0	2	−2	150
S_3	0	0	0	0	1	−1	1	125
A	1	0	0	0	0	−1	1	325

Interpretation: $A = 325$ $S_1 = 1400$
$B = 150$ $S_2 = 0$
$S_3 = 125$
$S_4 = 0$
Profit = £20 500

The optimal solution to the problem is to produce 150 units of B and 325 units of A, the minimum required. This will generate a profit of £20 500. There will be no surplus A production, so $S_4 = 0$. In terms of the three original constraints we have spare assembly hours (1400) and spare microchips (150) but no spare inspection time ($S_2 = 0$). Accordingly, the two binding constraints are the minimum A constraint (Eq. (8-5)) and the inspection time constraint. As usual with each binding constraint we would expect to be able to identify a scarcity value or opportunity cost. With S_2, which relates to a constraint taking the form $\leq$, we could apply the sensitivity analysis rules we developed in the previous section. There is an opportunity cost of £8.33 and we could determine the maximum change in available inspection time and the associated change in the optimal solution and the objective function. In this section, however, we shall examine Eq. (8-5). From the objective function row in Tableau 8-2 we see that S_4 also has a non-zero value, at $-£60$. We also know that this surplus variable relates to Eq. (8-5) and because $S_4 = 0$ we also know this constraint is binding. However, it obviously makes no sense to talk, in this context, of acquiring additional units of a resource as we can do for the inspection constraint. Instead we refer to unit changes in the right-hand side of the constraint. Because this constraint is binding, and as we know from our original problem, this minimum production requirement is adversely affecting profit. Suppose we were to increase this restriction by an extra unit, i.e. require at least 326 units of A. The opportunity cost figure indicates that profit would then *fall* by £60. On the other hand, if we were to relax this constraint to 324 units profit would then *increase* by £60. We can see the logic in this fairly readily. We know from the original problem (Tableau 8.1) that optimal production was 300 units for A and 200 for B. Such a solution (and the associated profit) is no longer feasible because of the new constraint requiring production of A to be at least 325 units. Equation (8-5) forces us—no matter what the effect on profit—to produce this minimum number of A. The fact that this is a binding constraint—there is no surplus A production—indicates that we are producing this quantity of A not because it is profitable to do so but because we are forced to. The opportunity cost figure of £60 indicates that if we were to relax this constraint (to require one unit less of Model A) then total profit would increase as a result. We can also determine from Tableau 8-2 what the effect on the rest of the optimal solution will be. The S_4 column coefficients, relating to this binding constraint, will allow us to quantify the precise effect of changing this constraint on the current values of the variables in the optimal solution. If this constraint changes to 324 then the column coefficients indicate that production of A will fall by 1 unit and that of B will increase by 2 units.

Student activity
Determine why this change in optimal production will occur.

The current solution is also constrained by inspection hours ($S_2 = 0$) which are all currently utilized. Producing 1 unit less of A will therefore release 12 inspection hours (Eq. (8-3)), which can then be used to produce 2 additional units of B, given that each unit of B needs only 6 inspection hours. The effect on profit will be an extra £100 from 2 units of B, less £40 for 1 unit less of A, i.e. £60 net. S_1 and S_3 (spare resources) will also decline by 56 and 1 unit respectively. Referring back to the problem formulation we know that 2 additional units of B will require 84 assembly hours and 2 microchips. Producing 1 unit less of A will require 28 fewer assembly hours and 1 microchip less. So the marginal effect on these resources (S_1 and S_3) will be to use an extra 56 assembly hours and 1 extra microchip. (Note that if the minimum production constraint were *increased* by one unit to 326, the S_4 column coefficients would again allow us to identify the effect on the current solution but in this case we would have to reverse the signs of the coefficients to identify the effect. That is, A would now increase by 1 and B would decrease by 2, while the new solution would require 56 fewer assembly hours and 1 less microchip than currently. Profit would decline by £60.) As before we also require to identify the maximum change in this constraint that can occur before the optimum point and the currently binding constraints change totally and our sensitivity analysis becomes invalid. We can proceed as before, using the S_4 column coefficients which are *negative* and the current values of the basic variables to identify the maximum change in this constraint that can occur.

Student activity
Calculate the appropriate ratios from Tableau 8-2 and determine the maximum change in the RHS of Eq. (8-5) that can occur and the associated effect on the current optimal solution.

Taking appropriate ratios (remembering that we are concerned only with the negative column coefficients) we have:

$$\frac{1400}{56} = 25$$

$$\frac{125}{1} = 125$$

$$\frac{325}{1} = 325$$

to find that the maximum change in constraint Eq. (8-5) is 25 units (given as before by the smallest of the ratios). The new solution would give B at 200 and A at 300 (i.e. the minimum value for A is now $325 - 25 = 300$). This obviously is the original optimum solution. Profit would be £20 500 + (60 × 25) = £22 000 and in terms of spare resources S_1 and S_2 will now be zero. There are no unused assembly or inspection hours but there are 100 unused microchips ($S_3 = 100$). At this stage it will again be worth reiterating the importance of such sensitivity analysis as a source of management information. Assume that IMC has a contract with a customer to supply at least 325 units of Model A per week. We can—as in Tableau 8-2—find the optimal production combination under the existing constraints. But, having conducted our sensitivity analysis, we can now see a way of improving profit further. This contract has an opportunity cost to IMC of £60 per unit. That is, the contract is preventing IMC from achieving higher profits than it is currently attaining. Accordingly, it will be worth while trying to renegotiate this contract with the customer. If IMC can reduce this contractual obligation to less than 325 units then their profit will increase as a result (with a reduction to 300 units being most desirable). Management may even wish to consider paying the customer to renegotiate the contract. A renegotiation fee of anything up to £1500 (25 units at £60) would be in IMC's interests.

Constraints =

Finally, for maximization problems we illustrate sensitivity analysis with an equality constraint. We amend our original problem (formulated in Eqs. (8-1) to (8-4)) such that we have a formulation and an optimal tableau as shown below:

Maximize $40A + 50B$

subject to: $28A + 42B \leq 16\,800$

$12A + 6B \leq 4\,800$

$1A + 1B \leq 600$

$1A + 1B = 450$ \hfill (8-6)

You will remember that we examined this constraint earlier in Chapter 7 where, because of a change in marketing strategy, we required an exact production level to use up all available packing cartons in the next production period. The final tableau for this problem is derived as Tableau 8-3.

Tableau 8-3 Optimal solution

	A	B	S_1	S_2	S_3	A_4	Value
PROFIT	0	0	−0.7143	0	0	−1020	−21000
B	0	1	0.07143	0	0	−2	300
S_2	0	0	0.4286	1	0	−24	1200
S_3	0	0	0	0	1	−1	150
A	1	0	−0.07143	0	0	3	150

Interpretation: $A = 150$ $S_1 = 0$

$B = 300$ $S_2 = 1200$

$S_3 = 150$

Profit = £21 000

Here we are producing 150 units of A and 300 units of B to meet the exact production requirement of Eq. (8-6). This generates a profit of £21 000 and requires all assembly resources ($S_1 = 0$) but leaves spare inspection ($S_2 = 1200$) and microchip resources ($S_3 = 150$). The binding constraints, therefore, are the assembly constraint and, of necessity, the production constraint of 450 units. As can be seen from the tableau, S_1, which relates to a constraint taking the form $\leq$, has a shadow price of £0.7143 and, again, we could carry out full sensitivity analysis in exactly the same way as before. But what of the other binding constraint relating to our exact equality requirement? It also must have a scarcity value. However, the only other non-zero coefficient in the objective function row in the final tableau relates to the artificial variable, A_4, with a coefficient of −£1020. This, in fact, is the opportunity cost for the production constraint ($A + B = 450$), which, you will remember, had neither slack nor surplus variables associated with it but does have an artificial variable, A_4, in the Simplex formulation. The associated coefficient of −£1020, however, includes the arbitrary penalty value that we incorporated into the original objective function. To identify the true opportunity cost for this constraint we simply remove the initial penalty value (£1000) to give a figure of −£20. Interpretation is then identical to any other opportunity cost figure. The figure indicates the effect on the objective function value if the right-hand side of this (necessarily) binding constraint changes. We can use the opportunity cost of A_4 to assess the impact of pushing the production constraint upwards to 451: that is, requiring $A + B = 451$. The coefficients in the A_4 column can be interpreted as the change in the current basic variables that would occur as a result of changing this binding constraint. There would be a decrease in B of 2 units, and an increase in A of 3 (i.e. a net change in total production of $+1$ unit as required by the new RHS). This change in production would require an extra 24 inspection hours (spare inspection hours, S_2, are reduced by this amount) and an extra 1 microchip (spare microchips, S_1, are reduced by this amount). The opportunity cost of £20 can also be confirmed. An extra 3 units of Model A will be produced (profit £120) and two units of B less (loss of profit of £100) with the net effect on profit, therefore, of £20, confirming the opportunity cost coefficient identified in the tableau.

Student activity
Determine the maximum possible increase in the RHS of constraint Eq. (8-6).

The maximum increase in this constraint can again be determined from the lowest ratio of values to negative A_4 column coefficients. Here, this will be 50 (1200/24) and implies a change in the solution to B at 200 and A at 300 if the equality constraint is amended to $A + B = 500$. It is apparent that this will bring us back to the original problem solution shown in Tableau 8-1. Again, it is worth while stressing the potential management importance of such sensitivity analysis. Management have adopted a policy of requiring all the old-style packing cartons to be utilized in the next production period. From the sensitivity analysis we know that this decision is costing IMC £1000 in lost profits (£20 × 50 units). It is now up to management to decide whether this opportunity cost—incurred by requiring existing packing cartons to be used up—is worth while. We could equally examine the effect of reducing the total level of production, reducing constraint Eq. (8-6) to 449 units. This implies less production and hence less profit and the shadow price indicates the reduction in profit that would occur. How would this be achieved? Again the column coefficients indicate the effect on the current solution but in this case the signs of the coefficients must now be reversed to identify the direction of the effect. Thus, production of A will fall by 3 units, B will increase by 2 units and so the net effect on profit will be $-£20$ ($-3 \times 40 + 2 \times 50$). This new level of production will require 24 fewer inspection hours, so S_2 will increase by 24. Similarly, 1 less microchip will be required, so S_3 increases by 1. Again, full sensitivity analysis can be undertaken, but we should remember that in this case we would be looking for the smallest ratio of values to *positive* coefficients, here at 50 (150/3) for S_3. This indicates that the production constraint can be forced downward by 50 (to $A + B = 400$) before the current optimal tableau changes and the sensitivity analysis is no longer valid. At this point we would be producing 400 units of B and zero units of A.

8-2 MINIMIZATION PROBLEMS

You will be gratified to know that sensitivity analysis carried out on minimization problems is virtually identical to that undertaken on maximization problems. The logic of the analysis follows the same pattern as before. We only need to amend some of the approaches slightly. Again, we will examine such analysis in the light of each of the three types of constraint, $\leq, \geq, =$.

Constraints ⩽

Let us examine the problem we have just used in the previous section but with a change to the objective function. In this case, given the same exact production requirement of $A + B = 450$, the company has decided to identify the optimum solution in terms of minimum cost rather than maximum profit, so the problem becomes:

$$\text{Minimize} \quad 219A + 299B \tag{8-7}$$
$$\text{subject to:} \quad 28A + 42B \leqslant 16\,800$$
$$12A + 6B \leqslant 4\,800$$
$$1A + 1B \leqslant 600$$
$$1A + 1B = 450$$

By introducing an artificial variable for the last constraint and using the method of penalties (with an arbitrary penalty value of 1000), the final tableau is as shown by Tableau 8-4.

Tableau 8-4 Optimal solution

	A	B	S_1	S_2	S_3	A_4	Value
Cost	0	0	0	13.3333	0	621	−106 550
S_1	0	0	1	2.33333	0	−56	2 800
A	1	0	0	0.16667	0	−1	350
S_3	0	0	0	0	1	−1	150
B	0	1	0	−0.16667	0	2	100

Interpretation: $A = 350$ $S_1 = 2800$
 $B = 100$ $S_2 = 0$
           $S_3 = 150$
           $A_4 = 0$
 Cost = £106 550

The solution to meet these constraints, whilst simultaneously minimizing cost, therefore requires A to be 350 units and B 100. Associated cost will be £106 550 and the two binding constraints will be inspection hours and the equality constraint ($S_2, A_4 = 0$). There will be spare assembly hours and spare microchips. Remembering that with minimization problems opportunity costs in the final tableau will be *positive*, we can see from the coefficients in the OF row that one of the binding constraints is the constraint relating to inspection time, which takes the form ⩽, with an associated opportunity cost of £13.33. Interpretation of this coefficient is virtually the same as with a maximization problem. If we change the right-hand side of this constraint costs will change by £13.33. The coefficients in the S_2 column, as usual, indicate the effect on the current basic variable values. So, for example, if we can acquire an extra hour of inspection time then the current optimal solution will change such that we will increase production of Model A by 0.166 67 units, decrease that of Model B by the same amount and require 2.3333 fewer hours of assembly time (i.e. S_1 increases). As a result costs *fall* by £13.33. We can readily confirm the logic of this. Reducing the output of Model B will release 1 inspection hour (0.166 67 units × 6, the inspection hours required per unit of B). To this we add the extra inspection hour that we have added to the RHS of this constraint and these 2 hours allow us to produce an extra 0.16667 units of Model A (given that each unit of A requires 12 hours of inspection time). This switch in production from B to A will release 2.3333 assembly hours (+ 0.16667 × 28 − 0.16667 × 42). There will be no change in the number of microchips required, as both models have the same per-unit resource requirements. The total cost will obviously fall as we are switching production away from B (a high-cost model) to A (a low-cost model). A decrease in the supply of this resource, however, will have exactly the opposite effect and, again, we would reverse the signs of the various coefficients to predict that with 1 less inspection hour available production of A would decline and that of B increase with an increase in the demand for assembly hours. Net effect on costs would be an *increase* of £13.33.

Student activity
Calculate the maximum possible change in this binding constraint and the new optimal solution.

Again, we can carry out full sensitivity analysis on this constraint in the usual way. The maximum increase in inspection hours will be given by the lowest ratio of values to negative S_4 column coefficients. Here with only one negative coefficient this would be:

$$100/0.16667 = 600$$

implying that the maximum potential increase in inspection hours is 600. The new solution with these additional resources would be:

$$A = 450 \quad S_1 = 4200$$
$$B = 0 \quad S_2 = 0$$
$$\qquad\qquad S_3 = 150$$
$$\qquad\qquad A_4 = 0$$
$$\text{Cost} = £98\,550$$

Our new solution, given the extra 600 inspection hours, would be to produce 450 units of A and no units of B (the total production constraint of 450 units, of course, is still binding). This will incur costs of £98 550, increase the unused amount of assembly hours and leave the number of unused microchips unchanged. The managerial implications of this analysis are clear. If management insist on this total production limit of 450 units then they should seek to acquire additional supplies of inspection hours to bring total costs down by enabling increased production of A at the expense of B. Clearly, A is the least-cost model but also requires more inspection hours per unit than B.

Constraints ⩾

To illustrate sensitivity analysis for this type of binding constraint let us examine the minimization problem below and its optimal tableau (Tableau 8-5).

$$\text{Minimize} \quad 219A + 299B$$
$$\text{subject to:} \quad 28A + 42B \leqslant 16\,800$$

$$12A + 6B \leq 4800$$
$$1A + 1B \leq 600$$
$$1A \geq 100 \qquad (8\text{-}8)$$
$$1B \geq 150 \qquad (8\text{-}9)$$
$$1A + 1B = 450$$

Tableau 8-5 Optimal tableau

	A	B	S_1	S_2	S_3	S_4	S_5	A_4	A_5	A_6	Value
Cost	0	0	0	0	0	0	80	1000	920	781	−110550
S_1	0	0	1	0	0	0	14	0	−14	−28	2100
S_2	0	0	0	1	0	0	−6	0	6	−12	300
S_3	0	0	0	0	1	0	0	0	1	−1	150
A	1	0	0	0	0	0	1	0	−1	1	300
B	0	1	0	0	0	0	−1	0	1	0	150
S_4	0	0	0	0	0	1	1	−1	−1	1	200

The interpretation of the tableau is:

$A = 300 \qquad S_1 = 2100 \qquad A_4 = 0$
$B = 150 \qquad S_2 = 300 \qquad A_5 = 0$
$\qquad\qquad\quad S_3 = 150 \qquad A_6 = 0$
$\qquad\qquad\quad S_4 = 200$
$\qquad\qquad\quad S_5 = 0$
$\text{Cost} = £110\,550$

The binding constraints relate to the production combination constraint ($A + B = 450$) and the minimum production constraint, $B \geq 150$. It is the latter we wish to investigate. We see from the S_5 column in Tableau 8-4 that this binding constraint has an opportunity cost of £80. How can this be interpreted? As with maximization problems this figure indicates the effect on the objective function of changing the right-hand side of a constraint taking the form $\geq$. If we examine S_5 then if we increase this constraint to:

$$B \geq 151$$

costs will increase by £80. However, in order to assess the impact on the current values of variables in the solution we must *reverse* the signs of the coefficients in the S_5 column. That is, if we are required to produce an extra unit of B then:

S_1 decreases by 14
S_2 increases by 6
S_3 remains unchanged
A decreases by 1
S_4 decreases by 1

Again, the logic of these changes is apparent. The other binding constraint in this problem is that requiring production to be exactly 450 units. Accordingly, if we wish to increase production of B by 1 unit then A must decrease by 1 unit. This will affect the demand for production resources: we will require 14 hours *more* of assembly time

(42 − 28), 6 hours *less* of inspection time (6 − 12) and no change in the number of microchips (1 − 1). Again, full sensitivity analysis can be undertaken, but in this case we would identify the maximum increase in this constraint by finding the smallest ratio of values to *positive* S_5 coefficients. In this case the smallest of these ratios will be 150 (= 2100/14 for assembly) and the new optimal solution would then be:

$$A = 150 \quad S_1 = 0 \quad A_4 = 0$$
$$B = 300 \quad S_2 = 1200 \quad A_5 = 0$$
$$ \quad S_3 = 150 \quad A_6 = 0$$
$$ \quad S_4 = 50$$
$$ \quad S_5 = 0$$
$$\text{Cost} = £122\,550$$

Student activity

Determine the new optimal solution if this constraint changes to:

$$B \geqslant 149$$

In the case of a reduction in the RHS of this type of constraint in a minimization problem we can interpret the column coefficients directly without having to reverse their signs. However, in order to assess the effect on the objective function we must reverse the sign of the appropriate opportunity cost coefficient, here £80. The effect of changing this constraint, therefore, will be:

B decreases by 1
S_1 increases by 14
S_2 decreases by 6
S_3 remains unchanged
A increases by 1
S_4 increases by 1
Cost decreases by £80

Again, the potential management importance of such sensitivity analysis becomes apparent. It is clear from our understanding of this solution (and the previously related problems) that the minimum production requirement for B (currently at 150) is adversely affecting cost. If possible we should try to reduce this minimum requirement below 150 units and thereby reduce total costs. We can readily confirm that maximum worthwhile reduction would be 50 units of B.

Constraints =

Finally, to illustrate sensitivity analysis in a minimization problem involving constraints taking the form =, let us return to Tableau 8-5 and the problem it represents. In that problem we had a constraint such that:

$$A + B = 450$$

and from the final tableau we see that this constraint of necessity is binding. As with a maximization problem this constraint has neither a slack nor a surplus variable associated with it but only an artificial variable, A_6. From Tableau 8-5 we see that the artificial variable has an opportunity cost of £219 (£1000 – £781, where £1000 is the arbitrary penalty value we used). This indicates that if we change the right-hand side of this constraint the objective function will change by £219. For example, if we now require to produce a total of 451 units of A and B total cost will increase by £219. The coefficients in the A_6 column indicate how this extra production will be achieved and the effects on all the current basic variables. The effects will be:

> 1 unit extra of A;
> no change in production of B;
> 28 extra hours of assembly are required (S_1 decreases by 28);
> 12 extra hours of inspection are required (S_2 decreases by 12);
> 1 extra microchip is required (S_3 decreases by 1);
> 1 extra surplus unit of A (S_4 increases by 1).

Naturally, the net effect on costs can readily be confirmed to be £219. Again, we would identify the smallest ratio of values to negative A_6 coefficients to identify the maximum change in this constraint. Here, it would be 25 (300/12), indicating that the maximum increase in the RHS of this constraint would be 25 (to 475) before we exhaust the available supply of unused inspection hours. Similarly, we could examine the effect of reducing the RHS of this constraint to 449 units. In this case we would need to reverse the signs of the appropriate coefficients in order to complete the analysis.

8-3 SUMMARY OF THE INTERPRETATION OF CHANGES IN BINDING CONSTRAINTS

You may feel that sensitivity analysis is a particularly complex task. In practice, if you fully understand the technique and its analysis then you should have no difficulty interpreting the final tableau in terms of changes in any one of the binding constraints. In fact we can neatly summarize sensitivity analysis as we have examined it thus far. Table 8-1 summarizes the effect of changing the RHS of a binding constraint in a maximization problem whilst Table 8-2 shows the equivalent effects in a minimization problem.

The general rules in Tables 8-1 and 8-2 can readily be applied to examine a *decrease* in the RHS of a binding constraint simply by reversing the direction of each number. You should use such rules cautiously, however, rather than mechanically. It is particularly important that such sensitivity analysis is always interpreted in the context of the problem under investigation. Failure to do so may lead not only to a misinterpretation of the importance of such information but may also fail to reveal an incorrect formulation of the original problem.

8-4 CHANGES IN THE OBJECTIVE FUNCTION: BASIC VARIABLES

In addition to examining changes in the RHS of a particular constraint management will also be interested in applying equivalent sensitivity analysis to the objective function. Such an interest may arise from a desire to develop contingency plans: for example, how should

Table 8-1 Maximization problems: interpretation of the effects of a 1 unit *increase* in the RHS of a binding constraint

Constraint type $\leq$
- The relevant column is that of the associated slack variable.
- The opportunity cost coefficient will be negative.
- The coefficient indicates the increase in the objective function.
- The column coefficients indicate the change in the values of the basic variables.
- The maximum change is determined by the smallest ratio of value to negative coefficients in the slack variable column.

Constraint type $\geq$
- The relevant column is that of the associated surplus variable.
- The opportunity cost coefficient will be negative.
- The coefficient indicates the decrease in the objective function value.
- The column coefficients must have their signs reversed to indicate the change in the values of the basic variables.
- The maximum change is determined by the smallest ratio of value to positive coefficients in the relevant column.

Constraint type $=$
- The relevant column is that of the associated artificial variable.
- The opportunity cost coefficient will be negative (after removing the arbitrary penalty value used).
- The coefficient indicates the increase in the objective function value.
- The column coefficients indicate the change in the values of the basic variables.
- The maximum change is determined by the smallest ratio of values to negative coefficients in the relevant column.

Table 8-2 Minimization problems: interpretation of the effects of a 1 unit *increase* in the RHS of a binding constraint

Constraint type $\leq$
- The relevant column is that of the associated slack variable.
- The opportunity cost coefficient will be positive.
- The coefficient indicates the increase in the objective function value.
- The column coefficients indicate the change in the basic variables.
- The maximum change is determined by the smallest ratio of values to negative coefficients in the relevant column.

Constraint type $\geq$
- The relevant column is that of the associated surplus variable.
- The opportunity cost coefficient will be positive.
- The coefficient indicates the increase in the objective function value.
- The column coefficients must have their signs reversed to indicate the change in the basic variables.
- The maximum change is determined by the smallest ratio of values to positive coefficients in the relevant column.

Constraint type $=$
- The relevant column is that of the associated artificial variable.
- The opportunity cost coefficient will be positive after the penalty value has been incorporated.
- The coefficient indicates the increase in the objective function value.
- The column coefficients indicate the change in the basic variables.
- The maximum change is determined by the smallest ratio of values to negative coefficients in the relevant column.

the company react, in terms of its current optimal production combination, should the relevant costs or prices of one of the two products change? Suppose the profit margin on Model B increases. Whilst this will naturally increase the total profit earned by IMC, will it require a change in the optimum production levels of the two models? Equally, management may wish to undertake such analysis on the objective function because, as we have indicated previously, the parameters used may not be strictly deterministic. There may be some uncertainty about specific values in the objective function (Are we *absolutely* sure that Model A earns *exactly* £40 profit, for example?) and we may wish to examine the extent to which the current optimal solution will change in response to changes in the objective function coefficients used. As before, we could work through the amended problem from the very beginning, reformulating, resolving and reinterpreting the new problem, but, again, the information needed is available directly from the final tableau. However, for this aspect of sensitivity analysis we must distinguish two separate situations:

- Changes for basic variables (those variables in the current optimum solution).
- Changes for non-basic variables (those not in the current optimum solution).

To illustrate sensitivity analysis involving the objective function we shall use an amended version of our original problem. IMC are considering producing a third type of computer monitor, Model C, which will be a mid-range product in between Models A and B. It has a profit contribution of £45 and requires 40 hours of assembly time, 10 hours of inspection time and 1 microchip. The new problem formulation is shown below and its corresponding optimal solution in Tableau 8-6.

$$\text{Maximize} \quad 40A + 50B + 45C \quad (8\text{-}10)$$

$$\text{subject to:} \quad 28A + 42B + 40C \leq 16\,800 \quad (8\text{-}11)$$

$$12A + 6B + 10C \leq 4\,800 \quad (8\text{-}12)$$

$$1A + 1B + 1C \leq 600 \quad (8\text{-}13)$$

Tableau 8-6 Optimal tableau

	A	B	C	S_1	S_2	S_3	Value
PROFIT	0	0	−6.1905	−1.07143	−0.83333	0	−22000
B	0	1	0.5952	0.03572	−0.08333	0	200
A	1	0	0.5357	−0.01786	0.125	0	300
S_3	0	0	−0.1309	−0.01786	−0.0417	1	100

The interpretation of the tableau is:

$$A = 300 \quad S_1 = 0$$
$$B = 200 \quad S_2 = 0$$
$$C = 0 \quad S_3 = 100$$
$$\text{Profit} = £22\,000$$

Thus the solution to this new problem is effectively the same as to our original problem. We are producing 300 units of A, 200 units of B and 0 units of C. The assembly and inspection constraints are binding and profit is £22 000. However, our focus at this stage of the analysis is upon the objective function, Eq. (8-10). It is clear from our knowledge of the technique that a change in one of the parameters of the objective function—one of the profit figures in this case—*may* lead to a change in the optimal allocation of resources. We have to say 'may' because, at this stage, we have no means of knowing for certain what the consequences of a change in one of the three profit figures will be. Effectively, we wish to determine how sensitive the current optimal solution is to changes in these coefficients. We shall first examine the relevant coefficients for the basic variables—those variables taking non-zero values in the optimal solution: here Models A and B.

Changes in coefficients: basic variables

If we wish to determine how sensitive the current optimum solution is for a basic variable— that is, one taking a non-zero value in the current optimum solution—the approach we can take is to calculate by how much the contribution coefficient of that variable in the objective function could change before affecting the current optimum resource allocation. In our problem we have two basic variables. Effectively we wish to determine by how much profit per unit of Model A or B must change before affecting our optimum product mix of 300 units of A and 200 units of B. Let us examine Model A, currently contributing £40 per unit profit. As we saw in Chapter 5 when we introduced the graphical method, the optimal solution is determined both by the feasible area and by the slope of the objective function. Assuming the profit coefficients for Models B and C remain constant, we can see that if A's profit coefficient increased there would come a point where the slope of the objective function changed so much that we would move to a different optimum point—that is, to a different corner of the feasible area. In effect, producing A would become so much more profitable that we would abandon production of B entirely. Conversely, if A's profit contribution fell then the reverse would eventually happen: we would cease production of A. The important point, of course, is to be able to determine when this switch of production will occur. To examine how we can assess such a change we shall work through the problem and the various tableaux with a new profit coefficient for Model A. Let us assume that A's profit figure is represented as £$(40 + k)$ where k is an appropriate number representing the change in A's profit figure. k could be large or small and, importantly, could be positive or negative. Thus our objective function becomes:

$$\text{Maximize} \quad (40 + k)A + 50B + 45C \tag{8-14}$$

with the rest of the problem formulation unchanged. We shall now proceed to work through the various Simplex iterations to examine the effect that k has on the solution. The reason for doing this, remember, is to try to ascertain what value(s) k must take in order for the current optimal solution to change. Effectively we are trying to determine by how much A's profit contribution must change in order to alter the optimal solution. You are strongly advised to work through the subsequent calculations yourself as we progress. Our initial tableau is then as in Tableau 8-7, and using the Simplex program the pivot element is 42 (column B, row S_1) and the new tableau is as shown by Tableau 8-8. The next pivot element is 8 (column A, row S_2) with the subsequent tableau as Tableau 8-9.

Apart from the objective function row, Tableau 8-9 is recognizably the same as Tableau 8-6 which represented the original optimal solution. Let us examine the OF row in

Tableau 8-7 Initial tableau

	A	B	C	S_1	S_2	S_3	Value
PROFIT	(40 + k)	50	45	0	0	0	0
S_1	28	42	40	1	0	0	16 800
S_2	12	6	10	0	1	0	4 800
S_3	1	1	1	0	0	1	600

Tableau 8-8 First iteration

	A	B	C	S_1	S_2	S_3	Value
PROFIT	(6.6667 + k)	0	− 2.619 05	− 1.190 476	0	0	− 20 000
B	0.666 67	1	0.952 38	0.023 81	0	0	400
S_2	8	0	4.285 71	− 0.142 857	1	0	2 400
S_3	0.333 333	0	0.047 62	− 0.023 81	0	1	200

Tableau 8-9 Second iteration

	A	B	C	S_1	S_2	S_3	Value
PROFIT	0	0	(− 6.190 479 − 0.5357k)	(− 1.071 43 + 0.017 86k)	(− 0.833 33 − 0.125k)	0	− 22 000
B	0	1	0.595 24	0.035 72	− 0.083 33	0	200
A	1	0	0.535 71	− 0.017 86	0.125	0	300
S_3	1	0	0.130 95	− 0.017 86	− 0.041 67	1	100

Tableau 8-9 in detail. We have three non-zero values in this row: for C, S_1 and S_2. In order for the Simplex program to stop at this stage (in other words, for Tableau 8-9 to be optimal) then we require all such coefficients to be negative. Let us examine each in turn. For C we have $(-6.1905 - 0.5357k)$ where k represents the change in A's profit contribution. We therefore require:

$$(-6.190\,479 - 0.5357k) \leq 0$$
$$-0.5357k \leq 6.190\,479$$
$$k \leq 6.190\,479/-0.5357$$
$$k \leq -11.56$$

In other words, as long as k is less than − £11.56 then the coefficient associated with C will remain negative and, therefore, will not require a subsequent iteration. We can repeat this analysis on the other two non-zero coefficients.

Student activity
Determine the appropriate limits for k for the other two non-zero coefficients in Tableau 8-9.

For S_1 the appropriate calculations are:

$$(-1.071\,43 + 0.017\,86k) \leq 0$$
$$0.017\,86k \leq 1.071\,43$$
$$k \leq 1.071\,43/0.017\,86$$
$$k \leq 59.99$$

and for S_2:

$$(-0.833\,33 - 0.125k) \leq 0$$
$$-0.125k \leq -0.833\,88$$
$$k \leq -0.833\,33/0.125$$
$$k \leq -6.67$$

So, summarizing the values for k we have:

$$\begin{array}{ll} C & k \leq -\pounds 11.56 \\ S_1 & k \leq \pounds 59.99 \\ S_2 & k \leq -\pounds 6.67 \end{array}$$

The k values we have calculated indicate the change in A's profit coefficient that can occur before the current optimal solution changes and one of the current non-basic variables (C, S_1, S_2) becomes basic. Thus, for example, if A's profit contribution were to fall to below £28.44 (i.e. £40.00 − £11.56) then C would become basic and enter the solution (thereby forcing A out of the solution and changing the optimal production combination). A similar interpretation can be placed on − £6.67. For the figure of £59.99 the opposite interpretation is appropriate. If A's profit increases to more than £99.99 (i.e. £40.00 + £59.99) then the current optimal solution will change. A will become so profitable that we will cease production of B and devote all our scarce resources to production of A. It is apparent in this example that we have two negative values for k. It is clear that it is the least negative of these (i.e. the one closest to zero) that will be critical in terms of assessing the maximum possible reduction in A's profit contribution. Here the figure of − £6.67 indicates the maximum reduction in A's profit. Had we had two positive k values then we would again have chosen the least positive (i.e. closest to zero) as being the most restrictive. This approach, therefore, allows us to determine the maximum changes (both increase and decrease) in a basic variable's OF coefficient that are possible before the current optimal solution changes. It is also apparent that the method we have developed thus far is somewhat clumsy and tedious, having to introduce k into the objective function and recalculate the various Simplex tableaux. In fact this is not necessary once we understand the principles of sensitivity analysis on the objective function. We can derive exactly the same figures for k from the original optimal tableau. If we return to Tableau 8-6 and examine the OF row and the A row (given that we are undertaking analysis on the A coefficient) then we can simply divide the OF row by the A row:

	A	B	C	S_1	S_2	S_3
PROFIT	0	0	− 6.1905	− 1.07143	− 0.83333	0
A	1	0	0.5357	− 0.01786	0.125	0
Ratio	0	0	− 11.56	59.99	− 6.67	0

to arrive at the same figures as we did by manipulating the tableaux involving the k value. We now know, therefore, that as long as A's profit is between £33.33 and £99.99 then the current optimal solution will remain unchanged. We could equally undertake such analysis on the other basic variable, B. In this case we would use the B row coefficients to determine the range of maximum variation in B's profit contribution before the current optimal solution changes. This is left as an end-of-chapter exercise.

Changes in coefficients: non-basic variables

Our attention, however, in such analysis will not always focus solely upon basic variables. We may be equally interested in the current non-basic variables. In our example Model C is non-basic. That is, under the existing problem parameters it is not profitable to produce Model C. The question naturally arises: when will it be profitable to produce this model? In the context of the sensitivity analysis we have undertaken we would wish to be able to determine by how much C's objective function coefficient must change in order for the current optimal solution to change. We could easily repeat the illustrative method developed in the previous section—altering C's profit contribution by k and working through the Simplex program to determine the effect this will have on the final tableau and then assessing the implications of the value of k for the current optimal solution. At this stage, however, this approach is not necessary (although it is set as an end-of-chapter exercise to confirm what we are about to do). Let us return to the optimal tableau for the problem, Tableau 8-6, and examine the OF row. We see that C has a coefficient of $-£6.1905$ in the optimal solution. Given that this is negative we know that C remains non-basic. However, the coefficient does indicate directly by how much C's profit contribution must change in order for it to enter the solution. C's profit contribution—currently of £45—must increase by more than £6.1905 in order for C to enter the solution. The coefficient in the OF row in the optimal tableau, in other words, indicates the necessary increase in this variable's OF coefficient. Note that we realize that the coefficient of £6.1905 indicates the necessary increase in C's contribution given that at £45 it is unprofitable to produce this model. Other things being equal, only an increase in C's contribution will bring it into the solution.

Minimization problems

Comparable sensitivity analysis can be carried out on the objective function coefficients in a minimization problem. In such a case all the OF row coefficients in the optimal tableau will be positive. Division of these coefficients by the row coefficients of a basic variable will, again, indicate the range of variability in the OF coefficient of that variable. Similarly, the OF coefficient of a non-basic variable will indicate by how much that variable OF coefficient must change in order for it to enter the optimal solution. In this case the coefficient will represent the reduction in the non-basic variable's coefficient that is required, given that the reason this variable is not in the current optimal solution must be that its OF coefficient is too high (relative to all the other parameters of the problem).

8-5 SUMMARY OF SENSITIVITY ANALYSIS

We have seen that sensitivity analysis—based on information available in the final tableau—can provide useful management information over and above the optimal solution to the problem under investigation. Such sensitivity analysis allows management the opportunity to plan—in advance—their optimum reaction to changing circumstances and to identify potentially profitable reallocation of resources easily and efficiently, without the need for a complete recalculation of the basic problem. It is important, however, to realize that, in sensitivity analysis, all our calculations are based on the assumption that only *one* aspect of the problem changes at any one time—all other factors remain constant. If this were not the case, and more than one factor changed, then we would have to reformulate the entire problem and recompute the new solution. If, for example, the profit contribution of both models were to change at the same time then this approach could not be used to identify the changes in the optimum solution that would occur. It is also important to realize that in the real world such sensitivity analysis calculations will typically be undertaken by the relevant computer software automatically. An adequate understanding of the logic of the analysis is still required, however, in order to ensure that this information is utilized in an appropriate way.

8-6 SENSITIVITY ANALYSIS: AN EXAMPLE

We shall conclude this chapter by undertaking a complete sensitivity analysis on one of the problems we investigated earlier as a student exercise in Chapter 6. You will remember that IMC were investigating a suitable stock control problem for one of their high street stores and we shall briefly summarize the problem. In addition to selling their computer equipment the store also stocks and sells a range of computer supplies: boxes of floppy disks, PC cleaning kits, boxes of printer paper and anti-glare screens for monitors. Each of these items has been found to contribute to the store's profit at the rate of £0.40, £2.20, £1.75 and £3.60 per item sold, respectively. IMC is trying to decide what quantity of each item should be held in stock in order to meet sales on a weekly basis. Additional relevant factors are as follows. The store has 350 cubic feet of storage space available and the 4 items take up respectively 0.5, 0.1, 1.3 and 0.4 cubic feet per unit stocked. The store has determined that, regardless of profitability, at least 200 boxes of disks should be stocked each week and at least 50 boxes of printer paper. It is felt that such items—frequently required by customers—should always be available. However, because of fire regulations the store is allowed to stock no more than 500 boxes of disks and 100 boxes of paper at any one time. Finally, the accounting department has been analysing the cash flow situation in the store. Holding items in stock naturally incurs costs (security, insurance, handling charges, etc.). The accounting department has decided that these stock costs should be no more than £75 per week given that the 4 items respectively incur stockholding costs of £0.06, £0.18, £0.10 and £0.25 per item per week. We are required to advise on a suitable quantity of stocks to be held. Denoting the 4 items as X_1, X_2, X_3 and X_4 we have the following formulation and the optimal solution shown in Tableau 8-10.

$$\text{Maximize} \quad 0.4X_1 + 2.2X_2 + 1.75X_3 + 3.6X_4 \tag{8-15}$$

$$\text{subject to:} \quad 0.06X_1 + 0.18X_2 + 0.10X_3 + 0.25X_4 \leq 75 \tag{8-16}$$

$$0.5X_1 + 0.1X_2 + 1.3X_3 + 0.4X_4 \leq 350 \tag{8-17}$$

$$1X_1 \leq 500 \tag{8-18}$$

$$1X_3 \leq 100 \tag{8-19}$$

$$1X_1 \geq 200 \tag{8-20}$$

$$1X_3 \geq 50 \tag{8-21}$$

Tableau 8-10 Optimal solution

	X_1	X_2	X_3	X_4	S_1	S_2	S_3	S_4	S_5	S_6	A_5	A_6	Value
PROFIT	0	−0.392	0	0	−14.4	0	0	−0.31	−0.464	0	−0.464	0	−1018.20
X_4	0	0.72	0	1	4.0	0	0	−0.40	0.24	0	−0.24	0	212
S_2	0	−0.188	0	0	−1.6	1	0	−1.14	−0.404	0	0.046	0	35.2
S_3	0	0	0	0	0	0	1	0	1	0	−1	0	300
S_6	0	0	0	0	0	0	0	1	0	1	0	1	50
X_1	1	0	0	0	0	0	0	0	−1	0	1	0	200
X_3	0	0	1	0	0	0	0	1	0	0	0	1	100

From the optimal tableau the solution is readily identified: we should stock 200 boxes of disks, zero units of the cleaning kits, 100 boxes of printer paper and 212 units of the anti-glare screens. This will generate a profit of £1018.20 per week. But what other advice or decision implications can we extract from the solution? Let us examine the binding constraints. These are Eqs (8-16), (8-19) and (8-20). In other words, the binding constraints relate to the maximum holding cost of £75 per week, the maximum holding of 100 units of X_3 and the minimum holding of 200 units of X_1. We can immediately see that the storage space constraint is not critical. In fact, we would advise management that they have some 35 cubic feet of storage space which is surplus to current requirements and could, presumably, be used for other purposes. We can also undertake sensitivity analysis on the binding constraints. If we examine constraint Eq. (8-16) we identify an opportunity cost of £14.40. Interpretation is simple. If we relax the requirement to keep weekly stockholding costs to no more than £75 then profit will increase by £14.40 for each £1 reduction in this constraint figure. The extra profit is achieved through extra sales of 4 units of X_4. The maximum feasible change in this constraint is 22 (i.e. to £97) when all the current unused storage space (S_2) will have been utilized.

Similarly, if we examine the second binding constraint, Eq. (8-19), relating to the maximum stocks of X_3 then we see that an increase in the RHS of this value (i.e. to 101) will lead to an increase in profit of £0.31. This will be achieved by increasing stocks of X_3 by 1 and reducing X_4 by 0.4 units. The maximum possible change in this constraint will be 30 (i.e. to 130), at which time again the spare storage space will be fully utilized. The management implications are clear. The current fire regulations restrict X_3 to no more than 100 units. It would be worth while investigating ways of removing or relaxing this restriction to allow more of X_3 to be stocked (thereby increasing profit)—perhaps by improving fire safety in the store.

Finally, in terms of the binding constraints we examine Eq. (8-20) relating to the minimum stock levels of X_1. The current problem formulation requires X_1 to take a minimum value of 200 units, the value that X_1 actually does take in the current solution. This implies (as is confirmed by the appropriate opportunity cost of £0.464) that we are stocking X_1 not because it is profitable but because we are required to. The implications again are clear. Reducing this requirement will increase profit with a maximum feasible reduction of 200 (200/− 1). This would actually lead to a position where zero units of X_1 were stocked and were replaced by extra stocks of X_4. However, as we were originally told, this stock item is regarded by IMC as a form of 'loss leader'—concerned more with providing a service to customers than with necessarily earning profit directly from sales of this item. Management would obviously need to re-evaluate this policy in the light of the information thrown up by the tableau.

192 LINEAR PROGRAMMING

Let us now examine the objective function. Variable X_3, relating to cleaning kits, is not in the current solution. We see from the OF row in Tableau 8-10 that its profit coefficient would have to rise by more than £0.392 (to more than £2.592) in order for it to enter the solution. For each of the three remaining variables which are basic we can determine the range of their profit contribution:

X_1:   Maximum decrease in coefficient = none
         Maximum increase in coefficient = £0.464

X_3 Maximum decrease in coefficient = $-$ £0.31
         Maximum increase in coefficient = none

X_4 Maximum decrease in coefficient = $-$ £0.544
         Maximum increase in coefficient = £0.775

We see that for X_1 there is no limit to the possible decrease in the profit coefficient. This relates to the fact that we must have at least 200 units of X_1 (Eq. (8-19)) and this is what we currently have in the optimal solution. No matter how low X_1's profit coefficient becomes it must remain a basic variable. On the other hand, if X_1's profit coefficient increases by more than £0.464 then the current optimal solution will change. Similarly, with X_3. There is no limit to the increase in this profit coefficient given that we face a maximum restriction on the X_1 value, although if the profit coefficient falls by more than £0.31 then the current solution will change. Finally, we see that for X_4 the current solution will remain optimal as long as the profit coefficient falls by no more than £0.544 and increases by no more than £0.755. Management know, therefore, that the current optimal solution will remain unaffected as long as any profit coefficient changes occur within these specified ranges.

8-7 CONCLUSION

We have seen in this chapter how powerful the tools of sensitivity analysis are in LP. The last example illustrates clearly the additional management information that can readily be obtained from the current optimal solution. Not only does such analysis provide the decision-maker with information about possible courses of action; it also goes a considerable way to removing some of the restrictive assumptions inherent in the technique, particularly with regard to deterministic problem formulation. It is important to remember that such sensitivity analysis allows us to examine only one change in the current problem at a time. Whilst there are methods available for introducing more than one such change they are beyond the scope of our analytical skills and are best resolved through a complete reformulation and new solution process. The importance of the analysis we have illustrated in this chapter, however, should not be underestimated.

STUDENT EXERCISES

8-1 Using the optimal solution shown in Tableau 8-1 explain why the opportunity cost of constraint 3 (relating to microchips) is zero.

8-2 Confirm the analysis of A's profit contribution undertaken in Tableau 8-9. Reformulate and re-solve the problem using a profit coefficient for A of £33.34 and then again for £33.33. Comment on the changes that have occurred.

8-3 Using Tableau 8-6 evaluate the maximum changes in B's profit contribution that could occur before altering the current optimal solution. Confirm your calculations by reformulating the problem using the new profit coefficients and re-solving.

8-4 Add the term k to C's profit coefficient in the problem formululated in Eqs (8-10) to (8-13). Derive the appropriate final tableau and confirm the increase in C's profit contribution that would be necessary in order for this variable to become basic.

8-5 Return to the problem formulated in Eqs (8-14) to (8-20) and its optimal solution. For the analysis undertaken on the objective function coefficients confirm these figures by amending the original objective function and re-solving the problem.

8-6 Amend the problem formulation shown in Eqs (8-14) to (8-20) such that total stock costs must not exceed 10 per cent of weekly profit. Determine the new solution and carry out a full sensitivity analysis. Draft a report to management detailing the implications of the optimal solution.

8-7 Return to each of the detailed problem formulations that we have been examining in Chapters 6 and 7. For the optimal solution you obtained for the appropriate student exercise in Chapter 7 undertake a full and complete sensitivity analysis:

(a) For each binding constraint determine and interpret in the context of the problem the relevant opportunity cost.
(b) Determine the maximum change possible in each binding constraint.
(c) Undertake a full analysis on the basic and non-basic variables in terms of their objective function coefficients.

Interpret your results in the context of the problem set.

Draft a management report summarizing the results of your sensitivity analysis and the implications for management and providing guidelines as to the management options that are available.

9

EXTENSIONS TO LINEAR PROGRAMMING

In this chapter we extend the basic LP model we have developed thus far in a number of ways. In the previous chapter we examined in detail the forms of sensitivity analysis that can readily be undertaken on the optimal solution to an LP problem and confirmed the usefulness of such analysis to the decision-maker. The methods of assessing and evaluating such sensitivity information were stated simply and then explained logically. In this chapter we shall examine the concept of the *dual* in linear programming and we shall see that the dual provides the important theoretical underpinning for the sensitivity analysis that we have undertaken. We shall also examine the problems that can arise when applying LP in practice and consider how such problems affect the usefulness of the technique and how they can be resolved. Finally, we shall examine the underlying assumptions of the LP model and assess how these affect the practical application of the technique to business problems. We begin by considering the dual.

9-1 THE DUAL

For the moment we simply state that the original formulation of an LP problem (the types of formulation we have so far considered) is known as the *primal* and that every primal problem formulation has an associated and corresponding formulation known as the *dual*. We shall see shortly the relationship that exists between the primal and dual formulations and that the solution to either problem will also provide the solution to the other. Effectively, we can regard the dual problem (and its solution) as a mirror image of the primal and we shall see how the dual actually provides the theoretical underpinning for much of the sensitivity analysis we have already introduced. Let us return to the IMC problem which we first examined in this section of the text. The problem formulation is duplicated below, and the optimal Simplex tableau is shown as Tableau 9-1.

$$\text{Maximize} \quad 40A + 50B \tag{9-1}$$
$$\text{subject to:} \quad 28A + 42B \leq 16\,800 \tag{9-2}$$
$$12A + 6B \leq 4\,800 \tag{9-3}$$
$$1A + 1B \leq 600 \tag{9-4}$$
$$A, B \geq 0$$

Tableau 9-1 Optimal solution

	A	B	S_1	S_2	S_3	Value
PROFIT	0	0	−1.0714	−0.8333	0	−22 000
B	0	1	0.0357	−0.0833	0	200
A	1	0	−0.01786	0.125	0	300
S_3	0	0	−0.01786	−0.0417	1	100

$$A = 300 \quad S_1 = 0$$
$$B = 200 \quad S_2 = 0$$
$$S_3 = 100$$
$$\text{Profit} = £22\,000$$

We have seen previously from the optimal tableau that the coefficients of 1.0714 and 0.8333 for S_1 and S_2 respectively represent the opportunity costs of the corresponding binding constraints—the value to IMC of extra supplies of scarce resources. In order to develop the dual formulation to this problem we shall examine IMC's situation from a different—but related—viewpoint. It is clear that our optimal production decision generates maximum profit from the production of the two types of monitor. Such profit must be generated within the limits imposed by the currently available resources. Such resources, however, have to be acquired and paid for and it is evident that IMC would be unwilling to produce either monitor if the necessary resources could not be acquired at reasonable cost. Naturally, this begs the question of what represents a *reasonable* cost for the company. The objective function for the problem (Eq. (9-1)) shows the per-unit profit that can be achieved from the production of either type of monitor and such profit figures clearly incorporate the costs of the required resources. (We saw earlier in Chapter 5 that these profit coefficients represent the difference between the unit selling price and the unit production and labour cost.) It is important, however, to recognize that such costs are a reflection of current, external market prices. That is, they represent the value of a resource as perceived by the economic market rather than by the company itself. Such market prices may not reflect the true value of the appropriate resources to the company. Consider, for example, someone employed in the assembly department. From the original problem formulation we know that current wage rates are £4 per hour. This is the value placed on this resource by the economic market system. IMC, however, may well value this resource differently. What is important from the company viewpoint in assessing the value of such a resource is what they get in return. In other words what extra production (and hence extra profit) such assembly time will generate. The value placed on this resource, therefore, may well be different from the current market price of this resource. (Some readers may see obvious parallels here with the economic concepts of marginal revenue and marginal cost.) On the other hand, as we saw in the last chapter, the opportunity cost figures generated by the Simplex method indicate the effect on IMC's profit as a result of acquiring extra units of some scarce resource. Such opportunity costs (often referred to more meaningfully in this context as *shadow prices*) measure the marginal value to the company of a particular resource and represent the prices that are appropriate to the company's management in trying to determine how much more of a resource to acquire. That is, in assessing that resource's value to the decision-maker, a value which may be very different from the market price. Let us examine Eq. (9-2), which relates to the currently available supply of assembly time. At the moment IMC has 16 800 assembly hours available. Let us denote U_1 as this resource's shadow price—the maximum price that IMC is willing to pay for additional supplies of this particular resource. It follows, therefore, that IMC should be willing to pay a total of:

$$16\,800 \times U_1$$

for the current assembly time capacity. In a similar way if we let U_2 denote the shadow price of inspection time and U_3 the shadow price of the microchip component then the company should pay a total of:

$$4800 \times U_2$$

for the current total inspection hours and:

$$600 \times U_3$$

for the current supply of microchips. The total payment for all three resources, therefore, will be given by:

$$16\,800U_1 + 4800U_2 + 600U_3 \qquad (9\text{-}5)$$

and it is clear, in the context of our current problem, that the company will wish to *minimize* these costs. However, there are also restrictions which apply to the way in which this cost function can be minimized and these relate to the two models IMC wishes to produce. If we examine Model A in the original (primal) formulation we see that each unit of A produced requires 28 hours of assembly time, 12 hours of inspection time and 1 microchip. Logically, IMC will be prepared to pay $28U_1$ for the assembly hours required, $12U_2$ for the inspection hours and $1U_3$ for the microchip. So the total amount the company will be prepared to pay for the resources required to produce one unit of A will be:

$$28U_1 + 12U_2 + 1U_3$$

However, acquiring and using these resources in the production of A will generate a profit of £40. It is evident that the value of the resources used to produce one unit of A must be at least equal to the profit that can be earned from this production. That is, we require:

$$28U_1 + 12U_2 + 1U_3 \geqslant 40 \qquad (9\text{-}6)$$

It is important to appreciate the logic implied in this constraint. The LHS indicates the value that IMC places on this quantity of resources. If this value turns out to be less than £40 then, logically, A should not be produced. Only if the company places a value of *at least* £40 on these resources will it be worth while using them to produce Model A (and generate a profit of £40). Similarly, for the alternative use of these resources (in production of Model B) we require:

$$42U_1 + 6U_2 + 1U_3 \geq 50 \qquad (9\text{-}7)$$

We can summarize the problem, therefore, as:

$$\text{Minimize} \quad 16\,800U_1 + 4800U_2 + 600U_3$$
$$\text{subject to:} \quad 28U_1 + 12U_2 + 1U_3 \geq 40$$
$$42U_1 + 6U_2 + 1U_3 \geq 50$$
$$U_1, U_2, U_3 \geq 0$$

This problem formulation is known as the *dual*. It is clear that the primal and dual formulations represent different perspectives on exactly the same problem. In the context of this problem the primal seeks to determine how much of each product should be produced in order to maximize the profit value of this production within the constraints limiting production to the available resources. The dual, on the other hand, seeks to determine the values (the shadow prices) associated with each input resource such that the total value of resources required is minimized whilst the constraints insist that the resource input value for a product is at least as high as the profit value of that product.

9-2 THE DUAL FORMULATION

It is apparent that the problem we have considered thus far as the primal formulation is conveniently simple and hence the derivation of the dual is straightforward. As we have seen, however, not all LP problems are this convenient to handle and it is necessary to examine how we can derive the dual from the primal of any problem. Assume that we have a primal problem such that, in general:

$$\text{Maximize} \quad c_1 X_1 + c_2 X_2 + \ldots + c_n X_n$$

$$\text{subject to:} \quad a_{11}X_1 + a_{12}X_2 + a_{13}X_3 + \ldots + a_{1n}X_n \leq b_1$$
$$a_{21}X_1 + a_{22}X_2 + a_{23}X_3 + \ldots + a_{2n}X_n \leq b_2$$
$$a_{31}X_1 + a_{32}X_2 + a_{33}X_3 + \ldots + a_{3n}X_n \leq b_3$$
$$\vdots$$
$$a_{m1}X_1 + a_{m2}X_2 + a_{m3}X_3 + \ldots + a_{mn}X_n \leq b_m$$
$$X_1, X_2, X_3, \ldots, X_n \geq 0$$

where the X_i's are the decision variables, the c_i's the objective function coefficients, the a's the technical coefficients and the b's the RHS constraint coefficients. Such a formulation is known as the *canonical primal*. The dual to such a formulation will then be given as:

$$\text{Minimize} \quad b_1 U_1 + b_2 U_2 + b_3 U_3 + \ldots + b_m U_m$$

subject to:
$$a_{11}U_1 + a_{21}U_2 + a_{31}U_3 + \ldots + a_{m1}U_m \geq c_1$$
$$a_{12}U_1 + a_{22}U_2 + a_{32}U_3 + \ldots + a_{m2}U_m \geq c_2$$
$$a_{13}U_1 + a_{23}U_2 + a_{33}U_3 + \ldots + a_{m3}U_m \geq c_3$$
$$\vdots$$
$$a_{1n}U_1 + a_{2n}U_2 + a_{3n}U_3 + \ldots + a_{mn}U_m \geq c_n$$
$$U_1, U_2, U_3, \ldots, U_m \geq 0$$

and the following general rules apply in deriving the dual from the canonical primal:

- The maximization objective in the primal becomes a minimization objective in the dual.
- The number of constraints in the dual will be the same as the number of decision variables (n) in the primal.
- The number of decision variables in the dual is the same as the number of constraints in the primal (m).
- The coefficients of the decision variables in the primal (c_i) become the values for the right-hand side of the constraints in the dual.
- The values in the right-hand side of the constraints in the primal problem (b_i) become the coefficients for the objective function in the dual.
- The $\leq$ constraints in the primal are replaced by $\geq$ constraints in the dual.
- The coefficients of the decision variables in the *rows* of the primal problem constraints become the coefficients of the decision variables in the *columns* of the dual constraints.

Thus if the problem for which we wish to derive the dual formulation fits into the canonical primal form we can readily determine the appropriate transformation.

Student activity
Using the above rules find the dual of the formulation shown in Eqs (9-5) to (9-7). What conclusion do you come to about this formulation and the original primal?

However, suppose that our primal problem does not fit into the canonical form. What then? Suppose, for example, that we have a primal minimization problem, or primal constraints which take the form $\geq$ or $=$? The easiest solution is to amend the original primal problem so that it is canonical. This can be done using a set of transformation rules.

Transformation rules

Constraints taking the form $\geq$ Assume we have a constraint for our primal problem such that:

$$A + B \geq 300$$

The direction of the inequality can be reversed simply by multiplying the constraint through by -1. That is:

$$A + B \geq 300$$
and
$$-A - B \leq -300$$

represent exactly the same restriction and the constraint now conforms to the constraint format required by the canonical and the dual is readily obtained.

Constraints taking the form = Assume a constraint for the primal problem such that:

$$A + B = 300$$

Such an equality constraint can be replaced with two inequality constraints of the opposite direction:

$$A + B \geqslant 300$$
$$A + B \leqslant 300$$

as it is apparent that only values that satisfy the strict equality will satisfy both these constraints simultaneously. Given that the canonical requires all constraints to be in the $\leqslant$ form these would become:

$$-A - B \leqslant -300$$
$$A + B \leqslant 300$$

Minimization functions If the primal problem involves a minimization objective function then (as we saw earlier in Chapter 7) we can convert this into a maximization function by multiplying through by -1. If, for example, we had a function such that:

$$\text{Minimize} \quad 219A + 299B$$

then this would become:

$$\text{Maximize} \quad -219A - 299B$$

To illustrate these rules consider the problem below (which we examined in detail in Chapter 7).

$$\text{Minimize} \quad 219A + 299B \qquad (9\text{-}8)$$
$$\text{subject to:} \quad 28A + 42B \leqslant 16\,800 \qquad (9\text{-}9)$$
$$12A + 6B \leqslant 4\,800 \qquad (9\text{-}10)$$
$$1A + 1B \leqslant 600 \qquad (9\text{-}11)$$
$$1A \geqslant 100 \qquad (9\text{-}12)$$
$$1B \geqslant 150 \qquad (9\text{-}13)$$
$$1A + 1B = 450 \qquad (9\text{-}14)$$

Student activity
Obtain the canonical primal form of the problem formulated in Eqs (9-8) to (9-14).

Using the transformation rules the problem becomes:

$$\text{Maximize} \quad -219A - 299B \tag{9-15}$$
$$\text{subject to:} \quad 28A + 42B \leq 16\,800 \tag{9-16}$$
$$12A + 6B \leq 4800 \tag{9-17}$$
$$1A + 1B \leq 600 \tag{9-18}$$
$$-1A \leq -100 \tag{9-19}$$
$$-1B \leq -150 \tag{9-20}$$
$$1A + 1B \leq 450 \tag{9-21}$$
$$-1A - 1B \leq -450 \tag{9-22}$$

and the dual of the problem is now readily found.

Student activity

Obtain the dual of the primal problem shown in Eqs (9-15) to (9-22).

The dual, therefore, is given as:

$$\text{Minimize} \quad 16\,800U_1 + 4800U_2 + 600U_3 - 100U_4 - 150U_5 + 450U_6 - 450U_7 \tag{9-23}$$
$$\text{subject to:} \quad 28U_1 + 12U_2 + 1U_3 - 1U_4 + 0U_5 + 1U_6 - 1U_7 \geq -219 \tag{9-24}$$
$$42U_1 + 6U_2 + 1U_3 + 0U_4 - 1U_5 + 1U_6 - 1U_7 \geq -299 \tag{9-25}$$

Three points are worthy of note at this stage. The first is that it is not strictly necessary to convert a primal problem into its canonical form before finding the dual. There are methods of transforming the different types of primal constraints and objective functions into their dual equivalents directly. However, we feel that the primal canonical form is the easiest way at this stage for the student to obtain the dual formulation given its simple and straightforward format. The second point relates to the fact that, as we saw in Chapter 7, the Simplex method cannot cope directly with constraints that involve negative RHS values (as in Eqs (9-24) and (9-25)). Should we wish to solve the dual problem we have just derived using the Simplex method then we would have to eliminate these negative RHS values first. The last point relates to the use of computer software. Many programs these days will have an option to provide the dual to the original problem automatically thus removing the need for a manual dual formulation. As ever though, the user needs to be familiar with the process of dual formulation that we have discussed in order to make sense of the appropriate computer output.

9-3 THE RELATIONSHIP BETWEEN THE PRIMAL AND DUAL PROBLEMS

You may be forgiven, at this stage, for wondering why we actually bother deriving the dual formulation at all. After all, the Simplex method will provide the optimal solution to the original primal problem and we have already developed the ability to undertake sensitivity analysis on the primal problem optimal tableau. We shall shortly see, however, that such sensitivity analysis is directly related to the dual and draws upon the dual formulation and solution. Let us return to the problem we examined at the start of this chapter. The primal and dual formulations were:

Primal

$$\text{Maximize} \quad 40A + 50B \tag{9-1}$$
$$\text{subject to:} \quad 28A + 42B \leq 16\,800 \tag{9-2}$$
$$12A + 6B \leq 4\,800 \tag{9-3}$$
$$1A + 1B \leq 600 \tag{9-4}$$

Dual

$$\text{Minimize} \quad 16\,800U_1 + 4800U_2 + 600U_3 \tag{9-5}$$
$$\text{subject to:} \quad 28U_1 + 12U_2 + 1U_3 \geq 40 \tag{9-6}$$
$$42U_1 + 6U_2 + 1U_3 \geq 50 \tag{9-7}$$

Student activity
Using the Simplex method derive the final, optimal tableau for the dual problem.

The optimal tableau for the primal problem is duplicated in Tableau 9-2 whilst the corresponding tableau for the solution to the dual is shown in Tableau 9-3.

Tableau 9-2 Primal solution

	A	B	S_1	S_2	S_3	Value
PROFIT	0	0	−1.0714	−0.8333	0	−22 000
B	0	1	0.0357	−0.0833	0	200
A	1	0	−0.01786	0.125	0	300
S_3	0	0	−0.01786	−0.0417	1	100

Tableau 9-3 Dual solution

	U_1	U_2	U_3	S_1	S_2	Value
Cost	0	0	100	300	200	−22 000
U_2	0	1	0.0417	−0.125	0.0833	0.8333
U_1	1	0	0.01786	0.01786	−0.0357	1.0714

(Note that the artificial variables have not been shown in Tableau 9-3. They play no part in the solution and have been removed to facilitate understanding.) It is immediately apparent that the two solutions contain virtually the same coefficients. Let us examine the optimal values for the sets of variables in detail.

Primal

Objective function = 22 000

A = 300
B = 200

Dual

Objective function = 22 000

$U_1 = 1.0714$
$U_2 = 0.8333$

$S_1 = 0$
$S_2 = 0$
$S_3 = 100$

$U_3 = 0$
$S_1 = 0$
$S_2 = 0$

It is clear that the two formulations lead to the same optimal value for the objective function: £22 000. This is true not only for our problem but for all primal–dual problems and leads to the first important property of the primal–dual relationship.

Property 1 *If the primal problem has an optimal solution then the dual has an optimal solution and vice versa. The OF values of the two optimal solutions are equal.*

Property 1 of the primal–dual relationship indicates that we can determine the value of the objective function from *either* of the two problem formulations. Equally, given that Property 1 indicates that the full optimal solutions are available, we can determine the appropriate values for the primal decision variables (A, B) from the dual solutions and for the primal slack variables (S_1, S_2, S_3). It is evident that the coefficients in the OF row in Tableau 9-3 columns are the same as the optimal values for S_1, S_2, S_3 and for A and B from the primal solution. This leads to the second property of the relationship.

Property 2 *The coefficients in the OF row in the optimal dual solution are the optimal values for the slack variables and decision variables in the primal problem.*

That is, we can determine from the OF row Tableau 9-3 that:

S_1 (from the U_1 column) = 0
S_2 (from the U_2 column) = 0
S_3 (from the U_3 column) = 100
A (from the S_1 column) = 300
B (from the S_2 column) = 200

So, again, either of the two solutions will provide values for the primal decision variables and for the primal slack values. The third and potentially most important aspect of the primal–dual relationship relates to the values of the dual decision variables (U_1, U_2, U_3). Remember that these relate to the shadow prices of the different resources used in the production process. We see from Tableau 9-3 that these are £0.833 for U_2, £1.0714 for U_1 and 0 for U_3. (U_3 does not appear in the dual basis and, therefore, takes a zero value.) However, it is also evident that we have encountered these coefficients previously when we were examining the primal solution in terms of sensitivity analysis. This leads to the third property of the primal–dual relationship.

Property 3 *The optimal values for the dual decision variables represent the shadow prices (opportunity costs) of the corresponding constraints in the primal problem.*

This last property is particularly important. We saw in the sensitivity analysis we undertook previously how we could utilize the opportunity cost coefficients to assess the effect of a change in the RHS of a binding constraint. We were not able, at that time, to provide other than an intuitive explanation of why these coefficients could be interpreted in such a way. We are now able, with the use of the dual, to confirm that such coefficients do in fact relate directly to the appropriate binding constraints. Given that the RHS value of a constraint in the primal problem is the corresponding coefficient for a dual variable in the objective function it follows that a unit change in this RHS value leads directly to a change in the dual's objective function value (which, through Property 1, implies an equivalent change in the objective function of the primal problem). To illustrate this important principle, let us consider U_1. This is the dual decision variable (the shadow price/opportunity cost) relating to the assembly time constraint in the primal problem. The dual objective function is given by:

$$16\,800U_1 + 4800U_2 + 600U_3$$

or, given the optimal values for these dual variables, as:

$$16\,800(1.0714) + 4800(0.8333) + 600(0) = 22\,000$$

Let us examine the effect on the dual problem of acquiring one extra assembly hour: i.e. the RHS of the primal constraint changes to 16 801.

Student activity
From the new primal formulation determine the new dual objective function.

Naturally this change in the primal problem will affect the dual. Given that we are altering one of the RHS constraint values in the primal then this will alter the objective function in the dual which will now be:

$$16\,801U_1 + 4800U_2 + 600U_3$$

and which, given the current optimal values for the dual decision variables, gives the objective function a value of:

$$16\,801(1.0714) + 4800(0.8333) + 600(0) = 22\,001.0714$$

This in turn (Property 1) must be the value of the objective function in the primal problem. An extra assembly hour will lead to a change in the dual's objective function of £1.0714. Given that the optimal solution to the dual is the same as that of the primal then it follows that this change in resource availability will increase total profit by this amount. The logic of the shadow prices—which are the decision variables in the dual—should be apparent. U_1 represents the value to IMC of this particular resource and we have confirmed, therefore, the sensitivity analysis approach we introduced in Chapter 8—assessing the opportunity cost relating to binding constraints.

9-4 THE DUAL AND COMPUTATIONAL EFFICIENCY

A second, useful aspect of the dual relates to the impact it has on the solution process for large-scale problems. Where a problem has relatively few decision variables but a large number of constraints (and, on reflection, you will understand that this is likely to apply to a considerable number of real business applications of the technique) it will often be easier to formulate, solve and interpret the *dual* rather than the *primal* problem. Consider a situation where the canonical primal consists of 100 decision variables and 500 constraints. Given that each constraint will be of the form ≤, we shall also require 500 slack variables. The central part of the tableau, therefore, will consist of 300 000 coefficients (the a's). Equally, at each iteration, 500 basic variables will be required. The dual, on the other hand, will be much smaller. We shall require 100 constraints of the form ≥, 500 decision variables, 100 surplus variables and 100 artificial variables. The central part of the tableau, therefore, will comprise only 70 000 coefficients and at each iteration only 100 basic variables will be required. Whilst the developments over the last few years in terms of cheap and available computing power make this less of a problem than it used to be there will also be benefits at the interpretation stage in using the dual. The amount of information to be assessed (and contained in the optimal tableau) will be much less, thus allowing the analyst and management to focus quickly upon the relevant information rather than being overloaded with information from the larger primal tableau. It is not surprising, therefore, that the dual is frequently used in practice in place of the primal formulation.

So far in this chapter we have introduced the concept of the dual formulation to an LP problem and examined the relationship that exists between the primal and the dual solutions. Whilst the dual may offer considerable computational advantage over the primal in practice (in terms of size, speed and time) its real importance lies elsewhere. The dual provides the theoretical underpinning for most of the sensitivity analysis that can be undertaken on the optimal solution to an LP problem and which we have already examined. Such sensitivity analysis, relying as it does on the dual, is a particularly important feature of the technique. In addition, much of the more advanced work that can be undertaken via sensitivity analysis (examining, for example, multiple changes in aspects to the formulation or changes in the constraint coefficients) can only adequately be undertaken through the use of the dual solution.

9-5 SPECIAL PROBLEMS

In applying LP (both in business and the classroom) certain problems can arise when attempting to find an optimal solution. In this section we shall examine the difficulties arising from *unbounded* problems, *infeasible* problems, *alternate* optimal solutions and *degenerate* problems. Each of these will be discussed in turn and we shall examine how we can ascertain that such a problem exists and identify the approach to be taken to try and resolve the difficulty. It should be remembered that such problems are likely to be spotted and flagged by the computer package you are using to solve a particular problem. You will need to be aware, though, of what the problem means and what action is necessary to try to resolve it.

Unbounded problems

A solution to an LP problem is said to be *unbounded* if the value of the solution can be increased without violating any of the problem constraints. If, for example, we had a profit maximization problem then such a situation would imply that there was no upper limit to the profit that could be attained. Consider the problem given below.

EXTENSIONS TO LINEAR PROGRAMMING

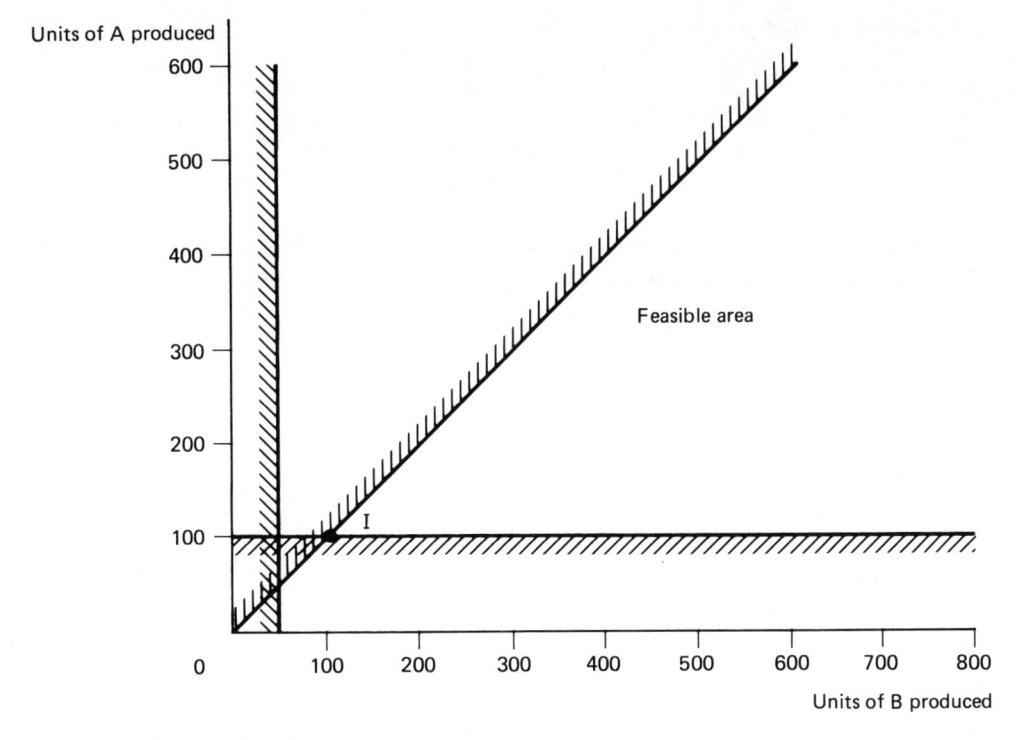

Figure 9-1 Unbounded problem

$$\text{Maximize} \quad 40A + 50B \tag{9-26}$$
$$\text{subject to:} \quad A \leq B \tag{9-27}$$
$$A \geq 100 \tag{9-28}$$
$$B \geq 50 \tag{9-29}$$
$$A, B \geq 0$$

The company has amended its production decision problem such that it now requires that production of A is always less than that of B (Eq.9-27) but also that production of A must be at least 100 units (Eq.9-28) and of B at least 50 units (Eq.9-29). Figure 9-1 shows the graph for this problem and it is immediately apparent that the feasible area has no upper boundary. Given that the objective is one of maximization it is clear that the iso-profit line will continue to move upward and outward away from the origin indefinitely and still represent feasible solutions. There is no upper limit on profit in other words. How would we recognize such a problem in the Simplex method, however?

Student activity
Using the method of penalties (with a penalty value of $-£100$), obtain Tableau 9-4 for this problem.

Tableau 9-4 Unbounded problem

	A	B	S_1	S_2	S_3	Value
PROFIT	0	0	5	15	0	−1500
A	1	0	0	−1	0	100
S_{U3}	0	0	−1	−1	1	50
B	0	1	−1	−1	0	100

Tableau 9-4—the fourth iteration for this problem—is shown here (again the artificial variable columns have been omitted for clarity). The current solution is:

$$\text{Profit} = £1500$$
$$A = 100 \qquad S_1 = 0$$
$$B = 100 \qquad S_2 = 0$$
$$\qquad\qquad S_3 = 50$$

At the moment the solution shown in Tableau 9.4 represents point I in Fig. 9.1. The solution, however, is clearly not optimal given the existence of positive coefficients in the objective function row. Consider the next sequence in the Simplex algorithm. We identify the pivot column (the entering variable) by selecting the variable with the highest positive coefficient in the OF row. Here this will be S_2. We next search for the pivot row (the variable to leave the basis) by computing ratios of values to *positive* column coefficients. However, in the case of S_2 there are no positive coefficients to be used. All are negative and the Simplex method can proceed no further. In fact this lack of suitable positive coefficients actually indicates that the problem is unbounded. It is of little help to consider the other column with a positive coefficient in the OF row, S_1. There are still no positive coefficients available for use in this column either. So, identifying that a problem is unbounded in the Simplex process is straightforward (even more so given that computer programs will automatically flag that the problem is unbounded). The Simplex algorithm, in trying to force a new variable into the basis, will fail to find positive coefficients in the appropriate pivot column. How is the problem to be resolved? Generally, such a situation has two possible causes: either we have incorrectly formulated the problem or we are trying to apply LP to a problem for which it is not suitable. We have discussed at length earlier in the text the difficulties that problem formulation creates in practice and it is only fair to point out that determining the precise cause of such unboundedness is often far from easy when dealing with problems that have a considerable number of complex constraints. However, an unbounded solution implies that we may have omitted some critical aspect of the problem from the mathematical model. If only a business could attain a position of unlimited profits! Equally, it may be that we are trying to apply the LP model to a business problem for which it is not appropriate. We shall discuss the key assumptions behind the LP model in detail in the next section. Suffice it to say here that LP—like any model—tries to simplify reality. It tries to determine the salient aspects of a business problem and use this to assist the decision-maker. Aspects of the problem that LP ignores may well be extremely relevant to the decision-maker and may thus cause the LP model to be inappropriate. For example, in practice we may well face a *non-linear* objective function rather than a strictly linear one. Such a feature may be sufficient to generate an unbounded solution to the model. The correct methodological approach (as discussed in detail in Chapter 1) clearly comes into its own in this context.

Infeasible problems

The second category of problem relates to those LP formulations for which an optimal solution cannot be found. That is, there are no values for all the decision variables that simultaneously satisfy all the constraints. Consider the problem shown below.

$$\text{Maximize} \quad 40A + 50B \qquad (9\text{-}30)$$
$$\text{subject to:} \quad A \leq B \qquad (9\text{-}31)$$
$$B \leq 100 \qquad (9\text{-}32)$$
$$B \geq 50 \qquad (9\text{-}33)$$
$$A + B \geq 250 \qquad (9\text{-}34)$$

The problem requires maximization of profit subject to output of A being less than that of B, output of B between 50 and 100 units and total output being at least 250 units. The appropriate diagram for this problem is shown in Fig. 9-2 and it is clear that no feasible area exists. On reflection it is evident that the problem constraints are inconsistent. We require B to be no more than 100 units, A must be less than B (i.e. no more than 100 units) and yet require total output to be at least 250 units which is clearly impossible. Again, however, it is necessary to examine how such infeasibility can be identified from the Simplex method.

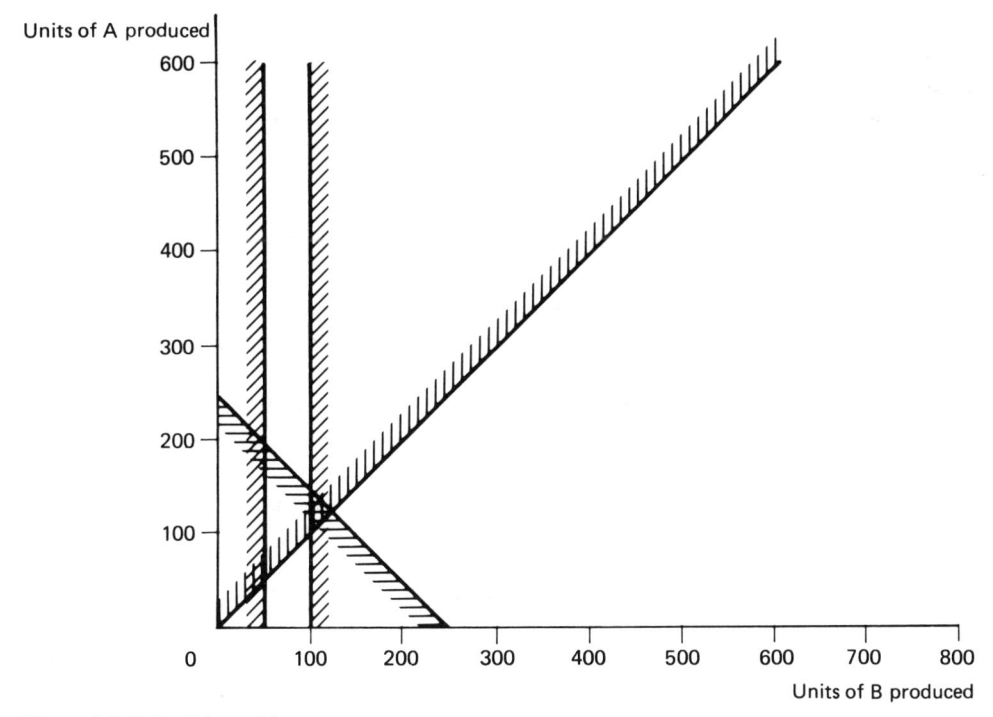

Figure 9-2 Infeasible problem

Student activity
Formulate this problem for the Simplex method and produce the appropriate tableau for iteration 4. Use the penalty method with a value of 100.

From the Simplex tableau we can easily recognize an infeasible solution by the fact that it will contain at least one artificial variable in the basis. Recollect the use of artificial variables in the Simplex algorithm discussed in Chapter 7. There, we saw that the artificial variables were necessary to allow us to use the algorithm when we had an infeasible solution. As we move closer to a feasible corner point then the artificial variables gradually disappear. It follows, therefore, that if an artificial variable remains then that solution is infeasible. Tableau 9-5 shows the final iteration for this problem. The current solution is:

Tableau 9-5 Infeasible solution

	A	B	S_1	S_2	S_3	S_4	A_3	A_4	Value
PROFIT	0	0	-140	-290	0	-100	0	0	-4000
A	1	0	1	1	0	0	0	0	100
S_{U3}	0	0	0	1	1	0	-1	0	50
B	0	1	0	1	0	0	0	0	100
A_4	0	0	-1	-2	0	-1	0	1	50

Profit £4000
$A = 100$ $S_1 = 0$ $A_3 = 0$
$B = 100$ $S_2 = 0$ $A_4 = 50$
$S_3 = 50$
$S_4 = 0$

We see that A is 100 units and B is 100 units. This satisfies constraints Eqs (9-31) to (9-33). The solution still contains an artificial variable, however, and is therefore infeasible. If we try to apply the usual Simplex rule to determine which variable enters the basis next, we examine the coefficients in the OF row but find none of them positive. No variable, in other words, can enter the solution at this stage, which implies that the artificial variable remains. As with unbounded problems, an infeasible solution suggests an incorrect formulation of the problem. In a classroom environment it is necessary to re-examine the formulation to see what has gone wrong (given that your lecturer is unlikely deliberately to give you an infeasible problem to try and solve). In a practical business situation, however, the infeasible solution may in fact be correct. There may well be no solution to the problem we have set. It is not possible to optimize the objective given the specified constraints. An indication of where the problem lies may be given by examining the constraint(s) associated with the artificial variable(s) remaining in the tableau. In Tableau 9-5 the artificial variable A_4 takes a value of 50. The implication is that the corresponding constraint (Eq. (9-34)) requires 50 more units of A and B than are possible if we are to satisfy all the constraints. In complex problems, however, the use of the artificial variable in this way should be treated with caution. Even in our simple problem we can see that it is not Eq. (9-34) by itself that is causing the difficulty. If we amend Eq. (9-32), for example, to $B \leqslant 150$ then an optimal solution becomes available. It is also worth noting that infeasible solution can occur only when we have constraints requiring artificial variables. Problems formulated only with constraints taking the form $\leqslant$ will always generate a feasible solution (even if this solution requires decision variables to take zero values in the case of a minimization problem).

Alternate optimal solutions

We state that if we have an LP formulation which has more than one optimal solution then it has alternate optima. Consider the problem below:

$$\text{Maximize} \quad 50A + 50B \tag{9-35}$$
$$\text{subject to:} \quad 28A + 42B \leq 16\,800 \tag{9-36}$$
$$12A + 6B \leq 4\,800 \tag{9-37}$$
$$1A + 1B \leq 450 \tag{9-38}$$

The earlier problem has been amended such that both products have the same profit margin (Eq. (9-35)) and the supply of microchips is now 450 (Eq. (9-38)). The corresponding diagram for the problem is shown in Fig. 9-3, which also has the iso-profit line superimposed. It can be seen that the OF line is parallel to the line of one of the constraints—that relating to the microchip availability. As we seek to push the profit line outward there will come a stage when it coincides *exactly* with this constraint line and, in this example, this will represent the optimum value for the objective function. It is evident, however, that there are actually an infinite number of optimal solutions to the problem.

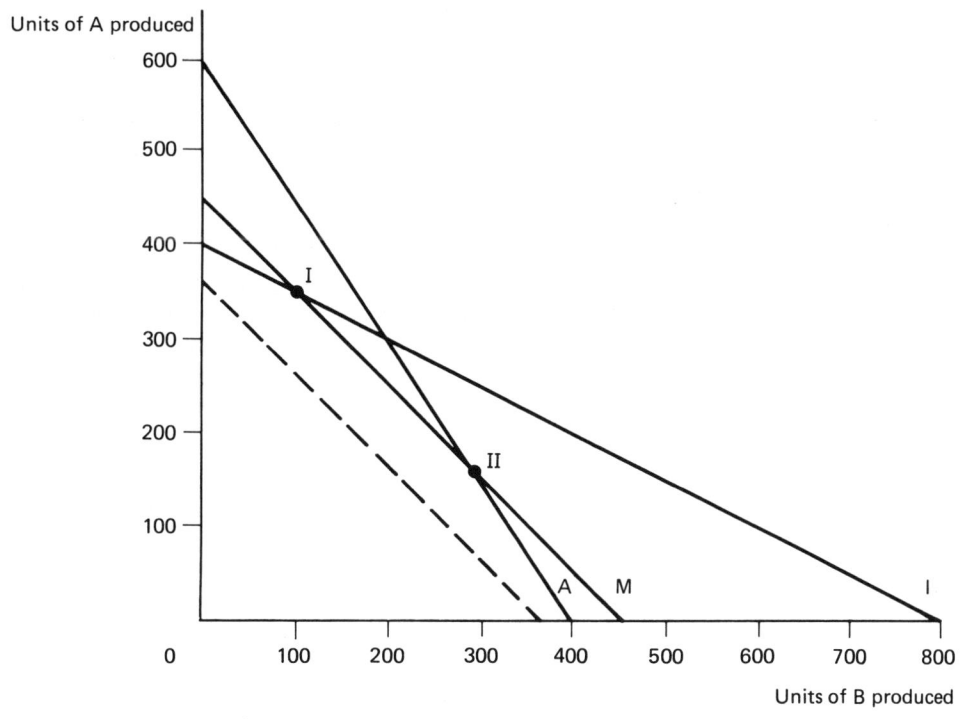

Figure 9-3 Alternate optima

Any combination of A and B that occurs between points I and II in Fig. 9-3 will generate exactly the same profit and represent an optimal solution on the boundary of the feasible area. Simply, such a situation occurs whenever the ratio of coefficients in the OF is the same as the ratio of coefficients in (what turns out to be) a binding constraint. Once again, we need to be able to recognize such a situation when using the Simplex method. In contrast to the case in other special situations the existence of alternate optima is unlikely to be flagged by a computer program.

Student activity
Formulate and solve the problem using the Simplex method. Examine the opportunity costs of the binding constraints.

Tableau 9-6 Alternate optima

	A	B	S_1	S_2	S_3	Value
PROFIT	0	0	0	0	−50	22 500
S_1	0	0	1	2.333	−56	2 800
A	1	0	0	0.1667	−1	350
B	0	1	0	−0.1667	2	100

Tableau 9-6 shows the optimal tableau for this problem. The solution is:

$$\text{Profit} = £22\,500$$
$$A = 350 \qquad S_1 = 2800$$
$$B = 100 \qquad S_2 = 0$$
$$\qquad\qquad\; S_3 = 0$$

From the tableau we can readily confirm we have the optimal solution as the OF row contains only zero or negative coefficients, implying that no new variable can be brought into the basis that will increase profit further. Production is set at $A = 350$ units and $B = 100$ units. Binding constraints are Eq. (9-37) ($S_2 = 0$) and Eq. (9-38) ($S_3 = 0$), with spare capacity in Eq. (9-36). Profit is maximized at £22 500. But how can we determine that alternative optima exist? Let us examine the binding constraints. We know that these represent scarce resources and are restricting profit from increasing. As such these two resources will have an opportunity cost—an indication of the value to IMC of acquiring extra supplies of these resources and thereby increasing production and profit further. If we examine S_3 we see it has an opportunity cost of £50 and, in the usual way, we could undertake a full sensitivity analysis on the effects of changing the RHS of this constraint. But let us consider the other binding constraint represented by S_2. From the tableau this has an opportunity cost of 0. How can this be? The implication is clear (if puzzling). Extra supplies of inspection time will not lead to a change in profit even though we are currently using all the available supplies of this resource, although they will lead to a change in the optimal values for the basic variables. In fact, such an opportunity cost indicates that alternative optimal solutions exist to this problem. Effectively, variable S_2 could enter the basis and have a zero effect to profit (i.e. profit would remain unchanged at £22 500). The corresponding column coefficients could also be used in the usual way to determine what this alternative solution would be.

Student activity
Using the S_2 column coefficients determine the alternate optimal solution and locate this on Fig. 9-3.

Note also that the Simplex tableau will determine one of the alternate optimal solutions which occurs at a corner point of the feasible area. The zero opportunity cost for the appropriate binding constraint will indicate one of the alternative optima at another corner point. But, in fact, there will be an infinite range of possible values between these two corner points, all generating exactly the same value for the objective function. Equally, it should be noted that such alternatives do not present a problem as such to the decision-maker. They simply provide information that the same target (as represented by the OF) can be attained in a variety of ways. The decision-maker can then choose the optimal solution most appropriate to his/her needs.

Degenerate problems

Finally in this section we consider the problem of *degeneracy*. You will remember that when we introduced the Simplex method we saw that we distinguish at each iteration between basic and non-basic variables. Basic variables appear in the current solution whilst non-basic variables do not and automatically take a value of zero. It may happen, however, that in a particular solution (either in an intermediate tableau or in the optimal tableau) a basic variable also takes a zero value. Normally this will not cause difficulties for the Simplex algorithm in its search for an optimal solution—we shall still arrive at an optimal solution—but as ever we need to be able to recognize the situation. Consider the following problem.

$$\text{Maximize} \quad 40A + 50B \tag{9-39}$$
$$\text{subject to:} \quad 28A + 42B \leq 16\,800 \tag{9-40}$$
$$12A + 6B \leq 4\,800 \tag{9-41}$$
$$1A + 1B \leq 500 \tag{9-42}$$

You will recognize that this problem is similar to one we examined earlier, with the difference that Eq. (9-42) has been altered slightly. The RHS of this constraint has been reduced from 600 to 500.

Student activity
Formulate and solve this problem using the Simplex method. Use the penalty method with a value of 100 and obtain the tableau for the second iteration as well as for the optimal.

As we use the Simplex method to solve this problem the degenerate nature gradually becomes evident. Tableau 9-7 shows the second tableau. It is apparent that this tableau is not optimal. Variable A has a positive OF coefficient at 6.667 and is clearly set to enter the basis. If we apply the standard Simplex rule to determine which variable will leave the basis

Tableau 9-7 Second iteration

	A	B	S_1	S_2	S_3	Value
PROFIT	6.667	0	−1.19	0	0	−20 000
B	0.6667	1	0.024	0	0	400
S_2	8	0	−0.14	1	0	2 400
S_3	0.3333	0	−0.02	0	1	100

we calculate the ratios of value to positive A column coefficients and select the smallest. This gives:

$$\begin{array}{ll} B & 400/0.6667 = 600 \\ S_2 & 2400/8 = 300 \\ S_3 & 100/0.333 = 300 \end{array}$$

We appear to have a problem. Two currently basic variables have the same ratio of 300: S_2 and S_3. Such a situation—where there is a choice as to which of two or more variables should leave the current solution—is an indication that the solution is degenerate. How do we resolve the dilemma of which variable to choose to leave the basis? In practice, although there are a number of alternative 'rules' to apply to such a situation it usually does not matter. We can arbitrarily select one of the tying variables as the pivot row. If we choose S_3 we then obtain Tableau 9-8.

Tableau 9-8 Optimal solution

	A	B	S_1	S_2	S_3	Value
PROFIT	0	0	−0.71	0	−20	−22 000
B	0	1	0.071	0	−2	200
S_2	0	0	0.429	1	−24	0
A	1	0	−0.071	0	3	300

We can confirm that this is indeed the optimal solution, given that no further variables have a positive coefficient in the OF row. We can see also the effect of degeneracy on the optimal solution. S_2 is shown in the basis but actually takes a zero value. A number of points need to be mentioned at this stage. The first is that a sensible computer package should be able to resolve the problem of a tie between pivot rows in a computationally efficient manner and that this will usually happen without the user being aware of the problem. Second, with a degenerate problem, there may, on rare occasions, be the problem of *cycling*. That is, the algorithm may return to a previous solution in its search for the optimum. Again, in practical terms the LP computer package you are using should be able to avoid this difficulty. Finally, it is important to note the effect that degeneracy has on any sensitivity analysis we may wish to carry out on the optimal solution.

Student activity
For each of the binding constraints in this problem reformulate the problem changing the RHS of each constraint in turn by + 1 and using a computer package to determine the new optimal solution. Compare the change in the objective function with the opportunity costs shown in Tableau 9-8.

If we examine the effect of changing the RHS of each constraint in turn (given that all

Table 9-1 Changes in objective function

Constraint	Change in OF	Opportunity cost from Tableau 9-8
1 (Eq. (9-40))	+0.71	+0.71
2 (Eq. (9-41))	0	0
3 (Eq. (9-42))	+20	0

three constraints are binding at the optimum—S_1, S_2 and $S_3 = 0$) then, by reformulating and solving each problem again, we obtain the changes in the objective function shown in Table 9-1.

It is evident that the opportunity cost figures from the tableau are no longer reliable in terms of assessing the effect of a unit change in a binding constraint. In this example, they appear to be valid for constraints 1 and 2 but not for constraint 3. In fact, the opportunity cost figures will depend in part upon the arbitrary choice of pivot row when we have tied variables. The situation is actually worse than it appears, for if we were to undertake sensitivity analysis in terms of a unit reduction in each constraint then we would find constraint 3's opportunity cost was correct but those of constraints 1 and 2 were not. The reason for this is effectively to be found in the dual formulation and solution. A degenerate primal problem implies that the optimal values of the dual solution are not unique. Property 3 of the primal–dual relationship (which allowed us to use such opportunity cost values) is strictly true only for non-degenerate problems. It is particularly important, therefore, that you are able to identify a degenerate solution from the optimal Simplex tableau if you are undertaking sensitivity analysis.

9-6 ASSUMPTIONS OF THE BASIC LP MODEL

It has become evident as we have progressed in the development and evaluation of the LP model that it is underpinned by a number of critical assumptions. In this section we shall examine each of these in turn. It is tempting for the model-builder and decision-maker to ignore such assumptions or, at best, treat them as an insignificant aspect of the business problem for which we are seeking a solution. However, the validity of such assumptions in the context of the application become critical. Not only may we waste our time trying to apply the model to a business problem for which it is unsuited but we may also interpret and use information generated by the technique with a far higher degree of confidence than is actually warranted. It is vitally important in practice to assess how well the model's assumptions compare with the key factors of the business problem. A word of encouragement is probably necessary at this stage. As we progress through this section it may appear that the list of assumptions behind the technique is indeed a formidable one and that few, if any, real-world problems can meet such requirements. In practice, there are methods of overcoming most of the difficulties encountered when a particular assumption is violated which do not prevent LP from being an extremely useful tool for the business decision-maker. As ever, though, it is of critical importance for the decision-maker to be aware of such limitations in order to be able rationally to assess the suitability of the model to a

Linearity

Although it may appear so obvious as to be hardly worth pointing out, LP is a technique involving *linear* relationships. Both the objective function and the constraints must be capable of being expressed mathematically in a linear form. This has implications both for the constraints and for the objective function. In fact there are two associated aspects of this linearity feature. These relate to the properties of *proportionality* and *additivity*. The proportionality concept implies a constant relationship between variables and their corresponding technical coefficients. Thus, for example, if one unit of Model A requires 28 hours of assembly time, 2 units require 56 hours, 3 units 84 hours, and so on. Equally, in terms of the objective function each unit produced contributes the same (fixed) amount to the objective function. Clearly, this implies that such factors as increasing or decreasing returns to scale do not exist, that there are no set-up or establishment costs, and so on. The concept of additivity is equally straightforward. This implies that the individual component parts of some relationship are equal to the total. Simply, profit earned from Model A plus profit earned from Model B is equal to total profit from both activities. Equally, the assembly time needed to produce Model A plus the assembly time needed to produce Model B is equal to the total assembly time required.

Taken together, both concepts imply linear relationships. Clearly there are many business situations where such linear relationships are appropriate. Wage rates, for example, may well follow a linear pattern, at least within a defined level of working. Machine production capacity per hour or per day is likely to be linear also. It is also apparent, however, that such relationships may well be non-linear. Wage rates may well be linear for the 'normal' working week but become non-linear when overtime or bonus payments are paid. Linear production functions do not allow for economies of scale, i.e. for the fact that at higher levels of output production equipment may become more (or less) efficient in terms of per-unit output. Equally, it may be unrealistic to assume that the per-unit profit contribution remains constant. In order to sell more of one item the company may well have to lower its unit selling price, which in turn may affect its profit contribution. Hidden behind the additivity assumption lies another implied relationship: that of independence. The objective function, for example, implies that the decision variables are independent of each other in terms of attaining the declared objective. In terms of profit this may be unrealistic. IMC, we are told, sell two products that may well compete against each other as well as against those of competing firms. It may well be, therefore, that selling more of Model A results in lower sales—and hence lower profit per unit—for Model B. The two profit coefficients, therefore, may well be interrelated and the corresponding objective function may take a form such as:

$$\text{Profit} = 40A + 50B - 0.1AB$$

which is clearly non-linear. The decision-maker, therefore, needs to assess carefully whether the relationships built into the model are realistically linear in practice. If in fact they are not then the model may still be useful. We have seen—when looking at detailed problem formulations—that it is often possible to manipulate non-linear relationships into

Assembly labour cost (£)

16 800   21 800

Assembly time (hours)

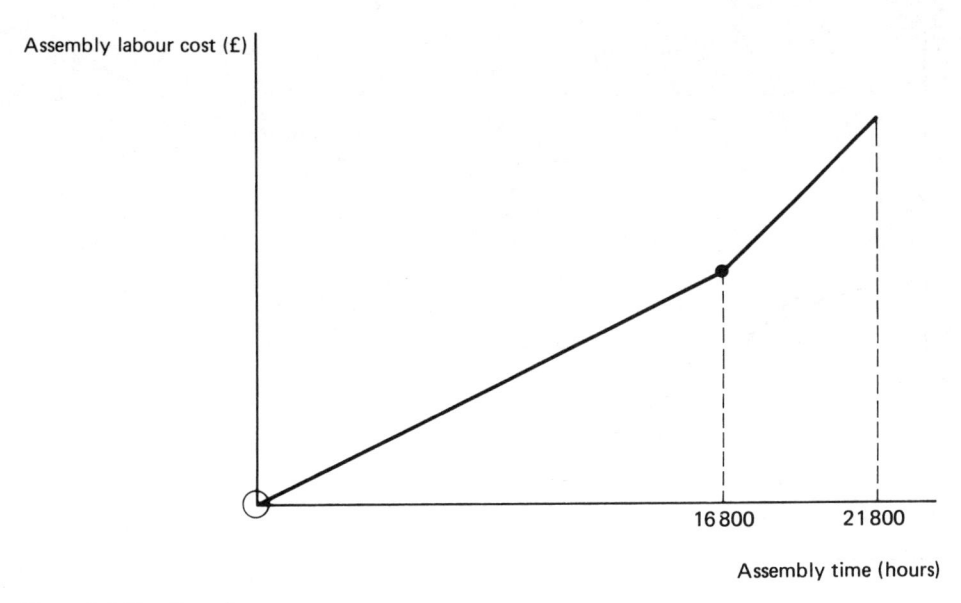

Figure 9-4 Non-linearity

a suitable linear form. Equally, through certain 'tricks' of formulation we may still be able to represent a non-linear relationship in a linear form. Consider the following illustrations. Returning to the original IMC problem that we first introduced in Chapter 5, we saw that the profit contributions for A and B were made up of selling price less component costs, assembly time costs and inspection time costs. Assembly time was costed at £4 per hour required. Let us assume that such labour costs still apply but that now, in addition, it is possible for IMC to pay their assembly staff overtime rates at £5 per hour and thus make an extra 5000 assembly hours available. The proportionality concept is now clearly violated given that assembly time cost per hour (and hence also profit contributions) will not be constant but will depend upon the total number of assembly hours being used. The situation is illustrated in Fig. 9-4.

The diagram shows that assembly costs rise at one rate up to 16 800 hours and then at another, different rate thereafter. However, by an appropriate formulation we can resolve this technically non-linear situation. Let us now define 4 decision variables: A and B measuring the output of the two models utilizing 'normal' assembly time and A_0 and B_0 showing output of the two models utilizing overtime assembly hours. The formulation of the problem would then become:

$$\text{Maximize} \quad 40A + 50B + 12A_0 + 8B_0$$
$$\text{subject to:} \quad 28A + 42B \leq 16\,800$$
$$28A_0 + 42B_0 \leq 5\,000$$
$$12A + 12A_0 + 6B + 6B_0 \leq 4\,800$$
$$1A + 1A_0 + 1B + 1B_0 \leq 600$$
$$A, B, A_0, B_0 \geq 0$$

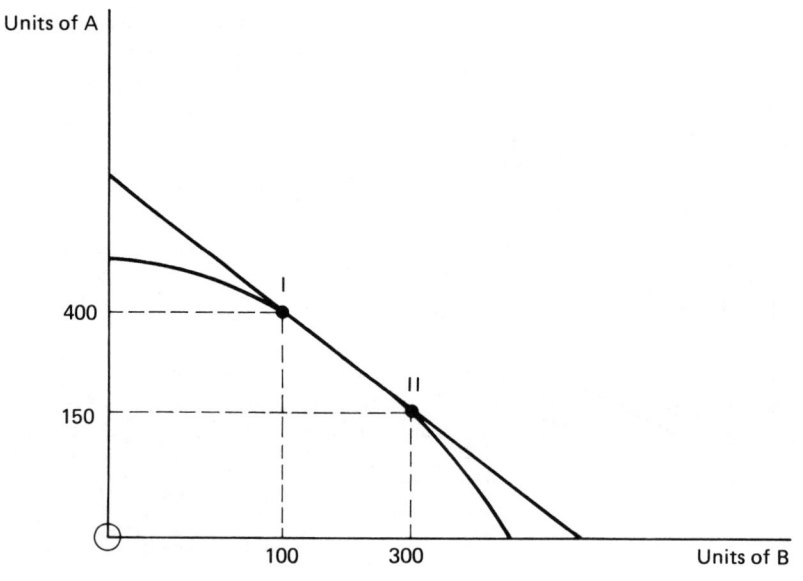

Figure 9-5 Non-linear constraint

and it is evident that the problem is now fully linear (although you may realize that the formulation as shown is actually incomplete given that there is no requirement for A to take a value before A_0 becomes non-zero). Turning to a different approach to resolve non-linearity, consider the situation shown in Fig. 9-5.

We can assume that we face a constraint where some resource, say inspection time, can be allocated between two competing products—Model A and Model B. The straight line indicates the linear relationship constraint we have used thus far:

$$12A + 6B \leq 4800$$

However, as we have discussed this implies a constant trade-off in terms of using this resource between the two competing requirements. For example, by sacrificing 1 unit of A we release 12 inspection hours, thereby allowing the production of two units of B. The implication of the constraint equation is that such a trade-off (1 A for 2 B) applies at every and any production level. Clearly, because of economy-of-scale factors and set-up costs this may well not be the case. We may face instead a trade-off relationship as shown by the non-linear function shown in the same diagram. This clearly indicates that the extra production of B that is made available per unit of A sacrificed depends on the level of production of the two products. At some levels of production the unit of A sacrificed will allow more than 2 units of B to be produced and at other levels of production less than 2. However, it may be possible—and realistic—to resolve the difficulty thus caused by the use of another assumption. It is likely that, in many practical situations, we shall be using LP as a 'fine-tuning' technique, that is, to make minor adjustments to the operational decisions that we have been taking for a considerable time before utilizing the technique. Equally, it may simply not be a management option—at least in the short term—to concentrate production on only one product even if the model solution indicates this is optimal. In other words, the range of production of A and B that we would actually consider will be limited: perhaps between points I and II as in Fig. 9-5. That is, we do not expect output of A to fall outside the range 150–400 or that of B outside the range 100–300. Clearly, using appropriate constraints we can build these requirements and assumptions into the model. It is also clear that within these limits we can actually approximate the true non-linear relationship that exists between A and B with a suitable linear function. Accordingly, the LP model is again appropriate as long as we remember—from the decision-making perspective—that the information it provides is valid only within the specified production ranges. And if all else fails then we can turn to those mathematical programming models that can deal explicitly with such non-linear relationships. We introduce some of these in Part C of the text.

Divisibility

The second key assumption behind the LP model relates to *divisibility*. This implies that all variables and activities are technically continuous: they can take any value both fractional as well as integer. The IMC problem illustrates this. Conveniently (!), the optimal solution to the IMC production problem required $A = 300$ units, $B = 200$ units. Given that this is a textbook example its features were carefully controlled (as were most of the other examples) to ensure integer—and hence sensible—values. There is no reason, however, why the technique should not generate solutions which, for example, required $A = 329.67$ units. (Indeed, you will already have encountered such solutions if you have completed the student exercises set at the end of each chapter.) Such a solution, however, is clearly impossible from a practical perspective. IMC cannot produce fractional units of the product. Equal considerations apply to resources. In practice we may generate a solution that requires one-quarter of a microchip, for example. Naturally, this assumption is not always a problem. We may well have constraints and an objective function that are expressed in units where non-integer values are realistic: monetary values (e.g. £'s), labour time (hours), and so on. However, when such values are not realistic then the temptation may well be simply to round the optimal solution to 'sensible' values. Whilst this may well be applicable to some solutions it will not necessarily apply to all. Consider, for example, a situation where we were using LP to evaluate some capital budgeting problem. IMC may have funding available to construct a new factory on one of three alternative sites. We may be able to formulate this problem in LP terms (with constraints relating to costs, finance, timescale, manpower, etc., and an objective function relating to the profit or return generated from each site). The optimal solution, however, might well indicate that we should use our resources to build half of a factory on one site and half on another. Rounding the solution in such a case will not help. We must build one factory on one site or not at all. Where such divisibility is a real difficulty then we must turn to another branch of the mathematical programming family: *integer programming*.

Certainty

The third assumption (and one frequently overlooked) relates to the certainty of the data used in the problem formulation. We imply in the original IMC problem that we know *precisely* and *with certainty* the values of the key parameters of the problem. This implies, for example, that we *know* that Model A generates *exactly* £40 profit and that each unit produced requires *exactly* 28 assembly hours. Clearly this is nonsense. No business organization will have such certain data available. At best such parameter values will be estimates or forecasts subject to the uncertainty that surround the techniques that can generate such information. To a large extent the use of sensitivity analysis will overcome this problem. Such analysis will, as we have seen, allow the decision-maker to assess by how much key parameters in the problem will have to change before the solution changes. If these parameters are known to be only estimates then such a sensitivity approach is particularly useful. It is equally important, however, that the decision-maker is familiar with the structure and logic of the LP model. After all, it is the decision-maker who will be most likely to be in the position of being able to evaluate the reliability of the data being used. He or she is obviously best suited for then assessing the potential reliability of the information generated by the model. This presupposes an adequate familiarity with the technique (a familiarity we have tried to develop in this text). It is worth while pointing out, however, that alternatives to the basic LP model do exist. In particular, the *stochastic programming* model offers the opportunity of incorporating uncertainty about parameters into the structure of the problem. Equally, *chance constrained programming* explicitly tries to incorporate an assessment (measured in probability terms) of the reliability of key parameters.

Single objectives

The final major assumption implied in the LP model is that of a suitable single objective. Equally, there is an implication that this objective can be accurately quantified. As ever, this may be a gross over-simplification of the business decision-making process. In some situations it is clear that a single objective may well be entirely appropriate. A production manager, for example, with a clear, fixed production target to be met may well be able to quantify an appropriate objective much as we have done in terms of profit or cost. In more complex situations, however, the decision may involve several—often conflicting—objectives. IMC may well want to maximize their profit from production and sales but equally they may have a policy of trying to increase market share even if, in the short term, this may not generate maximum profit. Clearly, LP cannot deal with such a conflict. It requires from the decision-maker a single, clear and unambiguous target to be attained. Equally, there is the implication that such a target can be quantified (in terms of profit, cost, etc.). In strict business applications this may not be unduly difficult. In other application areas, however, it may prove more problematic. Determining a policy that provides a 'good' service to customers, or a 'high' quality of output, may well be realistic—but difficult to quantify—management targets. Once again, whilst it may be difficult to apply LP to those business problems that do face multiple objectives, management scientists have developed a branch of mathematical programming to try to deal with multiple objective problems. *Goal programming* is one of these and will be examined in more detail later in the text.

Whilst an awareness of such assumptions is of especial importance to the practitioner it must be remembered that they have not prevented LP from being applied across a diverse range of business areas. What is important is to be aware of how much such assumptions limit the reliability of the information thrown out by the technique. In practice this can best be achieved by those who are most familiar with the business problem under investigation.

9-7 SUMMARY

In this section of the text we have introduced and developed the LP model as a powerful tool for the decision-maker. We have examined the logic and method of the technique and we have illustrated its potential across a variety of typical business problems. We have stressed throughout that, in order to gain maximum benefit from this powerful analytical tool, the decision-maker needs to be familiar with both the methodology and solution process. Unlike the earlier models of assignment and transportation, LP requires a reasonable degree of expertise from the decision-maker. However, as we have tried to show, the development of such expertise does not necessarily imply theoretical mathematical underpinning. It is possible—not to say desirable—for the manager to develop the skills necessary to formulate, solve and interpret the solution of LP applications to his/her own business problems. The benefits arising from applying the technique in business no doubt explain in part the tremendous growth in the variety and extent of LP applications over the past few years. The technique offers a tremendous amount of information directly relevant to the decision-maker that is difficult, if not impossible, to obtain from any other source. Even the inherent limitations of the technique (defined by its key assumptions) have not proved a major hindrance in applying the technique to a considerable diversity of business areas (although this is not a justification for blandly assuming that such assumptions are unimportant). Without doubt the other key factor has been the arrival of inexpensive and efficient computer power on the decision-maker's desk in the form of a PC or a direct, interactive link to the company's mainframe or minicomputer system. Arguably more than any other model, LP has developed over the past decade from a model used by the management science specialist to a general operational tool used by the manager.

STUDENT EXERCISES

9-1 In order to gain familiarity with both the dual formulation and its direct relationship with the primal you should return to some of the more complex problems we have examined:
(a) Put the primal problem into the standard canonical format.
(b) Obtain the dual formulation.
(c) Input this dual formulation into a computer package and solve for the optimal solution.
(d) Compare the dual solution with the primal.

9-2 For each of the major student exercises set you should return to the original formulation and assess the implications of the key assumptions behind LP in terms of its likely impact on the reliability of the information generated in the optimal tableau.

9-3 Examine each of the solutions you have generated using the Simplex program to determine whether any of the problems (unboundedness, alternate optima, etc.) apply and if so what difficulties they cause.

9-4 Consider the problem shown below:

$$\text{Maximize} \quad 40A + 50B$$
$$\begin{aligned}\text{subject to:} \quad 28A + 42B &\leq 16\,800 \\ 12A + 6B &\leq 4\,500 \\ 1A + 1B &\leq 600\end{aligned}$$

Required:
(a) Find the optimal solution.
(b) Comment on the practical implementation of this solution.
(c) Round the solution upward to the nearest integer value. Check the feasibility of this solution against the original constraints.
(d) Round the solution downward. Check the feasibility against the original constraints. What conclusion do you come to about the practical optimal solution?
(e) Determine the value of the objective function from (d) above. Now test the feasibility of the solution $A = 261$ and $B = 226$ and determine the corresponding value of the objective function. What conclusion do you now reach?

PART C

FURTHER MATHEMATICAL PROGRAMMING MODELS

In Part B of the text we saw how powerful and useful the general linear programming (LP) model was for the decision-maker. Not only was it readily adaptable to a tremendous variety of business problems but it also provided a considerable amount of detailed information pertaining to the problem under investigation. Moreover, we found that it was relatively straightforward to use and required little formal mathematical underpinning. However, we also concluded that a degree of caution needed to be exercised when applying LP to ensure that the principles and assumptions underpinning the technique were appropriate to the problem under investigation. Because of the potentially restrictive nature of the basic LP model it is not surprising that considerable effort has been given to the development of further—more specialized—mathematical programming models. It is to some of these that we turn in this section.

The first area we consider is that of integer programming. Chapter 10 examines the way in which the requirement for integer values in mathematical programming can arise and the ways in which such a requirement can be incorporated into the model formulation. Chapter 11 then examines some of the solution programs that are available for dealing with integer programming formulations.

Chapter 12 introduces the area of goal programming where we are concerned with problems where multiple objectives may be appropriate. We consider how a variety of often conflicting goals can be incorporated into a mathematical programming model and how the solution of such a formulation can be determined.

In Chapter 13 we address the problem of non-linearity in mathematical programming and consider the approaches that can be taken with non-linear programming.

Finally, in Chapter 14 we turn to dynamic programming which is fundamentally an approach concerned with accommodating changes in the parameters to the model over time.

It is important to realize that it is not our intention in this part of the text to provide a fully comprehensive coverage of these topics in terms either of formulations or of solution methods. The reasons for this will become clear as we progress. In the first instance such models become increasingly complex in terms of their mathematical underpinning. We saw that one of the advantages of LP was that it could be approached on an intuitive rather than mathematical basis. This is, unfortunately, not the case with the more advanced and the more useful models which require considerable mathematical dexterity in terms of their formulation, the solution approach adopted and the solution interpretation.

In addition it will also become apparent that there is generally no single solution method for these models. Instead, solution methods have been developed for different groups of problems. This in itself raises difficulties for the decision-maker who may be considering applying such techniques to business problems. The objective of this part, therefore, is to provide an outline of the nature of these more advanced models, to examine the effect such problems have on the general LP method and to examine a number of possible solution approaches. It is *not* our intention to provide a detailed and rigorous examination of this subject area or to examine the solution algorithms in detail. Such an examination lies beyond the scope of this text and of our intended audience. However, by the end of this part the decision-maker will appreciate the potential of these models and will be in a position to assess the trade-off that exists between applying the general LP model to a problem (with its inherent assumptions and possible inaccurate representation of reality) and applying a more complex—but potentially more realistic—model.

10

INTEGER LINEAR PROGRAMMING

In earlier chapters we saw how linear programming, either directly or via one of its special variants for dealing with transportation and assignment problems, could be used to tackle many of the business problems that face the modern manager. LP was shown to be able to model an extensive range of business situations and to provide detailed information that the manager could consult and use before taking any final decision. A second look at these models reveals, however, that we were fortunate to produce solutions that the manager could immediately recognize as 'sensible'. After all, in none of these did we attempt to account for the fact that some—possibly all—of the decision variables must represent *whole numbers* of units. Consequently, had we given any further thought to the outcome of our analyses, we would have had no reason to expect solutions in which variables took appropriate *integer* values. In Chapter 5, for example, the reader could not reasonably have expected an LP investigation of the International Monitor Company's monitor assembly problem to result in directly implementable production quantities for Model A and Model B monitors. A different choice of figures for the available weekly supplies of labour and microchips, or for the unit resource inputs to the two models, could have led to an optimal solution in which the variables took fractional values implying that, at some stage, IMC should produce incomplete pieces of monitor. In such a case it may occasionally be possible to interpret the solution realistically, for example to mean that some monitors are left unfinished on a Friday afternoon and completed the following week. More realistically, however, it should be recognized that, because of the magnitude of the numbers involved, it is often permissible to round off the optimal values and create a solution which, though no longer technically optimal, is both directly implementable and sufficiently close to optimality for all practical purposes. For example, the profit-maximizing combination of the two monitors in Chapter 5 turned out to be $A = 300$ and $B = 200$. Had these been $A = 300.4$ and $B = 200.7$ instead, then a simple rounding down to the original values would, in all probability, have resulted in an acceptably small reduction in profit potential and an insignificant shift in the production schedule.

However, there are many instances of problems where linear programming will not lead to acceptable practical solutions, either by a judicious interpretation of fractional values or by skilful rounding. In such cases we need to develop a suitable linear model where integer conditions are imposed on some or all of the variables. Although these models of *integer linear programming* (ILP) are disarmingly similar to those of ordinary LP, the solutions derived from them may be very different. The natural consequence of this is that solution procedures may also prove to be different. We shall examine these in some detail in the next chapter. It would be entirely wrong, however, to believe that integer linear programming exists simply to fill a gap in the armoury of ordinary linear programming. That is far too negative a view. ILP can—and does—provide a means of addressing whole new categories of business problem that fall outside the boundaries of classical LP. The rest of the chapter illustrates this by introducing a series of problem scenarios. Our intention is to extend the reader's modelling expertise one step at a time so that, by the end of the chapter, you will have mastered many of the concepts and constructions that make ILP such a powerful tool. We do not pretend that our treatment is comprehensive—ILP can be applied to so diverse a set of problems that no treatment could possibly cover all the ground—but we have attempted to identify a significant subset of common modelling situations in which there are standard and effective ILP approaches. Lastly, a word of warning—and a challenge. By comparison with LP the logic of ILP is, generally speaking, on a higher plane of subtlety. In the later sections of the chapter we shall make considerable demands on the reader's powers of reasoning and concentration as we build ILP models of some complexity. Once again, we can only reiterate our original advice—keep up with both the activities and exercises.

10-1 LP AND ILP: THE GULF BETWEEN

The purpose of this section is to confirm that LP and ILP, despite their obvious similarities, may produce very different results and, therefore, that there is a need for an approach to ILP problems in their own right. Consider the dilemma that faces the production manager at IMC's Northtown factory. Constrained by an annual budget of £300 000 on capital expenditure, he needs to acquire certain up-to-the-minute items of equipment to improve production capacity and match the output of his counterparts at Midtown and Southtown. His shortlist consists of two machines: the X and the Y. Machine X costs £100 000 and could increase annual output by 8000 monitors. Machine Y costs £120 000 but could raise annual output by 10 000. If we assume that the manager is willing to consider purchasing any combination of Xs and Ys, and that his primary objective is to maximize Northtown's production capacity, his problem can be approached in classical LP fashion. If X and Y respectively denote the numbers of machines X and Y purchased, then in order to optimize annual production capacity while remaining within the budgetary constraint, the manager must:

$$\text{Maximize} \quad 8000X + 10\,000Y \tag{10-1}$$

$$\text{subject to:} \quad 100\,000X + 120\,000Y \leqslant 300\,000 \tag{10-2}$$

$$X, Y \geqslant 0$$

It is also evident that, in the context of the problem, X and Y should be whole numbers but we will ignore this requirement for the moment. Instead we investigate the solution that results when the manager's problem is treated as a straightforward LP.

Student activity
Find and interpret the LP solution to this problem. Comment on the realism of the solution generated.

The reader will be aware that this is a particularly small problem of its kind: it has just two variables and only one constraint. Such single-constraint LP problems are rapidly solved by common sense and the use of a little arithmetic. In this case, X improves annual capacity by 8000/100 000 of a monitor for every £1 spent, while the same investment in Y produces an increase of 10 000/120 000. The choice is therefore between 0.08 per £1 spent on machine X, and 0.083 for machine Y. It is apparent that the manager should spend all his budget on Y, so enhancing annual capacity by $300\,000 \times 10\,000/120\,000$ (i.e. 25 000) monitors and buying 300 000/120 000 (i.e. 2.5) machines of type Y. We conclude that the optimal LP solution is:
$$X = 0, \quad Y = 2.5$$

However, no amount of imaginative interpretation can make any practical sense of the fractional result generated by the LP model. The manager either buys a machine or he doesn't—half-measures are meaningless. But what of rounding? Could we round the value of Y up or down to produce an optimal *integer* solution? Clearly the only feasible rounding is downward—otherwise we exceed the manager's budget—and so the model indicates that the manager should consider purchasing two machines of the Y type. A moment's reflection, however, shows that, though integer, this is by no means the optimal solution. Two Y's would increase capacity by 20 000 monitors a year, but for a capital expenditure of £300 000 the manager could buy three X's and add 24 000 to Northtown's output potential. It is clear that this last suggestion is indeed the optimal solution for the appropriate problem formulation:

$$\text{Maximize} \quad 8000X + 10\,000Y \qquad (10\text{-}1)$$

$$\text{subject to:} \quad 100\,000X + 120\,000Y \leqslant 300\,000 \qquad (10\text{-}2)$$

$$X, Y \geqslant 0 \text{ and integer}$$

In such a case the LP and ILP solutions to what is ostensibly the same problem are very different indeed. It is quite evidently beyond the realms of expert interpretation or creative rounding to produce the one directly from the other. This fact alone is enough to set ILP apart from LP, and warrant its investigation as a distinct and separate approach to modelling. Even so the following sections provide further justification for the study and use of ILP as we examine the way in which it creates new opportunities for the application of mathematical programming to business problems.

Student activity
Construct a graph for this problem. Show the feasible area relating to Eq. (10-2) and the objective function line. Show also all the possible combinations of X and Y that represent integer solutions and confirm the conclusions of this section.

10-2 BINARY DECISION VARIABLES

Of central importance to ILP is a new kind of decision variable that has no counterpart in LP. This is the *binary* or *zero-one* variable. As its names imply it can take only two values: 0 or 1. Such a variable may be used for a variety of purposes. In all cases, however, it may be regarded as a switch that is set either to 'off' (i.e. its value is 0) or to 'on' (i.e. its value is 1). This provides the modeller with a means of representing decisions that comprise a simple choice between alternatives—between 'yes' and 'no', 'do' and 'don't' or 'stop' and 'go'. Because so many of the problems and opportunities confronted by business decision-makers contain elements of this type, the binary variable is an invaluable new weapon in the modeller's armoury. As an illustration of the application of binary variables consider the range of investment opportunities currently under discussion by IMC's board of directors. In a move to expand the company's manufacturing base potential factory sites have been identified in the USA, France and Italy. Further, each site has been subjected to a detailed analysis of costs and returns taking account of initial legal and land purchase charges, local labour and transportation costs, regional subsidies and likely market conditions over the next 5 years. As a result, estimates covering initial outlays and expected net present values* have been derived. These are shown in Table 10-1.

Table 10-1 IMC investment data—new factory proposals

Country	Site	Initial outlay (£m)	Net present value (£m)
USA	Pasadena	30	81
	Seattle	27	72
France	Lille	15	48
	Orléans	18	54
	Grenoble	20	60
Italy	Rome	16	50
	Milan	22	64

IMC's financial advisers anticipate that the company could raise £100m to cover the initial outlay on its chosen sites. However, this is clearly not enough to permit expansion in all directions at once, and so the board must select those sites which it considers to give best value for money. We translate this objective quite reasonably as the desire to maximize the total net present value of the chosen sites subject to the availability of finance. The corresponding ILP model begins as follows:

---

* For those readers who have not previously met the concept, we should point out that NPV is a measure of the overall value of an individual project. Briefly, the NPV allows for the fact that any investment will generate a series of cashflows (i.e. cash payments and returns), occurring at different points in time over a possibly lengthy period, by down-weighting or 'discounting' future amounts according to the time at which they occur. The NPV of an investment is the amount of cash that, if received right now, would exactly match the net benefits over time attributable to the investment.

Define $\quad X_P = 1\quad$ if the Pasadena site is selected
$\qquad\qquad\qquad\quad\; 0\quad$ otherwise

and $\qquad\quad X_S = 1\quad$ if the Seattle site is chosen
$\qquad\qquad\qquad\quad\; 0\quad$ otherwise

Similarly, we introduce variables X_L, X_O, X_G, X_R and X_M for the remaining sites, Lille through to Milan. Clearly the X's are 'do/don't' variables, representing the fact that the board will finally decide: 'We do/don't go ahead and build a factory on this site.' The complete model is:

Maximize $\quad 81X_P + 72X_S + 48X_L + 54X_O + 60X_G + 50X_R + 64X_M \qquad$ (10-3)

subject to: $\quad 30X_P + 27X_S + 15X_L + 18X_O + 20X_G + 16X_R + 22X_M \leq 100 \qquad$ (10-4)

$$X_P, X_S, X_L, X_O, X_G, X_R, X_M \quad binary$$

The structure of the model is straightforward. It is essentially that of the example we discussed in the previous section—a single-constraint problem. Indeed, we may even alter the wording of our variable definitions—without actually changing their meaning—to bring them into line with earlier usage. For example, X_P could be viewed as the number of times the Pasadena site is selected, X_S the number of times the board selects Seattle, and so on. The objective function represents the total net present value, measured in £ million, achieved by the set of chosen sites. Since Pasadena's NPV is £81 million if selected and £0 million if not, the first term of the function—$81X_P$—is the contribution to total NPV made by the Pasadena site, whether or not it is selected. The same considerations apply to each of the other sites. The logic of the constraint follows an identical pattern. Its left-hand side:

$$30X_P + 27X_S + 15X_L + 18X_O + 20X_G + 16X_R + 22X_M$$

represents the total initial outlay in £ million on selected sites and is made up of the individual outlays, site by site, whether or not any particular site is selected. Since at most £100 million is available, the inequality follows.

Student activity
For strategic reasons IMC's board of directors has agreed to develop at least one site in each of USA, France and Italy. Incorporate this additional information into the investment model by devising additional constraints.

10-3 SPECIFICATION OF VARIABLE TYPES

We will be returning to IMC's investment problem in a later section when we investigate a further development of the model. However, it is essential to emphasize one final feature of the way in which we presented it. Note that, as in LP, it is customary to complete the description of the model by specifying the *type* of variables involved in it. In LP the variables were always simply non-negative and we indicated the fact by writing $x_1 \geq 0$, $x_2 \geq 0$, and so on. Since this was unfailingly the case the reader may have wondered why we took the trouble to mention it explicitly in every problem. In ILP, however, the specification of variable types is no mere convention. It is a vital piece of information without which the model is incomplete. Unless we are told the nature of the variables, we have no means of knowing whether they are binary, non-negative integer, or merely non-negative, and, as we saw in the previous section, this may have a considerable effect on the solution we derive. We could have chosen to specify the variables of IMC's investment problem as non-negative integers. Had we done so, however, we would have been forced to include additional constraints of the form:

$$X_P \leq 1, \quad X_S \leq 1, \quad \text{and so on}$$

to ensure that the X's took appropriate—i.e. zero–one—values. Notice also that there is nothing to stop us using a mixture of variables of different types. Where we feel the need, we shall not hesitate to build models that employ variables of all types: binary, integer and ordinary non-negative. Such models are normally described as 'mixed integer' and account for a sizeable proportion of all ILP in current use. Detailed examples of these will be discussed in later sections.

10-4 A FURTHER USE FOR BINARY VARIABLES

We next investigate the use of binary variables in a rather more complex setting, illustrating certain new types of constraint which LP was unable to model. In Chapter 4 we met the basic assignment problem and saw how the particular structure of the resulting model was exploited in a special solution technique: the Hungarian method. When the assumptions of the basic model are relaxed to account for the complications that may occasionally arise in practice—for example, where several resources may be assigned to the same task, or vice versa—then the methods associated with the model may still be applicable even when the Hungarian method is not. There are, however, certain difficulties that cannot be overcome in this way and that, because of the essentially integer nature of the variables involved, demand the use of ILP. Consider the following example. IMC recently received 4 substantial orders for monitors all urgently requesting delivery by the end of the month. The numbers of monitors required by the orders are:

Order	A	B	C	D
Monitors required	230	350	210	290

In the interests of speed and convenience an initial decision has been taken to assign each order *in its entirety* to a particular factory. Thus, for example, order A will go to just one of Northtown, Midtown and Southtown and will not be split between them, however cost-effective such a tactic might be if more time were available. It has also been decided that, in order to spread the workload, each factory should be allotted at least one order. Further, since orders A and B are regarded as prestige assignments, no single factory is to be given both. We assume that the three factories have spare capacity this month, as follows:

	Northtown	Midtown	Southtown
Spare capacity (number of monitors)	450	500	550

Table 10-2 IMC's unit supply costs (£)

	Order			
	A	B	C	D
Northtown	200	250	320	220
Midtown	190	260	290	220
Southtown	210	240	300	210

Estimates of unit supply costs, comprising both production and transportation costs and based on a recent analysis by IMC's accounting department, are given in Table 10-2.

Student activity
Explain why the assignment, transportation and standard LP models are inappropriate for this order assignment problem.

Assuming that IMC wishes to minimize the total supply cost incurred in meeting the four orders, we proceed to model IMC's decision problem. We define:

$X_{AN} = 1$ if order A is assigned to the Northtown factory
        0   otherwise

The remaining variables, X_{AM} to X_{DS} follow in similar fashion. The total supply cost (in £) is the objective function:

$$\text{Minimize} \quad 230(200X_{AN} + 190X_{AM} + 210X_{AS}) + \\ 350(250X_{BN} + 260X_{BM} + 240X_{BS}) + \\ 210(320X_{CN} + 290X_{CM} + 300X_{CS}) + \\ 290(220X_{DN} + 220X_{DM} + 210X_{DS}) \quad (10\text{-}5)$$

This results from the fact that the cost of supplying, for example, the 230 monitors of order A from Northtown will be:

$$£(230 \times 200 \times X_{AN})$$

whether or not order A is assigned there. This can be rewritten as:

$$\text{Minimize} \quad 46\,000X_{AN} + 43\,700X_{AM} + 48\,300X_{AS} + \\ 87\,500X_{BN} + 91\,000X_{BM} + 84\,000X_{BS} + \\ 67\,200X_{CN} + 60\,900X_{CM} + 63\,000X_{CS} + \\ 63\,800X_{DN} + 63\,800X_{DM} + 60\,900X_{DS} \quad (10\text{-}6)$$

In formulating the model's constraints we need to ensure four things: firstly, that we do not exceed the capacities of the factories; secondly, that the requirements of each order are satisfied somewhere; thirdly, that each factory takes at least one order; and finally, that A and B are assigned to different factories. The first of these stipulations leads to:

$$230X_{AN} + 350X_{BN} + 210X_{CN} + 290X_{DN} \leq 450 \quad (10\text{-}7)$$

$$230X_{AM} + 350X_{BM} + 210X_{CM} + 290X_{DM} \leq 500 \quad (10\text{-}8)$$

$$230X_{AS} + 350X_{BS} + 210X_{CS} + 290X_{DS} \leq 550 \quad (10\text{-}9)$$

The left-hand side of each constraint represents the total number of monitors produced at the corresponding factory for the orders assigned there. Since production is limited by capacity the inequality follows. Inexperienced modellers are inclined to neglect the second stipulation in problems of this kind—possibly because there is no explicit statement of it in the original decision problem. In fact we need:

$$X_{AN} + X_{AM} + X_{AS} = 1 \tag{10-10}$$

$$X_{BN} + X_{BM} + X_{BS} = 1 \tag{10-11}$$

$$X_{CN} + X_{CM} + X_{CS} = 1 \tag{10-12}$$

$$X_{DN} + X_{DM} + X_{DS} = 1 \tag{10-13}$$

The left-hand side of each of these constraints is the total number of times the corresponding order is undertaken by IMC at its three factories. Naturally, since IMC undertakes each order once and once only, the given equations result. If we were to omit any one of these constraint equations then we could not guarantee that our solution would supply all the orders. A more compact way of writing these constraints is in the form:

$$X_{iN} + X_{iM} + X_{iS} = 1: \quad \text{for } i = A, B, C, D \tag{10-14}$$

To meet the third stipulation we have:

$$X_{AN} + X_{BN} + X_{CN} + X_{DN} \geq 1 \tag{10-15}$$

$$X_{AM} + X_{BM} + X_{CM} + X_{DM} \geq 1 \tag{10-16}$$

$$X_{AS} + X_{BS} + X_{CS} + X_{DS} \geq 1 \tag{10-17}$$

In these equations the left-hand side represents the number of orders assigned to a particular factory: Northtown, Midtown and Southtown respectively. In every instance this must be at least one. Again, this can be generalized to:

$$X_{Aj} + X_{Bj} + X_{Cj} + X_{Dj} \geq 1: \quad \text{for } j = N, M, S \tag{10-18}$$

Next we include:

$$X_{AN} + X_{BN} \leq 1 \tag{10-19}$$

$$X_{AM} + X_{BM} \leq 1 \tag{10-20}$$

$$X_{AS} + X_{BS} \leq 1 \tag{10-21}$$

which ensure that at most one of orders A and B is undertaken at any factory. Again, writing this in its compact form we have:

$$X_{Aj} + X_{Bj} \leq 1: \quad \text{for } j = N, M, S \tag{10-22}$$

Finally, of course, we complete the formulation with the specification of variable types:

All X's are binary

The full model is therefore:

$$\text{Minimize} \quad 46\,000X_{AN} + 43\,700X_{AM} + 48\,300X_{AS} + \\
87\,500X_{BN} + 91\,000X_{BM} + 84\,000X_{BS} + \\
67\,200X_{CN} + 60\,900X_{CM} + 63\,000X_{CS} + \\
63\,800X_{DN} + 63\,800X_{DM} + 60\,900X_{DS}$$

subject to:
$$230X_{AN} + 350X_{BN} + 210X_{CN} + 290X_{DN} \leq 450 \\
230X_{AM} + 350X_{BM} + 210X_{CM} + 290X_{DM} \leq 500 \\
230X_{AS} + 350X_{BS} + 210X_{CS} + 290X_{DS} \leq 550$$

$$X_{iN} + X_{iM} + X_{iS} = 1 \\
X_{Aj} + X_{Bj} + X_{Cj} + X_{Dj} \geq 1 \\
X_{Aj} + A_{Bj} \leq 1$$

X_{ij} binary; $\quad i = A, B, C$ and D; $j = N, M$ and S

Constraints of these types expressed in these ways are extremely common in ILP problems. They provide the decision-maker with a modelling capability that LP alone cannot match.

Student activity

Modify the order assignment model to allow for each of the following changes:

1. Order A cannot be supplied by Northtown.
2. Because business at Southtown is particularly slack, at least two orders should be assigned there.
3. A and D are related orders. Customers have requested that they are undertaken at the same factory but have left IMC to decide which this should be.

10-5 CONDITIONAL LOGIC IN DECISION MODELS

To digress for a moment, one of the major reasons for the success of computing systems in areas of business activity is the presence in all programming languages of a construct of the form:

IF condition THEN action

This simple statement instructs the computer to take a particular action provided that a certain specified condition is true. If the condition is false then the computer will not take the action. By means of IFs computers can therefore be programmed to act in a manner appropriate to the circumstances in which they find themselves: that is, in a manner determined by conditions on the values of program variables. Unfortunately, in ordinary linear programming we find ourselves frustrated occasionally by our inability to apply a similar construct. There are no IF ... THEN ...'s in LP, much as we would sometimes like them. It would be useful, for example, to build decision models which permitted the manufacture of new products IF annual profits exceeded some specified level—but not otherwise. It would also be extremely convenient if we had a means of varying or entirely disregarding constraints in circumstances where they are altered by decisions that are themselves the subject of investigation within the same model—for instance, where a limit on the availability of some raw material is removed by a decision to replenish stocks. As we

232 FURTHER MATHEMATICAL PROGRAMMING MODELS

saw in Chapter 6, there are occasions when ingenuity and experience in the definition of variables and in the use of additional constraints may allow the formulation of the model we want. Such creativity is not always possible, however, and this is where ILP comes into its own. Through judicious use of binary variables—and admittedly a degree of ingenuity and experience as well—we can always arrange our models to represent the conditional logic—the IF . . . THEN . . .'s—that our decision problems demand. The remainder of the chapter is devoted to showing precisely how this is done in a range of typical business situations.

10-6 THRESHOLD CONSTRAINTS

To find a first illustration of conditional logic in ILP we return to IMC's investment selection problem of Section 10-2. Let us now assume, however, that in order to comply with regional development policy the French Government has imposed a severe condition on any investment IMC may contemplate in France. This is that unless IMC agrees to invest at least £30 million in its proposed French factories the company will not be welcome to invest in France at all. In terms of the IFs of the previous section, this may be summarized as:

IF there is any investment in France THEN it must total at least £30 million.

Note, of course, that this does not exclude the possibility that there is no investment in France. We must be careful to leave this option open when we come to build our model. The variables and constraint that we introduced in Section 10-2 are still perfectly valid. In other words, we start with the original formulation:

$$\text{Maximize} \quad 81X_P + 72X_S + 48X_L + 54X_O + 60X_G + 50X_R + 64X_M \tag{10-3}$$

$$\text{subject to:} \quad 30X_P + 27X_S + 15X_L + 18X_O + 20X_G + 16X_R + 22X_M \leq 100 \tag{10-4}$$

$$X_P, X_S, X_L, X_O, X_G, X_R, X_M \quad \text{binary}$$

At this point we might suggest an extra constraint:

$$15X_L + 18X_O + 20X_G \geq 30 \tag{10-23}$$

However, on reflection this will not suffice. It insists that, whatever else may happen, we *must* invest at least £30 million in French factories, and so precludes the very option—no French investment—that we wished to keep open. In fact there are several ways around this difficulty but the simplest and most instructive takes the following form:

Define $\quad Y_F = 1 \quad$ if there is any investment in France
$\qquad\qquad\quad\;\; 0 \quad$ otherwise

Now introduce two new constraints:

$$15X_L + 18X_O + 20X_G \leq 1000 Y_F \tag{10-24}$$

$$15X_L + 18X_O + 20X_G \geq 30 Y_F \tag{10-25}$$

and the type specification: Y_F is binary.

Both left-hand sides represent the total investment in France (in £ millions). The first constraint ensures that if such an investment is positive then Y_F cannot be 0 and, being binary, must therefore be 1. However, when Y_F is 1 then the second constraint guarantees that the investment will be at least the required £30 million. *Et voilà!* To condense the argument we see that, if IMC's French investment is positive, then it cannot fall below the minimum 'threshold' level dictated by the French Government. Although the argument is complete, there are several points of our presentation which demand further comment. Firstly, our use of Y_F instead of X_F merely emphasizes its distinctive role in the threshold constraints, Eqs (10-24) and (10-25). Secondly, note that these two constraints work together as a pair to produce the effect we want. Neither one, taken alone, could do so. Thirdly, why should we use $1000Y_F$ in the first constraint? In fact, many other numbers would have sufficed. The only significant characteristic of the number is its size. It must be large. Otherwise it might impose an unintended restriction on the French investment. For example, had we used $50Y_F$ instead, we would have precluded the possibility that IMC may select all three French sites—contrary to the board's wishes. In cases like this, it pays to play safe and make the number as large as possible—as large, that is, as the problem solver's computer will allow. The reader will recollect that the penalty value in the LP simplex method was subject to similar considerations. For this reason it is normal practice not to use a specific number at all, but to introduce a surrogate 'Big M'. The constraint then becomes:

$$15X_L + 18X_0 + 20X_G \leq MY_F \qquad (10\text{-}26)$$

Take care to note, however, that M is not a decision variable and will be replaced by a suitable number when a solution is required from the model. Finally, note that when we enter the model into a computer package for solution we will usually need to gather all variables together on the left-hand side. Thus the final form of the two constraints will be:

$$15X_L + 18X_2 + 20X_G - 1000Y_F \leq 0 \qquad (10\text{-}27)$$

$$15X_L + 18X_0 + 20X_G - 30Y_F \geq 0 \qquad (10\text{-}28)$$

Student activity
IMC's Italian backers have offered a grant of £5 million towards the initial costs of developing factory sites in Rome and Milan provided that the company's overall investment exceeds £25 million. Reformulate the model of Section 10-2.

Note that, in order to meet its backer's requirement, IMC would need to select both Italian sites. Using this observation produce an alternative formulation.

10-7 ADJUSTABLE CONSTRAINTS

In Section 10-4 we commented on the desirability of varying or, indeed, entirely disregarding constraints in circumstances where they are altered by decisions that are themselves the subject of investigation within the same model. To clarify this we turn again to the example of Chapter 5. You will recall that we wished to find the profit-maximizing mix of monitors—how many of Model A and how many of Model B IMC should produce in one week. Constraining IMC's ability to assemble unlimited numbers of the two models were restrictions on assembly and inspection hours and a small supply of microchip components. The resulting model was:

$$\text{Maximize} \quad 40A + 50B \tag{10-29}$$
$$\text{subject to:} \quad 28A + 42B \leq 16\,800 \tag{10-30}$$
$$12A + 6B \leq 4\,800 \tag{10-31}$$
$$1A + 1B \leq 600 \tag{10-32}$$
$$A, B \geq 0$$

Assume that business is currently rather slack in other areas of IMC's operation. As a result it will be possible, with a suitable training programme, to divert resources—in this case, manpower—to assembly or inspection. However, the move will be temporary and can benefit only one of the two departments. In other words, it must be either assembly or inspection but not both. Ten employees are involved in the move, with the result that 420 hours can be added to the time available in any week for assembly or inspection. In terms of conditional logic, we may find it useful to extend our IF ... THEN ... construct to:

$$\text{IF} \ldots \text{THEN} \ldots \text{ELSE} \ldots$$

In this case:

IF manpower is diverted to assembly THEN the constraint on assembly hours is relaxed to $(16\,800 + 420)$ hours ELSE the constraint on inspection becomes $(4800 + 420)$ hours.

An ILP formulation of this situation can be achieved in more than one way, but the following method is possibly the most instructive and can be extended easily to cover any number of 'adjustable' constraints.

We define $Y_1 = 1$ if manpower is diverted to assembly
$ 0$ otherwise

and $Y_2 = 1$ if manpower is diverted to inspection
$ 0$ otherwise

The assembly and inspection constraints now become:

$$28A + 42B \leq 16\,800 + 420Y_1 \tag{10-33}$$
$$12A + 6B \leq 4\,800 + 420Y_2 \tag{10-34}$$

and we must also add:

$$Y_1 + Y_2 = 1 \tag{10-35}$$

to be sure that just one of the two possible decisions is taken. To complete the model we also specify that:

$$Y_1, Y_2 \text{ are binary}$$

Student activity
Extend the treatment of this section to deal with the case of

1. 3 constraints, any 2 of which may be adjusted.
2. m constraints, any n of which may be adjusted.

Discardable constraints

So far our discussion has been restricted to the alteration of constraints in line with related decisions. The constraints have none the less remained in force, albeit in a modified form. We can use the same approach, however, to dispense entirely with a constraint that is not needed. For example, suppose that the number of employees diverted from other work is large—so large that the department receiving them no longer imposes any restriction on the mix of monitors that can be produced. In such a case the corresponding constraint should be removed from the problem—it has no further part to play. The dilemma, of course, is that we do not know in advance which constraint should leave and which should stay. This decision is inextricably bound up with the rest of the problem. However, the answer is clear enough. Using the 'Big M' approach once again, we have:

$$28A + 42B \leqslant 16\,800 + MY_1 \qquad (10\text{-}36)$$

$$12A + 6B \leqslant 4\,800 + MY_2 \qquad (10\text{-}37)$$

and
$$Y_1 + Y_2 = 1 \quad \text{as before}$$

As in Section 10-6 M is as big as we can conveniently make it. Thus, if Y_1 takes the value 1 the first constraint is effectively removed from the model—it has no chance of being binding in the optimal solution. However, since Y_2 must then be 0, the second constraint remains in force exactly as before. Reversing the values of Y_1 and Y_2 leaves the first constraint in place but discards the second.

Student activity
IMC's production manager has so far neglected the costs of training involved in diverting manpower from other areas of the company. However, for the week in question, these are:

	(£ per employee)
Assembly	100
Inspection	50

Assume that manpower will be diverted from other work only if it is economic to do so (i.e. if it results in greater profit overall) and reformulate the manager's model accordingly.

10-8 FIXED-CHARGE PROBLEMS

One of the best-known applications of ILP arises in situations where decision-makers are obliged to incur some fixed charge before they can undertake one or more of their activities. The preceding student activity provided a simple instance of this: IMC's production manager was forced to incur a certain fixed training cost per employee before (s)he could be set to work in another department. The following scenario, however, is a more detailed example of its type. It is a Monday morning and IMC's Midtown monitor assembly line is about to start up again. The question, as ever, is: what should it produce this week? The assembly line is currently set to produce the new Model C monitor, but since Model Cs were assembled last week stocks are more than adequate. This means that the choice is between Model A, Model B and some combination of the two. Unfortunately, whichever choice is made, the assembly line must undergo the appropriate set-up process—a rearrangement of work stations along the line, some of which need to be retooled and re-equipped. Inevitably, time is lost and cost is incurred as a result: IMC estimates that to set up for Model A costs £1200 overall and £1350 for Model B. Using our previous notation the profit for Model A is therefore:

$$0 \quad \text{if } A = 0$$

but

$$40A - 1200 \quad \text{if } A > 0$$

whereas for Model B we have:

$$0 \quad \text{if } B = 0$$

but

$$50B - 1350 \quad \text{if } B > 0$$

Our task is thus to incorporate these different forms in a single objective function. This is achieved once more by binary variables. We are yet again in a Yes/No situation: Yes, we do set up the production line for Model A; No, we don't. And similarly, of course, for B. We define:

$Y_A = 1$ if the line is set up to produce Model A at some time during the week
      0   otherwise
$Y_B = 1$ if the line is set up to produce Model B at some time during the week
      0   otherwise

The objective we seek is now clearly:

$$\text{Maximize} \quad 40A - 1200Y_A + 50B - 1350Y_B \tag{10-38}$$

If we also assume that the original restrictions on production still apply, then we must add:

$$\begin{align}
\text{subject to:} \quad 28A + 42B &\leq 16\,800 \\
12A + 6B &\leq 4\,800 \\
1A + 1B &\leq 600 \\
A, B &\geq 0
\end{align}$$

The formulation is still incomplete, however. The solution to the model as it currently stands is evident. There is nothing to prevent Y_A and Y_B from being zero, even when A and B are positive. Therefore the optimal solution $A = 300$, $B = 200$ remains in force, but with the somewhat pointless addition of:

$$Y_A = 0 \quad Y_B = 0$$

In other words IMC makes both types of monitor without setting up production of either. To ensure that Y_A and Y_B take values consistent with the problem, we include two further constraints:

$$A \leq MY_A \tag{10-39}$$

$$B \leq MY_B \tag{10-40}$$

Again, we meet the familiar 'big M' of previous sections. In this case, we may set M to any value no smaller than the weekly capacity of the assembly line for Models A and B. Using a lower value would impose an unintended restriction on the production of monitors. Whatever the M, it is apparent that if A is strictly positive then the first constraint can be satisfied only when $Y_A = 1$. Nevertheless, this is not enough to guarantee the whole of the relationship that we desire between A and Y_A—we also require that Y_A be 0 when A is 0. However, consider the form of the objective function. Y_A has a negative coefficient and so the effect of maximization will be to lower its value as far as possible—indeed, to reduce it to zero if this can be done without violating any constraint. Since Eq. (10-39), the only constraint in which Y_A appears, allows this to happen when A is 0, we can be certain that it will. In practical terms the argument becomes evident if we simply remark that IMC would scarcely incur a set-up cost for Model A if it intended to produce none of that product. Similarly, the combined effect of the second new constraint and the objective function is to force the correct relationship between B and Y_B, namely that the only pairs of values which can result from the model are:

$$B = 0, \quad Y_B = 0$$

and

$$B > 0, \quad Y_B = 1$$

For the sake of clarity and completeness, we present the whole of the model in its modified form.

$$\text{Maximize} \quad 40A - 1200Y_A + 50B - 1350Y_B$$

$$\begin{aligned}
\text{subject to:} \quad & 28A + 42B \leq 16\,800 \\
& 12A + 6B \leq 4\,800 \\
& 1A + 1B \leq 600 \\
& A - MY_A \leq 0 \\
& B - MY_A \leq 0 \\
& A, B \geq 0 \text{ and integer} \\
& Y_A, Y_B \text{ binary}
\end{aligned}$$

Student activity

This problem can be solved by ordinary linear programming (subject perhaps to a rounding of the final values of A and B) if we consider three separate cases, namely that the production line is set up for:

1. A alone,
2. B alone,
3. both A and B.

Each case leads to a distinct LP model, and so to a separate optimal solution. An overall optimum results when we deduct the appropriate fixed charges from the corresponding profits and compare. Solve the fixed charge problem in this way. Why is such an approach generally inferior to ILP?

10-9 COMBINATIONS OF FIXED CHARGES

There are many situations in which cost reductions or 'discounts' are available if two or more similar activities are undertaken simultaneously. To illustrate the point, consider IMC's latest ideas on research and development. Two new products—touch-sensitive (TS) and light-pen-controlled (LPC) screens—are the subject of a recent preliminary report from IMC's R & D department. The report, resulting from an initial feasibility study, proposes development programmes for both products and provides estimates of the associated costs and potential benefits. These are given in Table 10-3.

Note that the cost associated with the combined development programme is less than the sum of the costs of developing TS and LPC screens separately. A 'discount' is available, presumably because ideas and developments generated in one area will prove useful in the other, thereby reducing duplication and costs. The same cannot be said of the benefits, however. These are unaffected by the way in which development takes place. On the basis of the R & D report and projections concerning the availability of financial and other resources IMC has built a strategic model in which:

$$Y_T = 1 \quad \text{if TS screens are developed}$$
$$0 \quad \text{otherwise}$$

and T is the production quantity of TS screens in the long term. L and Y_L are defined for LPC screens in similar fashion. If IMC's aim is the long-term maximization of its profits, then the model's objective function must contain terms which evaluate to:

$$0 \quad \text{when both } T = 0 \text{ and } L = 0$$
$$60T - 1\,200\,000 \quad \text{when} \quad T > 0 \text{ and } L = 0$$
$$80L - 1\,500\,000 \quad \text{when} \quad T = 0 \text{ and } L > 0$$
$$60T + 80L - 2\,100\,000 \quad \text{when both } T > 0 \text{ and } L > 0$$

To achieve this we first define yet another binary variable:

$$Z = 1 \quad \text{if the combined development programme is undertaken}$$
$$0 \quad \text{otherwise}$$

Table 10-3 IMC new product development: costs and benefits

Programme	Estimated cost (£m)	Estimated contribution to profits per screen (£)	
		TS	LPC
TS alone	1.2	60	—
LPC alone	1.5	—	80
TS and LPC together	2.1	60	80

The part of the objective function relating to IMC's new products is then:

$$60T + 80L - 1\,200\,000Y_T - 1\,500\,000Y_L + 600\,000Z \quad (10\text{-}41)$$

Student activity
Verify that this expression meets the requirements of the cases identified above.

Note that the formulation is still incomplete. We have done nothing as yet to ensure the appropriate relationships between the variables. As we have already seen on a number of occasions it is not enough merely to attach suitable meanings to the variables when we define them. We must also construct our models in such a way that the variables are forced into taking values that are consistent with their meanings and which, in particular, bear the right relationships with other variables. In this example, the difficult task is to relate T, L, Y_T, Y_L and Z correctly. T and Y_T, L and Y_L are linked as in the previous section:

$$T \leq MY_T \quad (10\text{-}42)$$

$$L \leq MY_L \quad (10\text{-}43)$$

ensuring that TS and LPC screens are produced and sold only if they are first developed. Z, however, must be 1 if and only if both Y_T and Y_L are 1; otherwise it is 0. This is guaranteed by:

$$2Z \leq Y_T + Y_L \quad (10\text{-}44)$$

Simple as it may seem this constraint warrants a closer look. Firstly, note that if either Y_T or Y_L is 0 then the right-hand side of the constraint is 1 at most, and so Z cannot take the value 1. This ensures that $Z = 0$ unless both Y_T and Y_L are 1. To be certain that $Z = 1$ when both Y_T and Y_L are 1, notice that Z appears in the objective function with a positive coefficient. Z will therefore take the highest value that it can in keeping with any constraint in which it occurs. Since the new constraint—the only one containing Z—allows Z to be 1 when Y_T and Y_L are 1 this is clearly the value Z will take in such a case.

Student activity
Consider a model identical in structure to that of the preceding section, except that Z appears in the objective function with a negative coefficient.
Explain why Eq. (10-44) no longer ensures that Z is 1 when Y_T and Y_L are 1, and verify that:

$$Z \geq Y_T + Y_L - 1$$

is a suitable replacement.

Discounted fixed charges for multiple set-ups

It is instructive to observe that similar principles can be applied to the more general problem in which a discount is available only when at least m of a set of n projects are undertaken simultaneously. If we number the projects from 1 to n and define:

$Y_i = 1$ if project i is undertaken
$\quad\;\; 0$ otherwise
for $i = 1, \ldots, n$

and $\quad\quad\quad Z = 1 \quad$ if at least m projects are undertaken
$\quad\quad\quad\quad\quad\quad 0 \quad$ otherwise

then the required constraint is:

$$mZ \leq Y_1 + Y_2 + \ldots + Y_n \tag{10-45}$$

There is no end, of course, to the complexities that could be built into problems of this sort. It is conceivable, for example, that whole series of discounts come into play as the number of projects increases or that savings are made only when special combinations of projects are undertaken. In each case the difficulties of formulation can be addressed using ideas similar to those above. In particular the reader should remember that a new integer or binary variable, judiciously defined, may well resolve the problem. The hardest task is to incorporate such a variable into the model so that it is certain to take consistent values. This may be achieved in several ways—there are almost always alternative formulations of any given problem. One approach is to exploit what may be termed a 'constructive interaction' between objective function and constraints. Helpful insights are gained if we imagine the objective function forcing a particular variable up or down while some opposing constraint holds it down or up. Our explanation of the structure of IMC's research and development model employed precisely this idea. Indeed, the reader may already have used it when attempting the preceding student activity. Frequently, however, the approach is precluded by the structure of the model. If a variable is involved in a number of constraints, its value will be determined by a complex system of relationships and an appeal to 'constructive interaction' may prove misleading. In any case, it is usually wise to ensure the validity of the variable by means of the constraints alone, even though this may result in a larger, less elegant (and less efficient) model. This is considered in the next section.

10-10 COMMON RELATIONSHIPS IN ILP

When formulating ILP models we find that there are many problem structures which frequently recur. This is true, for example, of certain simple relationships between variables. We now investigate a sample of these and construct the constraint systems that allow us to ensure that our variables take consistent sets of values. Throughout the section we will assume that any X's are continuous or general integer variables, while any Y's and Z's are binary. We first extend our discussion of threshold constraints.

$$Z = 1 \quad \text{if and only if} \quad X \geq V$$

In this instance we wish to ensure that binary variable Z takes the value 1 if variable X equals or exceeds a specified constant V; Z will otherwise be 0. For a full discussion of this relationship we must consider three cases:

Case 1 Firstly, we suppose that Z's involvement in the model is particularly simple. Apart from any constraint(s) we may need to create in order to ensure the appropriate relationship with X, it appears only in the objective function. Assume also that V's coefficient in the objective function is such that Z's value is forced upwards, i.e. Z's coefficient is positive in a maximization or negative in a minimization. Note here that we return to the idea of 'constructive interaction' outlined in Section 10-9. This suggests that Z must be held down—i.e. be subject to some upper limit in the form of a $\leq$ constraint acting in opposition to the objective. In fact, the following is effective:

$$VZ \leq X \tag{10-46}$$

Because of the objective function, Z will take the highest value compatible with any constraint(s) which apply to it. Since it appears only in Eq. (10-45) Z will therefore take the value 1 if the constraint allows. It is clear, however, that this can be so only when X is V or larger: if X is strictly less than V then Z must take the value 0.

Case 2 In the second case we assume the same simplicity as in Case 1, but now suppose that Z is forced downward, i.e. Z's coefficient is negative in a maximization or positive in a minimization. We must therefore seek a constraint that holds up the value of Z in an appropriate way. One such is:

$$MZ \geq X - V' \tag{10-47}$$

where M is the arbitrarily large number of previous discussions and V' is a constant chosen to be slightly smaller than V. In this instance Z will take the smallest possible value consistent with Eq. (10-47). It will thus be 0 if Eq. (10-57) allows—i.e. if X is V' or less. If X is strictly greater than V' then Z must be 1. Note that the validity of the constraint depends on the closeness of V' to V. Invalid results will be obtained if X lies between these two values. In practice this is unimportant, however, since we may make the difference as small as we wish—or, at least, as small as the problem-solver's computer can manage.

Case 3 In the third case we make no assumption about the objective function. Instead we construct a pair of constraints which, whatever the involvement of Z in the rest of the model, ensure the desired relationship with X. These are, in fact, Eqs (10-46) and (10-47). The first guarantees that Z is 0 if $X < V$; the second that Z is 1 if $X > V'$. If V and V' are sufficiently close we may therefore conclude that these are effective. Note that the constraints will conflict if $V' < X < V$ but that this is once again unlikely to pose any practical difficulty.

> *Student activity*
> Modify Eqs (10-46) and (10-47) to deal with the case where $Z = 1$ if and only if $X > V$ (i.e. X is strictly larger than V).

Let us examine the situation where $Z = 1$ if and only if both Y_1 and $Y_2 = 1$. Reminding the reader that Z and the Y's are binary variables, we reintroduce the three cases considered in our discussion of the previous relationship:

1. Since Z is forced upwards by the objective function, it is enough to add:

$$2Z \leq Y_1 + Y_2 \tag{10-48}$$

Table 10-4 Feasible value sets for Eqs (10-48) and (10-49)

Z	Y_1	Y_2
0	0	0
0	1	0
0	0	1
1	1	1

2. Z will take the smallest value compatible with any constraint(s) that apply to it. The following therefore has the desired effect:

$$Z \geq Y_1 + Y_2 - 1 \qquad (10\text{-}49)$$

3. Eqs (10-48) and (10-49) together ensure that the only feasible values for Z and the Y's are those implied by the relationship. These are shown in Table 10-4.

Student activity
Explain fully how Eqs (10-48) and (10-49) achieve their effect in cases 1, 2 and 3 above. Assuming that Z has a positive coefficient in a maximization objective function but is not involved in any other part of the model, find a constraint to ensure the relationship:

$$Z = 1 \quad \text{if both } Y_1 = 0 \text{ and } Y_2 = 1$$
$$0 \quad \text{otherwise}$$

Let us now examine the situation where $Z = 1$ if and only if either $Y_1 = 1$ or $Y_2 = 1$. We stress here that we are dealing with the inclusive 'or'. In other words we mean:

$$\text{either} \quad Y_1 = 1 \quad \text{or} \quad Y_2 = 1 \quad \text{or both}$$

Here the three cases which we considered in our discussions of the previous relationships yield:

1. $$Z \leq Y_1 + Y_2 \qquad (10\text{-}50)$$
2. $$2Z \geq Y_1 + Y_2 \qquad (10\text{-}51)$$
3. Both Eqs (10-50) and (10-51).

Student activity
Confirm that Eqs (10-50) and (10-51) achieve the desired effects in the three cases above. Assuming no knowledge of the objective function, find constraints to ensure that:

$$Z = 1 \quad \text{if either } Y_1 = 1 \text{ or } Y_2 = 0$$
$$0 \quad \text{otherwise}$$

10-11 NON-LINEAR OBJECTIVE FUNCTIONS

In all our previous models we have assumed that the coefficients of the objective function remain fixed no matter how large or how small the values of the variables may be. In practice this is sometimes an unwarranted simplification. Indeed, there are many instances of objective functions which behave in a wholly non-linear fashion. Chapter 13 sets out the problems and principles of this difficult area in detail. In this section, however, we investigate two examples in which the methods of LP and ILP can be applied in spite of the fact that, by the strict definition of the term, the objective functions are non-linear. These examples illustrate the modelling of problems characterized by economies and diseconomies of scale and we shall see once again that binary variables play a vital role in ensuring appropriate relationships between variables.

Decreasing returns to scale

We return yet again to IMC's monitor mix problems. On this occasion, though, we shall assume that the situation is complicated by the presence of non-linearities in the objective function. It has been observed, in particular, that diseconomies of scale apply to the production of Model A monitors. IMC's chief economist has calculated that the marginal contribution (the contribution to IMC's fixed costs and profit attributable to the production of one extra monitor) per A monitor declines as production increases, as shown in Table 10-5.

The table is interpreted as follows. If the weekly production of A monitors falls in the range 0 to 50 then each additional monitor we produce contributes £45 to IMC's profits. For the ranges 51 to 150 and above 150 the corresponding contribution figures are reduced to £40 and £35 respectively. The reader should recognize that Table 10.5 is itself a model of the relationship between the production and marginal contribution of A monitors. A less approximate model might take the form of a mathematical 'marginal contribution function' whose graph would describe a smooth downward curve. We assume, however, that the table provides a sufficiently accurate representation for decision-making purposes. It is evident that the objective function of the original model will no longer suffice:

$$\text{Maximize} \quad 40A + 50B$$

The term $40A$ must be replaced by a valid expression for the total contribution derived from A monitors. This is achieved by defining new variables A_1, A_2 and A_3 such that:

$$A = A_1 + A_2 + A_3 \tag{10-52}$$

A is decomposed in the manner determined by the following cases:

If $\quad A \leq 50 \qquad$ then $A_1 = A, \qquad A_2 = 0, \qquad A_3 = 0$

Table 10-5 Decreasing marginal contributions: Model A monitors

Production range	$0 \leq A \leq 50$	$50 < A \leq 150$	$150 < A$
Marginal contribution per monitor (£)	45	40	35

If $50 < A \leqslant 150$ then $A_1 = 50$, $A_2 = A - 50$, $A_3 = 0$
If $150 < A$ then $A_1 = 50$, $A_2 = 100$, $A_3 = A - 150$

Thus, for example,

if $A = 170$ then $A_1 = 50$, $A_2 = 100$, $A_3 = 20$

IMC is evidently gaining contributions of £45 on each of A_1 monitors, £40 on each of A_2 monitors and £35 on each of A_3. The total contribution function is therefore:

$$45A_1 + 40A_2 + 35A_3 \tag{10-53}$$

and, assuming that the constraints of the original problem still apply, the completed model is:

$$\text{Maximize} \quad 45A_1 + 40A_2 + 35A_3 + 50B \tag{10-54}$$
$$\text{subject to:} \quad 28A_1 + 28A_2 + 28A_3 + 42B \leqslant 16\,800 \tag{10-55}$$
$$12A_1 + 12A_2 + 12A_3 + 6B \leqslant 4\,800 \tag{10-56}$$
$$A_1 + A_2 + A_3 + B \leqslant 600 \tag{10-57}$$
$$A_1 \leqslant 50 \tag{10-58}$$
$$A_2 \leqslant 100 \tag{10-59}$$
$$A_1, A_2, A_3, B \geqslant 0$$

It is vital to note, however, that this formulation is valid only because the objective function coefficients of the A's decrease as we move from A_1 to A_3. Without taking a closer look at the properties of the model we might suppose that some solution method could produce an optimum in which the values of A_1, A_2 and A_3 were inconsistent. For example, on applying the Simplex algorithm, we might discover that A_3 was positive even though A_1 and A_2 had not yet reached their limits, 50 and 100. In relation to the meanings of the variables this is clearly absurd. That such a situation never occurs is evident from the following argument. Any inconsistent solution can be transformed into a consistent one with the same value of A simply by defining A_1, A_2 and A_3 in the appropriate way. Because the value of A is unchanged, the constraints are unaffected, and so the new solution remains feasible. Moreover, this solution has a higher objective function, since the shift in values has been towards the variables with the larger coefficients. This shows that an inconsistent solution cannot possibly be optimal. Situations characterized by decreasing returns to scale can therefore be modelled without difficulty by introducing additional variables of the same type. A_1, A_2 and A_3 are all of the same type as A, whether this is continuous or integer. It is evident, however, that similar arguments would not apply if the coefficients of these variables were reversed. This is a case we now consider.

Increasing returns to scale

With increasing returns to scale the objective function grows at an increasing rate as production rises. In other words, the company benefits from economies of scale. Table 10-6 illustrates such a situation. Note that we have simply reversed the figures of Table 10-5.

Table 10-6 Increasing marginal contributions: Model A monitors

Production range	$0 \leq A \leq 50$	$50 < A \leq 150$	$150 < A$
Marginal contribution per monitor (£)	35	40	45

Although we have already observed that the previous method is ineffective in such a case it is clearly reasonable to define A_1, A_2 and A_3 as before, i.e.

$$A = A_1 + A_2 + A_3 \quad (10\text{-}60)$$

Our task is to ensure that A_1, A_2 and A_3 take consistent values in the optimal solution despite the opposing influence of the objective function. As in earlier sections we shall see that correct relationships between these variables can be guaranteed if we introduce appropriate binary variables and constraints. We define:

$$Y_1 = 1 \quad \text{if } A > 50 \qquad Y_2 = 1 \quad \text{if } A > 150$$
$$ 0 \quad \text{otherwise}   0 \quad \text{otherwise}$$

We must now combine the Y's with the A's so that A_2 is prevented from becoming positive while $A_1 < 50$, and A_3 remains zero while $A_2 < 100$. The following constraints achieve exactly this.

$$A_1 \geq 50 Y_1 \quad (10\text{-}61)$$
$$A_2 \leq M Y_1 \quad (10\text{-}62)$$
$$A_2 \geq 100 Y_2 \quad (10\text{-}63)$$
$$A_3 \leq M Y_2 \quad (10\text{-}64)$$

As long as A_1 remains below 50, Eq. (10-61) ensures that Y_1 is zero. If this is the case, however, then A_2 must also be zero because of Eq. (10-62). Once A_1 has reached 50, of course, then Y_1 may increase to 1, so allowing A_2 to become positive. We are therefore assured of the correct relationship between A_1 and A_2 provided we can be certain that A_1 will never exceed 50. However, an inconsistent solution such as this can never be optimal by an argument similar to the one we used in our discussion of decreasing returns. Equations (10-63) and (10-64) operate in an identical way to guarantee consistency between A_2 and A_3. The complete model is thus:

$$\text{Maximize} \quad 35A_1 + 40A_2 + 45A_3 + 50B \quad (10\text{-}65)$$
$$\text{subject to:} \quad 28A_1 + 28A_2 + 28A_3 + 42B \leq 16\,800 \quad (10\text{-}66)$$
$$12A_1 + 12A_2 + 12A_3 + 6B \leq 4\,800 \quad (10\text{-}67)$$
$$A_1 + A_2 + A_3 + B \leq 600 \quad (10\text{-}68)$$
$$A_1 - 50Y_1 \geq 0 \quad (10\text{-}69)$$
$$A_2 - MY_1 \leq 0 \quad (10\text{-}70)$$
$$A_2 - 100Y_2 \geq 0 \quad (10\text{-}71)$$

$$A_3 - MY_2 \leq 0 \qquad (10\text{-}72)$$

$$A_1, A_2, A_3 \text{ and } B \geq 0$$

$$Y_1, Y_2 \text{ binary}$$

10-12 SUMMARY

In this chapter we have extended our earlier discussion of linear programming to include models in which variables are permitted to take integer values. We have done this not only because many real problems contain decision variables whose values must be whole numbers but also because the integer properties of variables may be used to bring large and hitherto unattainable classes of business decisions within the ambit of mathematical programming. We have seen, in particular, how binary variables can model discrete decision alternatives—'Yes, we do'/'No, we don't' take a given course of action—and may also be used to ensure consistency in the relationships between other variables. It should have become clear from our many examples that building ILP models is a more subtle and more difficult art than LP modelling. We have attempted, however, to present a sample of problem situations that occur with reasonable frequency, in the expectation that the reader will be able to recognize familiar structures where they exist and have the skill to model them. As in other areas, skill in ILP modelling is gained through practice, experience and exposure to the tried and tested methods of others in the field. Reference to the bibliography will indicate the variety of ILP applications that have been investigated in the business world, many of them classical examples of their kind. Throughout this chapter we have assumed implicitly that, whatever model we produced, we could be sure of finding some suitable method to solve it. Since we have not actually solved any of our sample problems this may seem presumptuous. In the next chapter we discuss ILP solution algorithms and discover that, though the picture may not be so clear cut as in LP, there are several solution approaches we can adopt.

STUDENT EXERCISES

10-1 Worldwide Holdings Incorporated (WHI) is currently considering prospective investments in four developing countries. Details are given in Table 10-7. (For reasons of confidentiality the names of the countries cannot be divulged.) WHI has already decided that:

1. the total initial investment must not exceed £150m;
2. at least one investment of each type should be undertaken; and
3. at most one investment of each type should be undertaken in each country.

Formulate WHI's decision in terms of ILP.
Modify the model to deal with each of the following cases.

(a) Recent negotiations between WHI and country A resulted in a much publicized 'threshold agreement' whereby the company must, if it invests in A at all, commit at least £30m to its initial investment there.
(b) Because of political tensions, B refuses to allow investment by any company which invests in C.
(c) The government of D has promised a grant of £15m towards initial costs provided that WHI's total investment there exceeds £20m.

Table 10-7

Investment type	1	2	3	1	2	3
Country	Initial cost (£m)			NPV (£m)		
A	15	35	20	70	60	100
B	—	30	—	—	130	—
C	15	—	—	80	—	—
D	10	25	30	60	100	140

10-2 In the early 1980s British Lowland (BL) had factories throughout the UK. Hit by the recession, the company decided to close a number of its plants, details of which are shown in Table 10-8.

1. Factory closures were subject to the following conditions:
   (a) BL's total annual loss should be reduced by at least £15m.
   (b) Total annual output should not fall below £150m.
   (c) The burden of redundancies should be spread between regions. At least 1 factory should remain open in each.
   (d) Total redundancies should be kept to a minimum.

   Express BL's problem as an ILP.

2. Each region has 1 distribution depot. The details are as given in Table 10-9. Reformulate your model to include the potential closure of the depots, assuming that each depot must remain open if and only if the region retains at least 2 of its factories.

Table 10-8

Region	North			Midlands		Scotland	
Factory	A	B	C	D	E	F	G
Annual loss (£m)	5	3	1	8	4	5	9
Annual output (£m)	40	35	15	50	40	35	65
Workforce (000)	4	4	1	6	3	5	6

Table 10-9

Depot	North	Midlands	Scotland
Annual loss (£m)	2	3	4
Workforce (000)	1	2	2

10-3 In the following problems A and B are the quantities of two products whose production involves marginal costs $£C_1$ and $£C_2$ and certain fixed charges. The nature of the fixed charges changes from problem to problem. Assuming that the objective of production planning is to minimize total costs subject to a number of (unspecified) resource constraints, formulate the part of the model that deals with the relationships between costs and production quantities:

(a) The fixed charge $£K$ is incurred if and only if either $A>0$ or $B>0$.
(b) The fixed charge $£K$ is incurred if and only if both $A>0$ and $B>0$.

For (c) and (d) the fixed charges are indicated as follows:

	Fixed charge	Conditions
(c)	0	$A = B = 0$
	15	$A > 0, B = 0$
	20	$A = 0, B > 0$
	30	$A > 0, B > 0$
(d)	0	$A = B = 0$
	50	either A or $B > 0$ but not both
	60	A and $B > 0$ but $A + B < 100$
	80	A and $B < 0$ and $A + B \geq 100$

10-4 Micro MacMagic (MMM) is a small Scottish firm which markets two hand-held electronic games, Action Clan (AC) and Spey Invaders (SI). The chips required by both games may be produced on either of two processes whose costs are set out in Table 10-10.

Every Friday MMM plans production for the following week, taking account of current demands and resource levels. This week the firm has decided to produce at least 200 ACs and 100 SIs but, owing to a shortage of components, can make no more than 500 games in total. The two processes X and Y are currently set for AC production, but either or both may be converted to produce SIs at some time during the week. (Conversion costs are given in Table 10-10.) MMM's output is normally sold to MacRosoft Wholesale yielding unit contributions* for ACs and SIs of £6 and £8 respectively.

(a) Formulate MMM's planning problem as an ILP.

How might your model be altered in each of the following cases?

(b) Chip production and process conversion times in minutes are as shown in Table 10-11. Each process is limited to 40 hours of normal working per week, but overtime may be used at an additional cost of £5 per hour on each process.

(c) MMM has agreed to supply ACs direct to Asma Superstores. Asma's terms are:
   (i) All chips used must be made on process X.
   (ii) MMM must supply at least 150 ACs per week in batches of 30.
   (iii) Contribution* per AC is £5.50 for weekly supplies of under 240, but as an incentive to greater commitment from MMM rises to £6.50 for supplies in excess of 240.

Table 10-10

Process	Variable production costs (£)		Conversion cost (£)
	AC	SI	AC to SI
X	2	3	200
Y	1	2	300

Table 10-11

Process	Production		Conversion, AC to SI
	AC	SI	
X	30	40	90
Y	20	24	120

* Contribution figures before deduction of variable production costs.

11
SOLUTION METHODS FOR INTEGER LINEAR PROGRAMMING

In the previous chapter we extended our treatment of linear programming to cover problems in which the decision variables were required to take integer values. In the process we saw that a great many decisions that had hitherto defied the application of mathematical programming now fell within its ambit. Chapter 10, however, dealt only with the formulation of ILP problems and, apart from stressing the point that the resulting models cannot readily be solved in the manner of LP, offered no suggestions as to possible solution methods. It need scarcely be said that there is little purpose in building a decision model unless there is then some means of manipulating it to produce a solution to the decision-maker's problem.

In this chapter we look briefly at a number of approaches to the task of solving ILP models. Unlike LP, where the Simplex method in one form or another has dominated the solution process and is still considered to be the major practical way of solving real problems, ILP has given rise to a surprising diversity of approaches. In line with the objectives of this section of the text, it is not our intention to give a comprehensive description of any single approach, but rather to present a detailed discussion of the algorithm which, for each, represents in the simplest and most effective way the ideas that underpin it. The intention is clearly to provide an illustrative discussion rather than a detailed examination of the solution algorithm so that the decision-maker can appreciate the principles of the solution process. At this level actual solution of such models is inevitably computer-based. In the course of time there has been a natural tendency for such solution algorithms to be extended and enhanced in order to increase the efficiency of the solution process. Developments of this sort may be designed to take advantage of new computer architectures, or to exploit the special features of commonly occurring models. They may also, of course, result from an improved understanding of solution methods generally, and involve the use of ideas from other areas of research. However, because

250 FURTHER MATHEMATICAL PROGRAMMING MODELS

such developments almost inevitably manifest themselves as complications, obscuring the essential principles of the underlying approach, we do not detail them here.

We close the chapter by commenting on the success of the various approaches in solving problems of realistic size. Comparing the merits of solution algorithms is no simple matter. Several criteria may be used to assess the effectiveness of any algorithm, and there is no guarantee that a method that scores highly with respect to one criterion will not fall short with respect to a second. Further, certain approaches work well with particular types of problem but indifferently with others. Despite these caveats practical experience suggests that, at the present time, there is a preferred approach to ILP solution which is currently the basis of most commercial computer codes.

11-1 A BRANCH AND BOUND METHOD

We begin our discussion of ILP solutions by investigating an example of what is arguably the simplest approach. *Branch and bound* methods belong to the family of 'tree search' algorithms and can be applied to a very broad class of problems which includes ILP as a large and important subclass. In general they demand very little elaboration of the theory of linear programming, requiring only that the problem-solver has the means to solve considerable numbers of LP models in an acceptably short time. All methods of the branch and bound type exploit the fact that the set of feasible solutions to the problem can be represented as a 'tree' structure in which each new 'branch' corresponds to the restriction of a particular decision variable to a specified subset of values. The manner in which the tree is constructed is determined by rules governing the calculation and use of 'bounds'.

Starting the tree

To illustrate the principles on which the method is based consider the following simple problem.

$$\text{Maximize} \quad 7A + 6B \tag{11-1}$$

$$\text{subject to:} \quad 4A + 10B \leq 31 \tag{11-2}$$

$$6A + 5B \leq 30 \tag{11-3}$$

$$A, B \geq 0 \text{ and integer}$$

In the optimal LP solution the two constraints are binding and the optimal values of the variables are:

$$A = 3.625, \quad B = 1.65$$

Student activity
Confirm this result graphically and use your graph to deduce the optimal ILP solution.

Solving the problem—initially in the absence of the integer conditions—provides a starting point for the branch and bound method and corresponds to the 'root' of the tree

(A = 3.625
B = 1.65
Z = 35.275)

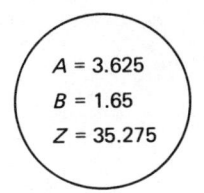

Figure 11-1 The first node of the tree

that will eventually lead to the solution we desire. We represent this as a circular 'node' or branching point as shown in Fig. 11-1.

Computing a bound

We have recorded the values of the variables inside the node and added the value of the objective function, which we denote by Z. The value of Z will play a crucial role in the progress of the algorithm guiding us to 'grow' and explore appropriate branches. It is Z, in fact, that provides the 'bound' that gives the method its title. The value 35.275 is the highest Z can achieve—even with the removal of the integer conditions on the variables. It is therefore an *upper bound* on the value achievable by Z in the ILP problem. It is evident that no additional restriction applied to a problem can ever result in an improved optimal solution, and the required integer conditions are such additional restrictions. We infer, therefore, that whatever the optimal ILP solution may be its objective function value cannot exceed 35.275.

The branching process

We next inspect the current values of the decision variables themselves. They are at present non-integer and so inappropriate for our problem. Had they been integer, of course, then our task would be complete already and we could conclude that the optimal LP solution was also optimal for the ILP. (As you will probably suspect, this is very rarely so in practice.) We therefore make an arbitrary choice of variable—in this case we choose A—and partition the set of feasible ILP solutions into two subsets, one containing points for which:

$$A \leq 3$$

and one for which:

$$A \geq 4$$

Clearly, since A cannot lie between consecutive integer values, one or other (but not both) of these conditions must apply to the optimal ILP solution—which is therefore certain to belong to just one of the subsets so defined. We represent these two possibilities as branches on the tree shown in Fig. 11-2.

Before progressing to the next step in the algorithm, we offer two comments. Firstly, it should concern you that we made an arbitrary choice of A as the 'branching' variable, i.e. as the variable with respect to whose values we partitioned the solution set. Had we chosen B instead, our tree would already represent an alternative view of the problem, and it is

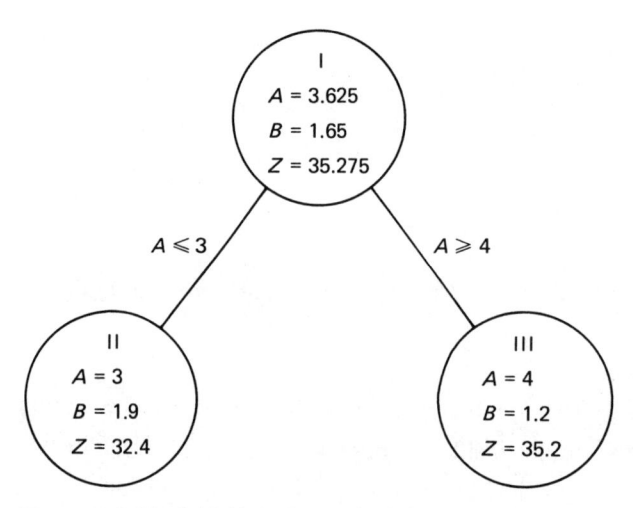

```
              ┌─────────────┐
              │      I      │
              │ A = 3.625   │
              │ B = 1.65    │
              │ Z = 35.275  │
              └─────────────┘
            A ≤ 3       A ≥ 4
          ┌────────┐  ┌────────┐
          │   II   │  │  III   │
          │ A = 3  │  │ A = 4  │
          │ B = 1.9│  │ B = 1.2│
          │ Z=32.4 │  │ Z=35.2 │
          └────────┘  └────────┘
```

Figure 11-2 The initial branches and subproblem solutions

reasonable to ask what difference this would ultimately make. The answer, of course, is that we cannot change the optimal solution simply by taking a different route on the way to it, but we can affect the length of the route by making judicious choices of direction at appropriate points along the path—and this is what we are doing when we select a particular branching variable. Naturally, the shorter the route, the faster we discover the optimal solution. (This is the same principle as applies, of course, to the Simplex algorithm if we are faced with a choice of variables to enter the basis.) In large problems this may be of critical importance in terms of the required computation time. However, because it has no significance for the structure of the method, we do not intend to take a detailed look at this task. In practice, a number of techniques have been tried. All are based on some *heuristic*—rule of thumb—which attempts to drive the algorithm as rapidly as possible towards the optimum. For example, in the simplest case, the chosen variable is that with the largest objective function coefficient. In more sophisticated approaches, the choice is based on penalty values calculated for each variable. Management science journals are frequently reporting the developments of such computationally more efficient algorithms.

Secondly, it may already be clear that our decision to use the values 3 and 4 when partitioning the solution set was by no means arbitrary. These are the integers on either side of the fractional value taken by A in the LP optimum. As we saw in the previous chapter, the ILP optimum may well differ greatly from the LP optimum. However, in seeking the former, we would be wise to look first in the vicinity of the latter before moving to parts of the feasible region further afield. In general this technique reduces the amount of computation required to reveal the final solution and we shall always use it when branching.

Computing further bounds

We now take a closer look at the two solution subsets corresponding to the branches of Fig. 11-2. If we progress down the left-hand branch to node II we restrict our attention to those cases in which, in effect, three constraints apply:

SOLUTION METHODS FOR INTEGER LINEAR PROGRAMMING

$$4A + 10B \leq 31 \qquad (11\text{-}2)$$

$$6A + 5B \leq 30 \qquad (11\text{-}3)$$

$$A \leq 3 \qquad (11\text{-}4)$$

In effect we have added a further restriction to the original LP problem. We cannot therefore hope to find any ILP solution along this branch that is superior to the optimum Z value we derived when solving the original problem at node I. This new augmented subproblem is the first of (potentially) many we may need to consider as we develop the tree. Each results from a further partitioning of the solution set and is represented by an additional branch. We can calculate a further upper bound on the value of Z—valid only for the left-hand subset—simply by ignoring the integer conditions once again and solving the node II subproblem as if it were an LP. The solution at node II indicates that the upper bound Z value along this branch is $Z = 32.4$. Applying the same analysis to the right-hand branch and its associated subproblem—the original problem augmented by:

$$A \geq 4 \qquad (11\text{-}5)$$

yields the corresponding right-hand bound and the solution shown in node III.

Student activity
Identify the two subproblems on your graph of the original problem and confirm the optimal solutions recorded in nodes II and III.

Although it is not an essential part of the ILP solution process, it is worth noting that both subproblems may be solved through some simple arithmetic. We illustrate the argument in the case of the left-hand subproblem: an exactly similar treatment applies on the right. Since, on the left, the new constraint $A \leq 3$ is all that prevents us from achieving the same objective function value as before, this constraint must be binding. If this were not so, we could remove it and leave the optimal solution unchanged. We can thus assume that $A = 3$. However, once A's value has been determined the subproblem is reduced to a one-variable LP and, as such, may be solved almost by inspection. Note first that, in order to maximize the objective function it is enough to find the largest value of B consistent with the constraints Eq. (11-2) and Eq. (11-3). Recalling that $A = 3$, we see that these constraints imply:

$$12 + 10B \leq 31 \qquad \text{i.e. } B \leq 1.9$$

and

$$18 + 5B \leq 30 \qquad \text{i.e. } B \leq 2.4$$

It follows that 1.9 is the optimal value of B. This simple technique can be used to confirm the optimal solutions of all the subproblems we shall meet in the current example.

Using the bounds

It is at this point in our development of the problem that we make use of the bounds for the first time. It is clear that the solutions at nodes II and III are still inappropriate given that we still do not have a fully integer solution (although note that we have progressed in this direction with one of the decision variables now integer). Let us compare the two bounds.

Inspection of the right-hand bound reveals that there is still some hope of finding an integer solution along the right-hand branch with a Z value as large as 35.2. By comparison, the left-hand branch is significantly less promising: the very most we can expect from the corresponding integer solution subset is 32.4. In the absence of more compelling reasons it would therefore seem advisable to investigate the right-hand branch further, leaving the left-hand branch for analysis at a later stage if the need arises. Whenever there are two or more branches that remain unexplored we shall be guided to the branch with the most promising bound. Since the current problem is a maximization, the most promising bound is the largest.

Introducing further branches

Restricting our attention, therefore, to the right-hand branch of Fig. 11-2 we now repeat the analysis and partition the current subproblem into two further subproblems. Since the value of A in node III is an integer, B is chosen as the branching variable yielding new constraints:

$$B \leq 1 \tag{11-6}$$

and
$$B \geq 2 \tag{11-7}$$

Note that as before the integers values of 1 and 2 are selected on either side of the fractional value of B. These define the new subproblems which are depicted once again as additional branches in the tree (Fig. 11-3). The new left-hand branch thus represents the original problem augmented now by two constraints, i.e.:

$$\begin{aligned}
\text{Maximize} \quad & 7A + 6B \\
\text{subject to:} \quad & 4A + 10B \leq 31 \\
& 6A + 5B \leq 30 \\
& A \geq 4 \\
& B \leq 1
\end{aligned}$$

The subproblem represented by the new right-hand branch is identical except that the last constraint, Eq. (11-6), is replaced by:

$$B \geq 2$$

Fathoming

We can now proceed to solve each of these two subproblems as an ordinary LP. For node IV the solution generates a value for Z of 35.17. In the case of node V, however, no such solution exists: the problem is infeasible. It would clearly be pointless to proceed any further along such a branch and so our search in this direction is terminated. The branch in question (or, more correctly, the path or sequence of branches which culminates in it) is said to be *fathomed*—in the literal sense that we have 'got to the bottom' of it—and the tree in Fig. 11-3 is amended accordingly. Note that, because it has proved to be a dead end, the fathomed branch is deleted from the tree. Infeasibility is a common cause of fathoming and often ensures that the size of the tree is kept within reasonable limits. However, there are

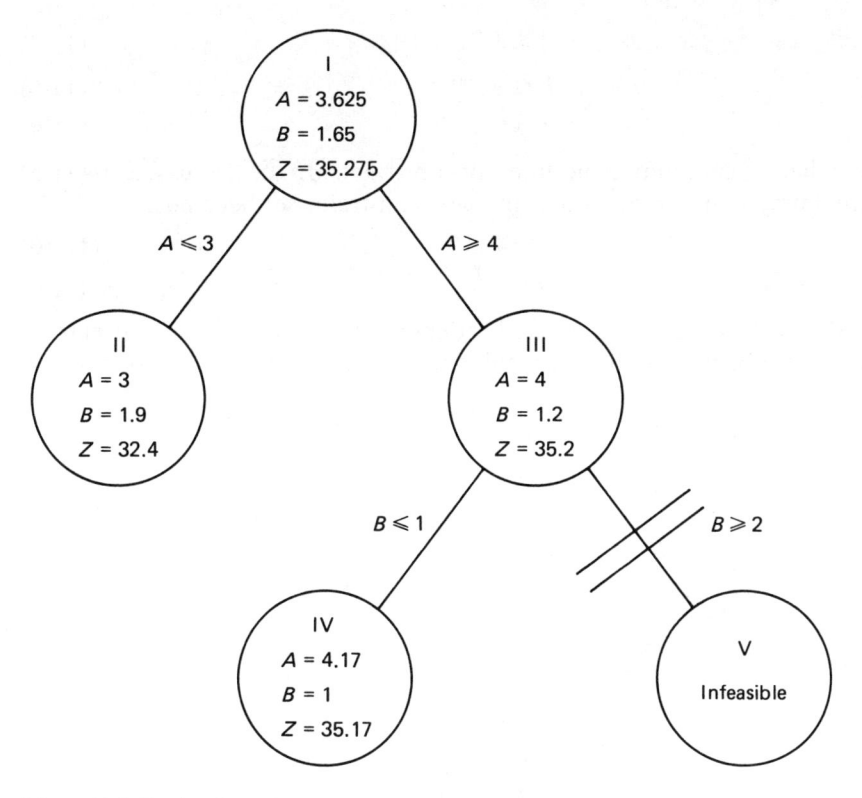

```
            I
        A = 3.625
        B = 1.65
        Z = 35.275
       /          \
   A ≤ 3         A ≥ 4
   /                \
  II                III
 A = 3            A = 4
 B = 1.9          B = 1.2
 Z = 32.4         Z = 35.2
                 /      \\
              B ≤ 1      B ≥ 2
              /            \
             IV             V
          A = 4.17       Infeasible
          B = 1
          Z = 35.17
```

Figure 11-3 Further branches and subproblem solutions

two other ways in which a branch may be fathomed and we shall shortly see how these can occur.

Student activity
Bring your graph of the problem up to date by including the new constraints and marking the regions of the graph that correspond to the new subproblems. In particular, note the infeasibility of node V's subproblem.

Completing the tree

At this stage we see that the tree once again contains two unexplored nodes—one originating from node IV and the other from node II. As before, we are guided to develop the node with the most promising bound ($Z = 35.17$), this time branching on the two alternative values of A. The subproblems that we introduce as a result are now the original problem augmented by the addition of three constraints. In the case of the left-hand node:

$$A \geq 4 \tag{11-5}$$
$$B \leq 1 \tag{11-6}$$
$$A \leq 4 \tag{11-8}$$

and
$$A \geqslant 4 \quad (11\text{-}5)$$
$$B \leqslant 1 \quad (11\text{-}6)$$
$$A \geqslant 5 \quad (11\text{-}9)$$

on the right. Note that we can simplify both sets of constraints. In the first case Eqs (11-5) and (11-8) clearly imply that $A = 4$, so that the new constraint set becomes:
$$A = 4 \quad (11\text{-}10)$$
$$B \leqslant 1 \quad (11\text{-}6)$$

In the second case Eq. (11-5) is rendered redundant by Eq. (11-9) and so may be ignored. The new subproblems and their optimal solutions extend the tree as shown in Fig. 11-4.

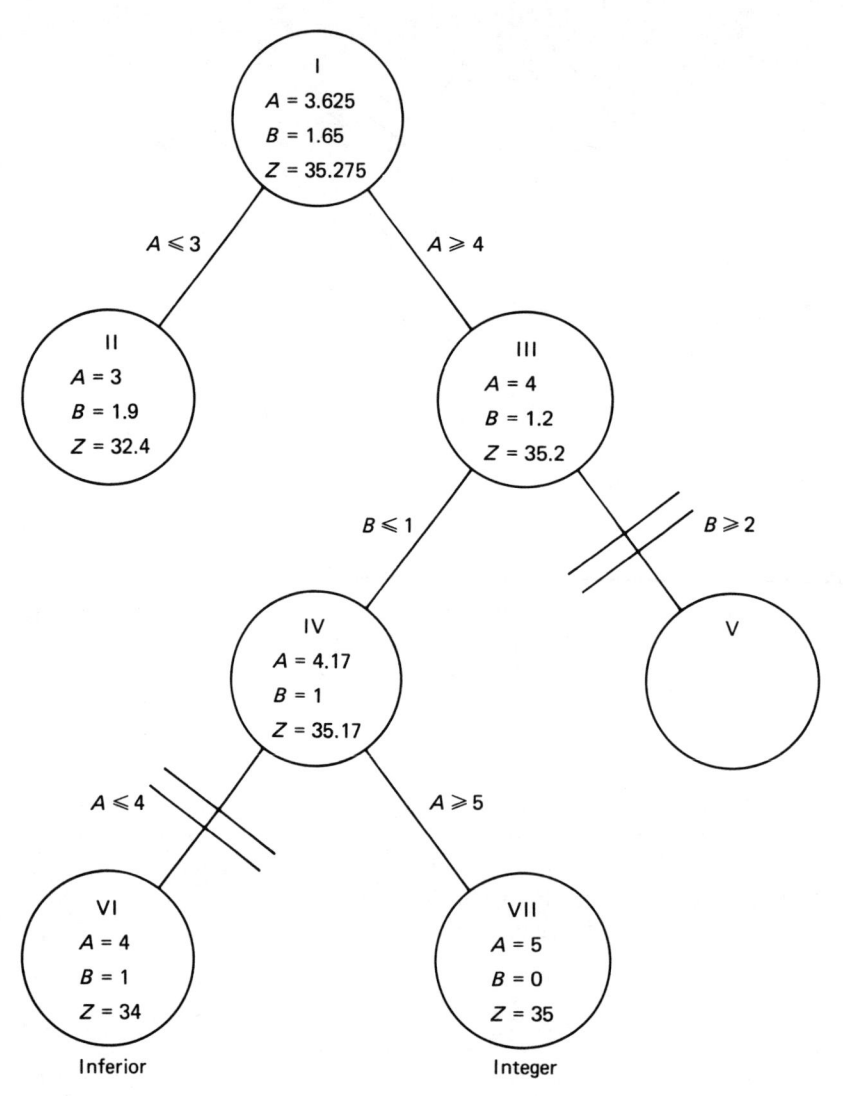

Figure 11-4 Third level of branches and subproblem solutions

The most striking fact about the new pair of solutions is that both are composed entirely of integer values. For the first time in our treatment of the problem we have discovered truly feasible solutions in that all the conditions we would wish to impose are satisfied. Notice also that, because any development of either branch could result only in Z values that were at best equal to 34 in the left-hand case or to 35 on the right, there is no point in pursuing them further. These integer solutions are already the best we can achieve along their respective paths. Their branches are therefore fathomed. We have found solutions of the kind we sought: integer, if not optimal—and we can terminate the search in these directions. In fact, the left-hand branch is also fathomed for a second reason, namely that its Z value is smaller than that of an integer solution which has already been revealed, i.e. the right-hand solution, for which Z is 35. Thus node VI cannot possibly be optimal and is deleted.

Just one further node remains to be considered—node II. However, the bound attached to node II is inferior to that of node VII, a Z value actually achieved by an integer solution, and so there is no hope of finding a better—or even an equally good—solution in this direction. The last of the nodes is therefore fathomed and the search is complete. Our method has proved that the ILP optimum is:

$$A = 5, \quad B = 0, \quad Z = 35$$

Student activity

Confirm the above analysis by representing all remaining subproblems on your graph.

Further remarks on fathoming

There are three ways in which paths through a branch and bound tree may be fathomed, all of them illustrated by the problem above. The fathoming of a branch may be due to the following:

1. Infeasibility The branching constraint most recently added results in an infeasible subproblem. Hence the branch cannot lead to any further feasible solution.

2. Inferiority The bound (i.e. Z value) attached to the branch is inferior to the objective function value of an integer solution already found in some other part of the tree. Developing the branch will not improve on the bound. Hence the branch cannot lead to an optimal solution.

3. Integrality The branch corresponds to a subproblem that results in integer values for all the variables. Once again, developing the branch will not improve on the bound. Hence the branch cannot lead to any better solution.

Branches that are fathomed because of infeasibility or inferiority are immediately deleted from the tree. On the other hand, branches fathomed because their solutions are integer are retained for future reference. Their Z values are noted and, at any point in the analysis, the best so far discovered may be used to check unexplored nodes for inferiority.

Also, of course, one or more of the integer nodes will ultimately prove to be optimal (provided there is a feasible solution to the problem).

Summary of the branch and bound method

A closer look at the branch and bound method presented above will convince you that, with only slight modifications, it can be made to apply to any mixed integer problem, i.e. any problem in which the variables are a mixture of integer and continuous types. The following summary is therefore couched in terms relevant to this broader class of problems, and we use the word 'appropriate' to indicate a solution in which all the necessary integer conditions are satisfied. The algorithm may be viewed as a sequence of steps:

1. Solve the problem as an ordinary linear program. If the solution is appropriate, then STOP. This is the optimal solution.
2. Create a node and inside it record the optimal LP solution, i.e. the values of all the variables and the objective function.
3. Select an integer variable—for convenience we shall denote it by X—whose value at this node is V, a fraction. (At least one such variable must exist, otherwise the solution in question would have been appropriate and the process would already have terminated.)
4. Construct two branches from the node.
   Label the left-hand branch: $X \leq \text{INT}(V)$
   Label the right-hand branch: $X \geq \text{INT}(V) + 1$
   where $\text{INT}(V)$ is the integer part of V.
5. Solve the LP subproblems corresponding to the left- and right-hand branches, remembering to include all previous branching constraints.
6. If either solution is fathomed because of infeasibility or inferiority, delete its branch. Otherwise create a new node and record the LP solution inside it.
7. If the solution is appropriate but not inferior then it must be the best so far. Note its objective function value for use in subsequent inferiority checks.
8. Search the tree for the node with the largest bound from which branching has not yet taken place. If the corresponding solution is appropriate, then STOP; this solution is optimal. Otherwise return to step 3.

It is clear that the branch and bound method offers a solution algorithm that is logical and straightforward as well as using the standard LP solution approach for each node.

11-2 A CUTTING PLANE METHOD

Although the branch and bound method of the previous section typically demands the solution of many LP subproblems, it does not rely on a particular LP solution technique. The LP optima could have been obtained by any available method—inspection, mental arithmetic, a graphical treatment, Simplex or indeed any other algorithm that might be devised. It does not depend, either, on any elaboration of the theory of linear programming, and for this reason it is often regarded as a rather crude and unsophisticated approach. By contrast, methods of the *cutting plane* type spring directly from a deeper understanding of the Simplex algorithm and are viewed—by mathematicians at least—as a more elegant and satisfying prospect. As with branch and bound, there are many variations on the cutting plane theme. We illustrate the use of the simplest (and oldest) of these methods, first proposed by Gomory in 1958, by means of the following example:

$$\text{Maximize} \quad 5A + 6B \quad (11\text{-}11)$$

$$\text{subject to:} \quad A + B \leq 4 \quad (11\text{-}12)$$

$$2A + 4B \leq 11 \quad (11\text{-}13)$$

$$A, B \geq 0 \text{ and integer}$$

All-integer problems

It is important to note that the problem above is entirely integer in character. All its coefficients and constants are whole numbers, as are its decision variables A and B. Furthermore, the same is true of any slack variables we may introduce for the purpose of solving the problem, for example:

$$S_1 = 4 - A - B \quad (11\text{-}14)$$

$$S_2 = 11 - 2A - 4B \quad (11\text{-}15)$$

It is evident that such calculations must produce integer results. *Gomory's all-integer method*, as its name implies, deals only with problems of this nature. Unless a problem can be converted to all-integer form, it cannot be solved by this method. Fortunately, most problems that involve integer variables exclusively can be transformed in an appropriate way. It is normally only a matter of multiplying the constraints by suitable factors to remove any awkward fractions that may be present. Thus, for example, the constraint:

$$5.25X + 6.5Y \leq 21.75$$

can be transformed by multiplying by 4 to produce:

$$21X + 26Y \leq 87$$

so that any corresponding slack variable will now be integer.

Beginning the process

As with branch and bound, the first step in the process is to find the LP solution of the problem, ignoring the integer conditions. In cutting plane, however, we require the whole of the final Simplex tableau, not merely the optimal values of the variables. This is shown in Tableau 11-1.

Tableau 11-1 Optimal solution

	A	B	S_1	S_2	Value
Z	0	0	−4	−0.5	−21.5
A	1	0	2	−0.5	2.5
B	0	1	−1	0.5	1.5

Observing the usual convention, we denote the objective function by Z. Slack variables S_1 and S_2 are defined in Eqs (11-14) and (11-15). Note that the optimal LP solution is: $A = 2.5$, $B = 1.5$. Had this been integer then the LP solution would have sufficed for the ILP problem and the process would terminate. Not surprisingly, this is almost never the case. We therefore take a closer look at the solution presented in Tableau 11-1. You will remember from our discussion of the Simplex method that any Simplex tableau, whether optimal or not, represents a set of simultaneous linear equations. This is most obvious for the initial tableau of the Simplex algorithm since it is always derived directly from the equations that result when the slack variables are introduced into the constraints. Exactly the same principle applies, however, in every other case. Each row of any tableau stands for a single equation whose coefficients are the entries in that row. In particular, the constraint rows of Tableau 11-1 may be translated as the following equation set:

$$1A + 0B + 2S_1 - 0.5S_2 = 2.5 \qquad (11\text{-}16)$$

$$0A + 1B - 1S_1 + 0.5S_2 = 1.5 \qquad (11\text{-}17)$$

The crucial point about these equations is that they are a logical consequence of the original set, resulting from a series of simple algebraic manipulations. (Simplex equations are presented in tabular form merely for ease and efficiency of computation.) They are valid whatever the type of the variables involved: continuous, integer, binary or a mixture of the three. The fact that the variables in Eqs (11-16) and (11-17) are integer, however, has further implications, which we shall now consider.

Creating a cutting constraint

Let us examine Eq. (11-16) and express it in the following way:

$$(1 + 0)A + (0 + 0)B + (2 + 0)S_1 + (-1 + 0.5)S_2 = 2 + 0.5$$

Notice that we have simply decomposed each of the numbers into integer and fractional parts, so that 1 has now become $1 + 0$ and 2.5 has become $2 + 0.5$. Notice also that the negative number -0.5 is represented as $-1 + 0.5$. The reasons for these changes will shortly be apparent. We next transpose the equation so that all fractional components appear on the left, while the integer terms appear on the right. Thus:

$$-0.5 + 0A + 0B + 0S_1 + 0.5S_2 = 2 - 1A - 0B - 2S_1 + 1S_2 \qquad (11\text{-}18)$$

Observe that the calculations on the right-hand side necessarily result in an integer. There is no way in which a fraction might be produced. Therefore, because we are dealing with an equation, the same must also be true of the left-hand expression. Further investigation of the left-hand side, however, shows that it may be viewed as:

$$-0.5 + (\text{an amount which cannot be negative})$$

This is an immediate consequence of the non-negative coefficients and variables involved. The left-hand side cannot therefore be less than -0.5, and again, because of the equation sign, the same is true of the right. Piecing together these deductions we see that both sides are:

1. integer, and
2. greater than or equal to -0.5

Since zero is the smallest number to satisfy these two requirements we conclude that both sides yield a value which is integer and greater than or equal to 0. If we denote this by a new variable, S_3, which is known as a *cutting slack*, then by definition S_3 is non-negative and integer and so is of exactly the same type as the other variables. From Eq. (11-18) and the definition of S_3, we have, therefore:

$$S_3 = -0.5 + 0.5S_2 \qquad (11\text{-}19)$$

and
$$S_3 = 2 - A - 2S_1 + S_2 \qquad (11\text{-}20)$$

Note that, having demonstrated the principles by which Eq. (11-18) was formed, we no longer explicitly include the terms with zero coefficients. Though it may not be obvious at this stage, we have in fact created a new constraint. Known as a *cutting constraint* or simply a *cut*, this takes either of the forms Eq. (11-19) or Eq. (11-20) and is a logical consequence of the integer nature of the variables.

Student activity
Employing the decomposition technique outlined above, use Eq. (11-17) to create an alternative cut (i.e. produce equations that are the equivalents of Eqs (11-19) and (11-20)).

It is instructive at this point to graph the original problem and investigate the significance of the new constraint for the integer optimum. To achieve this we must first express the cut in more familiar terms. We choose to deal with the version of the cut shown in Eq. (11-19) because of its greater simplicity. Note that, as S_3 is non-negative, Eq. (11-19) implies:

$$-0.5 + 0.5S_2 \geq 0 \qquad (11\text{-}21)$$

so that, on rearranging:
$$0.5S_2 \geq 0.5$$

and therefore:
$$S_2 \geq 1 \qquad (11\text{-}22)$$

Note also that, by definition:
$$S_2 = 11 - 2A - 4B \qquad (11\text{-}15)$$

Combining Eq. (11-22) and Eq. (11-15), we have:
$$11 - 2A - 4B \geq 1$$

from which it follows that:
$$2A + 4B \leq 10 \qquad (11\text{-}23)$$

Equation (11-23) is our cutting constraint expressed only in terms of the problem's decision variables. The graphs of the original constraints, together with the new cut, are

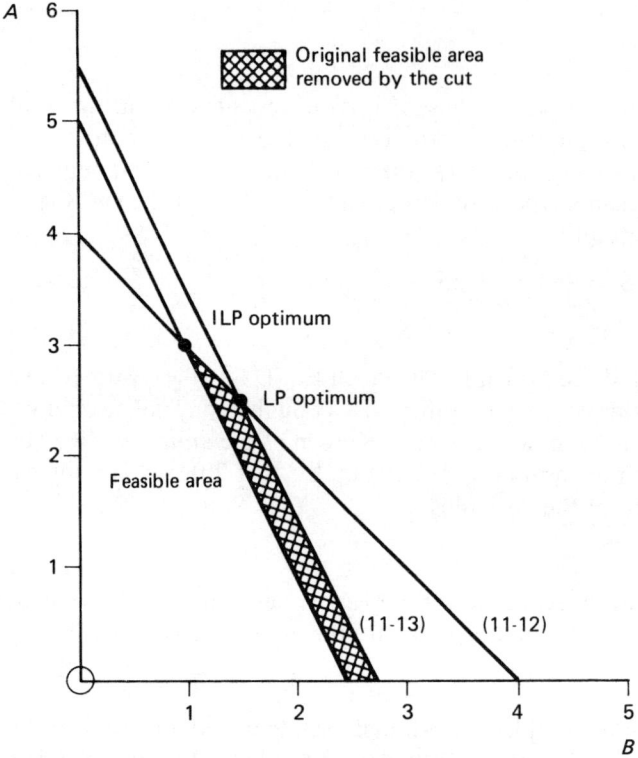

Figure 11-5 Original feasible area and the effect of the cut

shown in Fig. 11.5, which illustrates two essential facts. Firstly, the cutting constraint removes a portion of the old feasible region and so reduces the set of possible solutions among which we need to seek the optimum. The reason for the term 'cut' is now clear: each such constraint (and there will be more than one such in larger problems) slices away a part of the previous feasible set. In three or more dimensions the cut is represented not by a line but by a plane—hence the title 'cutting plane'. Because of the manner in which the cut is created the part that is cut away contains no integer points and so is redundant as far as the ILP problem is concerned. Close inspection of Fig. 11-5 reveals that there are no integer value combinations for A and B that have been cut away. Secondly, the previous (non-integer) LP optimum is removed by the cut so that at the next stage in the process the new LP optimum must be closer to the optimal integer solution.

Student activity
Solve the amended problem incorporating Eq. (11-23) using the standard LP approach.

Indeed for our illustrative example the new LP optimum for the problem formulation including Eq. (11-23) is already integer and so the process terminates. The final solution is:

$$A = 3, \quad B = 1$$

Student activity
Return to the original problem. Incorporate the alternative cut (which you derived earlier using Eq. (11-17)) and derive the optimal solution in the same way.

A general discussion of the method

In general, of course, it is rare for a cutting plane method to terminate after only one step. Even for two-variable problems of the sort illustrated above it is quite normal to add several cuts before the integer optimum is obtained. At each stage a new cut is created from the final Simplex tableau in the same manner as Eqs (11-19) and (11-20). The problem is then augmented by the addition of the cut and re-solved in LP fashion by the Simplex method. The process continues until the LP solution is found to be integer. By this point, successive cuts have typically removed much of the original feasible region. However, since all integer solutions remain intact, any LP optimum that happens to be integer must necessarily be the ILP optimum as well. It is clear that the description of the method begs a number of questions. Firstly, in order to create the cut in our example we made an arbitrary choice of row from the final Simplex tableau with which to create the cutting constraint. Clearly a different row will result in a different cut. Does the choice of cut affect the performance of the method in any way and, if so, is there a rational basis on which to choose the most suitable row? Secondly, the way in which we decomposed the numbers of the Simplex equations to produce the cut may still be something of a mystery. How is this done in general? Are there 'rules' that we can follow? Thirdly, you may wonder whether it is always necessary to recast the cut in terms of the main variables before it can be added to the problem. Or is there a less laborious way? Finally, if we continue to add more and more constraints to the problem, will it eventually become too large to solve? These points are considered below.

General principles for creating a cut

For the purpose of this section we assume that the variables of the problem are labelled X_1 to X_n. We make no distinction between main and slack variables: the X's include them all. Assume also that the entries of the particular row of the final Simplex tableau from which we wish to create a cut are the numbers a_1 to a_n together with the value b. Then the corresponding equation is:

$$a_1 X_1 + a_2 X_2 + \ldots + a_n X_n = b \qquad (11\text{-}24)$$

We now decompose each of the numbers $a_1, \ldots, a_n$ and b as follows. For each a_m, where $m = 1 \ldots n$, we write:

$$a_m = i_m + f_m$$

Similarly, for b we write:

$$b = i + f$$

The f_m, for $m = 1 \ldots n$, and f are fractions lying between 0 and 1. They are all strictly less than 1, but may equal 0. The i_m, for $m = 1 \ldots n$, and i are integers. Equation (11-24) can therefore be rewritten:

$$(i_1+f_1)X_1+\ldots+(i_1+f_n)X_n=i+f \qquad (11\text{-}25)$$

and, on rearranging, we obtain:

$$-f+f_1X_1+\ldots+f_nX_n=i-i_1X_1-\ldots-i_nX_n \qquad (11\text{-}26)$$

Note that in Eq. (11-26):

1. the right-hand side is an integer since all coefficients and variables are integers;
2. the left-hand side is

$$-f+(\text{an amount which is non-negative})$$

since all coefficients and variables are non-negative and must therefore be greater than or equal to $-f$.

It follows that both sides of Eq. (11-26) take a value that is integer and at least $-f$. Because 0 is the smallest number with such properties, we conclude that both sides of Eq. (11-26) are integer and non-negative. Denoting them by X_{n+1}, we have:

$$X_{n+1}=-f+f_1X_1+\ldots+f_nX_n \qquad (11\text{-}27)$$

and

$$X_{n+1}=i-i_1X_1-\ldots-i_nX_n \qquad (11\text{-}28)$$

Either of these equations may be taken as the required cutting constraint. X_{n+1} is the associated cutting slack.

Student activity
Confirm that Eq. (11-18) is correctly decomposed according to the rules laid down in this section.

Choosing a cut

The task of choosing a cut in a cutting plane method may be likened to that of choosing a branching variable in branch and bound—or indeed any of the solution algorithms that we have introduced. Any cut will lead to a solution closer to the ILP optimum but a sequence of injudicious choices will slow the process by forcing the addition of more cuts than are necessary. It is therefore important to recognize 'deep' cuts and to use them when they arise. The concept of 'depth' of cut is best understood in graphical terms. When we implement a cutting constraint we wish to slice as deeply as possible into the existing feasible region, removing as many redundant (i.e. non-integer) solutions as we can. Of course, in real applications there is no graph to aid the choice. The cut must be selected on the basis of some arithmetic criterion applied to the rows of the final Simplex tableau. To establish the 'rules' we consider Eq. (11-27). For convenience we repeat the equation here:

$$X_{n+1}=-f+f_1X_1+\ldots+f_nX_n \qquad (11\text{-}27)$$

The argument of the previous section showed that X_{n+1} is both integer and non-negative. It must therefore be true in particular that:

$$-f+f_1X_1+\ldots+f_nX_n\geq 0$$

and so:
$$f_1X_1 + \ldots + f_nX_n \geq f \qquad (11\text{-}29)$$

This is often the favoured way of expressing the cutting constraint and it is ideal for our purposes. In general, the constraint will be stronger (i.e. more restrictive), and the corresponding cut in the feasible region deeper, if either:

1. the constant f is larger, or
2. the coefficients f_m, for $m = 1 \ldots n$, are smaller.

Although the f's provide a means of distinguishing good cuts from bad they are often an ambiguous guide. It is normally true that the cut derived from a particular row of the tableau will be good only in parts. By comparison with the cuts of other rows, for example, it will have f_m values that are promisingly low in some cases but forbiddingly high in others. Finding a cut that is superior in all respects is rare. For this reason a heuristic criterion, based on the f's, is usually applied to select a suitable row. Several have been tried—with varying success—but the following has proved popular:

select the row for which the cut has f values such that
$$f/(f_1 + \ldots + f_n)$$
is as large as possible.

Such a criterion clearly responds to f and the f_m in the way that it should. It will tend to pick out rows with large f and small f_m's.

Augmenting the problem

From our earlier discussion the reader may have gained the impression that whenever a new cut is introduced it must first be expressed in terms of the main variables so that the augmented problem may be solved from scratch. In practice this is not the case; if it were, the method would be considerably less efficient than it is. In fact, after a minor rearrangement of Eq. (11-29) the cut may be inserted directly into the final tableau and, following a (typically) small number of additional Simplex iterations, the new LP optimum found. We illustrate this on our previous example. The cut we wish to use was derived from Tableau 11-1 and is:
$$S_3 = -0.5 + 0.5S_2 \qquad (11\text{-}19)$$

from which:
$$-0.5S_2 + S_3 = -0.5 \qquad (11\text{-}30)$$

Tableau 11-1 is now enlarged to include the cut as shown in Tableau 11-2.

Tableau 11-2

	A	B	S_1	S_2	S_3	Value
Z	0	0	-4	-0.5	0	-21.5
A	1	0	2	-0.5	0	2.5
B	0	1	-1	0.5	0	1.5
S_3	0	0	0	-0.5	1	-0.5

Notice that the tableau has gained an extra column for the variable S_3 and an extra row for the cutting constraint and that the latter is entered in the form of Eq. (11-30) in which S_3 appears with coefficient 1. Note also that, in the solution represented by Tableau 11-2, S_3 takes the negative value -0.5 in violation of the fact that S_3 is a non-negative variable. In other words the solution is infeasible. On reflection the reader will realize that this is only to be expected. Tableau 11-2 still represents the old optimal point—which the addition of the cut has excluded from the new feasible region. Infeasible solutions cannot be handled by the standard Simplex method. Fortunately, however, there is a variant of standard Simplex, the dual Simplex method, which is ideally suited to them. In dual Simplex we first choose the variable to leave the basis: in this case S_3, because of its infeasibility. The entering variable is then determined using the 'dual ratio test', an analogue of the ratio test in standard Simplex. In this example, S_2 is selected. Therefore, using -0.5 at the foot of S_2's column as the pivot, we iterate from Tableau 11-2 to produce Tableau 11-3.

Tableau 11-3

	A	B	S_1	S_2	S_3	Value
Z	0	0	-4	0	-1	-21
A	1	0	2	0	-1	3
B	0	1	-1	0	1	1
S_2	0	0	0	1	-2	1

Notice that the new tableau is both feasible and optimal, so that the search for the new LP optimum is already complete. It is also—as we might expect from our graphical treatment of the same problem—an integer solution and therefore the ILP optimum:

$$A = 3, \quad B = 1, \quad S_2 = 1$$

Cutting plane methods do not normally terminate quite so quickly, of course. In practice it will usually be necessary to add a series of cuts, increasing the size of the problem by a single constraint at each step. If left unchecked, the problem may soon become unmanageably large and the solution process extremely inefficient. A simple device will prevent this, however. Whenever any cutting slack appears in an optimal basis (i.e. takes a positive value in an LP optimum) we know that the associated cut has ceased to be binding once another cut has been made. It may thus be treated as a redundant constraint and removed from the problem by deleting the appropriate row and column. By this method an optimal basis can never—except temporarily—contain variables other than the original decision and slack variables, and must therefore be of limited size.

Summary of the cutting plane method

We complete our discussion of the cutting plane method by listing the steps of the process that we undertake:

1. If necessary, convert the problem to all-integer form, multiplying the constraints in which fractions appear by appropriate factors.
2. Solve the problem as a linear program by the Simplex method.
3. If all the variables have integer values, then STOP; the integer optimum has been found.

SOLUTION METHODS FOR INTEGER LINEAR PROGRAMMING **267**

4. Remove unwanted cutting slacks from the problem by deleting the row and column of any that have become basic.
5. Using a suitable heuristic, select a row of the final Simplex tableau and from it create a cutting constraint of the form:

$$-f_1 X_1 - \ldots - f_n X_n + X_{n+1} = -f$$

6. Augment the problem by enlarging the tableau, adding a column for the new cutting slack and a row for the cutting constraint.
7. Apply the dual Simplex method to find the optimal LP solution of the augmented problem, then return to step 3.

11-3 AN ENUMERATION METHOD

Enumeration methods constitute a third approach to the solution of ILP problems. Like branch and bound methods, they are tree search algorithms. Unlike both branch and bound and cutting plane, however, they place no reliance whatever on the solution of related linear programs. In this sense it could be argued that they are the only approach of the three to make full use of the integral nature of the variables. At first glance, however, enumeration methods suffer from one major disadvantage: they are applicable only to problems which may be formulated exclusively in terms of zero–one (i.e. binary) variables. To appreciate that this is less of a drawback than it might seem, note that provided we can assume an upper limit on the value of an integer variable we can express it as a linear combination of binary variables.

For those not familiar with binary arithmetic a short digression will be productive. In normal arithmetic we are used to dealing with numbers in terms of 1's, 10's, 100's, etc. The number 111, therefore, we would interpret as (reading from right to left):

        1 unit of the number   1
        1 unit of the number   10
        1 unit of the number 100

In binary arithmetic numbers are expressed in terms of 2's (and powers thereof) rather than in 10's. So in binary arithmetic the number written as 111 would equate to (again reading from right to left):

        1 unit of the number 1
        1 unit of the number 2
        1 unit of the number 4 (2×2),

implying that the binary number 111 was the equivalent to the decimal-based number 7 $(1 + 2 + 4)$. The second aspect of binary arithmetic is that the values of the binary number can only be 0 or 1. So, for example, the binary number 10100 equates to the decimal-based number 20:

        0 units of the number   1
        0 units of the number   2
        1 unit of the number   4 (2×2)

0 units of the number 8 $(2 \times 2 \times 2)$
1 unit of the number 16 $(2 \times 2 \times 2 \times 2)$

A variable may therefore be written:
$$X = 16X_1 + 8X_2 + 4X_3 + 2X_4 + X_5$$
where X_1 to X_5 are binary variables that represent the binary digits of X ranging from the most to the least significant. In particular, if $X = 20$, then:
$$X_1 = 1, \quad X_2 = 0, \quad X_3 = 1, \quad X_4 = 0, \quad X_5 = 0$$

In practice it is rare to find an integer variable for which we cannot estimate a reasonable upper limit. Virtually every all-integer model may thus be transformed into binary form and solved by enumeration methods. In this section we shall investigate a variant of the best-known method of its type: the so-called *additive algorithm* first described by Balas in 1965.

Student activity
Express the following problem in binary form:

$$\text{Maximize} \quad 4X_1 + 9X_2$$
$$\text{subject to:} \quad 7X_1 + 3X_2 \leq 42$$
$$2X_1 + 5X_2 \leq 30$$
$$X_1, X_2 \geq 0 \text{ and integer}$$

(Hint: use the constraints to deduce upper limits on the variables.)

A new canonical form

In order to apply Balas' algorithm the problem must be expressed in a particular canonical form:
$$\text{Minimize} \quad c_1 X_1 + c_2 X_2 + \ldots + c_n X_n$$
$$\text{subject to:} \quad a_{11} X_1 + a_{12} X_2 + \ldots + a_{1n} X_n \leq b_1$$
$$a_{m1} X_1 + a_{m2} X_2 + \ldots + a_{mn} X_n \leq b_m$$
$$X_1, X_2 \ldots X_n \text{ binary}$$

where $c_1, c_2 \ldots c_n$ are non-negative numbers.

Note the unusual combination of minimization and less-than-or-equal-to constraints. The significance of this will become apparent as we investigate the algorithm. The reader should also be assured that this new form in no way restricts the class of problems that may be solved by Balas' method: any binary problem can be converted to it if the following transformations are used:

1. If the problem is a maximization, multiply the objective function by -1. (Minimizing $-Z$ has precisely the same effect as maximizing Z.)
2. Multiply any $\geq$ constraint by -1. This will change the signs of all the constraint's coefficients and constant, and will reverse the inequality.

3. For any variable X_i whose objective function coefficient is negative, define a new variable X_i' as follows:

$$X_i' = 1 - X_i \qquad (11\text{-}31)$$

Clearly X_i' is another binary variable, taking the values 0 and 1 as X_i takes 1 and 0. It is also true that:

$$X_i = 1 - X_i' \qquad (11\text{-}32)$$

This equation should now be used to replace X_i wherever it occurs in the problem. As a result, the modified version of the objective function will contain terms all of whose coefficients are non-negative. The fact that it may also have acquired a constant term is of no importance, since any such constant may be ignored without changing the optimal values of the variables in any way. (After all, minimizing the variable portion of the objective function will minimize the whole of it.) Once the solution has been found, Eq. (11-32) is used to revert from X_i' to X_i, providing an interpretation consistent with the initial model.

Student activity

Convert the following problem to a form suitable for the application of Balas' algorithm.

$$\text{Maximize} \quad 3X_1 - 2X_2 - X_3$$
$$\text{subject to:} \quad X_1 + 5X_2 - 4X_3 \geq 2$$
$$-X_1 + X_2 + 5X_3 \leq 3$$

X_1, X_2, X_3 binary

First steps in the algorithm

We illustrate the use of the algorithm on the following problem:

$$\text{Minimize} \quad 3X_1 + X_2 + 7X_3 + 2X_4 + 5X_5 \qquad (11\text{-}33)$$
$$\text{subject to:} \quad 2X_1 - 3X_2 + X_3 + 5X_4 + 6X_5 \leq 4 \qquad (11\text{-}34)$$
$$X_1 + 3X_2 - 3X_3 - X_4 - 4X_5 \leq -1 \qquad (11\text{-}35)$$

All X's binary

Notice that the problem is already in canonical form so that no further transformation is needed. Notice also that, if the constant of Eq. (11-35) had been zero or positive then we could have achieved the optimal solution immediately simply by setting all variables to zero. The 'all zero' solution is clearly feasible and, because of the non-negative character of its coefficients, a zero value for the objective function could not possibly be bettered. In this and most other cases, at least one negative constant exists and so further development is necessary. We first define slack and objective function variables in the usual way but express them as the subjects of the resulting equations:

$$Z = 3X_1 + X_2 + 7X_3 + 2X_4 + 5X_5 \qquad (11\text{-}36)$$

$$S_1 = 4 - 2X_1 + 3X_2 - X_3 - 5X_4 - 6X_5 \qquad (11\text{-}37)$$

$$S_2 = -1 - X_1 - 3X_2 + 3X_3 + X_4 + 4X_5 \qquad (11\text{-}38)$$

A partial solution

To progress with Balas' method we must now define two new concepts: the *partial* solution and the *free* variable. A partial solution is an ordered set of variables to which values 0 or 1 have been assigned. The additive algorithm requires the consideration of a number of such partial solutions. The partial solution under consideration at any given time is said to be *current*, and all calculations based on Eqs (11-36) and (11-38) are taken to involve only those variables that are contained in it. A variable is free if it is not in the current partial solution, and is thus not involved in the calculation of Z and the S's. These ideas will become clearer as the method unfolds. We first consider a partial solution in which there are no variables at all: in other words every variable is free. The corresponding values of Z, S_1 and S_2 computed from Eqs (11-36) to (11-38) are:

$$Z = 0, \qquad S_1 = 4, \qquad S_2 = -1$$

These are recorded in the first node of a tree as shown in Fig. 11-6.

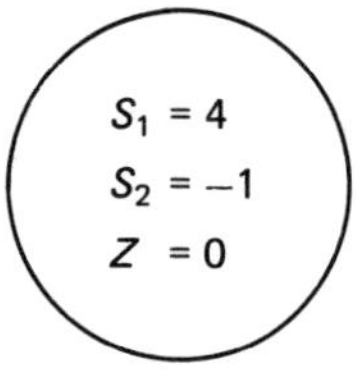

$S_1 = 4$
$S_2 = -1$
$Z = 0$

Figure 11-6 First partial solution

Adding a variable to a partial solution

We now investigate the set of free variables in the hope of finding suitable candidates for inclusion in the partial solution. A variable's suitability must be judged according to two criteria:

1. its ability to reduce the infeasibility of at least one slack;
2. that it will not result in too large an increase in the value of Z.

Until we have discovered a complete feasible solution, i.e. a partial solution in which all variables have been assigned values (so that none remains free) and all S's take appropriate non-negative values, we are not in a position to apply criterion 2. We have no idea at this stage what constitutes 'too large' an increase in Z. We therefore concentrate attention on criterion 1. In our example, S_2 is currently the only infeasible slack—at present it takes the value -1. From Eq. (11-37) it can be seen that its infeasibility is reduced if any of X_3, X_4 and X_5 is assigned the value 1 and added to the current partial solution. Note that this observation depends only on the signs of the coefficients in Eq. (11-38). Where a variable has a positive coefficient it offers a reduction in the infeasibility;

```
   ┌─────────┐
   │ S₁ = 4  │
   │ S₂ = −1 │
   │ Z  = 0  │
   └─────────┘
         \
          \ X₃ = 1
           \
         ┌─────────┐
         │ S₁ = 3  │
         │ S₂ = 2  │
         │ Z  = 7  │
         └─────────┘
```

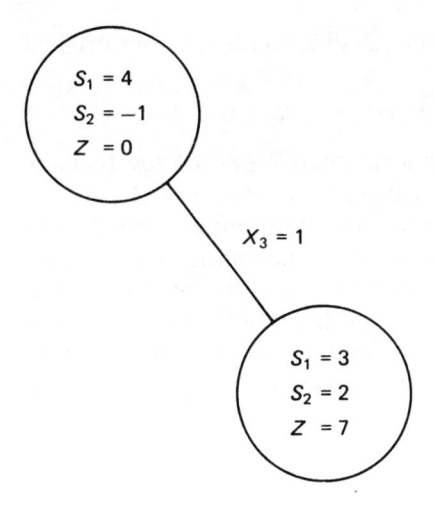

Figure 11-7 New partial solution

otherwise it does not. Evidently, if no such free variable exists then there is no way in which we can complete the current partial solution feasibly, and we will cease to investigate it. We shall discuss later what action we should take in these circumstances. In this case, in fact, setting any of X_3, X_4 and X_5 to 1 will remove S_2's infeasibility entirely. However, note their different effects on S_1. From Eq. (11-37), only X_3 will lead to a feasible value for this slack; setting X_4 or X_5 to 1 will force S_1 to be negative. Our choice is therefore clear: we form a new partial solution by assigning the value 1 to X_3. The resulting values of Z and the S's are recorded in a new branch of the tree as shown in Fig. 11-7.

In general it may well be true that there is no single variable that, on being set to 1, removes all infeasibility. In such cases it is normal practice to regard the most suitable candidate as the one that minimizes total resultant infeasibility. In other words, for each suitable candidate we sum the infeasibilities that would result if we were to set the variable to 1, and then select the candidate with the smallest total. This is the kind of heuristic procedure we encountered earlier. The choice of a variable for inclusion in the partial solution is the Balas equivalent of the 'branching variable' decision in branch and bound or the 'cut row' decision in cutting plane. Indeed, as Fig. 11-7 shows, X_3 is actually a branching variable but of a rather different sort.

> *Student activity*
> Verify that, if their suitability were to be measured by total resultant infeasibility, the variables X_3, X_4 and X_5 would be ranked in that order.

A complete feasible solution

Consider next the new partial solution which consists solely of the variable X_3, assigned the value 1. This is now our current partial solution. Figure 11-7 shows that if we were to assign the value 0 to all remaining free variables then the resulting partial solution would be complete and feasible and thus would represent one possible solution to our original problem:

$$X_1 = 0, \quad X_2 = 0, \quad X_3 = 1, \quad X_4 = 0, \quad X_5 = 0$$

with a corresponding value of $Z = 7$. This is valuable information. We now know that any partial solution with a Z value greater than 7 cannot be completed optimally. Because of the non-negative coefficients of the objective function there is no assignment of values to the free variables, which can reduce Z below 7 and so improve on the solution that we have already established. We shall use this fact when next we add a new variable to a partial solution. We remark also that our investigation of the right-hand branch of the tree is complete. There are no further solutions for which $X_3 = 1$ that we wish to consider. With the use of the same terminology as in Section 11-1, this branch has been fathomed. Fathoming can occur in other ways, as we shall shortly see.

Backtracking

Having fathomed the right-hand branch we turn our attention to the left. In general it will pay us to view this change of position in terms of *backtracking*. Backtracking is the process by which we work our way upwards through the tree (i.e. towards the root) along the branches that we constructed at earlier stages in our analysis until we arrive at a node from which further branching is possible. Because of the manner in which branching takes place, we shall always find that the single branch at such a node corresponds to the assignment of the value 1 to some variable X, let us say. A new partial solution is created by assigning a zero value to X and retaining the existing values of all variables associated with branches higher in the tree (i.e. closer to the root). This means, of course, that other variables associated with branches over which we have just backtracked are deleted from the old partial solution in forming the new. At this stage of our analysis, backtracking is particularly simple. It results in the additional branch shown in Fig. 11-8 where the partial solution in which X_3 is assigned a value 0 and all other variables are free is now current.

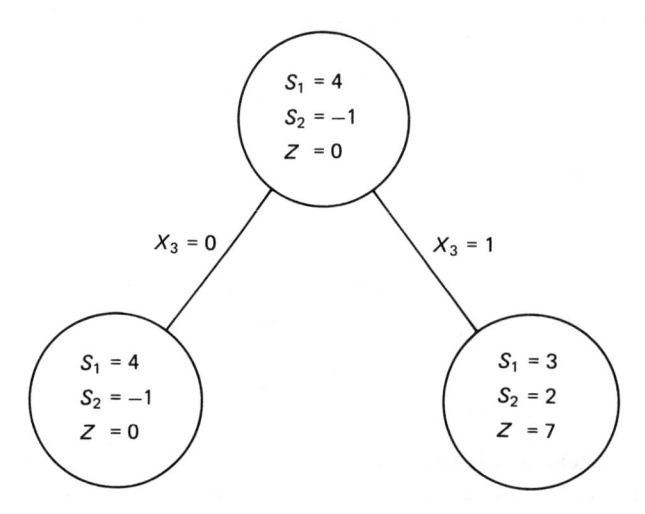

Figure 11-8 Backtracking

SOLUTION METHODS FOR INTEGER LINEAR PROGRAMMING 273

Backtracking is an important feature of Balas' method not only because it is one means by which the tree is extended but also because it will eventually indicate the termination of the algorithm. This occurs when there is no further unfathomed node from which to branch.

Creating further partial solutions

In our current partial solution S_2 takes the value -1 and so is once again infeasible. The set of free variables no longer contains X_3 and thus the candidates for inclusion in the partial solution are X_4 and X_5. The reader should confirm that both satisfy the criteria for suitability, i.e. both reduce the infeasibility of some slack—namely, S_2—and neither, if set equal to 1, would increase the value of Z beyond the 7 already achieved by a complete feasible solution. However, as shown in the previous student activity, X_4 has the smaller total resultant infeasibility and is therefore considered the better choice. Assigning 1 to X_4 creates another new partial solution, this time with:

$$Z = 2, \quad S_1 = -1, \quad S_2 = 0$$

Once more we must seek a candidate variable for inclusion in the solution. On this occasion we have no choice. X_2 is the only variable that satisfies the two criteria, and so we assign a 1 to it. At the next stage, however, there are no candidates at all: X_5 is the only variable to reduce an infeasibility, but to assign it a value of 1 would increase Z to 8, so proving that the current partial solution could not be completed optimally. The corresponding branch is therefore fathomed and we backtrack by assigning the value 0 to X_2. Again, though, there is no candidate variable—indeed there is no way at all of reducing the infeasibility in S_1—so this branch is also fathomed and we backtrack once more. It is instructive to present the current stage of our analysis visually as in Fig. 11-9.

Student activity
Using Eqs (11-36) to (11-38), confirm the findings of the previous paragraph and follow the development of the algorithm in Fig. 11-9.

Summary of the method

Although we have not yet completed our analysis of the problem, we now present a summary of the steps in Balas' algorithm. Our treatment to date has, in fact, made use of all the major points and an optimal solution may be found by repeatedly applying them. The steps, which should be enacted in sequence unless it is stated otherwise, are:

1. If necessary, convert the problem to the canonical form for Balas' algorithm.
2. Introduce a slack variable into each constraint and express it as the subject of the resulting equation.
3. Consider the partial solution for which all variables are free. If this can be completed feasibly by setting all main variables (i.e. the X's) to zero, then STOP. This complete solution is optimal.
4. Create a node and record the values of the objective function and slacks within it.
5. Search the set of free variables for members which, if assigned the value 1, would:

274 FURTHER MATHEMATICAL PROGRAMMING MODELS

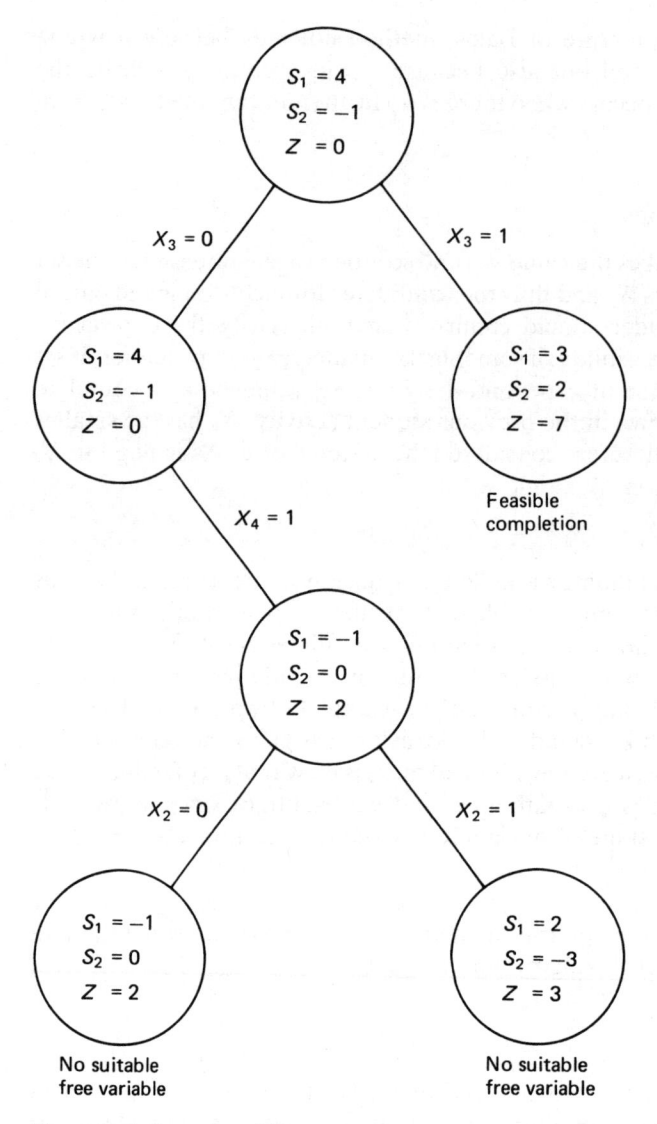

```
                    ┌─────────┐
                    │ S₁ = 4  │
                    │ S₂ = -1 │
                    │ Z = 0   │
                    └─────────┘
              X₃ = 0 /        \ X₃ = 1
                    /          \
            ┌─────────┐      ┌─────────┐
            │ S₁ = 4  │      │ S₁ = 3  │
            │ S₂ = -1 │      │ S₂ = 2  │
            │ Z = 0   │      │ Z = 7   │
            └─────────┘      └─────────┘
                              Feasible
                              completion
                    X₄ = 1
                         \
                          ┌─────────┐
                          │ S₁ = -1 │
                          │ S₂ = 0  │
                          │ Z = 2   │
                          └─────────┘
                    X₂ = 0 /    \ X₂ = 1
                  ┌─────────┐  ┌─────────┐
                  │ S₁ = -1 │  │ S₁ = 2  │
                  │ S₂ = 0  │  │ S₂ = -3 │
                  │ Z = 2   │  │ Z = 3   │
                  └─────────┘  └─────────┘
                  No suitable   No suitable
                  free variable free variable
```

Figure 11-9 Current position

(a) reduce the infeasibility of at least one slack—i.e. for some negative slack, either reverse its sign or move its value closer to zero, and

(b) not increase the objective function beyond the best value previously established for a complete feasible solution.

If no such variable exists, move to step 9.

6. Select a branching variable. (If several variables satisfy the criteria of step 4, apply a suitable heuristic. For example, choose the one that minimizes the total resultant infeasibility.)

7. Form a new partial solution by assigning the value 1 to the variable chosen at step 6.

Create a new branch to represent this, and record the values of the objective function and slacks within the node.
8. If the current partial solution can be completed feasibly by assigning the value zero to all the free variables, note its objective function value. (This must be the best so far.) Move to step 9.
   Otherwise return to step 5.
9. Backtrack to a node from which further branching is possible. If no such node exists, then STOP. The last complete feasible solution to be noted (as in step 8) is the optimal solution.
10. Form a new partial solution by assigning the value 0 to the variable associated with the node. Create a new branch to represent this, and record the values of the objective function and slacks within the new node. Return to step 5.

Student activity
Verify that Fig. 11-10 represents a full analysis of the example, and deduce that the optimal solution is:

$$X_1 = 0, \quad X_2 = 1, \quad X_3 = 0, \quad X_4 = 0, \quad X_5 = 1$$

11-4 COMPUTATIONAL EXPERIENCE

No matter how impressive the theory may appear, the acid test of an algorithm is its ability to perform well in practice. As mentioned in the introduction to this chapter, there are several measures by which the performance of any solution method may be judged. In particular it should be accurate and reliable for a wide range of problems, providing optimal solutions in an acceptable length of time. Because they both rely—though to varying extents—on the integer properties of the variables, cutting plane and enumeration methods often appear the more promising approaches. Balas' additive algorithm, particularly, reduces all computation to simple addition and subtraction and might therefore be expected to prove superior to techniques that, like Simplex, demand large numbers of multiplications and divisions—operations which, even by computer, take appreciably longer to perform. Furthermore, there are cutting plane and enumeration methods that apply to mixed integer as well as all-integer problems. Perhaps surprisingly, however, neither approach figures prominently in modern commercial software. In the case of cutting plane methods, this is probably due to two inherent disadvantages. Firstly, with most versions of the approach, difficulties may arise because of the rounding errors that result from the inclusion of new cuts in the final Simplex tableau and accumulate as the algorithm progresses. Secondly, the approach produces no feasible solution (in the sense of meeting all constraints and integer conditions) until the optimal solution itself is achieved. For large problems it is a considerable advantage to discover good—if not optimal—solutions at earlier stages in the method. These may still be of practical value to the problem-solver. For enumeration methods, despite the efficiency with which any particular partial solution can be analysed, the number of solutions that need to be considered approximates an exponential function of the number of variables, so that overall solution times are often prohibitive for large problems. As you will have inferred,

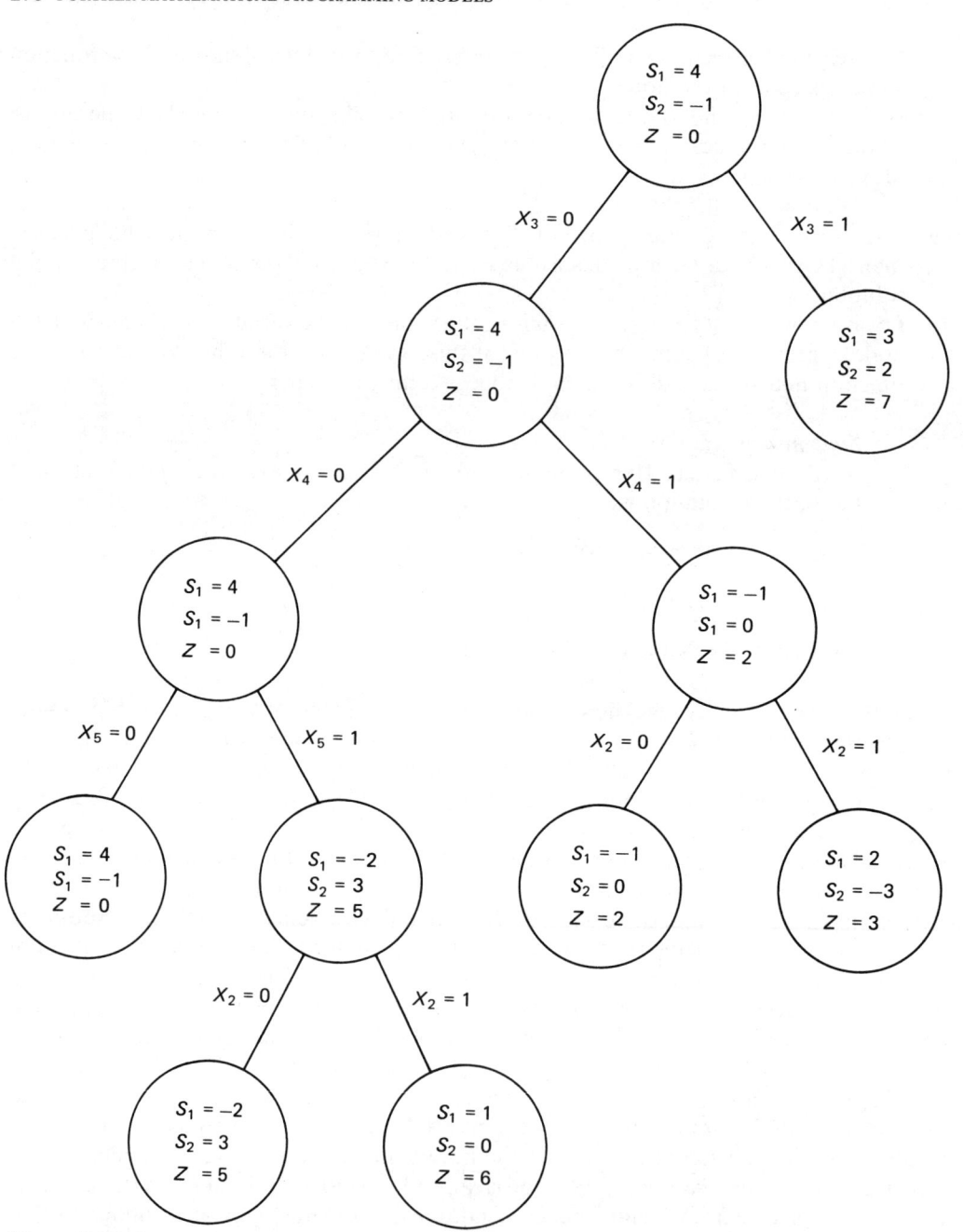

Figure 11-10 The complete tree

for problems of a realistic size the branch and bound approach has in general proved superior. It is currently the core of most commercial codes and, although research into alternative algorithms continues on a broad front, is likely to remain so for the foreseeable future.

11-5 SUMMARY

In this chapter we have introduced a number of methods for the solution of integer linear programs. We stress once again that each of these is merely one representative of a broad approach to ILP solution, and that many enhancements are possible in every case. Nevertheless, our examples have been chosen to illustrate the essential features of each approach and to emphasize the differences between them. Thus branch and bound methods are a simple, direct means of attacking ILP problems that require—in principle—very little theoretical elaboration, but may demand the solution of considerable numbers of linear programs. Cutting plane algorithms, by contrast, depend on elegant refinements of the theory of the Simplex method—but may still require a lengthy series of augmented problems and Simplex solutions. Finally, enumeration methods can be viewed as the only approach to make full use of the integer nature of the variables, but may yet necessitate the consideration of large numbers of partial solutions. Despite the greater theoretical appeal of cutting plane and enumeration methods, commercial ILP packages most often use branch and bound techniques as the basis of their solution procedures.

Of course, technical matters such as the choice of ILP solution algorithm are not necessarily ones over which the practising manager will wish to exercise judgement. It may well be enough to know that methods exist to solve ILP problems and that there are reliable computer programs which make use of them. For those who would like to see ILP play an increasing role in decision-making, the most encouraging trend of recent years has been the remarkable growth of computing power available to all areas of business rather than the development of enhanced solution procedures. With the ever greater speeds and capacities of modern computer architectures, the solution of moderately large ILP models may shortly be a practical desktop proposition bringing ILP to the same level of popularity as ordinary LP as far as the decision-maker is concerned. What is, at present, important from the perspective of the decision-maker is the ability to appreciate when ILP models are likely to play a useful role in providing useful management information and to have an understanding of the principles underpinning their solution. Without this the business decision-maker will not be in a position to evaluate either the usefulness of such models or the reliability of the management information they generate.

STUDENT EXERCISES

11-1 Cuttons Foundry holds stocks of steel bars, each 400 cm in length, which it cuts to the sizes required by customers. A particular order involves lengths of 124 and 68 cm, and Cuttons would like to know what cutting 'pattern' it should use to minimize the amount of waste from each bar. Such a pattern must allow for the fact that, to prevent excessive cutting and handling, the number of pieces cut from a bar should be limited to five at most. Show that Cuttons' problems can be formulated as:

$$\begin{aligned} \text{Maximize} \quad & 124A + 68B \\ \text{subject to:} \quad & 124A + 68B \leq 400 \\ & A + B \leq 5 \\ & A, B \geq 0 \text{ and integer} \end{aligned}$$

Graph Cuttons' problem and determine the optimal LP solution. Using this as your starting point, apply a branch and bound method to solve the problem and confirm your answer by reference to the graph.

11-2 Use a branch and bound method to solve the following problem:

$$\text{Maximize} \quad 4A + 3B$$
$$\text{subject to:} \quad 2A + 3B \leq 6$$
$$-3A + 2B \leq 3$$
$$2A + B \leq 4$$
$$A, B \geq 0 \text{ and integer}$$

You may solve the subproblems involved in your analysis either manually, using the arguments of Section 11-1, or by employing a suitable computer program.

11-3 Using a computer program to derive your subproblem solutions, solve the following ILP problem.

$$\text{Maximize} \quad 9A + 5B + 6C$$
$$\text{subject to:} \quad 7A + 3B + C \leq 20$$
$$2A + 4B + 5C \leq 24$$
$$A, B, C \geq 0 \text{ and integer}$$

How would your analysis and solution change if A were not required to be an integer?

11-4 Explain the view that 'Comparing the branch and bound technique with the cutting plane method is like comparing a hatchet with a razor. Branch and bound chops the problem into ever smaller, more manageable chunks, whereas cutting plane pares the problem down to its bare essentials.'

11-5 Consider the problem:

$$\text{Maximize} \quad 5A + 3B$$
$$\text{subject to:} \quad 9A + 5B \leq 24$$
$$7A + 5B \leq 23$$
$$A, B \geq 0 \text{ and integer}$$

When the integer conditions are ignored, the optimal Simplex tableau is:

	A	B	S_1	S_2	Value
Z	0	0	−0.4	−0.2	−14.2
A	1	0	0.5	−0.5	0.5
B	0	1	−0.7	0.9	3.9

Following the logic of your method with care, show that there is a cutting constraint of the form:

$$0.3S_1 + 0.9S_2 - S_3 = 0.9$$

where S_3 is a non-negative integer. Add this cut to the tableau and use it to solve the problem. (Hint: when you iterate to the next tableau, use S_2 as the entering and S_3 as the leaving variable.)

Illustrate the effect of the cut graphically and confirm your solution.

11-6 The LP solution of problem 11-2 has the final tableau:

	A	B	S_1	S_2	S_3	Value
Z	0	0	−0.5	0	−1.5	−9
B	0	1	0.5	0	−0.5	1
S_2	0	0	−1.75	1	3.25	5.5
A	1	0	−0.25	0	0.75	1.5

Derive cutting constraints from the two rows of the tableau with fractional values in the final column, and use the heuristic rule of Section 11-2 to confirm that S_2's produces the deeper cut. Use this to solve the problem. (Hint: S_1 replaces the cutting slack in the basis at the next iteration.)

11-7 Convert the following problem to a form suitable for the use of Balas' additive algorithm.

$$\text{Maximize} \quad A + 2B - 3C$$
$$\text{subject to:} \quad 20A + 15B - 12C \geq 5$$
$$-4A + 7B + 2C \leq 4$$
$$A, B, C \text{ binary}$$

Confirm that the optimal solution is:

$$A = 1, \quad B = 1, \quad C = 0$$

11-8 Using the second constraint to deduce upper limits on the values of the variables, transform the following model into a problem in binary variables.

$$\text{Minimize} \quad 3A + 5B + C$$
$$\text{subject to:} \quad 7A + 2B + 9C \geq 20$$
$$6A + 4B + 3C \leq 12$$
$$A, B, C \geq 0 \text{ and integer}$$

Confirm that the optimal solution is:

$$A = 0, \quad B = 0, \quad C = 4$$

11-9 Use Balas' additive algorithm to solve the following problem.

$$\text{Minimize} \quad 3A + 2B + 5C + 2D + 6E$$
$$\text{subject to:} \quad -A - B + C + 2D - E \leq 1$$
$$-7A \quad\quad + 3C - 4D + 3E \leq -2$$
$$11A - 6B \quad\quad -3D - 3E \leq -1$$
$$A, B, C, D, E \text{ binary}$$

11-10 Return to the problems introduced in Part B on linear programming. For each problem that resulted in a non-integer solution introduce the integer requirement and using one of the methods detailed in this chapter (and preferably a suitable computer package) re-solve the problem.

Assess the effect that the integer requirement has had on the LP optimal solution.

Evaluate the need for a strictly integer approach in the business context of the problem under investigation.

12
GOAL PROGRAMMING

When managers make decisions they normally have more than one objective in view. At the strategic level, for example, decision-makers will typically aim not only to increase profits but also to ensure a healthy return on capital investment, to enhance the dividend paid to shareholders, to promote an appropriate corporate image, to achieve an acceptable standard of service to clients and the community, and, if all else fails, to ensure that the organization at least survives. This is merely a small sample of the many objectives that may well be relevant to any decision at the highest organizational level. At the tactical and operational levels too, single-objective decisions are the exception rather than the rule. For these reasons, linear programming in all the forms that we have examined thus far is sometimes criticized as unrealistic. In order to represent the objective function, so the argument goes, any LP model must assume that the decision-maker has some unique and exclusive objective that (s)he is seeking to attain. It is therefore only in particularly simplistic situations that LP can provide a useful decision aid. In this chapter we show how this criticism can be refuted through the use of *goal programming*. Goal programming (GP) was developed expressly to deal with multi-objective decision problems. Despite the change of emphasis, however, GP is still a form of linear programming. In fact, this criticism is misconceived—it fails to appreciate the power and flexibility of the LP approach. Even without GP, modellers are able to throw light on problems with multiple objectives. For example, it is often possible to choose an objective of particular importance as the basis of the objective function, ensuring an acceptable level of performance with respect to the others by means of appropriate constraints. By switching the roles of objective and constraints and re-solving the problem the decision-maker may be presented with a range of solution options, and will then employ professional judgement and experience to select the 'best'. Indeed, GP is little more than a means of formalizing this approach and ensuring that the constraints that represent the problem's objectives receive the special treatment that is their due. We begin by extending the traditional concept of a constraint.

12-1 SOFT CONSTRAINTS

In all our previous discussions we have assumed that constraints are applied strictly and inescapably. When the International Monitor Company set budgets for its managers or noted limits on the availability of components, raw materials or labour hours, we inferred that no solution could possibly violate the constraints that these implied and still remain workable. In practice this is often not the case. Fresh stocks of components and raw materials can be ordered, staff may be willing to work overtime and even budgets are elastic on occasions. Of course, as this discussion indicates, violating a constraint will normally imply a cost of some sort—whether this is a special delivery surcharge, an overtime payment or some other monetary penalty. The essential point, however, is that our earlier idea of the constraint as a strict, inviolable requirement will need to be modified when the occasion demands it. The result is the so-called *soft constraint*. Consider once again the IMC problem of Chapter 5. The model we formulated earlier is reproduced below.

$$\text{Maximize} \quad 40A + 50B \tag{12-1}$$

$$\text{subject to:} \quad 28A + 42B \leq 16\,800 \tag{12-2}$$

$$12A + 6B \leq 4\,800 \tag{12-3}$$

$$1A + 1B \leq 600 \tag{12-4}$$

$$A, B \geq 0$$

Assume now that overtime may be worked in the assembly and inspection departments at marginal costs per hour of £1 and £2 respectively. Assume also that additional supplies of microchips may be procured if management is prepared to pay a special delivery surcharge of £1.5 per microchip. We consider first the effects of these changes on the constraints. Clearly Eqs (12-2) to (12-4) no longer apply: they are *hard constraints* and imply inviolable restrictions. In their place we introduce:

$$28A + 42B + D_1^- - D_1^+ = 16\,800 \tag{12-5}$$

$$12A + 6B + D_2^- - D_2^+ = 4\,800 \tag{12-6}$$

$$1A + 1B + D_3^- - D_3^+ = 600 \tag{12-7}$$

Equations (12-5) to (12-7) are soft constraints that, in effect, allow IMC to use any amounts of assembly and inspection time and any number of microchips they wish. The D's are *deviational* variables and are included for exactly this purpose. D_1^-, for example, represents the number of assembly hours that remain unused when production is complete, and will therefore take a positive value if utilized assembly time falls short of 16 800 hours. On the other hand, if this figure is exceeded, D_1^+ becomes positive, since it represents the number of assembly hours used by IMC over and above normal working. In fact, the deviational variables are no more than slack and surplus variables in disguise. Those with the superscript $^-$ perform the role of slacks, those marked by $^+$ act like surpluses. For the first time we see both types of variable in the same constraint, but this should not surprise us—after all, any soft constraint must combine both forms of inequality: $\leq$ and $\geq$. It should concern the reader, however, that there appears to be nothing to prevent both D_1^- and D_1^+, for example, from taking non-zero values in the same solution. To be consistent, we cannot permit this to happen. Assembly hours may be less than 16 800 or greater than 16 800, but cannot be both at the same time. The modified form of the objective function ensures this:

$$\text{Maximize} \quad 40A + 50B - 1D_1^+ - 2D_2^+ - 1.5D_3^+ \qquad (12\text{-}8)$$

We have subtracted the costs incurred by IMC when additional resources (D_1^+ assembly hours, D_2^+ inspection hours and D_3^+ microchips) are utilized. To keep these costs to a minimum the objective function will ensure that the D^+'s remain as small as possible. Thus each D^+ will take a positive value only when forced to do so, i.e. when the corresponding resource reaches its original limit and the associated D^- becomes zero. For the sake of clarity and completeness we repeat the new model below.

$$\text{Maximize} \quad 40A + 50B - 1D_1^+ - 2D_2^+ - 1.5D_3^+ \qquad (12\text{-}8)$$
$$\text{subject to:} \quad 28A + 42B + D_1^- - D_1^+ = 16\,800 \qquad (12\text{-}5)$$
$$12A + 6B + D_2^- - D_2^+ = 4\,800 \qquad (12\text{-}6)$$
$$1A + 1B + D_3^- - D_3^+ = 600 \qquad (12\text{-}7)$$
$$A, B \text{ and all } D\text{'s} \geq 0$$

Student activity
With the introduction of the D's, IMC's problem now has eight variables. Using a suitable software package, solve the problem and verify that the D's form a consistent set (i.e. at most one of each associated pair is positive).

12-2 CONSTRUCTING GOAL PROGRAMS

We now turn our attention to the objectives of a multi-objective decision problem. Instead of retaining the term 'objective', however, we substitute the word 'goal'. This is done for two reasons. Firstly, we wish to emphasize the move away from single-objective LP. Secondly, we must stress a fundamental difference between goals and the objectives of our previous problems: unlike objectives, we cannot guarantee that goals will be achieved. In general, each goal is represented by a target at which we can aim—but which we may fail to hit. To illustrate this point and demonstrate the formulation and solution of goal programs, we consider a modified version of IMC's monitor mix problem. We now assume that, for tactical reasons, there are three goals that IMC wishes to achieve. These are:

1. to meet the needs of a long-standing and important customer who has ordered 150 monitors of Model A,
2. to attain a reasonable level of profit, and
3. to use as little overtime as possible in the assembly department, where recent overtime payments have been excessive.

As in our original treatment of this problem we assume that there is no way of increasing the number of hours available in the inspection department. It is already working at full capacity and no further overtime is possible. Also, following the delivery of a large consignment of microchips there is no shortage of components.

Goals and targets

Before we attempt to construct a mathematical model of this problem, let us investigate IMC's goals a little further. Firstly, notice that there is a certain vagueness about goal 2. What do we mean by 'a reasonable level of profit'? To progress we must sharpen the statement of this goal by specifying the level of profit that IMC considers reasonable, and making this our target. Here we will assume that IMC has set its sights on a profit of at least £25 000. Similar targets already exist in the case of goals 1 and 3: we have a production target of 150 Model A monitors associated with goal 1, and, for goal 3, an overtime target of 0 overtime hours in the assembly department (alternatively, a target of at most 16 800 utilized assembly hours in total). We therefore draw a clear logical distinction between goals and targets. A goal is an expression of the organization's desire to reach, exceed or remain within some specified level of performance. The associated target is the numerical value that we attach to the level in question. Despite this we shall often use the two words interchangeably and take the terms 'attaining the goal' and 'attaining the target' to have the same meaning. It should be fairly clear that we cannot be sure of attaining all IMC's targets in a single solution. In fact, any attempt to do so by introducing suitable hard constraints (Eqs (12-9) to (12-12)) will lead to failure. It can readily be shown that the resulting problem is infeasible.

$$A \geq 150 \qquad (12\text{-}9)$$
$$40A + 50B \geq 25\,000 \qquad (12\text{-}10)$$
$$28A + 42B \leq 16\,800 \qquad (12\text{-}11)$$
$$12A + 6B \leq 4\,800 \qquad (12\text{-}12)$$

Student activity
Verify graphically that Eqs (12-9) to (12-12) represent an infeasible system of constraints.

Prioritizing the goals

Our discussion has led us to conclude that IMC has conflicting goals. In GP, however, this is no difficulty. We progress by assuming that it is possible to prioritize the goals in some way, and that each successive goal in the priority list is of insignificant importance by comparison with the one before it. In our example we prioritize the goals in order of appearance, and, so that our priorities are clear, represent them by P_1, P_2 and P_3. Such an ordering is entirely realistic. In IMC's long-term interests, it would be unwise not to meet the requirements of a valued customer, even if this meant sacrificing short-term profit. Similarly, it is arguably unreasonable to forgo additional profit for the sake of establishing a principle in the assembly department. (Naturally, in other companies, at other times, in other circumstances, priorities may differ.) To model P_1, P_2 and P_3 we first soften the corresponding hard constraints, Eqs (12-9) to (12-11). These now become:

$$A + D_1^- - D_1^+ = 150 \tag{12-13}$$

$$40A + 50B + D_2^- - D_2^+ = 25\,000 \tag{12-14}$$

$$28A + 42B + D_3^- - D_3^+ = 16\,800 \tag{12-15}$$

The variables that are particularly pertinent are D_1^-, D_2^- and D_3^+. These represent, respectively, the amounts by which IMC:

- undershoots its customer supply target (i.e. falls short of satisfying the important customer);
- undershoots its profit target;
- overshoots its assembly overtime target (i.e. uses any overtime at all in the assembly department).

The goals may thus be specified as:

$$P_1: \quad \text{minimize } D_1^-$$
$$P_2: \quad \text{minimize } D_2^-$$
$$P_3: \quad \text{minimize } D_3^+$$

which we represent as follows:

$$\text{Minimize} \quad P_1 D_1^- + P_2 D_2^- + P_3 D_3^+ \tag{12-16}$$

Note that this 'objective function' may be interpreted in either of two ways. We may view it as a purely formal expression of IMC's goal system, i.e. simply as a shorthand form for all that we have already said about IMC's goals and priorities. In this interpretation, we are not dealing with an objective function in the normal sense at all, and should not think of the P's as quantities. However, if we prefer a more conventional explanation, we may regard the P's as numerical weights of decreasing size, such that:

$$P_1 >>> P_2 >>> P_3$$

The symbol $>>>$ is translated as 'is very much greater than'. The weights have an effect similar to that of the penalties of Chapter 7 where we wished to ensure that the values of artificial variables were reduced to zero. Here they guarantee that D_1^-, D_2^- and D_3^+ are minimized (again, if possible, reduced to zero) in the appropriate priority order.

A complete model

We have now discussed the various parts of the model in some detail. For clarity and completeness we bring them together:

$$\text{Minimize} \quad P_1 D_1^- + P_2 D_2^- + P_3 D_3^+ \tag{12-17}$$

$$\text{subject to:} \quad A + D_1^- - D_1^+ = 150 \tag{12-18}$$

$$40A + 50B + D_2^- - D_2^+ = 25\,000 \tag{12-19}$$

$$28A + 42B + D_3^- - D_3^+ = 16\,800 \tag{12-20}$$

$$12A + 6B \leq 4\,800 \tag{12-21}$$

$$A, B \text{ and all } D\text{'s} \geq 0$$

Because of the absolute prohibition on overtime working in the inspection department Eq. (12-21) remains as the problem's only hard constraint. In general, of course, a GP model will contain a mixture of hard and soft constraints.

12-3 GRAPHICAL SOLUTION

Since our example has just two main variables, we may view the model graphically and this will prove to be particularly instructive. We present the graph in Fig. 12-1.

Inspection time's hard constraint is represented in the usual way by means of the solid line. The soft constraints, on the other hand, are shown as dotted or broken lines, indicating their less restrictive, more flexible nature. The lines are numbered with their corresponding equations to help identification. In so far as we are able to portray it in two dimensions the feasible region consists of the triangle formed from the origin to $A = 400$ to $B = 800$. In reality, however, our model exists in eight dimensions—it has the six D variables in addition to A and B—but two are enough to establish an optimal GP solution. We proceed as follows. Because of the stated priorities IMC will choose to address P_1 before turning its attention to the subsidiary goals. (Recall that each successive goal is of no importance compared with those ahead of it in the priority list.) Thus, setting out in Simplex fashion from the origin we increase the value of A in order to reach P_1's

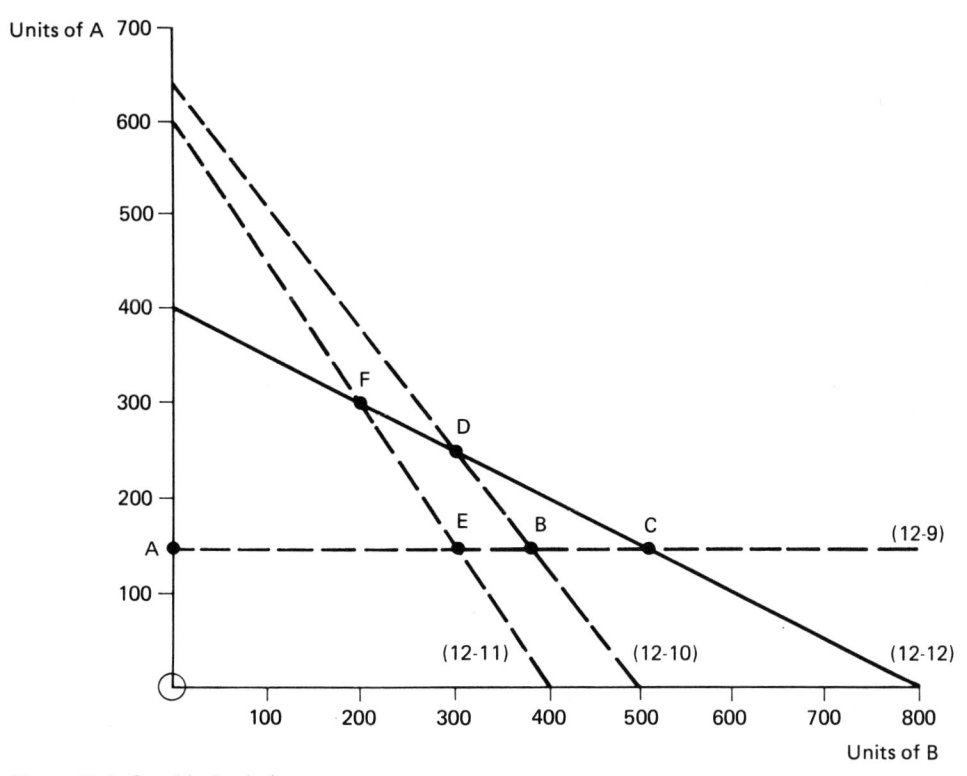

Figure 12-1 Graphical solution

production target as rapidly as possible. This takes us to the point A on the graph and the first goal is thereby achieved. From now on we must take care not to move below this point since this would detrimentally affect P_1, but there is nothing to prevent us from moving above this point. Now that the requirements of P_1 are satisfied, we can turn to P_2. In effect we have switched objective functions and, once again in Simplex fashion, will increase the variable that promises to take us by the quickest route to the target profit, £25 000. Because of the parameters of the profit function (shown in Eq. (12-1)) the preferred variable is B and so we move to the point B. We are now in a position where we have attained both the first and second goals. We now turn to P_3. Again, our priorities will ensure that we never fall below the discontinuous line that represents the £25 000 profit target or below the line representing minimum production of Model A. In effect, therefore, the two goals that we have already achieved restrict further movement only to the small area in the upper right-hand portion of the feasible region (the area marked as BCD). Any attempt to attain P_3, i.e. to arrive on the line labelled Eq. (12-11) can thus take us no closer than the point D without adversely affecting the first two goals. In fact this is where the process ends. The goal optimum at point D is:

$$A = 250, \quad B = 300$$

Student activity
Confirm arithmetically that the solution we have just derived achieves goals P_1 and P_2, and calculate the overtime requirement in the assembly department.

The solution to the goal program indicates that we have achieved the first two goals but that the third (at least in terms of our current priorities) cannot be achieved. Examination of the deviational variables confirms this. D_1^+ is 100 (indicating the number of units of Model A by which we exceed the minimum requirement), both D_2^- and D_2^+ are zero (indicating we are exactly meeting the profit target) whilst D_3^+ is 2800 (indicating the overtime hours required).

Changing the priorities

It is interesting and instructive to consider the effect of changing the priority order of the goals in our model. Assume, for example, that IMC has decided to put principle before profit and wishes to limit the assembly department to normal working if at all possible. Naturally, this will still be subject to meeting the requirements of IMC's important customer; if overtime is necessary to fill that order, then so be it. In terms of the variables of Section 12-2, our model is exactly as before, except for the objective function which now becomes:

$$\text{Minimize} \quad P_1 D_1^- + P_2 D_3^+ + P_3 D_2^- \tag{12-22}$$

Figure 12-1 is still of use in determining the GP optimal solution, but we must now reframe our argument, and allow for the change in goal priorities. P_1 is attained at point A as before, but the nature of the problem thereafter is very different. Notice first that, at point A, goal P_2 is already achieved. No overtime is worked at this point, and so nothing more need be done to attain the target assembly time. It should be stressed, however, that to maintain this state of affairs we cannot move beyond the line labelled Eq. (12-11). In other words we are limited to a small area of the feasible region in any future movement. Aiming to achieve P_3, we find that our objective function is, in effect:

$$40A + 50B$$

so we now increase B and move as far as point E on the graph. Without detracting from goals P_1 and P_2 we can, however, make an even closer approach to the profit target—i.e. P_3—by following the line of Eq. (12-11) up to point F. At this point no further progress is possible. The goal optimum is thus:

$$A = 300, \quad B = 200$$

Again, the original problem formulation confirms the appropriate values for the deviational variables.

Student activity
Using the graph of Fig. 12-1, find the goal optimum when the priorities of Section 12-2 (shown in Eq. (12-16)) are reversed.

12-4 GOALS WITH UNLIMITED TARGETS

It is quite common to find that at least one of the targets associated with a decision-maker's goals is unlimited. In IMC's monitor problem, for example, it is perfectly possible that the company may wish to substitute 'maximize' for 'attain a reasonable level of' in its profit-related goal. In such a case there is no specified finite target. The goal is to achieve as high a level of the appropriate measure as possible. (Notice that we have no difficulty with minimization; the target is zero.) With unlimited targets of this sort we reintroduce a device that we have used several times in the past—the 'Big M'. M is some number, chosen to be as large as practicable, which we include in the relevant constraint in place of the usual target. Thus for IMC's profit goal, Eq. (12-14) becomes:

$$40A + 50B + D_2^- - D_2^+ = M \tag{12-23}$$

If a computer is to be used to produce the goal optimum then M is normally the largest number with which it can cope. The reader should be aware, however, that where unlimited targets appear the decision-maker will constrain the attainment of lower-priority goals quite severely. This can be seen from the current example. If IMC wishes to maximize its profit goal P_2 then it will have no room for manœuvre at all when it comes to address P_3—the goal optimum will have been achieved already. Although this could be exactly what the decision-maker wants it may indicate that insufficient care has been given to the consideration of a suitable target.

Student activity
Confirm that, if IMC's second priority goal is the maximization of profit, then the search for the goal optimum ends with the attainment of P_2.

12-5 A SIMPLEX METHOD FOR GOAL PROGRAMMING

We now consider methods for solving GP problems of a realistic size. We shall assume for the purposes of this section that we are dealing with models in which all the variables are continuous. In principle, almost all our discussion of goal programming applies with equal force to problems involving integer variables. For example, the graphical treatment of previous sections remains valid provided we restrict attention solely to integer points. To solve larger integer or mixed integer GPs, of course, we must adopt one of the approaches outlined in Chapter 11. When solving GPs it is tempting to employ the alternative interpretation of the GP objective function mentioned in Section 12-2. Recall that, according to this view, the P's were regarded as quantities of sharply decreasing value, i.e.

$$P_1 >>> P_2 >>> \ldots >>> P_g$$

where g is the number of goals. For problems in which g is small—say 2 or 3—it may well be possible to define quantities of suitable relative size, insert them in the objective function in place of the P's and solve by Simplex in the normal way. This approach is unreliable, however, since we must ensure that each P is 'very much' smaller than the one before it, but may have little idea just how much 'very much' should be. When the number of goals is large—and in this context 5 or 6 may be considered so—P_1 will often need to be astronomically big, and P_g minutely small, to produce an appropriate set of P's.

However, a careful reading of the graphical treatment of IMC's problem will suggest a more promising solution method. Because of its overriding importance, any goal we have already attained must now become inviolate. Whatever move we make towards the achievement of lower-priority goals, we can never allow any deterioration in those of higher priority. The higher goals therefore assume the role of hard constraints and we may concentrate on achieving the lower goals by adopting, one by one, the objective functions which represent them. We could thus adopt the following method:

1. Introduce slack, surplus and deviational variables as appropriate into the model's hard and soft constraints.
2. Representing goal P_1 by a single objective function, solve the model by applying Simplex in the normal way.
3. Use the final objective function value to create a new constraint which ensures that P_1 is maintained. Add the new constraint to the model.
4. Represent P_2 by a single new objective function, and use it to replace the old.
5. Solve the new model by applying Simplex in the normal way.
6. Repeat steps 3 to 5 for lower-priority goals, creating a new constraint from each as we achieve it, and substituting the goal at the next priority level as objective function.

This outline method begs a number of questions, of course. It may not be clear, for example, precisely how we create the new constraints and objective functions from the goals. More seriously, it appears to imply that at each stage we must solve the resulting new model from scratch. In general this would be grossly inefficient, increasing the amount of computation necessary for large problems by a considerable factor. We can overcome these difficulties, however, by adopting an alternative form of Simplex procedure. We illustrate this by solving IMC's goal programming problem. For convenience now we repeat Eqs (12-17) to (12-20):

$$\text{Minimize} \quad P_1 D_1^- + P_2 D_2^- + P_3 D_3^+ \quad (12\text{-}17)$$

$$\text{subject to:} \quad A \quad\quad\quad\quad + D_1^- - D_1^+ = 150 \quad (12\text{-}18)$$

$$40A + 50B + D_2^- - D_2^+ = 25\,000 \quad (12\text{-}19)$$

$$28A + 42B + D_3^- - D_3^+ = 16\,800 \quad (12\text{-}20)$$

$$12A + 6B + S_1 = 4\,800 \quad (12\text{-}24)$$

$$A, B \text{ and all } D\text{'s} \geq 0$$

The initial Simplex tableau is shown in Tableau 12-1. Notice that in most ways it is just like any other. S_1 and the deviational variables with superscript $^-$ take on the role previously reserved for slacks alone. (We have already mentioned the similarity between slacks and deviationals.) The only important difference is that there are now three goal rows in place of the usual objective function. Each is represented in the left-hand column by the appropriate P and, because we are minimizing, by a negative value in the final column. (Using Eqs (12-17) to (12-20), we have expressed the deviational variables D_1^- and D_2^- in terms of the non-basic variables before entering the goal rows P_1 and P_2. The variable D_3^+ is already non-basic and so remains unchanged in P_3.)

In terms of our earlier graphical analysis the tableau represents the solution at the origin with:

$$A = 0, \quad B = 0, \quad S_1 = 4800$$

$$D_1^- = 150 \quad D_2^- = 25\,000 \quad D_3^- = 16\,800$$
$$D_1^+ = 0 \quad\; D_2^+ = \quad\;\; 0 \quad\; D_3^+ = \quad\;\; 0$$

Student activity
Interpret the values of the variables in the initial Simplex tableau and confirm that they are consistent.

The initial stages of the goal Simplex method are identical to those of standard Simplex—with the exception that we must remember not to treat the goal rows as constraints. Only the rows below the line are used in the ratio test to select a leaving variable. Applying the usual Simplex rules, we therefore see that A is the pivot column and

Tableau 12-1 Initial goal Simplex tableau

	A	B	S_1	D_1^-	D_1^+	D_2^-	D_2^+	D_3^-	D_3^+	Value
P_1	-1	0	0	0	1	0	0	0	0	-150
P_2	-40	-50	0	0	0	0	1	0	0	$-25\,000$
P_3	0	0	0	0	0	0	0	0	1	0
D_1^-	1	0	0	1	-1	0	0	0	0	150
D_2^-	40	50	0	0	0	1	-1	0	0	25\,000
D_3^-	28	42	0	0	0	0	0	1	-1	16\,800
S_1	12	6	1	0	0	0	0	0	0	4\,800

Tableau 12-2 Second goal Simplex tableau

	A	B	S_1	D_1^-	D_1^+	D_2^-	D_2^+	D_3^-	D_3^+	Value
P_1	0	0	0	1	0	0	0	0	0	0
P_2	0	−50	0	40	−40	0	0	0	0	−19000
P_3	0	0	0	0	0	0	0	0	1	0
A	1	0	0	1	−1	0	0	0	0	150
D_2^-	0	50	0	−40	40	0	0	0	0	19000
D_3^-	0	42	0	−28	28	0	0	1	−1	12600
S_1	0	6	1	−12	12	0	0	0	0	3000

D_1^- is the pivot row. The computations involved in producing the new tableau are exactly as normal and so we generate Tableau 12-2.

It is now clear from P_1's row that, as far as our first goal is concerned, we have achieved 'optimality'. In other words, the first goal has been attained. At the next step we therefore switch attention to P_2's row. This is, in effect, our new objective function, and we may use it in precisely the same way as we always have, provided that we never allow a deterioration in P_1. In the present case, there is no danger of this. Applying the usual Simplex rules once again, we find that the pivot column is B and the pivot row is D_3^-. Performing another iteration, we arrive at the third tableau (not shown) which corresponds to the solution:

$$A = 150, \quad B = 300, \quad S_1 = 1200$$

$$\begin{array}{lll} D_1^- = 0 & D_2^- = 4000 & D_3^- = 0 \\ D_1^+ = 0 & D_2^+ = 0 & D_3^+ = 0 \end{array}$$

The reader will note that D_2^- is positive, implying that we have not yet attained IMC's target profit. This will, of course, be obvious from the P_2 row of the tableau. In fact, at the next stage of the Simplex procedure, D_1^+ enters the basis while S_1 leaves. Once again, such a change is permissible since it will not affect P_1 in any way. The resulting fourth tableau represents the solution:

$$A = 300, \quad B = 200, \quad S_1 = 0$$

$$\begin{array}{lll} D_1^- = 0 & D_2^- = 3000 & D_3^- = 0 \\ D_1^+ = 150 & D_2^+ = 0 & D_3^+ = 0 \end{array}$$

P_2 is still not achieved, however, and so a further change of basis is required. On this occasion D_3^+ replaces D_2^- to produce the fifth of the Simplex tableaux, Tableau 12-3.

Tableau 12-3 Goal optimal solution

	A	B	S_1	D_1^-	D_1^+	D_2^-	D_2^+	D_3^-	D_3^+	Value
P_1	0	0	0	1	0	0	0	0	0	0
P_2	0	0	0	0	0	1	0	0	0	0
P_3	0	0	0.78	0	0	−0.93	0.93	1	0	−2800
A	1	0	0.14	0	0	−0.02	0.02	0	0	250
D_2^+	0	0	−0.78	0	0	0.93	−0.93	−1	1	2800
B	0	1	−0.11	0	0	0.03	−0.03	0	0	300
D_1^+	0	0	0.14	−1	1	−0.02	0.02	0	0	100

From P_2's row we see that the usual conditions for optimality are satisfied, so that the second goal has finally been attained and we may turn our attention to P_3. P_3's row shows that D_2^- is the only variable that can move the solution towards the achievement of the third goal. However, D_2^- has a positive coefficient in P_2's row, indicating that, if the variable were to increase from zero, this would detract from the higher-priority goal that we have just realized. The conclusion is clear: we can go no further—the goal optimal solution has been reached and is:

$$A = 250, \qquad B = 300, \qquad S_1 = 0$$

$$\begin{array}{lll} D_1^- = 0 & D_2^- = 0 & D_3^- = 0 \\ D_1^+ = 100 & D_2^+ = 0 & D_3^+ = 2800 \end{array}$$

12-6 SUMMARY

In this chapter we have recognized the need of decision-makers to confront problems with multiple objectives or 'goals'. In so doing we have introduced the concept of the soft constraint to allow for situations in which the restrictions on management's actions may not be absolute and inflexible. These same soft constraints permit us to construct a different type of linear programming model—the goal program—which may be applied to multi-objective problems if suitable priorities and numerical targets are associated with the decision-maker's goals. Two-variable goal programming models can be solved in a manner similar to the graphical technique of LP, using discontinuous lines to represent the soft constraints. However, as in all other areas of mathematical programming, a numerical method is required to solve problems of realistic size. In GP this is a variant of the Simplex algorithm which moves from goal to goal in priority order, ensuring that no goal of higher priority is ever compromised for the sake of one of lower priority. Although the examples and discussion of this chapter are couched in terms of continuous variables and 'ordinary' LP, the same principles apply equally well to integer and mixed integer programs. Clearly, in these areas practical solution methods require the use of approaches from Chapter 11 and thus necessitate a higher order of computational effort.

Apart from the obvious appeal of GP in allowing the decision-maker to model in multiple-objective terms, there is ample evidence of the increasing influence of GP in other ways. Even in situations where the assignment of goal priorities is open to argument—as it may well be if, for example, decisions are the result of group discussion—the imaginative use of GP very often provides a range of solution options from which decision-makers can agree a final, most suitable choice. It is usually a simple matter of generating the different solutions associated with distinct and different priority systems and subjecting their practical implications to close scrutiny. Indeed, it is frequently the case that the GP solutions differ less than the corresponding priority systems might suggest. However, the more significant point—a point we cannot emphasize enough throughout the whole of mathematical programming—is that any final decision of importance will almost always be the result of considered interaction between decision-maker and model. It is in this sense that mathematical modelling complements the experience and skill of the user rather than supplanting them.

STUDENT EXERCISES

12-1 A goal programming problem has been formulated as follows:

$$\text{Minimize} \quad P_1 D_1^- + P_2 D_2^-$$
$$\begin{aligned}
\text{subject to:} \quad & 4A + 5B && \geq 20 \\
& A && \geq 3 \\
& A + B + D_1^- - D_1^+ &&= 5 \\
& A + 2B + D_2^- - D_2^+ &&= 11
\end{aligned}$$
$$A, B \text{ and all } D\text{'s} \geq 0$$

(a) Interpret this problem and provide a graphical solution.

(b) Suppose that the original system of goals is replaced by:

$$\text{Minimize} \quad P_1(D_1^- + D_1^+) + P_2 D_2^-$$

Interpret these goals and solve the new problem graphically.

12-2 Chemanure is a small company which specializes in the production of artificial fertilizers. The requirements and contribution per tonne of each of its two most popular products, xylocine and ytoxin, are shown in the accompanying table.

	Xylocine	Ytoxin
Process time (hours)	0.5	1.0
Phosphate (tonnes)	0.5	0.5
Contribution (£)	50	70

An ongoing dock strike has caused shipping difficulties and Chemanure is unable to obtain further supplies of phosphate from its usual supplier. The company currently has only 60 tonnes of phosphate in stock. However, the supplier has promised that ample quantities will be available in a fortnight's time when, it is widely believed, the strike will be resolved. In the last few days there has been much discussion among senior management about the merits of approaching a competitor in the hope of purchasing additional phosphate from this source. It is clear that Chemanure would be charged considerably more than the normal market price, but no one is certain just how much. In any case, for reasons of company pride this is a move that management would rather not make.

Chemanure works a 40-hour week and runs a single process which produces either xylocine or ytoxin but not both. It was recently in dispute with its own labour force and since then has attempted to avoid the use of overtime where at all possible.

(a) Formulate Chemanure's problem as a goal programme, assuming that management's goals are:
  P_1 To allow no overtime working.
  P_2 To maximize the total contribution of its two products over the next fortnight.
  P_3 To buy in no additional supplies of phosphate.

(b) Solve this problem graphically.

(c) Solve the problem using the goal Simplex method. Is the route taken by the Simplex algorithm in reaching the optimal solution the same as in (b)?

12-3 In Chemanure's problem there are six different ways of ordering the priorities attached to management's goals. Using a graph, determine the corresponding goal optima, and compare and contrast the practical solutions they represent.

12-4 Having won £80 000 in a national competition, you are considering sound ways of investing it. You have shortlisted two market investments that your broker has recommended because of their recent performance. Details of these are given in the table. However, you are also thinking of starting a business of your own as a consultant in mathematical programming and estimate that this would cost an initial £10 000. In addition, you have taken a fancy to a stylish red Porsche that a friend has just put up for sale at £15 000. You are still considering

Investment	Expected return next year (%)	Estimated maximum loss next year (%)
A	20	30
B	15	20

your priorities but have already decided that, for next year, achieving an expected return of at least 12 per cent and avoiding a maximum loss of at most 25 per cent—both calculated on the basis of all that you spend—are your primary concerns (in that order).

Basing the remaining priorities on your own preferences and estimating any further data you require, formulate a mixed integer goal program to model your problem.

13
NON-LINEAR PROGRAMMING

In this chapter we shall provide both an introduction to and an overview of the approaches that are appropriate to the examination of *non-linear programming* models. It is not our intention to examine the solution methods available in detail as we did for the LP model. Rather we intend to encourage the manager and decision-maker to develop an appreciation of the potential of NLP models and their limitations both in a modelling sense and in the context of business decision-making. First of all we shall examine some of the ways in which non-linear relationships can develop in a business problem. We shall then examine the concept of optimization and investigate the use of Lagrange multipliers in this optimization process and show how they lead to the Kuhn–Tucker conditions which assist considerably in the identification of an optimal solution to a non-linear program. We shall then introduce one of the special types of NLP models—that dealing with quadratic programs. Finally, we shall examine the potential for transforming non-linear relationships into a linear format in order to use the powerful facilities of the standard model with which we are already familiar—the LP model.

13-1 NON-LINEAR OBJECTIVE FUNCTIONS AND CONSTRAINTS

Let us examine how non-linear relationships can arise in both the objective function and in constraints. We return to a simplified form of the IMC production problem that we used in Part B:

$$\text{Maximize} \quad 40A + 50B \tag{13-1}$$
$$\text{subject to:} \quad 28A + 42B \leq 16\,800 \tag{13-2}$$
$$1B \leq 300 \tag{13-3}$$
$$A, B \geq 0 \tag{13-4}$$

That is, we seek to maximize profit subject to the available assembly time and a maximum production limit on Model B. Let us examine the linear profit function in more detail. We originally derived this function in Chapter 5 by determining per-unit revenue and per-unit costs and finding the difference between the two. From the original problem the per-unit costs were £219 per unit of A and £299 per unit of B. Unit revenue in the original problem was given also at £259 and £349 respectively. It may well be unrealistic, however, to assume that the selling price of the two products is fixed regardless of the quantity actually sold. A more appropriate assumption might be that the selling price is a function of the quantity brought to the market and that, in line with standard economic theory, the more we try to sell the lower the price we must ask for the product. For Model A, for example, we might have a demand function such that:

$$P_a = 299 - 0.1A \tag{13-5}$$

where P_a is the selling price of the model and A represents the quantity we are trying to sell. It is evident that as we try to sell more of the product we must expect a lower price per unit. Economic demand theory would regard this as entirely logical. Similarly, for model B we might have a demand equation such that:

$$P_b = 399 - 0.15B \tag{13-6}$$

Total revenue is found by multiplying price per unit by quantity, giving:

$$TR_a = P_a \times A = (299 - 0.1A)A = 299A - 0.1A^2 \tag{13-7}$$

$$TR_b = P_b \times B = (399 - 0.15B)B = 399B - 0.15B^2 \tag{13-8}$$

Since profit is simply the difference between total revenue and total cost then for the two products we have profit equations such that:

$$\text{Profit (A)} = (299A - 0.1A^2) - 219A = 80A - 0.1A^2 \tag{13-9}$$

$$\text{Profit (B)} = (399B - 0.15B^2) - 299B = 100B - 0.15B^2 \tag{13-10}$$

giving a total profit equation:

$$\text{Profit} = 80A - 0.1A^2 + 100B - 0.15B^2 \tag{13-11}$$

Clearly this objective function is no longer linear. We could easily add further complexities to this objective function. We could legitimately expect per-unit costs also to be a function of output levels and not simply fixed regardless of the quantity produced. This would give rise to a non-linear cost element to be incorporated into the profit equation. Equally, we might expect the two demand functions (Eqs (13-5) and (13-6)) to include a third term showing the interaction of the two products on selling prices. That is, higher output of B might have an effect on the selling price of A and vice versa. Equally, we may encounter a constraint that is in some way non-linear. We discussed in Chapter 9 the implications of linear production constraints in terms of returns to scale (which may be increasing, decreasing or constant). Equation (13-2) may be better represented, for example, as:

$$28A + 42B + 0.05B^2 \leq 16\,800 \tag{13-12}$$

implying that as production of B increases an increasing quantity of this resource is required for each unit produced (hence we face decreasing returns to scale). The development of non-linear objective functions and constraints, therefore, is not something we encounter merely as an academic problem. Non-linear relationships are clearly needed to model economic and business behaviour in an accurate and realistic way and it is by now apparent that there can be no guarantee that all aspects of a mathematical programming problem will be linear. Some (or all) of the problem may be capable of being represented mathematically only in a non-linear form. It should also be evident that the *nature* of the non-linear relationship itself could be diverse. The illustrative examples we have used here are quadratic (involving variables no higher than power two). Higher-power variables, logarithmic variables and ratio variables all add to the complexity of NLP. Let us now examine some of the more obvious implications of such non-linearity for the solution approach we developed using the Simplex method. We turn first of all to the objective function (Eq. (13-11)). Figure 13-1 shows three iso-profit lines for this function: at £15 000, £20 000 and £25 000. (You may wish to confirm these yourself through your own calculations.) The diagram immediately reveals the non-linearity of this particular objective function. Moreover, it is apparent—in this example—that higher iso-profit lines gradually move inward and that the highest possible profit will actually be represented by a

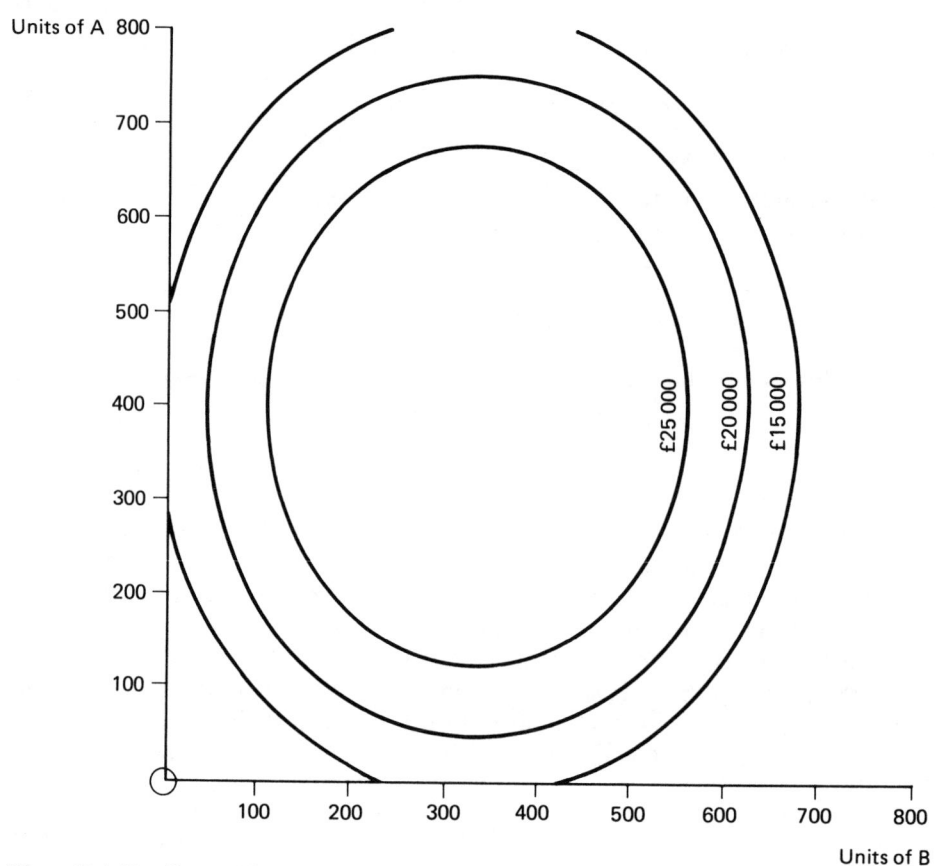

Figure 13-1 Non-linear objective function

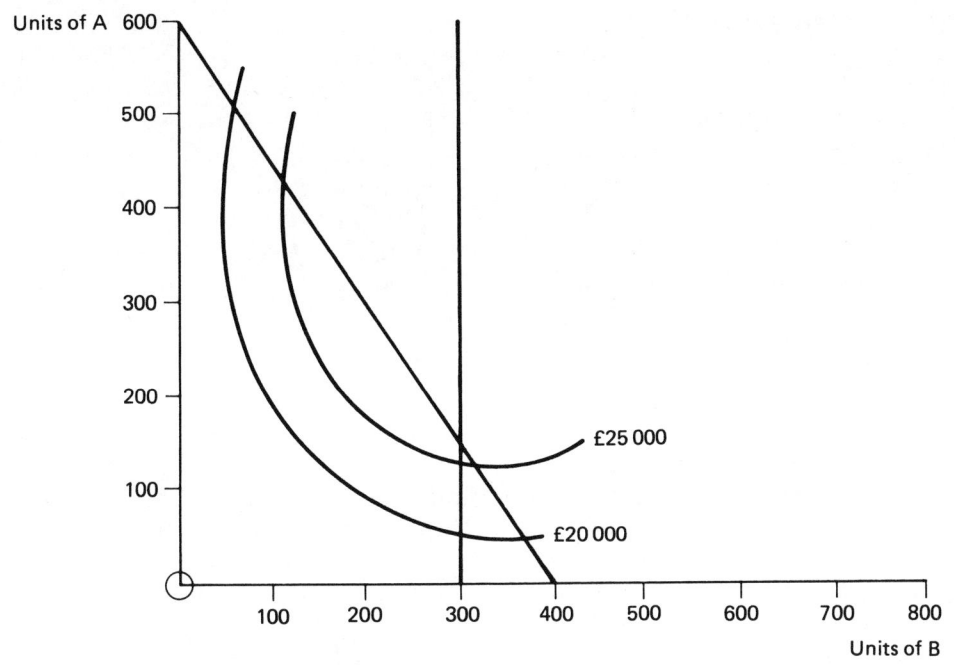

Figure 13-2 Feasible area and non-linear objective function

single point at the centre of this concentric process (although whether such a profit is attainable will depend upon the feasible area). Figure 13-2 shows both the feasible area (given by Eqs (13-2) to (13-4)) and the relevant parts of the iso-profit line for £25 000 and £20 000. It is evident that in searching for a solution we face a similar situation to that faced in the ordinary LP problem. We seek to push the objective function as far away from the origin as possible (given that we face a maximization problem) but will be constrained by the feasible area. However, unlike an LP problem there is no guarantee that the optimal solution will actually occur at a corner point of the feasible area (and you will recollect that this was a fundamental underpinning of the Simplex algorithm). The optimal point may well occur somewhere along the boundary of the feasible area rather than at a corner point *per se*. Naturally, we would expect this to create considerable difficulties when looking for a solution method to such a problem. In fact we can generalize somewhat. Let us restrict our attention for the moment to sets of linear constraints and to maximization problems. Figure 13-3 summarizes the general types of situation we may encounter. Figure 13-3a illustrates a situation where the optimal solution occurs at a corner point of the feasible area boundary. However, such a situation is by no means certain (and in practice rare). Figure 13-3b reveals a more likely situation where the optimal solution occurs at a point on the boundary of the feasible area (but not at a corner point). Finally, Fig. 13-3c illustrates a situation where the solution occurs *within* the feasible area rather than somewhere along its boundary. Naturally, in more complex problems there will be no immediate means of recognizing which type of situation we are likely to encounter. Equally, this has implications for the Simplex method used in LP problems. The algorithm is clearly inappropriate

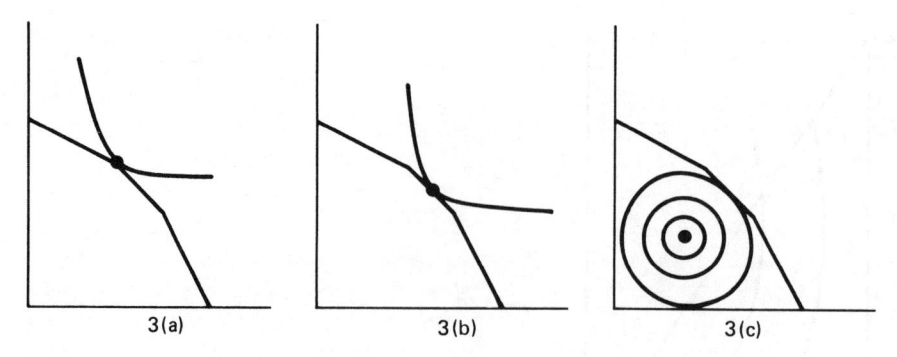

Figure 13-3 Optimal solutions: non-linear objective function

for NLP problems given that it searches for corner points of the feasible area and uses these to determine each basic solution.

A second problem relates to non-linear constraints and the distinction between *local* and *global* optima. Consider Fig. 13-4, which shows both the feasible area for some problem and the corresponding iso-line for some (linear) objective function. If we are dealing with a maximization problem then we seek to push the OF line as far outward from the origin as possible. As we seek to do this we encounter point I on the diagram. Such a point is known as a *local* optimum. From this point we might (following the logic of the Simplex algorithm) seek to establish whether a move in any appropriate direction on the boundary of the feasible area would lead to an increased value for the objective function. From point I we have two alternative moves: in direction A or in direction B. Both, however, lead to an immediate decrease in the value of the objective function and we would probably conclude that point I represented the optimal solution. Because of the complexity of the feasible area, however, it is apparent that the true optimal solution (the *global* optimum) actually occurs at point II. Naturally, whilst such a feature is evident from the graph, such a situation is far less obvious in complex problems.

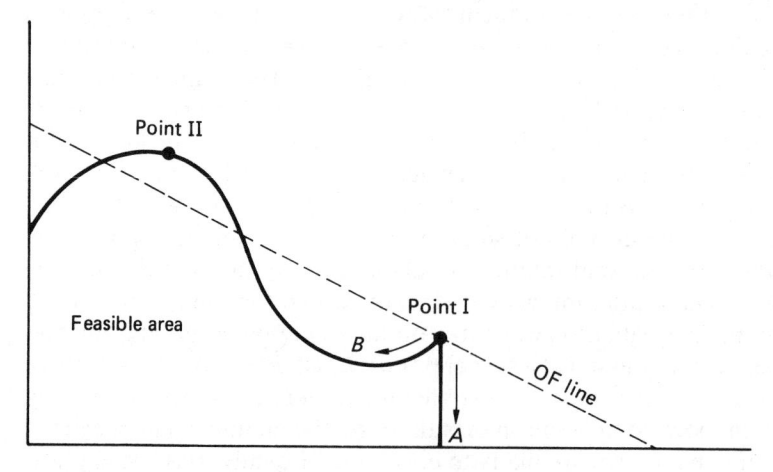

Figure 13-4 Local and global optima

You may be forgiven for wondering at this stage how we can resolve such difficulties. The answer is that methods are available for surmounting such problems but, as ever, at a cost. The cost in this context lies in the added mathematical complexity underlying such approaches and the fact that no single solution method can be applied to NLP problems as a group. A range of varying solution methods is available (with more becoming available each year as further theoretical developments take place in this field), depending on the exact nature of the non-linear relationships involved in the problem. The implications of this for the decision-maker (as opposed to the management science specialist) are severe. It implies that the decision-maker is likely to become familiar with few, if any, NLP techniques in detail and considerable doubt must then be expressed over the role of such techniques in a general management framework. (This is not to say, of course, that such techniques will not be applied by those with the appropriate training and mathematical background.) In contrast to LP the decision-maker is unlikely to be able to apply and use NLP solution methods himself/herself. Instead (s)he will be dependent upon the skills and expertise of the management scientist in modelling the business problem, deriving a solution and then interpreting that solution in its business context. However, the decision-maker *will* need to exercise judgement over the potential use of such NLP models in the organization and their usefulness in providing meaningful information. One of the main aims of this section, therefore, is to provide the decision-maker not only with the detailed mathematical skills necessary for NLP problems but with an adequate understanding and awareness of the general principles involved. This is an important issue which we shall return to later. However, let us now turn our attention to a number of approaches that, whilst not providing a generalized solution method, will at least provide a useful insight into the framework and methodology of NLP. Before doing so, however, it is necessary to review a number of important mathematical principles.

13-2 A REVIEW OF DIFFERENTIAL CALCULUS

In order to progress in our appreciation of how we can deal with non-linearity in mathematical programming it becomes necessary to introduce certain key elements of differential calculus. In this section we (very) briefly review the main concepts we require. If you are already familiar with this topic you can omit this section and move straight on to Section 13-3. Through our analysis of LP models you are already familiar with the concept of a linear relationship—its algebra and its geometry. Algebraically a simple linear equation can be represented as:

$$Y = f(X) = a + bX$$

where Y and X are the two variables and a and b are the parameters of the equation: the values which give the equation its specific characteristics. Graphically such an equation can be represented as an appropriate straight line. More importantly, however, the relationship between the two variables is summarized by the value of the b parameter and, in turn, through the gradient or slope of the line on the corresponding graph. In terms of both mathematics and business it is this relationship we are frequently interested in. Consider the equation:

$$Y = 500 + 30X \qquad (13\text{-}13)$$

It is apparent that for each unit change in the X variable Y will change by 30 (the b value). Equally, if X changes by 2 then Y will change by 30×2, and so on. The relationship between the two variables therefore (in terms of the rate of change between them) is constant. No matter what value X takes each unit change will always bring about the same response in Y. The same conclusions can be derived directly from the corresponding graph. The straight line that we could derive from this equation indicates a constant rate of change between the two variables. However, for non-linear equations this relationship does not remain constant: the slope will differ at each point along the function (that is, the slope will vary depending on the X value). Consider the equation shown below:

$$Y = 500 + 30X - 3X^2 \tag{13-14}$$

which is clearly non-linear (given it involves variables other than those to the power 1). The graph of this equation (for $X = 0$ to 10) is shown below in Fig. 13-5.

It is clear that the slope of this equation varies depending on the value of X. When X is less than 5 the slope is positive (but becoming less so as we approach $X = 5$). When X is greater than 5 the slope is negative and becomes more so as X increases. Because of our frequent interest in the slope (the rate of change of Y to X) it is patently useful to be able to determine the slope of such a function at any point along its length—that is, for any value of X. We can achieve this through the process of *differentiation* and the calculation of a *derivative*. Intuitively you should recognize that if we were to construct a straight line that was at a tangent to the original function at one particular point then the slope of this line and the slope of the function at that point will be identical. (Naturally, if we move to a different point on the function we will require a different tangent line.) All we now require is a means of determining such a tangent. The slope of this tangent is referred to as the

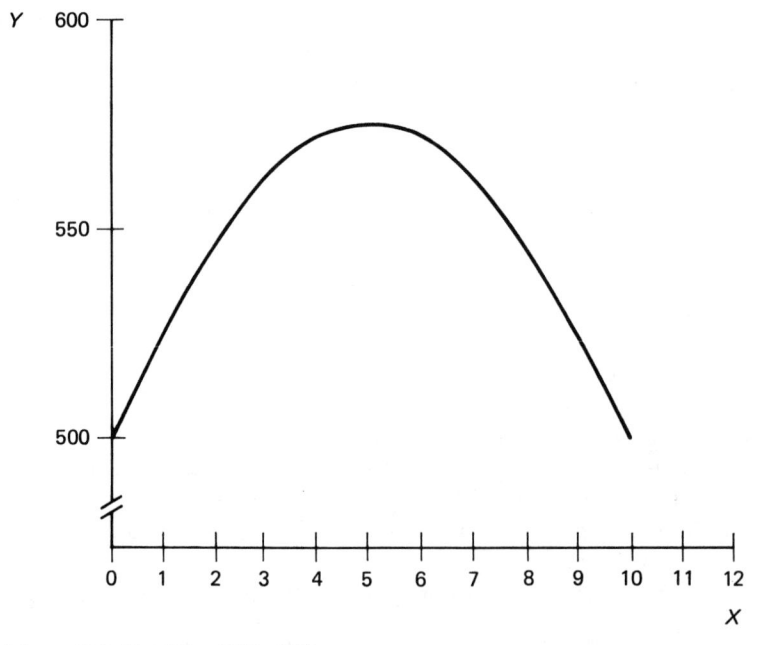

Figure 13-5 $Y = 500 + 30X - 3X^2$

derivative (technically the first derivative) of the original function and because the slope of the tangent indicates the rate of change of Y as X changes it represents the slope of the function at that point also. In practical terms there are a number of straightforward 'rules' for obtaining such a derivative. We shall look briefly at the first few of these (and simply present the rest later).

The derivative of a constant

We state that the derivative of a constant $= 0$. Consider the equation $Y = 500$. This equation will be represented graphically by a straight line parallel to the X axis. That is, as X changes Y remains constant. The slope of this line (which is what any derivative indicates) is zero. We denote the derivative as:

$$\frac{dY}{dX} \quad \text{(pronounced 'dee y by dee x')}$$

The symbol dY/dX is not indicative of arithmetic division but simply a standard notation used in differential calculus. An alternative symbol for indicating a derivative is that of:

$$f'(X)$$

where the f' symbol indicates the first derivative of the function with respect to X. We shall use this symbol from now on.

The derivative of a power term

Consider a power expression taking the general form:

$$Y = kX^n$$

where k and n represent some real numbers. We state that the derivative of such an expression is given by:

$$f'(X) = nkX^{(n-1)}$$

Consider $Y = 30X$. Here $k = 30$ and $n = 1$. Using this rule we have:

$$f'(X) = (1)30X^{(1-1)} = 30X^0 = 30$$

Consider the implication of this derivative. As we already know the original function is linear hence has a constant slope equal to 30. The derivative also measures the slope of the function, $f(X)$, at any point along its length and the derivative calculated, $f'(X)$, indicates also that the slope is constant at 30.

The derivative of a sum or difference

The derivative of a sum or difference is equal to the sum or difference of their derivatives. Consider the equation:

$$Y = 500 + 30X - 3X^2 \tag{13-15}$$

The equation is made up of three parts. If we differentiate each part in turn (using the

302 FURTHER MATHEMATICAL PROGRAMMING MODELS

appropriate rule) then the derivative of the function is equal to the sum of the part derivatives. That is:

$$\begin{aligned}
\text{derivative of } 500 &= 0 \\
\text{derivative of } 30X &= 30 \\
\text{derivative of } -3X^2 &= -6X \\
\text{derivative of } 500 + 30X - 3X^2 &= 0 + 30 - 6X = 30 - 6X
\end{aligned}$$

But how does this help in our search for a value for the slope? It means that if we wish to determine the slope at any specific point on the original function we can now use the derivative to find it. Assume that we wish to determine the slope when $X = 3$. Using the derivative we have:

$$f'(X) = 30 - 6X = 30 - 6(3) = 30 - 18 = 12$$

That is, at $X = 3$ the slope of the original function is 12. In terms of our original understanding of the slope this indicates that at this point a change in X will bring about a change in Y which is 12 times as large. An important point here, however, is that such an interpretation is appropriate only for *small* changes in X (anything other than a small change, of course, will move us away from the point $X = 3$ and so will require a new value for the slope from the derivative expression).

Student activity
From the original function calculate the Y value when $X = 2.9$ and again when $X = 3.1$. From these determine the slope of the function over this range of X values and compare it with the derivative value.

Table 13-1 summarizes some of the more common rules of differentiation for different types of expression.

Maxima and minima using the derivative

One important use of the derivative is that it enables us to determine a maximum or minimum point on the original function. Consider the function shown in Eq. (13-15) (and the corresponding diagram in Fig. 13-5). It is evident that the function reaches an optimum Y value when $X = 5$. But we can readily arrive at the same conclusion using the derivative.

Table 13-1 Derivative rules

Expression	Function $y = f(x)$	Derivative $f'(x)$
Constant	$y = a$	0
Power term	$y = x^n$	$nx^{(n-1)}$
Constant times power term	$y = kx^n$	$knx^{(n-1)}$
Sum or difference	$y = g(x) \pm h(x)$	$g'(x) \pm h'(x)$
Product	$y = g(x)h(x)$	$g(x)h'(x) + h(x)g'(x)$
Quotient	$y = g(x)/h(x)$	$\dfrac{h(x)g'(x) - g(x)h'(x)}{h(x)^2}$

Clearly, the slope of this function will be zero at the optimal point—known as a stationary point. Given that we have the derivative (which is a general expression for the slope) then if we set this to zero and solve it, it will provide the value for X which generates a zero slope. That is:

$$f'(X) = 30 - 6X = 0$$

and solving gives $X = 5$ at the optimal point. The derivative, therefore, can readily be used to determine such a point on (almost) any function. However, all that we have actually shown in this calculation is that when $X = 5$ the slope of the original function is zero. How do we know that this represents a maximum (as opposed to a minimum) stationary point? To answer this we turn to the *second derivative* and state that:

- if the second derivative is greater than zero the turning point is a minimum;
- if the second derivative is less than zero the turning point is a maximum.

The first derivative, you will remember, shows the slope of the original function. The second derivative shows the rate of change in the slope (the first derivative) as X changes. We can use our (intuitive) understanding of the rate of change of the slope to infer the shape of the original function at this point and thereby determine whether we have located a maximum or a minimum point. The second derivative is readily found. We simply differentiate the first derivative using the appropriate rule:

$$f(X) = 500 - 30X - 3X^2$$
$$f'(X) = 30 - 6X$$
$$f''(X) = -6$$

In this example the second derivative (denoted by $f''(X)$) is negative, indicating that the slope of the original function around this value of X is decreasing. From Fig. 13-5 we can readily see the logic in this. Around $X = 5$ we see that the slope changes from positive, through zero to negative (i.e. there is a decrease in the slope). If the second derivative had been positive it would have indicated that the point we had located with a zero slope was a minimum. Equally, we can use the second derivative to determine the general shape of the function at that point. A negative second derivative implies a *concave* shape (an inverted-U shape as in Fig. 13-5) whilst a positive second derivative implies a *convex* shape (a U-shaped function at this point) although it is important to remember we are often describing the shape of the function only in this localized area around the given value for X.

Local and global optima

We have already mentioned in this chapter that we may encounter problems in determining whether an optimal point represents a local or a global optimum. Technically the use of derivatives only allows us to derive the local optimum points. But by comparing these optima (if there is more than one) and calculating the Y value for each will allow us to determine the global optimum point. We shall illustrate this shortly.

Partial derivatives

Thus far, we have examined functions expressed in terms of a single variable, X. We have already encountered expressions involving more than one variable (Models A and B for example) and clearly need to be able to deal with these in a similar way. Consider the function:

$$Y = 500 + 30X_1 - 3X_1^2 + 25X_2 - 5X_2^2 + X_1X_2 \qquad (13\text{-}16)$$

The derivative of such a multi-variable function is known as a *partial* derivative and can be determined and interpreted in much the same way as before. We can find the derivative of each independent variable (X_i) in turn. For example, we can obtain the partial derivative with respect to X_1 and then again with respect to X_2. Such a derivative indicates the rate of change in Y as the X_i variable changes (and with the assumption that all other X variables remain unchanged). Effectively we are quantifying the change in Y as one of the X variables is allowed to change. Consider the partial derivative with respect to X_1. We simply treat X_2 as if it were a numerical constant (i.e. not affecting Y directly) and apply the standard differentiation rules. That is:

$$\frac{\partial Y}{\partial X_1} = 30 - 6X_1 + X_2 \qquad (13\text{-}17)$$

where we use the term $\partial Y/\partial X_1$ to indicate a partial derivative with respect to X_1. As before we shall use the alternative notation to represent the derivative: f_{X1}. Similarly, the partial derivative of X_2 is given as:

$$f_{X1} = 25 - 10X_2 + X_1 \qquad (13\text{-}18)$$

To reiterate, the partial derivative with respect to X_i reflects the rate of change in Y as X_i changes with other X variables remaining constant. Equally, we could find the second-order partial derivatives. In such a case, however, complications arise given that, for example, we could differentiate the first partial derivative (13-17) with respect either to X_1 or to X_2 (as we could with the second equation, Eq. (13-18)).

Student activity
Determine the appropriate second derivatives for each of the two first-order derivatives.

Thus we end up with the following second-order partial derivatives.

$$\begin{aligned} f_{X1X1} &= -6 \\ f_{X2X2} &= -10 \\ f_{X1X2} &= 1 \\ f_{X2X1} &= 1 \end{aligned}$$

Note that the last two second-order derivatives (the cross partial derivatives) are the same. This will typically be the case. We can now use the first- and second-order partial derivatives to determine optimality just as we did for a single variable equation. However, it may help your understanding of this process to refer to Fig. 13-6. This shows a schematic representation of some two-variable equation. Naturally, we have to represent this in

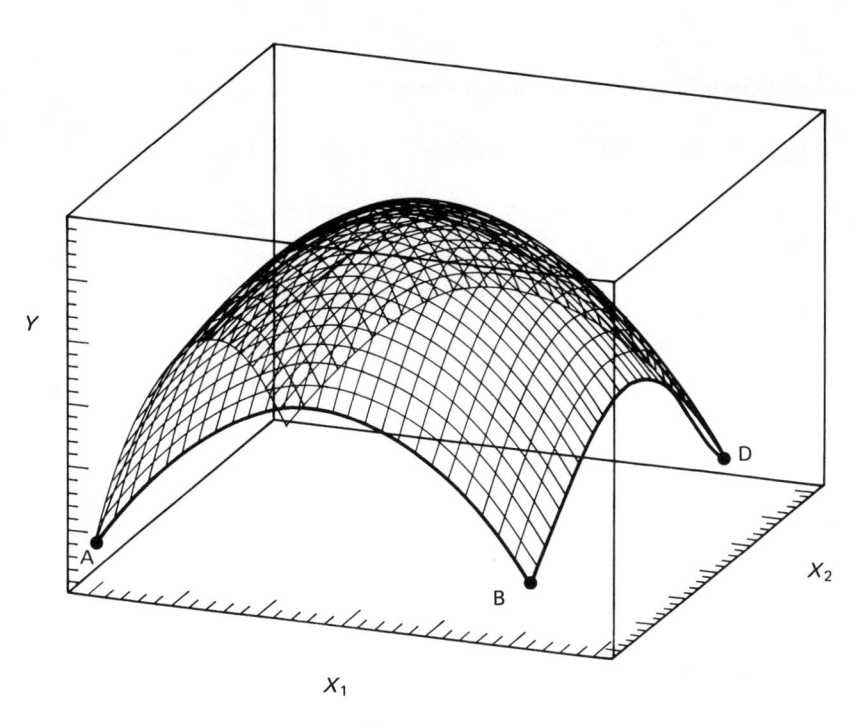

Figure 13-6 Multi-variable function

three dimensions: the vertical axis shows Y, the left-to-right horizontal axis shows X_1 and the front-to-back horizontal axis shows X_2. $f'(X_1)$ is the expression showing the slope of this function in the YX_1 plane (that is, in the arc from A to B). If we set this to zero (as we did previously with the first-order derivative) and solve it, it will give us a position where the slope on this arc is zero. Equally, the other first-order partial derivative—$f'(X_2)$—shows the slope in the YX_2 plane (in the arc from B to D). Again, setting this derivative to zero and solving will give us the position on this arc where the slope is zero. It is evident that if we perform both these calculations simultaneously—setting both first-order derivatives to zero and solving—this will give us the position over the whole surface where the slope is zero in both planes. In our illustrative diagram this will occur at the top of this figure. If we perform the appropriate calculations we have:

$$f_{X1} = 30 - 6X_1 + 1X_2 = 0$$
$$f_{X2} = 25 - 10X_2 + 1X_1 = 0$$

and solving gives $X_1 = 5.5085$ and $X_2 = 3.05085$ at the stationary point. However, we face a problem similar to that we faced before. How do we know whether this point of zero slope represents a maximum or a minimum? As before we must use the second-order derivatives to resolve this. Without proof we state that:

we calculate the value of the expression:

$$f_{X1X1} f_{X2X2} - (f_{X1X2})^2$$

- if this value > 0
  then we have a local maximum if both f_{X1X1} and f_{X2X2} are less than zero;
- if this value > 0
  then we have a local minimum if both f_{X1X1} and f_{X2X2} are greater than zero;
- if this value < 0
  then we have what is known as a *saddle point*—where one variable reaches a maximum and the other a minimum.

Applying this rule we see that:

$$f_{X1X1}f_{X2X2} - (f_{X1X2})^2 = (-6)(-10) - 1^2 = 59$$
$$f_{X1X1} = -6$$
$$f_{X2X2} = -10$$

so that the position of zero slope we have found represents a local maximum (i.e. the function takes a concave form around these values). Whilst the partial derivatives we have examined have related to two variable functions the same principles are readily extended to n-variable functions (although it is not necessary for us to do this).

13-3 LAGRANGE MULTIPLIERS

We are now in a position to return to the problems we were examining earlier. Let us assume that we seek a solution to the problem shown below (for which Fig. 13-2 is also relevant).

$$\text{Maximize} \quad 80A - 0.1A^2 + 100B - 0.15B^2 \quad (13\text{-}11)$$
$$\text{subject to:} \quad 28A + 42B = 16\,800 \quad (13\text{-}19)$$
$$1B = 300 \quad (13\text{-}20)$$
$$A, B \geq 0$$

That is, we seek to maximize the non-linear profit function derived earlier subject to the requirement that all assembly hours must be utilized and that exactly 300 units of B must be produced. This may seem a somewhat trivial example but the solution process will reveal a number of important principles. In fact, we can generalize this type of problem using some simple notation. We have:

$$\text{Maximize/minimize} \quad f(x_1 \ldots x_n)$$
$$\text{subject to:} \quad g_i(x_1 \ldots x_n) = b_i \quad (i = 1, 2, \ldots, m)$$

In general, such problems can be referred to as *constrained optimization* problems and we can solve such a problem using the method of *Lagrange multipliers*. This approach involves creating a new, single function by combining the objective function and the equality constraints and then using partial derivatives to optimize this new function. That is:

$$\text{Lagrange function} = L(x_1 \ldots x_n, \lambda_1 \ldots \lambda_n) = f(x_1 \ldots x_n) - \Sigma \lambda_i [g_i(x_1 \ldots x_n) - b_i]$$

where λ refers to the Lagrange multiplier(s). This (as usual) sounds more complex than it is. Let us return to the problem formulation. The Lagrange function for this problem is:

$$L = 80A - 0.1A^2 + 100B - 0.15B^2 \\ - \lambda_1(28A + 42B - 16\,800) - \lambda_2(1B - 300) \quad (13\text{-}21)$$

where λ_1 and λ_2 are the Lagrange multipliers associated with constraints Eq. (13-19) and Eq. (13-20) respectively. Note that we have rearranged the expression $g(X) = b$ to $g(X) - b = 0$. We state (without formal proof) that the optimal solution to the Lagrange function is determined by taking the partial derivatives of the function with respect to each of the variables in turn (including the Lagrange multipliers), setting each partial derivative to zero and finding the values such that all partial derivatives equal zero. (This is obviously the process we have just reviewed in the section on differential calculus.) Providing that the original objective function is *concave* for a maximization problem (or *convex* for a minimization) then this solution will be the solution to the original problem.

Student activity
From Eq. (13-21) derive the appropriate partial derivatives for A, B, λ_1, λ_2.

From the Lagrange function we determine each partial derivative in turn.

$$f_A = 80 - 0.2A - 28\lambda_1 = 0 \quad (13\text{-}22)$$
$$f_B = 100 - 0.3B - 42\lambda_1 - \lambda_2 = 0 \quad (13\text{-}23)$$
$$f_{\lambda 1} = -28A - 42B + 16\,800 = 0 \quad (13\text{-}24)$$
$$f_{\lambda 2} = -1B + 300 = 0 \quad (13\text{-}25)$$

We are now left with four equations and four unknowns and it becomes possible to solve these four equations simultaneously. If we do this (and you are recommended to use a suitable computer package to confirm the results) we get:

$$A = 150 \quad \lambda_1 = 1.785\,71$$
$$B = 300 \quad \lambda_2 = -65$$

that is, optimum production of A and B is set at 150 units and 300 units respectively. Substitution back into the objective function gives a profit of £26 250. Effectively we have used the first-order partial derivatives to derive a local optimal point. Given that there is only one such local optimum it must also be the global. But you may be forgiven, at this stage, for wondering why we bothered. Given our problem formulation it is evident that the solution (if there is a feasible solution) must occur at the interesection of the constraints since these constraints must be binding because of the equality requirement. The answer is that we shall shortly modify the Lagrange multiplier method to allow us to approach more typical mathematical programming problems. There is also a second reason for investigating this method. Let us examine the current values for the two Lagrange multipliers: 1.785 71 and −65. The first multiplier relates to the first constraint (Eq. (13-19)). Let us undertake some simple sensitivity analysis. Assume that 1 more hour of assembly time becomes available: i.e. the RHS of Eq. (13-19) increases to 16 801. In terms of the partial derivatives it can be seen that only Eq. (13-24) will change and the whole equation system can be re-solved to find the new optimal solution.

Student activity
Determine the new optimal solution and the change in the value of the objective function that has occurred.

This solution is:

$$A = 150.036$$
$$B = 300$$

which gives rise to a new value of the profit function of £26 251.80—an increase in profit of £1.80. Equally, assume that we change constraint Eq. (13-20) to 301. Again, the only partial derivative affected will be Eq. (13-25) and, again, we can re-solve to find:

$$A = 148.5$$
$$B = 301$$

and the new profit level at £26 184.6—a decrease of £65.375. It is evident that such sensitivity analysis indicates the change in the objective function value arising from unit change in the RHS of a constraint is virtually the same as the Lagrange multiplier for that constraint. In other words we can interpret and use the Lagrange multiplier values as dual values (opportunity costs) in exactly the same way as we did for LP problems. However, a word of caution is worthy of note at this stage. In interpreting such dual values we must remember that because they are calculus-based they are appropriate only for technically small changes in the corresponding b value. Given that in NLP we may wish to examine the change in such values in terms of discrete units the dual value is an approximate indicator of objective function change only. This is the reason why the changes in the objective function arising from the new solution are not identical to the Lagrange multiplier values from the original solution.

13-4 THE KUHN–TUCKER CONDITIONS

Whilst the Lagrange multipliers are a step forward, the approach at present is clearly limited given that the constraints were expressed as strict equations. However, we can adapt the method to deal with inequality constraints. Let us amend our problem as shown below:

$$\text{Maximize} \quad 80A - 0.1A^2 + 100B - 0.15B^2$$

$$\text{subject to:} \quad 28A + 42B \leq 16\,800 \quad (13\text{-}26)$$

$$1B \leq 300 \quad (13\text{-}27)$$

We can express such a problem in general as:

$$\text{Maximize} \quad f(x_1 \ldots x_n) \quad (13\text{-}28)$$

$$\text{subject to:} \quad g_i(x_1 \ldots x_n) \leq 0 \quad \text{for } i = 1 \text{ to } m, \; x_1 \ldots x_n \geq 0 \quad (13\text{-}29)$$

Note that we can express Eqs (13-26) and (13-27) in the format required by Eq. (13-28) simply by rewriting as $(28A + 42B - 16\,800 \leq 0)$. Following the same logic as we used in the Simplex method we can transform inequality constraints into equations by adding a slack variable to the LHS. Such a variable will represent the difference (if any) between 0 and $g_i(x_1 \ldots x_n)$ for any values of X_j. Logically, such a variable must be non-negative and because of the potential mathematical complexities of NLP problems the easiest way of ensuring such non-negativity is to add a slack variable in the form S^2 (given that any real number squared must be non-negative). Thus Eq. (13-29) becomes:

$$g_i(x_1 \ldots x_n) + S_i^2 = 0 \qquad (13\text{-}29a)$$

and we are able to create an appropriate Lagrange function:

$$L(x_1 \ldots x_n, S_i, \lambda_i) = f(x_1 \ldots x_n) - \Sigma \lambda_i [g_i(x_1 \ldots x_n) + S_i^2] \qquad (13\text{-}30)$$

In order to find a stationary point the partial derivatives should equal zero. This implies that:

$$\frac{\partial L}{\partial X_j} = \frac{\partial f}{\partial X_j} - \Sigma \lambda_i \frac{\partial g_i}{\partial X_j} = 0 \qquad (13\text{-}31)$$

$$\frac{\partial L}{\partial S_i} = -2\lambda_i S_i = 0 \qquad (13\text{-}32)$$

$$\frac{\partial L}{\partial \lambda_i} = -(g_i(x_1 \ldots x_n) + S_i^2) = 0 \qquad (13\text{-}33)$$

Equation (13-32) requires either λ or S (or both) to equal zero. Let us examine the implication of $S = 0$. If $S = 0$ then, from Eq. (13-33), $g_i(x_1 \ldots x_n)$ must equal zero also. This gives rise to the further implication that:

$$\lambda_i g_i(x_1 \ldots x_n) = 0 \qquad \text{if } S_i = 0$$

So, collecting these together we have the following necessary conditions for a given set of X values to represent a stationary point:

$$\frac{\partial L}{\partial X_j} = \frac{\partial f}{\partial X_j} - \Sigma \lambda_i \frac{\partial g_i}{\partial X_j} = 0 \qquad (13\text{-}31)$$

$$\lambda_i g_i(x_1 \ldots x_n) = 0 \qquad (13\text{-}34)$$

$$g_i(x_1 \ldots x_n) \leq 0 \qquad (13\text{-}29)$$

$$\lambda_i \geq 0 \qquad (13\text{-}35)$$

These conditions are known as the *Kuhn–Tucker conditions* and in addition become the conditions both necessary and sufficient for a local maximum if the objective function is concave and the constraints form a convex set. In other words, if we determine a set of X values that satisfy these conditions it *must* represent a maximum point (but not necessarily the global maximum). If we had been dealing with a minimization problem then Eq. (13-29) would be in the form:

$$g_i(x_1 \ldots x_n) \geq 0 \qquad (13\text{-}36)$$

and we would require the objective function to be convex. So, we are in a position to determine whether a particular solution to an NLP problem represents a local maximum (or minimum). It is important to realize at this stage, however, that the Kuhn–Tucker conditions do not in themselves provide a method of solution to NLP problems. They do provide a means of determining whether a solution is an optimal one. Let us return to our original problem. The appropriate Lagrangian function from Eqs (13-11), (13-26) and (13-27) becomes:

$$L = 80A - 0.1A^2 + 100B - 0.15B^2 \\ - \lambda_1(28A + 42B - 16\,800) - \lambda_2(1B - 300)$$

and the corresponding conditions are:

$$\frac{\partial L}{\partial X_j} = \frac{\partial f}{\partial X_j} - \Sigma \lambda_i \frac{\partial g_i}{\partial X_j} = 0 \qquad (13\text{-}31)$$

$$\lambda_i g_i(x_1 \ldots x_n) = 0 \qquad (13\text{-}34)$$

$$g_i(x_1 \ldots x_n) \leq 0 \qquad (13\text{-}29)$$

$$\lambda_i \geq 0 \qquad (13\text{-}35)$$

For our problem this translates to:

$$\frac{\partial L}{\partial A} = 80 - 0.2A - 28\lambda_1 = \quad 0 \qquad (13\text{-}37)$$

$$\frac{\partial L}{\partial B} = 100 - 0.3B - 42\lambda_1 - \lambda_2 = \quad 0 \qquad (13\text{-}38)$$

$$\lambda_1(28A + 42B - 16\,800) = \quad 0 \qquad (13\text{-}39)$$

$$\lambda_2(1B - 300) = \quad 0 \qquad (13\text{-}40)$$

$$28A + 42B \leq 16\,800 \qquad (13\text{-}26)$$

$$1B \leq \quad 300 \qquad (13\text{-}27)$$

$$\lambda_1 \geq \quad 0$$

$$\lambda_2 \geq \quad 0$$

Let us examine how we might determine a solution to this problem. Consider Eqs (13-39) and (13-40). These effectively relate to the constraints of the problem. It is evident that either the Lagrange multiplier or the bracketed expression must equal zero to satisfy these equations. This implies that, for Eq. (13-39) for example, the Lagrange multiplier must equal either zero or some positive value. If it equals some positive value then $(28A + 42B - 16\,800)$ must equal zero. This in turn implies that this constraint (Eq. (13-26)) is actually binding at that solution point. Equally, if the Lagrange multiplier is zero then that constraint is not binding. Logic suggests, therefore, that a comparison of all the solutions generated by examining combinations of binding constraints will lead us to an optimal solution. Let us examine each possibility in turn. (You may find it useful to refer to Fig. 13-2 in the following discussion and locate each solution point on the graph.)

Case 1 $\lambda_1 = 0, \lambda_2 = 0$ This implies that neither constraint is binding at this solution. If both multipliers are zero then Eqs (13-37) and (13-38) simplify to:

$$80 - 0.2A = 0$$
$$100 - 0.3B = 0$$

and solving gives:

$$A = 400 \qquad \lambda_1 = 0$$
$$B = 333.333 \qquad \lambda_2 = 0$$
$$\text{Profit} = £32\,666.67$$

but on reflection this solution violates Eqs (13-26) and (13-27) (i.e. lies outside the feasible area) and can therefore be rejected.

Case 2 $\lambda_1 = 0, \lambda_2 = 0$ This implies that the second constraint is binding whilst the first is not. Using the same principles Eqs (13-37), (13-38) and (13-40) simplify to:

$$80 - 0.2A = 0$$
$$100 - 0.3B - \lambda_2 = 0$$
$$\lambda_2(1B - 300) = 0$$

and from Eq. (13-40) if the Lagrange multiplier does not equal zero then the term in brackets must, giving $B = 300$ (as we already know if this constraint is forced to be binding). Given B we can determine the values for A and λ_2 as:

$$A = 400 \qquad \lambda_1 = 0, \lambda_2 = 10$$
$$B = 300$$
$$\text{Profit} = £32\,500$$

but, again, this solution lies in the infeasible area violating Eq. (13-26) and so can be rejected.

Case 3 $\lambda_1 = 0, \lambda_2 = 0$ Now we examine the solution generated if we require the first constraint to be binding. We have:

$$80 - 0.2A - 28\lambda_1 = 0$$
$$100 - 0.3B - 42\lambda_1 = 0$$
$$28A + 42B - 16\,800 = 0$$

and solving as a three-variable system gives:

$$A = 280 \qquad \lambda_1 = 0.8571, \lambda_2 = 0$$
$$B = 213.333$$
$$\text{Profit} = £29\,065$$

and checking against the Kuhn–Tucker conditions indicates that none of the conditions are violated. This solution represents (at least) a local optima. Let us now examine the last possibility.

Case 4 $\lambda_1 = 0, \lambda_2 = 0$ We now consider the case where both constraints are binding. We have:
$$80 - 0.2A - 28\lambda_1 = 0$$
$$100 - 0.3B - 42\lambda_1 - \lambda_2 = 0$$
$$28A + 42B - 16\,800 = 0$$
$$1B - 300 = 0$$

and solving gives:

$$A = 150 \quad \lambda_1 = 1.7857, \lambda_2 = -65$$
$$B = 300$$
$$\text{Profit} = £26\,250$$

It can be seen that the second Lagrange multiplier violates the necessary conditions in that it takes a negative value. (Recollection of our earlier discussion of the interpretation of such a multiplier implies that the second constraint is having an adverse effect on the value of the objective function. By implication allowing this constraint to be non-binding—$B < 300$—will allow profit to increase.) Accordingly, we are left only with Case 3 as a solution meeting all the conditions and, given that we already know that the objective function is concave and the constraints convex, the local solution must also be the global. It is clear that the Kuhn–Tucker conditions allow us to determine whether a solution represents an optimal position or not. The conditions, however, do not provide a solution method themselves and it is apparent that for more complex problems the step-by-step approach we adopted in this section will not suffice. A considerable number of computational algorithms have been developed to make use of the Kuhn–Tucker conditions in determining a solution to a given class of NLP problems. To illustrate the potential we shall examine the class of quadratic programming in the next section.

13-5 QUADRATIC PROGRAMMING

It is evident that, compared with the Simplex method, the approaches taken thus far in NLP problems are clumsy, inefficient and time-consuming. It is not surprising, therefore, that considerable effort has been devoted to devising computational algorithms to cope with NLP problems. To date no general solution method has been found, implying that NLP problems must be approached in groups or subsets. One such subset is the *quadratic programming* problem. In fact, without specifying it as such the problem we have been examining thus far is an example of this subset. Quadratic programming is concerned with problems that have a quadratic objective function and a set of linear constraints. As we shall see such a problem can be amended using the Kuhn–Tucker approach to make it amenable to solution through a variant of the Simplex algorithm. It is apparent why such an approach is attractive. Let us return to our problem.

$$\text{Maximize} \quad 80A - 0.1A^2 + 100B - 0.15B^2$$
$$\text{subject to:} \quad 28A + 42B \leq 16\,800 \quad (13\text{-}26)$$
$$1B \leq 300 \quad (13\text{-}27)$$

We shall illustrate the approach using this problem but we must stress that, again, we are not concerned with providing theoretical underpinning or with providing an exhaustive discussion of this topic. Rather we intend to illustrate the general approach and logic used. We shall make use of the partial derivatives we used in the Kuhn–Tucker approach and, for simplicity, we shall use the symbol L to denote the Lagrange multipliers. The first two partial derivatives are:

$$80 - 0.2A - 28L_1 \quad \text{or} \quad 0.2A + 28L_1 = 80$$
$$100 - 0.3B - 42L_1 - L_2 \quad \text{or} \quad 0.3B + 42L_1 + 1L_2 = 100$$

From the LHS of each of these expressions we subtract another L variable:

$$0.2A + 28L_1 - 1L_3 = 80 \tag{13-41}$$
$$0.3B + 42L_1 + 1L_2 - 1L_4 = 100 \tag{13-42}$$

We can regard these—together with Eqs (13-26) and (13-27)—as the appropriate constraints for our problem. As usual with the Simplex we need to add slack variables to constraints taking the form $\leq$ and artificial variables to constraints taking the form $=$. Using S_1 and S_2 to represent the two slack variables and A_1 and A_2 to represent the two artificial variables we now have:

$$0.2A + 28L_1 - 1L_3 + 1A_1 = 80 \tag{13-43}$$
$$0.3B + 42L_1 + 1L_2 - 1L_4 + 1A_2 = 100 \tag{13-44}$$
$$28A + 42B + 1S_1 = 16\,800 \tag{13-45}$$
$$1B + 1S_2 = 300 \tag{13-46}$$

and if we solve this with the objective function:

$$\text{Minimize} \quad A_1 + A_2 \tag{13-47}$$

then this provides the equivalent linear programming formulation to our original problem. (If you are especially interested in the theoretical justification for this you should refer to the appropriate section in the Bibliography.) In fact, in order to complete the formulation we must add certain additional requirements, which give a complete formulation of:

$$\text{Minimize} \quad A_1 + A_2$$
$$\text{subject to:} \quad 0.2A + 28L_1 - 1L_3 + 1A_1 = 80$$
$$0.3B + 42L_1 + 1L_2 - 1L_4 + 1A_2 = 100$$
$$28A + 42B + 1S_1 = 16\,800$$
$$1B + 1S_2 = 300$$
$$A, B, L_i, S_i, A_i \geq 0$$

and
$$AL_3, BL_4, S_1L_1, S_2L_2 = 0$$

The last constraint expression (generally referred to as complementary slackness) can be seen logically as an extension of the approach taken in the previous section. Each variable (A, B, S_1, S_2) is paired with its complementary Lagrange multiplier (L_3, L_4, L_1, L_2) and the product of these must equal zero. One of each pair must be zero in the solution

Tableau 13-1 Initial tableau

	A	B	S_1	S_2	L_1	L_2	L_3	L_4	A_1	A_2	Value
OF	0.2	0.3	0	0	70	1	−1	−1	0	0	180
A_1	0.2	0	0	0	28	0	−1	0	1	0	80
A_2	0	0.3	0	0	42	1	0	−1	0	1	100
S_1	28	42	1	0	0	0	0	0	0	0	16 800
S_2	0	1	0	1	0	0	0	0	0	0	300

in other words. Consider S_1 and L_1, its Lagrange multiplier. If $S_1 = 0$ then the complementary slackness constraint is satisfied and L_1 can take any non-negative value. But if $S_1 = 0$ then constraint (13-26) is binding and will have an appropriate opportunity cost. We have already seen that the Lagrange multiplier can be interpreted as the opportunity cost corresponding to a binding constraint. Equally if $L_1 = 0$ (i.e. a zero opportunity cost) we know that this constraint is not binding and so S_1 can take a non-negative value. But because of the complementary slackness requirement both of these variables cannot take non-zero values simultaneously (i.e. a non-binding constraint cannot have a non-zero opportunity cost). It is also evident that—apart from this complementary slackness constraint—the problem is readily amenable to solution via the Simplex algorithm. A few additional comments will be useful at this stage before we proceed. It is evident that the optimal solution to the formulated problem will occur when A_1 and A_2—the two artificial variables—are zero. This is equivalent to a solution where the two partial derivatives equal zero (the Kuhn–Tucker requirement). It may also be evident that we have been able to transform the original—quadratic—objective function into linear partial derivatives and it is this aspect that, in part, allows us to reformulate into a Simplex program. Our initial tableau, therefore, is given as Tableau 13-1.

As usual in the Simplex, the initial basis consists of the two artificial variables and the slack variables. The objective function row has been obtained in the usual way when dealing with artificial variables by adding the A_1 and A_2 rows together and subtracting the objective function of $(1A_1 + 1A_2)$. We can now proceed to apply the Simplex algorithm. On examining the OF row L_1 is set to enter the basis, given that it has the highest positive coefficient. However, L_1 is not permitted to enter the basis at this stage as its complementary variable—S_1—is already basic. In other words, this constraint is non-binding so must have a zero opportunity cost (L_1). The same logic applies to our next choice—variable L_2. Our third choice of entering variable, however, is free to enter—B. Using the standard Simplex rules B will enter and S_2 will leave the basis at the next stage. The Simplex tableau can be updated in the usual way.

> *Student activity*
> Obtain the optimal solution for this problem using the standard Simplex approach but ensuring complementary slackness.

If we proceed to do this and then to search through successive tableaux for a solution, we finally reach Tableau 13-2 on the fifth iteration.

We confirm that this represents the optimal solution given that no further positive coefficients remain in the OF row and that none of the complementary slackness conditions are violated. Our solution is interpreted as follows:

Tableau 13-2 Optimal tableau

	A	B	S_1	S_2	L_1	L_2	L_3	L_4	A_1	A_2	Value
OF	0	0	0	0	0	0	0	0	−1	−1.5	0
S_2	0	0	−0.01428	1	0	−1.333	−2	1.333	2	−1.333	86.67
L_1	0	0	−0.00001	0	1	0.01428	−0.01428	−0.01428	0.01428	0.01428	0.857
A	1	0	−0.02142	0	0	−2	−3	2	3	−2	280
B	0	1	0.01428	0	0	1.333	2	−1.333	−2	1.333	213.33

$$A = 200$$
$$B = 213.33$$

and the original profit function reveals a profit of £29 065 (you may wish to confirm these figures from the Lagrange multiplier solution we derived earlier). However, the potential benefits of using the Simplex method become apparent. We see from the solution that $S_2 = 86.67$—the second constraint is not binding (confirmed by the fact that its complementary opportunity cost, L_2, does not appear in the basis and is therefore zero). L_1, however, does appear, indicating that the first constraint is binding and, moreover, has an opportunity cost of £0.857. Whilst it goes beyond the technical competencies we have developed at this level it is evident that this approach leads directly into the area of sensitivity analysis of the current optimal solution and we have frequently seen how important such analysis is to the decision-maker. Whilst in this section we have used the Kuhn–Tucker conditions to develop a method of solving quadratic problems, the conditions are readily amenable to other groups of NLP problem. All you require is the mathematical skill to follow what is happening!

13-6 LINEAR APPROXIMATIONS OF NON-LINEAR FUNCTIONS

Given that no general purpose algorithm has yet been developed for NLP and given the considerable power and efficiency of the Simplex method it is perhaps not surprising that considerable attempts have been made to transform NLP problems into a format suitable for solution by the standard Simplex algorithm. We have already seen how this can be applied to quadratic programs but such an application is somewhat limited to those objective functions that are quadratic and cannot be applied at all to non-linear constraints. An alternative approach is to *linearize* a non-linear function (whether the objective function or constraint) and reformulate the problem so that it can be solved using Simplex. The key to such linearization lies in whether the non-linear function is *separable*. A function:

$$f(X) = f(X_1, X_2, X_3, \ldots, X_n)$$

is said to be separable if it can be written:

$$f(X) = f_1(X_1) + f_2(X_2) + f_3(X_3) + \ldots + f_n(X_n)$$

Consider our objective function:

$$f(A, B) = 80A - 0.1A^2 + 100B - 0.15B^2$$

This is separable and can be written as:
$$f(A, B) = f_1(A) + f_2(B)$$
where $f_1(A) = 80A - 0.1A^2$ and $f_2(B) = 100B - 0.15B^2$.

Whilst some non-linear functions are obviously separable, others may appear not to be. Consider the function:
$$f(A, B) = AB$$
which does not appear separable as $f(A, B) = f_1(A) + f_2(B)$. However, if we redefine the function as:
$$\ln[f(A, B)] = \ln(A) + \ln(B)$$
we see that it is. Equally, consider the function:
$$f(A, B) = 80A - 0.1A^2 + 100B - 0.15B^2 + 0.05(A + B)^2$$
By defining a new variable, $C = (A + B)$, we can write this function as:
$$80A - 0.1A^2 + 100B - 0.15B^2 + 0.05C^2$$
which is now separable (although we would need to add a further constraint to the problem in the form $A + B - C = 0$). Such mathematical 'tricks' allow a considerable variety of non-linear functions to be put into separable form. But how does such a separable function help? We shall consider two approaches.

Piecewise linear approximation

Let us return to our problem:

Maximize	$80A - 0.1A^2 + 100B - 0.15B^2$	(13-11)
subject to:	$28A + 42B \leq 16\,800$	(13-26)
	$1B \leq 300$	(13-27)

which, as we have seen, has a separable objective function. For each part of the separable OF we derive an approximation to the original function by piecewise linearization. Consider:
$$f_1(A) = 80A + 0.1A^2$$

From Eq. (13-26) we know that this variable cannot be greater than 600. Figure 13-7a shows this function for A from 0 to 600. We can approximate this function with a series of linear functions between:
$$0 \leq A \leq 200$$
$$200 \leq A \leq 400$$
$$400 \leq A \leq 600$$
and for each linear function we can determine the slope. These linear approximations are shown in Fig. 13-7a. For the first function we have:

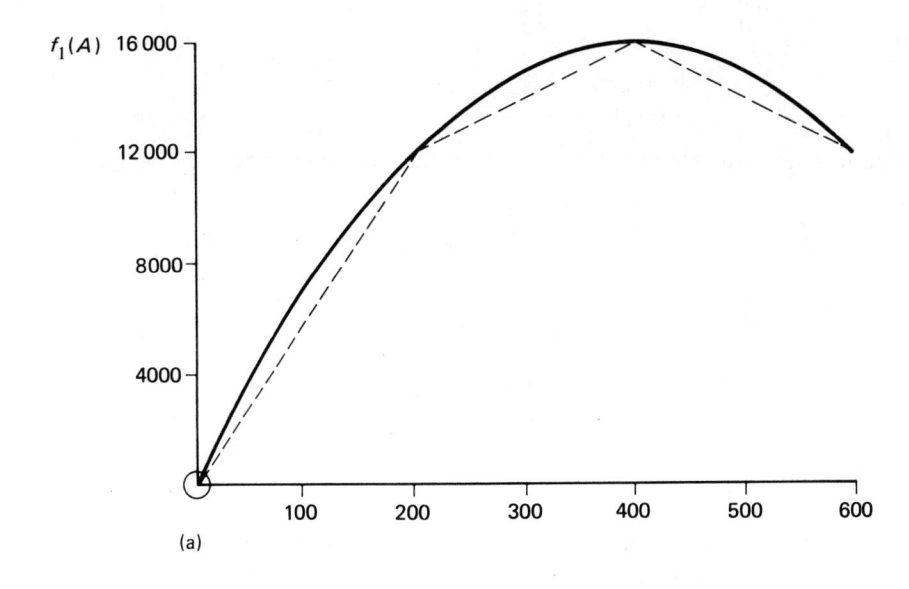

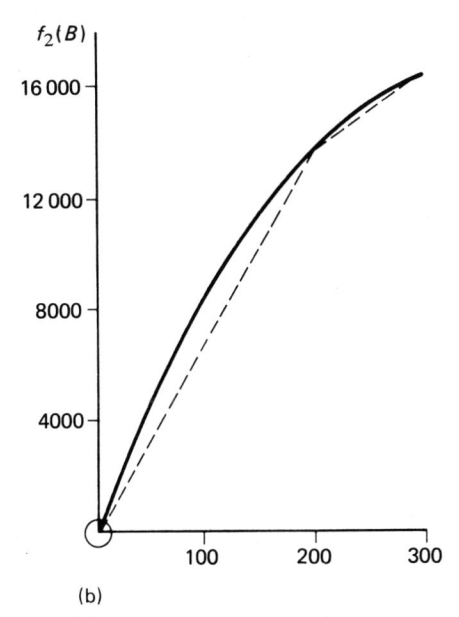

Figure 13-7 Linear approximation

$$\text{when} \quad A = 0, \quad f(A) = 0$$
$$\text{when} \quad A = 200, \quad f(A) = 12\,000$$

giving a slope of $12\,000/200 = 60$. Equally, for the other two linear functions we have:

$$\text{when} \quad A = 200, \quad f(A) = 12\,000$$
$$\text{when} \quad A = 400, \quad f(A) = 16\,000$$
$$\text{when} \quad A = 600, \quad f(A) = 12\,000$$

giving slopes of

$$4000/200 = 20 \quad \text{and}$$
$$-4000/20 = -20$$

If we now define a new variable (X_i) associated with each linear segment we have:

$$A = X_1 + X_2 + X_3$$
$$f_1(A) = 60X_1 + 20X_2 - 20X_3$$

with
$$X_1 \leq 200$$
$$X_2 \leq 200 \quad \text{(i.e. } 400 - X_1)$$
$$X_3 \leq 200 \quad \text{(i.e. } 600 - X_1 - X_2)$$

Student activity
Breaking the original function into two parts at $B = 200$, obtain an equivalent set of expressions for B.

Equally we can transform the second part of the original objective function into linear segments. B cannot exceed 300 units (Eq. (13-27)) and the corresponding graph is shown in Fig. 13-7b. In this case we generate two linear approximations: from $B = 0$ to 200 and $B = 200$ to 300. The slopes of the two linear functions can be calculated as before and if we denote X_4 and X_5 as the appropriate variables we have:

$$f(B) = 70X_4 + 25X_5$$

with
$$X_4 \leq 200$$
$$X_5 \leq 100 \quad \text{(i.e. } 300 - X_4)$$

Collecting these terms together with the original constraints, we now have a problem:

Maximize $\quad 60X_1 + 20X_2 - 20X_3 + 70X_4 + 25X_5 \quad$ (13-48)

subject to: $\quad 28X_1 + 28X_2 + 28X_3 + 42X_4 + 42X_5 \leq 16\,800 \quad$ (13-49)

$$X_4 + X_5 \leq 300 \quad (13\text{-}50)$$
$$X_1 \leq 200 \quad (13\text{-}51)$$
$$X_2 \leq 200 \quad (13\text{-}52)$$
$$X_3 \leq 200 \quad (13\text{-}53)$$
$$X_4 \leq 200 \quad (13\text{-}54)$$
$$X_5 \leq 100 \quad (13\text{-}55)$$
$$X_i \geq 0$$

and it is apparent that this can now be solved using the standard Simplex approach. Before we do this, however, a number of points are worthy of note. The first is that the solution generated will be an approximation only of the solution to the original problem. The second point relates directly to this. We can readily improve the accuracy of our approximation by breaking each separable function into more and more parts. From Fig. 13-7a we could readily have derived (say) 5 linear functions from $A = 0$–200, 200–300, 300–

400, 400–500, 500–600. The more such functions we use then the closer these linear functions become to the original non-linear function and the more accurate our approximate solution. As ever, there is a cost involved in doing this. The more linear functions we add then the more X variables appear in the problem formulation, making the problem more complex in terms of both solution and interpretation. In practice a compromise is necessary. We shall see shortly how such a compromise can be reached. The final point at this stage is one that may already have occurred to you. Consider B (represented by X_4 and X_5). There is nothing in the formulation to prevent X_5 taking a positive value whilst X_4 is still set at zero. Clearly this would be illogical as we would want X_4 to reach its maximum value before X_5 moves away from zero. However, as long as the objective function is concave (or convex for a minimization problem) we actually do not need to worry about this occurring. Under such conditions we see that X_4 has a higher OF coefficient than X_5 (note the same applies to X_1, X_2, X_3) and given that the constraint coefficients for these variables must of necessity be the same the Simplex method will always choose to increase X_4 in preference to X_5 as long as X_4 is below its upper limit.

Student activity
Solve the problem as formulated using the Simplex method. Evaluate the results.

Returning to our problem if we solve through the standard Simplex method we obtain a solution:

$$X_1 = 200 \quad \text{giving } A = 300, B = 200$$
$$X_2 = 100$$
$$X_4 = 200 \quad \text{Profit} = £28\,000$$

Given that we already know the solution to this problem ($A = 280, B = 213.3$) we see that the approximation generated is reasonable but not that accurate. In practice we would now use the current approximation to improve the accuracy of the solution generated. We now know the region of the feasible area where the actual solution exists. It would be sensible, therefore, to return to our separable linear approximations of the objective function and rework them. For A and B we might consider a series of functions:

$$0 \leq A \leq 250 \qquad 0 \leq B \leq 175$$
$$250 \leq A \leq 275 \qquad 175 \leq B \leq 200$$
$$275 \leq A \leq 300 \qquad 200 \leq B \leq 225$$
$$300 \leq A \leq 325 \qquad 275 \leq B \leq 300$$
$$325 \leq A \leq 600$$

and reformulate and resolve the problem. Given the new solution (which you may wish to confirm directly from your own calculations), we could focus further on the area around this next solution by better approximating the separable OF in this region. In this way we can proceed to approach the actual optimal solution to the original problem until we are satisfied that further linear approximations to improve accuracy are not cost-effective. Such piecewise linear approximation is also applicable directly to non-linear constraints.

Separable programming

A second, but related, approach involves separable programming. As with the piecewise method we begin by approximating each separate part of the linearized function. If we stay with our existing problem then the separable OF is:

$$f_1(A) = 80A - 0.1A^2$$
$$f_2(B) = 100B - 0.15B^2$$

and for the given values of A and B we have the appropriate values for $f_1(A)$ and $f_2(B)$ as:

A	0	200	400	600	B	0	200	300
$f_1(A)$	0	12 000	16 000	12 000	$f_2(B)$	0	14 000	16 500

If we examine these we see that, if we define appropriate X variables (1–4 for A, 5–7 for B) then any point on either of the two parts of the separable function can be approximated by a weighted average of these variables. For example, for A:

$$A = 0X_1 + 200X_2 + 400X_3 + 600X_4$$

and
$$f_1(A) = 0X_1 + 12\,000X_2 + 16\,000X_3 + 12\,000X_4$$

with
$$X_1 + X_2 + X_3 + X_4 = 1$$

where the last expression ensures the weights total to 1. For example, the point $A = 300$ (midway between $A = 200$ and $A = 400$) can be approximated, setting $X_1 = 0$, $X_2 = 0.5$, $X_3 = 0.5$, $X_4 = 0$ to give:

$$A = 0X_1 + 200X_2 + 400X_3 + 600X_4$$
$$= 0 + 200(0.5) + 400(0.5) + 0 = 300$$

with an equivalent approximated value for $f_1(A)$.

Student activity
Determine the corresponding expressions for B.

The corresponding expressions for B are given by:

$$B = 0X_5 + 200X_6 + 300X_7$$

and
$$f_2(B) = 0X_5 + 14\,000X_6 + 16\,500X_7$$

with
$$X_5 + X_6 + X_7 = 1$$

Our original, separable problem was:

$$\text{Maximize} \quad f_1(A) + f_2(B)$$
$$\text{subject to:} \quad 28A + 42B \leq 16\,800$$
$$1B \leq 300$$

Using the weighted average expressions we can now rewrite this as:

$$\text{Maximize} \quad 0X_1 + 200X_2 + 400X_3 + 600X_4 + 0X_5 + 200X_6 + 300X_7 \qquad (13\text{-}56)$$

subject to:
$$28(0X_1 + 200X_2 + 400X_3 + 600X_4) + 42(0X_5 + 200X_6 + 300X_7) \leq 16\,800 \quad (13\text{-}57)$$
$$0X_5 + 200X_6 + 300X_7 \leq 300 \quad (13\text{-}58)$$
$$X_1 + X_2 + X_3 + X_4 = 1 \quad (13\text{-}59)$$
$$X_5 + X_6 + X_7 = 1 \quad (13\text{-}60)$$

and, once again, the problem is ready for solution directly via the Simplex method. The solution to this problem gives:

$$X_2 = 0.5$$
$$X_3 = 0.5$$
$$X_6 = 1$$

which if we substitute back into the appropriate equations gives $A = 300$, $B = 200$ and which you will realize is the equivalent solution we generated using the piecewise approach with these linear approximations. The same comments are equally applicable. The solution must be seen as an approximation only although the accuracy of the approximation can be improved by breaking the separable functions into smaller and smaller linear segments. Once again, the method is appropriate for concave objective functions (convex for minimization problems). In the case of both of these linearization approaches the problems must have a concave objective function and a set of convex constraints although the approaches can be readily extended to deal with NLP problems which do not meet these criteria.

13-7 SUMMARY

In this chapter we have begun to explore the implications of non-linearity for mathematical programming and we have seen that a different formulation and solution approach is required. We have attempted in this chapter to provide an insight into some of the more common and potentially useful methods of approaching such NLP problems. However, whilst the use of differential calculus and Lagrange multipliers is of considerable theoretical importance these do not readily lend themselves to a general, efficient solution method. Indeed, attempts to provide an equivalent to the Simplex algorithm for NLP problems have so far been unsuccessful. The implications of this for the decision-maker are apparent. Efficient solution methods are limited to a small subset of NLP problems and each tends to require a considerable underpinning in the mathematical justification of the method used as well as in the ability to interpret and evaluate the complex solution thereby generated. The typical business decision-maker will simply not be in a position to develop a working knowledge of the considerable variety of such solution approaches available (as we were able to do with LP problems). The decision-maker faced with an NLP problem is therefore placed in a quandary. Either s(he) must devolve all responsibility for the formulation, solution and interpretation of such a problem to the 'expert' or s(he) must attempt to manipulate the problem so that it is compatible with the solution methods with which s(he) is familiar. The first option is not one that any decision-maker will relish given that s(he) will not be in a position to assess and evaluate directly either the reliability of the results or the usefulness of the information generated for the organization. It is evident why the second has considerable attraction and why considerable efforts are often made to linearize an NLP problem. In this chapter, we have tried to redress the balance somewhat by providing an overview and an appreciation of the NLP approaches that may be available. As we stated at the beginning, our intention was not to provide a detailed exposé of the subject content but to provide an outline of this programming area to enable the decision-maker to approach more rationally (and with a little more understanding) the NLP problems that may well be encountered. This may enable the decision-maker to determine whether a business problem does require a specialist NLP approach or whether it could reasonably be investigated using some form of LP.

STUDENT EXERCISES

Given the (often tedious) mathematical complexities of NLP, the number of exercises for this chapter is deliberately small. Further examples of non-linear problems can readily be obtained by referring back to one of the original problem formulations in Part B on LP and amending one or more aspects of that problem to be non-linear.

13-1 Consider the following problem formulation:

$$\text{Maximize} \quad 80A - 0.1A^2 + 100B - 0.15B^2$$

$$\text{subject to:} \quad 28A + 42B \leq 16\,800$$
$$12A + 6B \leq 4\,800$$

Required:
(a) Solve this problem using Lagrange multipliers and the Kuhn–Tucker conditions. Locate each solution combination on an appropriate graph.
(b) Solve this problem using the quadratic Simplex approach.
(c) Solve this problem using the piecewise linear approach.
(d) Solve this problem using separable programming.
(e) Draft a management report outlining the advantages and disadvantages of using each of these solution approaches from the viewpoint of both accuracy and the provision of useful management information.

13-2 The problem formulation is now amended to:

$$\text{Maximize} \quad 80A - 0.2A^2 + 100B - 0.1B^2$$

subject to the same constraints.
Determine the effect the new objective function has on your solution to **13-1**(a)–(d).

13-3 Consider the problem:

$$\text{Maximize} \quad 40A + 50B$$

$$\text{subject to:} \quad 28A + 42B + 0.05B^2 \leq 16\,800$$
$$12A + 6B \quad\quad\quad\; \leq 4\,800$$

Determine the optimal solution to this problem.

14
DYNAMIC PROGRAMMING

Throughout this text we have seen how mathematical programming can be applied to a broad range of business decision problems. We have noted in particular how such models represent problems in the form of algebraic models which, when subjected to the manipulations of appropriate algorithms, yield optimal solutions for the decision-maker's guidance. It would be remiss of us, however, to omit one final technique from our discussion. *Dynamic programming* (DP) is a legitimate branch of mathematical programming despite the fact that it differs in fundamental respects from the methods of earlier chapters. In the first place it may not require an algebraic model at all and we shall shortly examine a number of problems in which algebraic symbols make no appearance whatever. More importantly, DP is centred on a single, very simple—but broadly applicable—principle around which a general approach to problem solving has evolved. It is no one method but involves the use of techniques from a variety of sources—including LP, ILP and the rest. DP is particularly appropriate for problems in which decisions are to be taken in sequence, with each decision being dependent in some way on the one before it. Surprising as it may seem, DP could actually be used to solve all the problems discussed in this book—every one can be viewed as a sequential decision problem. We do not recommend the reader to attempt this feat, but make the point to emphasize DP's range of applicability. You may wonder at this stage why we do not use DP exclusively. The answer lies in the fact that other mathematical programming models may be more efficient at solving certain classes of problems. However, DP is also important in its own right. We shall investigate the use of DP in an important class of decision problems that other methods can rarely—if ever—address. These are stochastic problems in which chance and uncertainty play so large a part that it cannot be ignored and must be built into the decision model. First, though, we consider a classical routing problem.

14-1 A SHORTEST-ROUTE PROBLEM

For our first illustration of the use of DP we return to the International Monitor Company and investigate a problem faced daily by the Distribution Supervisor (DS). It is the responsibility of the DS to recommend suitable routes for IMC's drivers to follow when delivering customers' goods. In a typical case the DS has no more information than the map in Fig. 14-1 and will usually estimate the shortest route from factory to customer from a quick inspection of the road network.

However, it is clear that this rough-and-ready method may often lead to longer journeys than are necessary and may thus result in significant avoidable cost. Management will naturally wish to find a reliable way of identifying the shortest route between factory and customer, whatever the customer's location. Though there are several solution methods for problems of this sort, most depend on ideas of a DP type. We discuss a classic DP treatment below, but first present a schematic version of the DS's map in Fig. 14-2. This assumes that we may regard the driver's path from the Northtown factory to the customer's site as a sequence of routing decisions, each taken at a specified stage of the journey. A decision is made at Northtown governing the initial direction taken by the driver. This means that, at the second stage of the journey, the driver will find himself at A, B or C—where a second choice of direction must be made. At stage 3 the driver is at D, E or F and faces a final decision—whether to travel to G or to H before ending the journey at I. The numbers attached to the links in the network are distances in miles.

It is typical of the DP approach that the analysis of the problem proceeds from the last decision stage to the first. In other words we start with the end point of the problem and work our way backwards to the start of the problem. In our example there are three decision stages, as shown in Fig. 14-2, and so our discussion begins at stage 3. At this stage the driver must find himself in one of three locations: D, E or F. We consider the choice of route he may take from there in Table 14-1.

The table will repay close inspection. We note that there are 3 locations appropriate

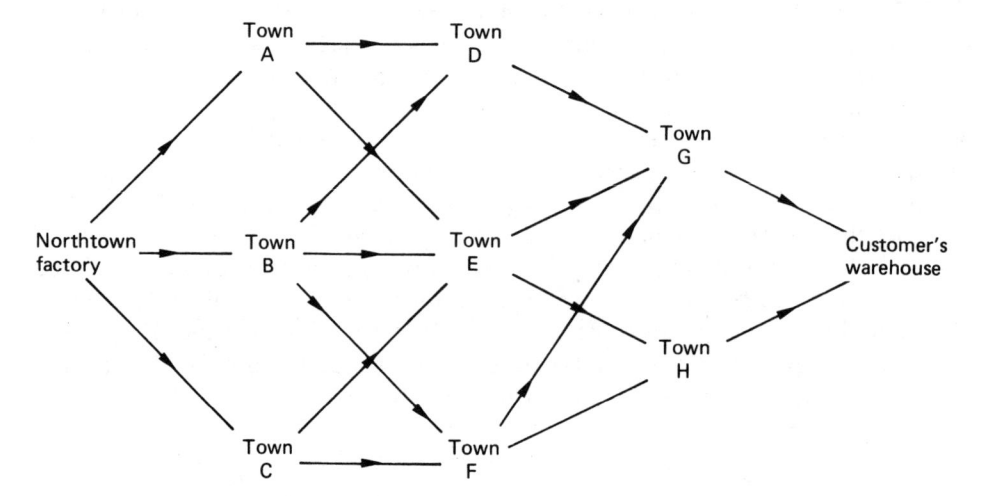

Figure 14-1 Road network linking factory to customer

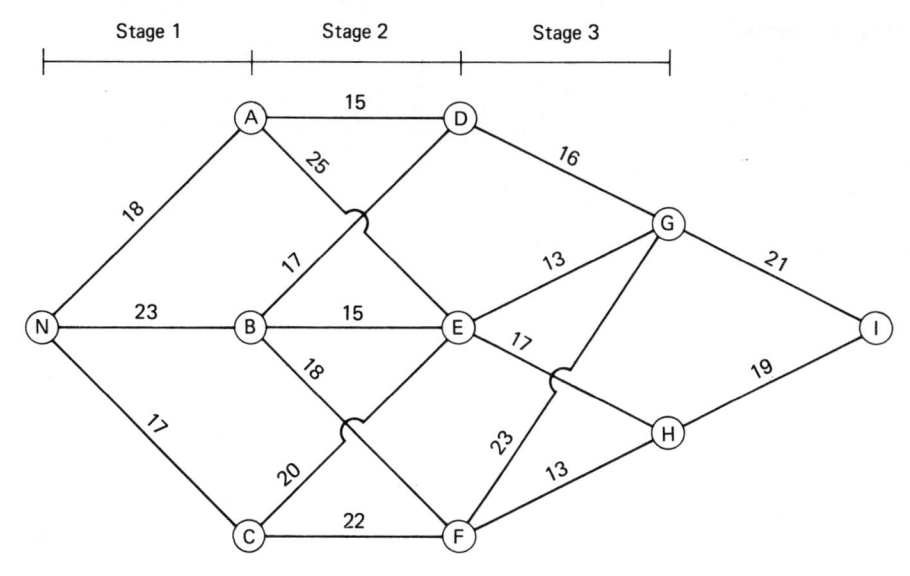

Figure 14-2 Route network and travel distances (miles)

Table 14-1 IMC's shortest-route problem: stage 3 analysis

Location	Decision	Remaining distance (miles) Now + later	Optimal decision	Optimal distance (miles)
D	Go to G	16 + 21	Go to G	37
E	Go to G	13 + 21		
	Go to H	17 + 19	Go to G	34
F	Go to G	23 + 21		
	Go to H	13 + 19	Go to H	32

for stage 3—D, E and F. Depending at which one of these locations the driver finds himself a decision must then be made as to whether to travel to G or to H. Note that according to the route diagram there is no alternative to the road to G if the driver finds himself in D. In each of E and F, on the other hand, two possibilities arise. The calculations of remaining distances is evident from Fig. 14-2. If the driver is at F, for example, and selects the road to G then the total length of the rest of the journey—from F to G to I—will be 23 + 21 miles. These simple computations are enough to establish an optimal decision for each location and a corresponding optimal distance for the remaining part of the journey. Table 14-2 summarizes the results of this analysis. These will be used to determine optimal routing decisions at stage 2.

Having completed the stage 3 analysis we now go back to the earlier stage—stage 2. In other words we suppose that the driver has arrived at A, B or C and must select a suitable road to D, E or F.

Table 14-2 Stage 3 results

Location	Optimal decision	Optimal distance (miles)
D	Go to G	37
E	Go to G	34
F	Go to H	32

Table 14-3 Stage 2 analysis

Location	Decision	Remaining distance (miles) Now + later	Optimal decision	Optimal distance (miles)
A	Go to D	15 + 37		
	Go to E	25 + 34	Go to D	52
B	Go to D	17 + 37		
	Go to E	15 + 34		
	Go to F	18 + 32	Go to E	49
C	Go to E	20 + 34		
	Go to F	22 + 32	Go to E or F	54

Student activity
Perform the equivalent calculations for stage 2.

We present our analysis in Table 14-3 using the same format as before.

Bellman's principle of optimality

Notice that we have evaluated all reasonable options at each possible stage 2 location and have once again identified the optimal decision(s). In the case of location C, for example, the driver may select either of two equally good routes—both entail a trip of 54 miles from C to the destination. The important point about this analysis, however, is the use that it makes of stage 3 results. When calculating the remaining distance, we argue that the driver must first travel the road to the next stage—this leads to the distance 'now' in Table 14-3—but must then, if he is to act optimally, cover the 'later' distance shown in Table 14-2 for the location in which he finds himself. Trivial as it may seem this illustrates the central principle of dynamic programming. This is *Bellman's principle of optimality*—named after Richard Bellman, a pioneer in the field of DP. The principle states that:

> Any optimal decision sequence is such that, whatever the stage and state of the problem, the decision-maker will always act in a manner which is optimal with respect to that stage and state.

At any stage in the decision process our analysis of a particular decision depends on

Table 14-4 Stage 2 results

Location	Optimal decision	Optimal distance (miles)
A	Go to D	52
B	Go to E	49
C	Go to E or F	54

Table 14-5 Stage 1 analysis

Location	Decision	Remaining distance (miles) Now + later	Optimal decision	Optimal distance (miles)
Northtown	Go to A	18 + 52		
	Go to B	23 + 49		
	Go to C	17 + 54	Go to A	70

knowing what will be done at the next stage when we arrive there. Such knowledge exists because we have already undertaken the relevant analysis and have the optimal results available. By Bellman's principle these are all we need to know about the succeeding stage. Stage 2 results are summarized in Table 14-4. As you will now realize, these will shortly be used in our analysis of stage 1.

The analysis of stage 1 follows an identical pattern. Note, however, that we need consider only one location. There is no doubt about the driver's whereabouts at stage 1: the journey begins at Northtown.

We are now in a position to present the solution of the problem as a whole. In DP this is done by *backtracking* through the tables of stage results, incorporating appropriate optimal decisions at each stage. For our shortest-route problem we begin at Table 14-5. It is clear from the stage 1 analysis that the optimal route length is 70 miles and that the driver should select the road to A as the first leg of his journey. This decision will place him in A at stage 2, of course, whereupon—by reference to Table 14-4—he will know to continue via D. In D at stage 3, however, Table 14-2 provides the information necessary for an optimal end to his trip: he should reach I by way of G. To summarize, the driver's route is:

$$\text{Northtown–A–D–G–I}$$

with the distance travelled minimized at 70 miles.

Student activity
Confirm the result of the DP analysis by identifying all possible routes from Northtown to the customer's site and comparing their lengths.

Computational advantages

The preceding student activity—the method of identifying, evaluating and comparing all the solutions to a problem—is usually known as *complete enumeration*. Where the solution set is small, as it is in IMC's routing problem, complete enumeration is a viable approach. Indeed, it is frequently the simplest and best way of solving the problem. Unfortunately, for larger problems—and even for many smaller ones—the number of solutions is so great that enumerating them all is a practical impossibility. This, of course, is the fundamental reason for the use of mathematical programming in business decision-making. There are simply too many options to consider every one individually and we must therefore find means of dealing with them *en masse* and selecting the ones that deserve closer attention. Even in IMC's problem, however, certain computational advantages are evident. There are, in fact, 12 routes from Northtown to I in Fig. 14-2, each involving 4 legs of the journey. A complete enumeration approach must therefore require, in addition to the identification of the routes:

and
$$36 \text{ additions}$$
$$11 \text{ route-to-route comparisons.}$$

The first of these numbers follows because each route necessitates 3 additions. For example:

$$18 + 15 + 16 + 21$$

to calculate the distance from Northtown to I via A, D and G. The second is a result of the fact that we choose the optimal route by making a series of pairwise comparisons between their lengths. For example, between Northtown–A–D–G–I and Northtown–A–E–G–I as the first step, then between the better of these and Northtown–A–E–H–I, and so on. Now consider the equivalent numbers of operations in the DP approach. These are shown in Table 14-6.

Although the reader may still feel that, in this case, the reduction in computation fails to justify the additional logical complexity of DP, it is apparent that for larger problems the savings could be considerable. In fact, for general sequential decision problems of a realistic size a typical DP analysis is vastly more efficient than complete enumeration, and in many instances represents the only satisfactory method of deriving a solution. It is to this that we now turn.

Table 14-6 IMC's shortest-route problem: DP computations

Stage	Additions	Comparisons
1	5	2
2	7	4
3	3	2
Total	15	8

14-2 CHARACTERISTICS OF THE DYNAMIC PROGRAMMING APPROACH

In this section we take a closer look at the structure of the method we adopted for IMC's routing problem and draw certain general conclusions about the nature of DP and the problems that it is able to solve. Before doing so, however, we stress that for particular types of problem special DP treatments may exist that fail to exhibit one or more of the characteristics we are about to discuss. In such cases it is fair to say that these are omitted in the interests of even greater efficiency, but that the basic principles and structure of the approach remain the same. The most obvious point about IMC's routing problem is that it consists of a sequence of stages. The reader will notice that we introduced this notion in moving from Fig. 14-1 to Fig. 14-2. Such a structure was not immediately apparent from the map itself. In fact, this is typical of many of the problems to which DP is applied—they are not normally thought of in terms of stages, but may be viewed in this way for the purpose of DP analysis. The next point to note is that at each stage the problem is in one of a number of states. The states of IMC's problem were the various locations in which the driver could find himself at particular stages of his journey. They were defined in an obvious, natural manner and we saw no reason to describe them as 'states of the problem' at the time. Although the success of the approach depends on them, it is not always so easy to find appropriate definitions.

In each state at each stage some decision needs to be made. This is selected from a known set of options which in general depend on the particular state and stage of the problem. In IMC's case the options comprised the locations to which the driver might travel next and clearly varied from state to state and stage to stage. Taking a decision effects a transformation of the problem. In fact, the problem is transformed from its current state at the current stage into some other state at the following stage. IMC's driver takes the chosen road and finds himself at some other location at the next stage of the problem. Associated with each transformation is a return of some sort. IMC's returns were distances in miles, but they could have taken several other forms. In particular, it is clear that the standard by which the company's journeys ought to be judged is that of cost. As the name suggests, it is usual to measure the return in monetary terms—normally as revenue, cost or profit. It is the decision-maker's objective to pass from stage to stage making the sequence of decisions that will optimize the overall return. Thus, for example, the decision-maker may wish to maximize the sum of a sequence of profits or minimize some total cost.

There is one final characteristic of the approach without which DP analysis would be impossible. It concerns the way in which the states of the problem are defined. As we indicated earlier, formulating state definitions is not always as straightforward as it was in IMC's case. In particular, we must ensure that the description of each state contains sufficient information to evaluate all the state's decision options. In our routing problem it was enough to know the driver's location—and nothing more—in order to identify and evaluate the options open to him. We did not, for example, require details of the earlier states and stages of his journey. These were an irrelevance as far as the next decision was concerned. In DP this must always be the case. When analysing the decision options in the current state at the current stage, the particular sequence of stages, states and decisions through which the problem has already passed must be of no significance—all that matters is the state itself. We illustrate this point by modifying the routing problem in a simple but important way. Assume that several of the routes from Northtown to I cross international boundaries. In particular, locations A and G lie in different countries which are presently hostile to one another. Diplomatic relations have been broken off and customs officers at D have instructions to confiscate the passport of any traveller who has recently passed through A. Of course, this new information changes our perception of the problem quite radically. A number of the routes we considered earlier are now out of bounds—the feasible set has been reduced. In particular, if the driver finds himself in location E at stage 3, we cannot evaluate the two decision options 'Go to G' and 'Go to H' unless we know whether he has already passed through A. In other words our definition of the state is inadequate. We lack the information on which to make the decision. A knowledge of the location alone is not enough. In situations such as this it may be possible to redefine the states of one or more stages to provide appropriate information. In the modified routing problem, for example, we can replace the locations D, E and F by new states:

$$(D, A) \quad (E, A) \quad (F, A)$$
$$(D, \text{not } A) \quad (E, \text{not } A) \quad (F, \text{not } A)$$

which specify not only the location of the driver but also whether or not he has passed through A. The analysis of the 'not A' states is exactly the same as that of locations D, E and F in our original treatment, but in the case of the others only one decision is possible—the driver must go to H. In general, defining states in terms of two or more parameters in this way will lead to a larger number of states and produce a more complex, less efficient solution procedure. We therefore avoid it if possible, but recognize that there are many occasions on which it may be inevitable.

14-3 KNAPSACK PROBLEMS

In Chapter 10 we introduced the ideas of integer linear programming and formulated a number of decision problems in terms of integer and binary variables. The simplest of its kind was the example used in Section 10-1, which we presented to illustrate the gulf between LP and ILP solutions. In fact, this was a particularly small example of a *knapsack problem*—so called because of its resemblance to the task of cramming items of greatest overall utility into a hiker's backpack of strictly limited size. Such problems are also known as *cargo-loading* or *flying-doctor* problems after certain simple applications of ILP. They may involve any number of variables but only one constraint and occur with remarkable frequency not so much as decision problems in their own right but as subproblems arising in the solution of much larger models. Despite its popularity for solving ILP models in general the branch and bound approach is not especially good with knapsack problems. In fact a dynamic programming technique is usually preferred and we now investigate such a method. The example we choose by way of illustration is an extension of the problem of Section 10-1. You will remember that the basic problem centred around the purchase of two alternative pieces of equipment, both of which could be used to produce monitors. The Type X machine costs £100 000 and can produce 8000 monitors a year. The Type Y machine costs £120 000 and can produce 10 000 monitors. The production manager has a capital budget of up to £300 000 to purchase some quantity of the two types of equipment. We now assume that the production manager has added a third piece of equipment to his shortlist: machines of Type Z cost £80 000 each and have an annual production capacity of 6500 monitors. The manager wishes to maximize the total production capacity of the machines that he decides to purchase subject to remaining within budget. His decision model is:

$$\text{Maximize} \quad 8000X + 10\,000Y + 6500Z \tag{14-1}$$

$$\text{subject to:} \quad 100\,000X + 120\,000Y + 80\,000Z \leq 300\,000 \tag{14-2}$$

$$X, Y, Z \geq 0 \text{ and integer}$$

For ease of analysis we scale the model as follows:

$$\text{Maximize} \quad 8X + 10Y + 6.5Z \tag{14-3}$$

$$\text{subject to:} \quad 100X + 120Y + 80Z \leq 300 \tag{14-4}$$

$$X, Y, Z \geq 0 \text{ and integer}$$

so that the objective function is now measured in thousands of machines per year and the constraint in £000. In order to apply dynamic programming we must first think in terms of a sequence of stages at each of which some decision is taken. In this problem these are the points at which we assign values to the three variables. Clearly, we may give values to X, Y and Z in any order we please. Here we shall assign values in alphabetical order: to X at stage 1, to Y at stage 2 and to Z at stage 3. Once we have completed the DP analysis you may wish to convince yourself that we would reach the same solution by assigning values in a different sequence and re-solving. The analysis begins as usual at the final stage, and assumes that earlier decisions—concerning the values of X and Y—have already been taken. The current task is to assign a value to Z. At this and all other stages we define the state of the problem as the amount of the manager's budget as yet unspent. Since there is no need to look ahead and reserve any part of the budget for future allocation—this is the final decision, after all—it is evident that the manager should spend as much of the remaining budget on Z-type machines as he can. In other words, if we denote the state of the problem by £S thousand, the manager will undoubtedly buy:

$$Z^* = \text{INT}(S/80) \text{ machines}$$

where by INT(expression) we signify the integer part of any value V, and by Z^* the optimal value of Z. As a result the machine capacity will be:

$$6.5 \, \text{INT}(S/80) \text{ thousand monitors per year}$$

Thus, for example, if £190(000) of the original budget remains at this stage, then:

$$Z^* = \text{INT}(190/80) = 2 \text{ machines}$$

must be bought and the resulting machine capacity will be:

$$6.5 \times 2 = 13(000) \text{ monitors per year}$$

Student activity
Evaluate the optimal decisions at stage 3 for the following values of S, in terms of number of units of Z and associated capacity:

$$0 \leqslant S < 80$$
$$80 \leqslant S < 160$$
$$160 \leqslant S < 240$$
$$240 \leqslant S \leqslant 300$$

These simple observations conclude the analysis of stage 3 and are typical of the initial phase of the DP treatment. We next move to stage 2 but in this case require a more extensive presentation. At this point in the decision process we assume that the first decision has already been taken and we are now required to consider the second—that is, we have already assigned a value to X and must now choose one for Y. Again, we define the state of the problem as the remaining amount of the manager's budget and denote this by £S thousand. The algebra is no longer quite so simple, however, and we are forced to identify several possibilities. These are shown in Table 14-7.

There are several points about Table 14-7 that are worthy of note. Firstly, we remark that the table could have been made considerably more extensive than it is. Since all the monetary amounts in the problem are multiples of £20 thousand, it would have been reasonable—if rather long-winded—to consider each individual value of S ranging from 0 to 300 in steps of 20. Had we done so, however, we would have seen that the analyses of consecutive states were very often identical. For example, if the problem is in either of states 160 and 180—that is, the manager has just £160 000 or £180 000 left to spend—then there are only two decisions he can take and only two possible outcomes. If he chooses to buy no Type Y machines (i.e. $Y = 0$), he leaves himself with enough to purchase two of Type Z (i.e. $Z = 2$) and the outcome from this and later stages is a total annual capacity of 13 000 monitors. On the other hand, if he buys one Y (i.e. $Y = 1$) then the remaining moneys are insufficient to meet the cost of any Z's at all and the result is a total annual capacity of 10 000. The discussion above also illustrates a second point. Whenever we evaluate the decision options available in any state, we constantly refer to the results of the stage 3 analysis. Thus when we consider the effect of the decision to set $Y = 1$ in state 240, we achieve an annual capacity 'now'—that is, from Type Y machines—of 10 000, but leave the manager in state 120 at stage 3, whereupon he purchases:

$$Z^* = \mathrm{INT}(120/80) = 1 \text{ machine of Type Z}$$

and adds an annual capacity 'later'—that is, from Type Z machines—of 6500. In this example the results of stage 3 are so obvious that we may be tempted to perform these calculations intuitively. It is important, however, to recognize and understand the logical link between the analysis of stage 2 and our previous discussion of stage 3. In general the later stages of a DP treatment do not permit intuitive computation of this sort and we shall need to be very clear about the dependence of stage N on stage $N + 1$.

We make one final point concerning Table 14-7. We could have reduced the size of the table if we had looked ahead to our discussion of stage 1. When the manager decides on the number of X's, he has only four options from which to choose: 0, 1, 2 and 3. There are therefore just four states that could possibly arise at stage 2 (in terms of the available budget, S)—300, 200, 100 and 0—and it would suffice to consider these and no others in the stage 2 table. We have chosen quite deliberately not to simplify the analysis in this way, since to do so is misleading. It is only at the penultimate stage of a DP treatment that

Table 14-7 Stage 2 analysis

State (£000)	Decision Y	Total capacity Now (000)	+	Later (000)	Optimal decision Y*	Optimal capacity (000)
$S < 80$	0	0	+	0	0	0
$80 \leq S < 120$	0	0	+	6.5	0	6.5
$120 \leq S < 160$	0	0	+	6.5		
	1	10	+	0	1	10
$160 \leq S < 200$	0	0	+	13		
	1	10	+	0	0	13
$200 \leq S < 240$	0	0	+	13		
	1	10	+	6.5	1	16.5
$240 \leq S < 280$	0	0	+	19.5		
	1	10	+	6.5		
	2	20	+	0	2	20
$280 \leq S \leq 300$	0	0	+	19.5		
	1	10	+	13		
	2	20	+	0	1	23

simplification of this sort is practicable: at earlier stages of the analysis identifying the states in this manner is normally too complex, time-consuming and prone to error.

The preceding paragraph has already set the scene for stage 1. Before we embark on a full analysis, however, we summarize the results of stage 2 in Table 14-8.

Note that for simplicity's sake we have represented each range of similar states by the first state in the range. Thus [120 stands for the range [120, 160 which includes 120 but excludes 160, i.e. it is the set of S values for which:

$$120 \leq S < 160$$

Table 14-8 is crucial to the analysis of stage 1 presented in Table 14-9. Notice that as usual there is only one state to consider. When the manager makes his first decision, the whole of the budgeted amount is available for spending. Notice also that the evaluation of total annual capacity now covers the entire set of machines. For example, if the decision is taken to set $X = 2$, then the resulting capacity of Type X machines is 16 000, but this leaves the problem in state 100 at stage 2, whereupon, from Table 14-8, a further capacity of 6500 is added. This 'later' capacity is the best that can be achieved at stages 2 and 3 when decisions on machine Types Y and Z are made.

Table 14-8 Stage 2 results

State S	[0	[80	[120	[160	[200	[240	[280
Optimal Z^*	0	0	1	0	1	2	1
Optimal capacity (000)	0	6.5	10	13	16.5	20	23

Table 14-9 Stage 1 analysis

Stage (£000)	Decision X	Total capacity Now (000)	+ Later (000)	Optimal decision X*	Optimal capacity (000)
300	0	0	+ 23		
	1	8	+ 16.5		
	2	16	+ 6.5		
	3	24	+ 0	1	24.5

The optimal solution to the problem as a whole is now clear. The manager should purchase 1 machine of Type X, transforming the problem into state 200 at stage 2. At this point he should buy 1 Type Y machine, so that at stage 3 the problem is in state 80. Finally, he uses all the remaining moneys to acquire 1 machine of type Z. (As in IMC's routing problem, note the way in which we backtrack through the stage tables to complete the solution.) The total capacity of the three machines is evident from Table 14-9: 24 500 monitors per year.

14-4 THE CURSE OF DIMENSIONALITY

In general the DP approach to such a problem is computationally more efficient, requiring in all a much smaller number of arithmetic operations for the same final result. It is perfectly reasonable to ask, therefore, whether DP can be extended to cope with larger integer programming problems to similar effect. The answer, unfortunately, is No. If we move out of the realm of knapsack problems by including additional constraints then we will find it necessary to define the states of the problem in terms of more than one parameter. In our discussion of the production manager's decision, it was possible to describe the states by reference to the amount of the budget as yet unspent. This was sufficient by itself to enable a full analysis of the decision options at each stage. However, where several constraints are present, the states must normally be defined in terms of them all. In other words the states must become multi-dimensional, the number of dimensions equalling the number of constraints. In consequence, the states involved in the DP treatment quickly proliferate as the size of the problem increases and soon become too numerous to analyse. This phenomenon, called the 'curse of dimensionality' by Richard Bellman, is a major reason why DP is less prominent as a solution method with problems of these sorts than its wide applicability might suggest.

14-5 A PROBLEM IN ORDER SCHEDULING

In our earlier discussions of the nature and purpose of DP, we stressed its suitability for situations in which it is required to take—or at least to implement—a sequence of decisions. In the case of IMC's routing problems such a sequence arose fairly naturally from the problem itself. With our knapsack problem, on the other hand, we were forced to impose an arbitrary sequence so that we could apply the DP treatment. We now investigate a situation in which the decision sequence is an inevitable consequence of the nature of the problem: the scheduling of orders for material resources. Our scenario is as follows. At the beginning of March this year IMC's Midtown production manager produced estimates of the factory's microchip requirements for the following 3 months. These were (in thousands):

March	April	May
1	4	3

Since stocks were on the verge of running out it was clear that replenishments were urgently needed, but the manager was determined that the choice of ordering strategy should be approached in a rational manner. The chips in question are generally scarce. IMC's supplier, who in normal circumstances can deliver just once at the beginning of the month, reported that she could supply up to 6000 chips in March but no more than 4000 in each of April and May. None the less, she was prepared to offer the usual bulk discounts for larger orders—with the proviso that, for particularly sizeable order quantities, IMC should pay an additional surcharge to cover the cost of a double delivery. Table 14-10 gives details of cost projections for different sizes of order. Note that these are in general a little higher for April and May, reflecting the increasing shortage of chips.

In addition to purchasing, of course, the manager was aware that IMC incurred costs associated with holding unused chips in stock. It is a reasonable approximation to assume that the company incurred £500 for every thousand chips in store at the end of a month. Given the structure of the data, the manager's decision problem is clear: what size of order should he have placed with IMC's supplier in each of the three months? We readily infer that the solution will be a series of decisions implemented in sequence at the beginnings of March, April and May.

Student activity
On the basis of the information provided, determine an intuitive solution to this problem.

In the DP treatment of a problem such as this the stages are defined in a particularly obvious manner: stages 1, 2 and 3 occur at the beginnings of March, April and May

Table 14-10 Purchasing cost projections: microchips

Order size (000)	Total purchasing cost (£000)		
	March	April	May
1	8	10	10
2	13	14	16
3	18	18	20
4	25	23	24
5	29	—	—
6	33	—	—

respectively. The states of the problem are perhaps a little less obvious and could, in fact, be determined in a number of ways. We might, for example, define them in terms of the level of microchip stocks or as the number of chips already ordered. However, for the purpose of this analysis we shall find it convenient to use the total number of chips still to be ordered before the end of May as our state definition. The results of the stage 3 analysis (for May) are contained in Table 14-11. For simplicity we assume that the manager always orders in multiples of 1000 chips.

Note that we need not consider any further states. Since the factory requires only 3000 chips in May something must have gone very badly wrong if the problem were to arrive in state 4 or higher at stage 3. By this point in our discussion of DP the reader will be reasonably familiar with the kind of analysis required at stage 2 (for April). We therefore present the results alone—but strongly recommend that you reconstruct each calculation and confirm the findings of Table 14-12.

By way of assistance, however, we shall undertake the calculations of state 5. This should reveal all the factors that play any part in the analysis. We remark first that, if the problem finds itself in state 5 at stage 2, then at the beginning of April the manager still has to order a further 5000 microchips by the end of May. There are exactly three decision options from which he may choose: order 2000, 3000 or 4000 chips now. All other possibilities are excluded for two reasons—at least 2000 chips are needed to satisfy April's requirement (given that the other 3000 are for use in May) and IMC's supplier can deliver no more than 4000 that month. The costs arising from these decisions are shown in Table 14-13.

Table 14-11 Stage 3 results (May)

State (000 chips to be ordered)	0	1	2	3
Optimal order quantity (000)	0	1	2	3
Optimal cost (£000)	0	10	16	20

Table 14-12 Stage 2 results (April)

State (000 chips)	0	1	2	3	4	5	6	7
Optimal order (000)	0	0	2	3	4	2/4	3	4
Optimal cost (£000)	0	10	15	19.5	24.5	34	38	43

Table 14-13 Costs of decisions

Decision (order size)	Total costs (£000)	
	Now	+ Later
2000	(14 + 0)	+ 20
3000	(18 + 0.5)	+ 16
4000	(23 + 1)	+ 20

Note that, as usual, the evaluation of each decision consists of two components: the 'now' and the 'later'. In this case the cost 'now' comprises the purchasing cost associated with the size of order and any additional stockholding cost that might be incurred at the end of April. For the decision to order 3000, for example, IMC incurs an initial cost of £18 000 for the purchase and an extra £500 for the 1000 chips that must be held in stock until May—the other 2000 will have been used up by that time. The cost 'later' is, of course, the cost which must be incurred at stage 3 if such a decision is taken. The total of these various amounts is therefore the aggregate of all the costs that will be incurred at this and all later stages. On this basis it is evident that there are two optimal order sizes for this state: the manager will be indifferent between ordering 2000 and 4000 chips. The rest of stage 2's results are derived in much the same way.

Student activity
Confirm the results of Table 14-12 from your own calculations.

Because the total chip requirement for April and May is 7000 we need not consider any further states in Table 14-12. Again, the problem can find itself in a higher state only if some disaster befalls the company and the Midtown factory fails to receive its quota of chips in March. The reader will also notice that we need not have troubled ourselves with states 0 and 1, since these could only arise if IMC were to order more than 6000 chips in March—that is, more than the supplier can deliver that month. As we pointed out in the preceding section, however, this is knowledge that we would normally have only at the penultimate stage in a DP treatment and to use it here may be misleading. We are now in a position to complete our treatment by compiling the stage 1 analysis. Once more we present the results alone. These are contained in Table 14-14.

Backtracking through the tables from Table 14-14 to Table 14-11 reveals the optimal solution to the problem as a whole. The manager should have used the following order schedule:

Table 14-14 Stage 1 results (March)

State (000 chips)	8
Optimal order (000)	5
Optimal cost (£000)	50.5

Month	March	April	May
Order size	5000	3000	0

The total cost of this sequence of decisions was £50 500.

Student activity
Confirm the results of Table 14-13 and the optimal order schedule and compare the optimal solution with your own intuitive solution derived earlier.

State-free problems

A salient feature of the optimal order schedule we have just examined is that each order quantity precisely matches the amount needed to satisfy Midtown's requirements over a whole number of months. Thus 5000 microchips will meet the factory's needs in March and April, 3000 in May. In our particular example, in fact, this is pure coincidence. However, if we were to change the conditions of the problem and assume a fixed delivery charge per order and a fixed purchase price—both regardless of order size—then the optimal solution would necessarily exhibit such a property. Furthermore, no order will ever be placed until existing stocks have run out. (Note that throughout our discussion of order scheduling we have assumed implicitly that stocks will always be on hand when IMC needs them. There are no difficulties with the supplier's lead times.) Both these facts are easily proved, though we do not present the proof here. In such cases, therefore, the full DP treatment is no longer essential. Whenever an order is placed it is enough to decide how many periods' demands the order should satisfy. This leads to a radical simplification of the DP analysis in which the stages remain as (potential) decision points—i.e. the beginnings of the periods—but the concept of the state is no longer required. At a particular stage in the decision process, with stock level at zero, the decision-maker's choice of order quantity transforms the problem into another zero stock situation at some later stage—not necessarily the next. The decision options at each stage are the aggregate demands for all possible numbers of periods, beginning with the current stage, and are evaluated once again on the basis of cost 'now' + cost 'later'. In this case, though, the cost 'now' includes all delivery, purchase and stockholding charges incurred before the next order point, whereas the cost 'later' is derived from a previous analysis of the stage at which this occurs. In other words the analysis is still performed by working backwards from the final stage to the first. As we wish to present a unified discussion of DP we will not probe this problem here. However, it is useful to know that there is a sizeable category of problems amenable to the use of DP to which a similar state-free analysis can be applied. For details of such problems and their DP treatments the reader is referred to the Bibliography.

14-6 THE MATHEMATICS OF DYNAMIC PROGRAMMING

In the earlier sections of this chapter we have deliberately avoided the mathematical representation of DP models in an attempt to present the essential features of the approach in as clear and simple a manner as possible. Although every DP treatment can be formulated algebraically, it is an unfortunate truth that this often serves to obscure the analysis rather than to clarify it. Now that the basic principles of DP are well established and the reader has developed a certain confidence in using them, we feel justified in presenting our earlier models in a more formal manner. The great merit of this lies in the ability of mathematics to express the structure and dynamics of any DP model in a succinct and unambiguous way. Once the reader has become familiar with the notational conventions of DP and has gained a clear understanding of the way in which they relate to our previous analyses, s(he) will appreciate their expressive power. We consider first the knapsack problem of Section 14-3.

Knapsack problems revisited

As a reminder of the production manager's machine selection problem we repeat the model (in its scaled-down version) below.

$$\text{Maximize} \quad 8X + 10Y + 6.5Z \qquad (14\text{-}3)$$

$$\text{subject to:} \quad 100X + 120Y + 80Z \leq 300 \qquad (14\text{-}4)$$

$$X, Y, Z \geq 0 \text{ and integer}$$

We began the mathematics of the DP treatment of this model in Section 14-3 when we noted that at stage 3 the best Z value is:

$$Z^* = \text{INT}(S/80) \qquad (14\text{-}5)$$

and that the corresponding optimal machine capacity in thousands of monitors per year is

$$6.5 \, \text{INT}(S/80)$$

Here the state of the problem at stage 3, defined as the amount of the budget as yet unspent, is £S thousand. We find it more convenient, however, to extend our notation as follows. Since S denotes the state at stage 3, it will be helpful to emphasize this by adding an appropriate subscript: thus S becomes S_3 and, by the same token, we shall use S_2 and S_1 as the state variables for stages 2 and 1. Further, (14-5) reveals that Z^* is a function of the state variable. We represent this by rewriting the equation as:

$$Z^*(S_3) = \text{INT}(S_3/80) \qquad (14\text{-}6)$$

The optimal machine capacity is also a function of S_3 and is denoted as f_3^*. In other words we have:

$$f_3^*(S_3) = 6.5 \, \text{INT}(S_3/80) \qquad (14\text{-}7)$$

The problem's stage 2 analysis, previously presented in Table 14-7, begins with the observation that the total machine capacity resulting from the decision to buy Y machines of Type Y will be:

$$10Y + f_3^*(S_2 - 120Y)$$

The two terms of this expression correspond to the 'now' and 'later' capacities of the table. While the 'now' is obvious, the 'later' may require explanation. Recall that S_2 is the amount of the budget as yet unspent at this stage. If the manager buys Y machines of Type Y, however, he will be left with just £$(S_2 - 120Y)$ thousand at stage 3, whereupon he will take the appropriate optimal decision for that state with the corresponding optimal return (i.e. capacity). We can introduce an additional 'return function' at this point such that:

$$f_2(S_2, Y) = 10Y + f_3^*(S_2 - 120Y) \qquad (14\text{-}8)$$

to stress the dependence of the return on both state S_2 and decision Y. The critical issues, however, are the optimal value of Y for any given S_2 and the associated optimal capacity. If we use the same conventions as in stage 3, these are denoted by:

$$Y^*(S_2) \qquad \text{and} \qquad f_2^*(S_2)$$

$f_2^*(S_2)$, of course, is the largest value that $f_2(S_2, Y)$ can achieve. We indicate this by

$$f_2^*(S_2) = \max_{Y} \{f_2(S_2, Y)\} \tag{14-9}$$

or equivalently

$$f_2^*(S_2) = \max_{Y} \{10Y + f_3^*(S_2 - 120Y)\} \tag{14-10}$$

The symbolism

$$\max_{Y} \{\ldots\}$$

is interpreted as the largest value achieved by the function in the brackets $\{\ldots\}$ as Y ranges over the appropriate set of values for the state in question. In this case Y can take any integer value from 0 up to $\text{INT}(S_2/120)$. By definition, $Y^*(S_2)$ is the particular value of Y that achieves the largest return. This fact is enough to specify $Y^*(S_2)$—we do not need to write down any more specific algebraic expression for it. The same principles apply equally to stage 1. We have:

$$f_1(S_1, X) = 8X + f_2^*(S_1 - 100X) \tag{14-11}$$

and so

$$f_1^*(S_1) = \max_{X} \{8X + f_2^*(S_1 - 100X)\} \tag{14-12}$$

with X ranging over the values from 0 to $S_1/100$. $X^*(S_1)$ is the best such value. The treatment is complete if we note that the starting state—that is, the only state—at stage 1 is:

$$S_1 = 300 \tag{14-13}$$

Indeed, if we wish, we may replace S_1 by 300 in each of Eqs (14-11) and (14-12).

The general knapsack problem

By definition the general knapsack problem may be expressed as follows:

$$\text{Maximize} \quad C_1 X_1 + C_2 X_2 + \ldots + C_n X_n \tag{14-14}$$

$$\text{subject to:} \quad A_1 X_1 + A_2 X_2 + \ldots + A_n X_n \leq B \tag{14-15}$$

$$\text{All } X\text{'s} \geq 0 \text{ and integer}$$

Employing the ideas and conventions of the machine selection problems, we can formulate the DP treatment of the model in the following way. We have, for the final stage, stage n:

$$X_n^*(S_n) = \text{INT}(S_n/A_n) \tag{14-16}$$

and

$$f_n^*(S_n) = C_n \, \text{INT}(S_n/A_n) \tag{14-17}$$

and for the remaining stages, stage i, for $i = n - 1$ down to 1:

$$f_i^*(S_i) = \max_{X_i} \{C_i X_i + f_{i+1}^*(S_i - A_i X_i)\} \tag{14-18}$$

where X_i ranges over the values 0 to $\text{INT}(S_i/A_i)$, and $X_i^*(S_i)$ is the best such value. Finally, to complete the treatment we specify the initial state S_1, namely:

$$S_1 = B \qquad (14\text{-}19)$$

These equations are said to be *backward recursive*—backward because we begin with the final stage and work backwards to the first, and recursive because each optimal return function f_i^* is defined recursively in terms of the succeeding member of the set f_{i+1}^*. The reader should recognize, however, that no matter how sophisticated the formulation of the DP treatment may now appear, the calculations that it implies are exactly equivalent to those of Tables 14-7 and 14-9. In other words, we have not reduced the number or complexity of the computations in any way. We have, however, presented the solution program in a succinct, precise and unambiguous manner.

Student activity
Verify that Eqs (14-6), (14-7), (14-10), (14-12) and (14-13) are implied by Eqs (14-16) to (14-19).

Order scheduling revisited

In order to reinforce the ideas just introduced we present the mathematical formulation of the order scheduling problem of Section 14-5. In this case, you will recall, the state of the problem is defined at any stage as the number of microchips still to be ordered by the end of May. Our objective is to minimize the total cost of ordering all the chips IMC requires for March, April and May. The first step in the formulation is to introduce suitable notation. Representing the beginnings of March, April and May as stages 1, 2 and 3, we define the following:

S_i = the state variable at stage i, i.e. the number of chips required by the end of May but not yet ordered.
X_i = the decision variable at stage i, i.e. the number of chips to be ordered at this stage.
$C_i(X_i)$ = the cost of ordering X_i chips at stage i.
R_i = the sum of all monthly chip requirements from month i onwards.
$f_i(S_i, X_i)$ = the return function, i.e. the total cost (at this and all later stages) which IMC incurs as a result of taking decision X_i in state S_i at stage i.
$f_i^*(S_i)$ = the optimal return function, i.e. the smallest value that $f_i(S_i, X_i)$ takes as X_i ranges over all feasible sizes of order for state S_i.
X_i^* = the optimal value of X_i for state S_i.

Note that we have deliberately defined the cost function $C_i(X_i)$ to permit a succinct presentation of the model. The values of this function are the figures contained in Table 14-10. The reason for introducing R_i will become clear as our treatment progresses. The analysis of stage 3 gives:

$$X_3^*(S_3) = \min\{4000, S_3\} \qquad (14\text{-}20)$$
and
$$f_3^*(S_3) = C_3(X_3^*(S_3)) \qquad (14\text{-}21)$$

(Notice that we are being somewhat pedantic in these two equations. As we pointed out in our previous treatment of this problem, IMC's decisions at stages 1 and 2 would have gone badly wrong if we were to find $S_3 > 4000$ at stage 3. It is therefore admissible to assume that $X_3^*(S_3) = S_3$.) For stage 2:

$$f_2(S_2, X_2) = C_2(X_2) + f_3^*(S_2 - X_2) \tag{14-22}$$

This is as usual the return 'now'—that is, the cost of buying X_2 chips in April—plus the return 'later'. The later return takes the given form because, by definition of S_2, purchasing X_2 chips in April will leave the problem in state $(S_2 - X_2)$ at the beginning of May—and Bellman's principle allows us to assume an optimal sequence of decisions thereafter. The optimal return is therefore:

$$f_2^*(S_2) = \min_{X_2} \{f_2(S_2, X_2)\}$$

i.e.
$$f_2^*(S_2) = \min_{X_2} \{C_2(X_2) + f_3^*(S_2 - X_2)\} \tag{14-23}$$

with X_2 ranging from

$$\max\{0, S_2 - R_3\} \quad \text{to} \quad \min\{4000, S_2\}$$

The first value of this set follows from the fact that IMC need order nothing if $S_2 \leq R_3$, since it already has enough to satisfy April's requirements, but must order at least $S_2 - R_3$ otherwise. The final value arises because IMC can order at most 4000 chips in April and will certainly order no more than the S_2 it needs to meet all remaining demand before the end of May. It is sufficient to define $X_2^*(S_2)$ as the optimal value within the range. In similar fashion, at stage 1, we have:

$$f_1(S_1, X_1) = C_1(X_1) + f_2^*(S_1 - X_1) \tag{14-24}$$

so that

$$f_1^*(S_1) = \min_{X_1} \{C_1(X_1) + f_2^*(S_1 - X_1)\} \tag{14-25}$$

where X_1 ranges from

$$\max\{0, S_1 - R_2\} \quad \text{to} \quad \min\{6000, S_1\}$$

and $X_1^*(S_1)$ is the best such value. Finally, we add that the initial state of the problem is:

$$S_1 = 8000$$

Perhaps the most striking feature of the DP treatment above is the care needed. This is particularly true of the value sets over which the decision variables are allowed to range. In general, such ranges are obvious enough when we take a purely numerical approach to the solution program—as we did in Section 14-4—but they become more difficult and unwieldy when we need to specify them correctly in algebraic form. The benefits of mathematical formulation are measured not only in an increase in precision, however, but also in terms of the small amount of effort needed to generalize the treatment. With very little extra work it is possible to extend the analysis of this section to cover any number of months' requirements.

Student activity
Introducing a further parameter Q_i to represent the maximum permissible order quantity at stage i, rewrite the equations of stages 2 and 1 more succinctly (i.e. in a similar manner to our treatment of the general knapsack problem). Extend your formulation to cover n stages (i.e. months).

14-7 A PROBLEM IN RELIABILITY

In all our examples thus far the calculation of the return function has required no more than a simple addition: we have always summed the returns 'now' and 'later' to produce the overall return resulting from a particular state–decision pair. Although extremely common in DP problems, this is by no means an essential feature of the approach. In fact, we shall now investigate a case in which returns are computed multiplicatively, taking the opportunity as we do so to introduce the concept of probability into our mathematical programming problems for the first time. Familiarity with the elementary theory of probability would therefore be an advantage but we are confident that even without it the reader will be able to follow the thrust of our analysis. IMC has been invited by NASA (the National Aeronautics and Space Administration) to participate in a new and highly prestigious venture which will place a manned space station in orbit around the moon. IMC has been asked, in particular, to design and assemble the station's monitors. Naturally, reliability is a prime design requirement—the station will remain in orbit for a year and its monitors will be in almost continuous use for the whole of that time. In order to increase monitor reliability IMC has decided that it should provide back-up systems for certain critical circuits and chips by including redundant components. In general, this is done by constructing arrays of identical components operating in parallel so that, if one component fails, the array can continue to function without interruption. The critical components of Model D monitors are circuits A and B and microchip C. IMC is to design an array for each component type and must decide how many of that type the array should contain. Weight and—appropriately—space constraints permit at most 4 components of any single type and no more than 6 in total. For the purpose of this problem it is convenient to define the term 'reliability' to mean 'the probability that a component/array/monitor continues to function effectively for at least one year'. In designing the Model D monitor IMC will wish to maximize monitor reliability by assigning appropriate numbers of A's, B's and C's to their respective arrays. We assume that, as a result of exhaustive testing, the reliabilities of these components are known to be:

Component	A	B	C
Reliability	0.8	0.7	0.75

Table 14-15 shows the reliabilities of the various component arrays for different numbers of components. These are the results of applying basic probability theory to the figures above. For the B array, for example, the argument is as follows. By definition of reliability, the probability that a B component will fail to function within a year is 0.3, i.e. $(1 - 0.7)$. Assuming that the components of any particular array operate—and fail—independently, the probability that all the array's components will fail within a year is therefore 0.3^m, where m is the number of components in the array. Once again by definition, array reliability is thus:

$$1 - 0.3^m$$

since the array will presumably continue to function as long as at least one component remains in working order. This explains the figures in the B column of the table.

Once the array reliabilities are known, it is a simple matter to compute a reliability for the monitor as a whole. For example, if the arrays contain respectively 1, 2 and 3 components then monitor reliability is:

$$0.8 \times 0.91 \times 0.98 = 0.713\,44$$

This follows because we assume that the monitor will continue to function if and only if all the arrays remain operative. The analysis of the preceding paragraphs demonstrates that, in general, problems of this nature may be formulated in the following manner:

$$\text{Maximize} \quad R_1(X_1) \times \ldots \times R_n(X_n) \qquad (14\text{-}26)$$

$$\text{subject to:} \quad X_1 + \ldots + X_n \leq c \qquad (14\text{-}27)$$

$$X_i \leq c_i; \, i = 1, \ldots, n \qquad (14\text{-}28)$$

$$X_i \geq 0 \text{ and integer}; \, i = 1, \ldots, n$$

where: n is the number of component types (and arrays),
X_i is the number of components assigned to the i-th array,
$R_i(X_i)$ is the corresponding reliability of the i-th array and may be represented by $(1 - P_i^{X_i})$ where P_i is the probability that a component of the i-th type will fail within the relevant period (for IMC's space monitor problem the values of $R_i(X_i)$ are contained in Table 14-15),
c_i is the maximum number of components permitted in the i-th array, and
c is the maximum number of components permitted overall.

You should note the similarity between this formulation and the knapsack model of Section 14-6. Both are problems involving integer variables and, Eq. (14-28) apart, a single constraint. (In many situations Eq. (14-28) can be removed from the model as there are no restrictions on permitted numbers of specific components.) The major difference lies, of course, in the nature of the objective function. Here it is highly *non-linear*, so that the

Table 14-15 IMC's space monitors: array reliabilities

Components	Array		
	A	B	C
0	0	0	0
1	0.8	0.7	0.75
2	0.96	0.91	0.9375
3	0.992	0.973	0.9844
4	0.9984	0.9919	0.9961

techniques of ILP, for example, offer no hope of solution. Indeed, the objective function is multiplicative rather than additive, and it is in this regard that DP can provide the analysis we need. For the DP treatment we define the stages in the obvious way, i.e. as the points at which IMC decides how many components it should assign to the arrays. At stage i—the point at which IMC assigns components of Type i to the i-th array—the state variable S_i is defined as the total number of components that may yet be assigned to the monitor without violating the overall constraint on component numbers. The backward recursive equations for the general reliability problem are as follows.

For stage n:
$$X_3^*(S_n) = \min\{S_n, c_n\} \tag{14-29}$$
and
$$f_n^*(S_n) = R_n(X_n^*(S_n)) \tag{14-30}$$

For stage i, with $1 \leq i < n$:
$$f_i(S_i, X_i) = R_i(X_i) \times f_{i+1}^*(S_i - X_i) \tag{14-31}$$
Thus
$$f_i^*(S_i) = \max_{X_i}\{R_i(X_i) \times f_{i+1}^*(S_i - X_i)\} \tag{14-32}$$

where X_i^* ranges over the values: 0 to $\min\{S_i, c_i\}$, and $X_i^*(S_i)$ is the best such X_i.

Finally, at stage 1 we have:
$$S_1 = c$$

Student activity
Verify the above formulation. In particular, explain why the term:
$$f_{i+1}^*(S_i - X_i)$$
appears in Eq. (14-31).

In order to exemplify the numerical calculations that underlie the formulation above, we set out in Tables 14-16 to 14-18 the results of the stage analyses for IMC's space monitor problem. We assume arbitrarily that stages 1 to 3 correspond to the assignment of components A, B and C in that order.

Table 14-16 IMC's space monitors: stage 3 results

State	S_3	0	1	2	3	4	5	6
Optimal decision X_3^*	(S_3)	0	1	2	3	4	4	4
Optimal return f_3^*	(S_3)	0	0.75	0.9375	0.9844	0.9961	0.9961	0.9961

Table 14-17 IMC's space monitors: stage 2 results

State	S_2	0	1	2	3	4	5	6
Optimal decision X_2^*	(S_2)	0	0/1	1	2	2	3	3
Optimal return f_2^*	(S_2)	0	0	0.525	0.6825	0.8531	0.9122	0.9578

Table 14-18 IMC's space monitors: stage 1 results

State	S_1	6
Optimal decision X_1^*	(S_1)	2
Optimal return f_1^*	(S_1)	0.8190

Backtracking through these tables, we see that the optimal solution is to place two components of each type in the monitor, and that the overall reliability will then be 0.8190.

Student activity

The analysis may be simplified if we note that each array must contain at least one component to ensure a non-zero reliability. Modify the mathematical formulation and Tables 14-16 to 14-18 to take advantage of this fact.

What improvement in monitor reliability would result if the total number of components were increased by 1?

14-8 A STOCHASTIC PLANNING PROBLEM

In this section we turn our attention to a second problem in which chance plays a major role—but on this occasion in a very different way. In the course of our investigation we shall see that DP can cope with situations in which we cannot predict the outcome of a decision with certainty—where, in fact, taking a specific decision in a specific state at a specific stage can be assumed only to transform the problem into one of several states at the next stage. We encounter the concept of expected monetary value and see how it may be used to construct a rational objective for such decision problems. The scenario is as follows.

Sensitive to current environmental issues, IMC has decided to cease production of one of its monitor cleaning kits, which contains a chemical detrimental to the ozone layer. The product will be phased out gradually over the next two quarters: production and sales will continue during spring and summer, but any stocks remaining at the beginning of autumn will be destroyed. (We assume that this can be done at negligible cost to the company.) Market demand for the kit is not seasonal in any way but shows considerable random variation, as indicated by the following table:

Quantity demanded (000)	1	2	3	4
Probability	0.2	0.4	0.3	0.1

IMC schedules production runs once a quarter incurring a set-up cost of £3000 and a marginal production cost of £3 per kit. The company has decided to maintain the sales price at £10 and at the present time—the beginning of spring—has 3000 kits in stock. Given IMC's stated policy on kits, the company clearly faces two decisions: it must determine how many kits to produce in each of its spring and summer production runs. It is evident that IMC's problem has two stages. It is also fairly clear that we may define the states of the problem in terms of the amount of stock on hand. We begin with the final stage as usual, noting that the problem may—in theory—be in any state at all. The number of kits in stock at the beginning of the summer quarter will depend on the numbers produced and sold in spring. To simplify our analysis we make two assumptions: firstly, that all production and sales quantities are multiples of 1000, and secondly, since it would otherwise be certain of having stocks of unsaleable kits at the beginning of autumn, that IMC will decide not to produce more than 5000 in the spring run. There are therefore just nine states at stage 2: the stock level lies in the range 0 to 8 thousand. We consider two of these in detail.

A. State = 1000 kits Suppose first that IMC begins the summer with 1000 kits in stock. Since quarterly demand is 4000 at most there is clearly no sense in producing more than 3000 additional kits and so the company has four decision options from which to make a choice: produce 0, 1000, 2000 or 3000 kits in the summer run. We analyse each in turn:

1. Produce 0 In this case IMC incurs no cost, but has only 1000 kits with which to meet summer demand. From the demand distribution, it is clear that the company will sell all its stock, receiving a total of £10 000 in revenue. As far as the summer quarter is concerned this may be regarded as pure profit.

2. Produce 1000 IMC incurs the production set-up cost of £3000 and an additional variable cost of £3000, but begins the quarter with 2000 saleable kits. The resulting revenue cannot be predicted with certainty. However, the demand distribution implies that two levels are possible: IMC can sell either 1000 or 2000 kits and receive either £10 000 or £20 000. Further, these two possibilities occur with probabilities 0.2 and 0.8 respectively. The expected value of IMC's revenue is thus:

$$£(10\,000 \times 0.2 + 20\,000 \times 0.8)$$

i.e. £18 000

This may require a little explanation. Firstly, a revenue of £20 000 accrues if summer demand is 2000 kits or more. The probability of achieving such a revenue, therefore, is:

$$0.4 + 0.3 + 0.1 = 0.8$$

More importantly, though, we cannot introduce the concept of the expected value without comment. It is a vital element in almost all *stochastic* problems—i.e. those in which chance plays any part. Briefly, the expected value is a notional mean (and indeed is often referred to as 'the mean' in the literature). In this case it measures the mean revenue that IMC would receive if it were to find itself in the same situation—with 2000 kits for sale in the quarter—a large number of times. Admittedly, IMC will not find itself in this situation more than once, but the expected value still provides a reasonable measure on which to base the analysis. Indeed, if decisions are consistently geared to the optimization of expected values then, in general, the company will succeed in optimizing actual values in the long term. Hence if the company aims to maximize the expected value of profit, it is likely—in the long term—to maximize its actual profit. A word of warning, however.

348 FURTHER MATHEMATICAL PROGRAMMING MODELS

Somewhat confusingly, an expected value is not necessarily a value that we can expect to actually occur. In the majority of cases the expected value is not even a value that can occur at all. IMC's expected revenue is £18 000, but £10 000 and £20 000 are the only revenues that can actually arise. In other words 'expected value' is a technical term and should be used with care. To summarize, if IMC chooses to produce 1000 kits, its expected revenue will be £18 000 and its (actual) cost will be £6000. Thus its expected profit will be £12 000.

3. Produce 2000 In this case initial costs total:

$$£(3000 + 2 \times 3000) = £9000$$

while the expected revenue is:

$$£(10\,000 \times 0.2 + 20\,000 \times 0.4 + 30\,000 \times 0.4) = £22\,000$$

The latter calculation follows from the fact that IMC begins the summer with 3000 kits in stock and will therefore sell 1000, 2000 and 3000 with probabilities 0.2, 0.4 and 0.4 respectively. (These are the figures appropriate to demands of 1000, 2000 and at least 3000 and are taken from the demand distribution table.) We conclude that the expected profit is £13 000.

4. Produce 3000 Here costs total £12 000 and the expected revenue is £23 000, with the result that expected profit is £11 000. Comparing the expected profits accruing from the four decision options, we see that the optimal decisions for this state is to produce 2000 kits.

B. State ⩾ 4000 kits With 4000 kits or more in stock at the beginning of summer, IMC will decide to produce nothing. According to the demand distribution, any production would simply result in additional waste at the beginning of autumn. There will therefore be no initial cost, but IMC will be able to meet all the quarter's demand, receiving a total expected revenue of:

$$£(10\,000 \times 0.1 + 20\,000 \times 0.4 + 30\,000 \times 0.3 + 40\,000 \times 0.1)$$

i.e. £23 000

The ideas and arguments we have used in the preceding paragraphs may be applied to all the remaining states of stage 2. The results are summarized in Table 14-19.

Student activity
Confirm the results of Table 14-19 by performing a full analysis of stage 2.

Table 14-19 IMC's cleaning kits: stage 2 results

State (kits in stock)	0	1000	2000	3000	⩾ 4000
Optimal decision (kits produced)	3000	2000	0	0	0
Optimal expected profit (£000)	10	13	18	22	23

At stage 1—the beginning of spring—there is only one state: there are 3000 kits in stock. As previously remarked, IMC will not wish to produce more than 5000 kits at this point. It would otherwise be certain of destroying surplus kits at the beginning of autumn. Consequently there are just six decision options: produce any multiple of 1000 from 0 up to 5000. To demonstrate the principles involved in the analysis, we present a detailed discussion of one such decision to produce 1000 kits.

As in previous problems, when we progress backwards through the stages we need to evaluate the decision options in terms of returns 'now' and 'later'. In this instance, returns 'now' consist of any profits made by the company during spring, and so are calculated from the costs and expected revenues for this quarter alone. Returns 'later' are those accruing from stage 2 (and, in general, beyond) and will be computed on the basis of our existing stage 2 results. But first the returns 'now'. Starting with 3000 kits and producing a further 1000, IMC has a total of 4000 with which to meet demand during spring. Its expected revenue is therefore:

$$£(10\,000 \times 0.2 + 20\,000 \times 0.4 + 30\,000 \times 0.3 + 40\,000 \times 0.1)$$

i.e. £23 000

Costs amount to £6000 in total and so the expected profit is £17 000. This is the 'now' return. To calculate the return 'later' we proceed as follows. Since spring demand, like that of any other quarter, is unpredictable, we cannot say with certainty to which state the problem will be transformed at the next stage. We can say, however, with what probabilities the problem will find itself in particular states at stage 2. These are:

State (kits in stock)	0	1000	2000	3000	≥ 4000
Probability	0.1	0.3	0.4	0.2	0

and follow directly from the quarterly demand distribution. For example, in order for the problem to arrive in state 1000, spring demand must be 3000—an occurrence whose probability is 0.3. The optimal expected profit associated with each of the stage 2 states is shown in Table 14-19. These can now be used to calculate the expected return 'later':

$$£(10\,000 \times 0.1 + 13\,000 \times 0.3 + 18\,000 \times 0.4 + 22\,000 \times 0.2)$$

i.e. £16 500

Note that, once again, the concept of the expected value comes to our aid in a situation characterized by chance. Similar calculations are needed, of course, for each of the other decision options. An analysis of stage 1 showing a moderate level of detail is contained in Table 14-20.

Our analysis reveals clearly that the optimal decision in spring is to produce no cleaning kits at all and that the resulting expected profit is £34 800. For summer, however, the picture is not nearly so clear-cut. In our previous examples, a decision taken at stage 1 of the problem leads with certainty to a single state at stage 2. In this case any decision has several possible outcomes and we must therefore know how to proceed whichever occurs. It is a feature of the DP treatment, of course, that such information is already available in

350 FURTHER MATHEMATICAL PROGRAMMING MODELS

Table 14-20 IMC's cleaning kits: stage 1 analysis

State (kits in stock)	Decisions (kits to produce)	Expected profits (£000)	
		Now	+ Later
3000	0	22	+ 12.8
	1000	17	+ 16.5
	2000	14	+ 20.1
	3000	11	+ 22.2
	4000	8	+ 22.9
	5000	5	+ 23

the stage 2 results table, and we may quote the appropriate 'decision rule' whatever the state of the problem at that stage. Thus if IMC discovers at the beginning of summer that stocks of kits have run out, an appeal to Table 14-19 will show that it should produce a further 3000. In other words solutions to stochastic problems of this type are different in kind from those of our previous examples—they comprise sets of decision rules rather than individual decisions.

14-9 SUMMARY

In this chapter we have introduced a radically different form of mathematical program. Dynamic programming is based on a particularly simple principle, but is widely applicable and may be used to solve an immense variety of decision problems. The chief characteristic of such problems is that they may be considered to consist of a series of stages, at each of which the problem is in one of a number of states. A decision is taken at each stage and this results in some form of return to the decision-maker while transforming the problem into some further state at the next stage. Although small problems may be solved by more direct means, DP often reduces the volume of calculation required quite dramatically. As a result, DP can be used for many types of problem that other methods cannot handle. In certain instances, however—in particular, where the states of the problem must be defined in terms of several parameters—the DP treatment suffers from the 'curse of dimensionality' and the number of states becomes prohibitive.

Despite the fundamental simplicity of DP, it has certain unusual features which are best approached at first through purely numerical examples. In this chapter we have dealt exclusively with backward recursion in which each decision sequence is analysed in reverse order. This is the usual form of analysis in DP, though in fact there are many problems that are equally amenable to forward recursion. A numerical approach, we believe, helps the student to appreciate the logic of DP without becoming too embroiled in the niceties of mathematics. Mathematical formulation is nevertheless an essential addition, since it permits the problem-solver to create models with far greater precision and succinctness. In the later sections of the chapter we saw, for the first time in this book, a number of decision situations in which chance or uncertainty played a substantial part. The methods of LP and its extensions are unable, in general, to address such stochastic problems. With the aid of probabilities and expected values, however, DP was seen to provide a suitable solution method.

If DP is such a versatile approach to problem solving, you may be forgiven for asking why it is not dominant in the field of mathematical programming. There are several reasons for this. It may be difficult to keep the number of states within bounds for a comprehensive treatment of a specific problem. However, the primary reason, we believe, is the lack of a standard, well-understood form for DP models. Almost every DP problem is sufficiently different in kind to require its own distinctive mathematical formulation. In general, problem-solvers—particularly those new to modelling—find the demands of DP formulation forbidding and are often reluctant to use it. Given such reluctance it is scarcely surprising that, although there are large numbers of LP packages in existence, general DP computer programs are a considerable rarity. Once again, the implications for the decision-maker's ability to understand and use such models are evident.

Before we close the chapter and the text, it is important to reiterate that our discussion of DP (and indeed the other more advanced mathematical programming models in this part of the text) is by no means comprehensive. We have deliberately done no more than to introduce the major concepts and principles on which the DP approach is based, and to illustrate its application in a small sample of decision problems. There are many other important practical aspects to DP that we have not discussed. Of course, it was never our intention to study the more advanced areas of these models but rather to provide the foundation on which the reader may build if he or she wishes and to provide the decision-maker with an appreciation of the principles of such models. Armed with such an awareness—and coupled with a rigorous understanding of LP—the decision-maker will be in a position to assess the potential usefulness of such models in the business organization and to evaluate the usefulness of information generated by the application of such models. By this stage we anticipate that the decision-maker will no longer have to rely solely on the opinion of the 'expert' within the organization to decide how best to incorporate such models and information into the decision-making process.

STUDENT EXERCISES

14-1 Return to IMC's routing problem where restrictions were introduced depending on whether the driver had passed through A. Solve this modified problem.

14-2 Solve IMC's knapsack problem by the branch and bound method of Chapter 11, using a suitable software package to supply solutions to the subproblems. From your knowledge of the Simplex method, which of the two approaches do you consider the more efficient in terms of the number computations involved?

14-3 Admax Limited is planning a 4-week sales campaign in an area comprising towns A, B, C and D, each of which has its own weekly newspaper. The company has decided to insert a total of 7 identical advertisements and wishes to allocate them between these 4 local papers. Admax's representatives in the 4 towns estimate that sales are affected by the placing of advertisements in the manner shown in Table 14-21.

(*a*) Assuming that Admax wishes to maximize the number of sales resulting from the campaign, use DP to discover the optimal allocation of advertisements.
(*b*) Formulate Admax's problem mathematically, extending your model to cover any number of towns and their papers.

14-4 During the summer Duvals bakery produce beignets for sale on popular Brittany beaches. The demand for beignets is particularly sensitive to price. From long experience Duvals estimate that for a single seller the hourly

Table 14-21

Number of advertisements in the town's paper	Town			
	A	B	C	D
0	200	400	360	600
1	240	450	370	610
2	250	470	390	620
3	260	480	420	630
4	270	480	430	640

demand distributions associated with different prices are as shown in Table 14-22. Thus, for example, at a price of 3 francs per beignet, there is a 0.3 probability of a demand for 40 beignets in an hour. Similarly, if the price is set at 2 francs, 60 beignets are sold in an hour with probability 0.6. The beignet sellers employed by Duvals are students on vacation. The company has therefore decided to lay down simple rules that will enable sellers to charge a price appropriate to the time of day. The sellers begin work at 2.00 p.m. with their afternoon quota of beignets. Duvals set an initial price, but each seller is required to review his/her stock at 3.00 p.m. and adjust the price according to the number of beignets still unsold. Sellers finish work at 4.00 p.m., at which point any remaining beignets are worthless.

(a) Duvals currently provide each seller with 80 beignets at 2.00 p.m. Assuming that the company wishes to maximize its revenue, use DP to determine the optimal initial price and specify optimal pricing rules that Duvals' sellers should apply.

(b) Extend your analysis to determine the optimal number of beignets sellers should be given at 2.00 p.m., assuming that the per-beignet production cost is 1.5 francs.

Table 14-22

Hourly demand (beignets)	Price (francs)		
	4	3	2
0	0.3	0.1	0
20	0.5	0.4	0
40	0.1	0.3	0.4
60	0.1	0.2	0.6

14-5 Durham Homes have just completed a small housing development. The market is sluggish and four properties—all priced at £100 000—are still to be sold. In an attempt to attract buyers, Durhams are planning a promotional campaign for July and August. Best professional advice indicates that, in either month, advertising expenditure and demand for Durhams' houses are related as in Table 14-23.

Table 14-23

Expenditure (£000)	Demand for houses			
	0	1	2	3
25	0.3	0.4	0.2	0.1
50	0.1	0.3	0.4	0.2
75	0	0.1	0.6	0.3

The figures in the body of the table are probabilities. For example, if £75 000 is spent on advertising in a particular month, there is a 0.6 probability that two houses will be demanded in that month.

The company's objective is to maximize its expected net income (i.e. expected income from house sales minus advertising expenditure) over the next two months. Use DP to determine the optimal advertising expenditure during July and an optimal set of decision rules for August's campaign.

APPENDIX

COMPUTER SOFTWARE

To accompany the text the authors have developed a set of IBM PC compatible software for the main mathematical programming models covered in the text. The authors feel that the availability and use of such software as an integrated part of the student's study of these models not only relieves the tedium of manual calculations (although these are sometimes important to reinforce concepts), but also develops the student's understanding of the solution algorithm and the principles underpinning the solution method. The software covers the models of:

Transportation
Assignment
Linear programming (Simplex and Dual)
Integer programming
Goal programming

In addition the disk contains a number of datafiles relating to the examples and exercises used throughout the text. Full details of these are contained in the README file on the disk.

The program is largely menu-driven and has been written in such a way as to make it as free standing as possible and the student (and lecturer) should be able to use the software by following the relevant on-screen instructions. The program is loaded and run by the following sequence:

1. ensure the default drive is set to A:
2. type the command START and press the ENTER key
3. the program should now load and you should follow the detailed on-screen instructions to continue.

The program is a compiled version written in TurboBasic and requires a fully compatible PC running with DOS 2.0 or higher. The program supports most graphics facilities and colour (where available).

Lecturers who are recommending the text for class use can obtain a free copy of the software and a site licence by contacting McGraw-Hill Book Company (UK) Limited, Shoppenhangers Road, Maidenhead, Berks SL6 2QL. Comments, suggestions or difficulties about the software itself should be communicated to the authors.

BIBLIOGRAPHY

We have not attempted to provide a comprehensive or exhaustive bibliography for the mathematical programming models we have covered in the text. Indeed, the areas of applications of these models are expanding at such a rate that it is difficult, if not impossible, for a textbook to keep up to date. What we have attempted to do is reference some of the key texts and articles in the historical development of these models and to provide a cross-section of the business applications of these models. The journal references in particular are quite diverse, both in terms of content and mathematical approach, and will repay closer inspection.

It is also advisable to monitor the content of a number of journals on a regular basis as they frequently contain articles in this field:

Accounting and Business Research
European Journal of Operational Research
Interfaces
Journal of the Operational Research Society
Management Science

Management science methodology

Beale, E. M. L.: The Evolution of Mathematical Programming Systems, *Journal of the Operational Research Society*, vol. 36, no. 5, 1985, p. 357

Dyer, J. S. and Shapiro, R. D.: *Management Science/Operations Research Cases and Reading*, Wiley, 1982

Hall, R. W.: What's So Scientific about MS/OR? *Interfaces*, vol. 15, no. 2, 1985, p. 40

Lee, S. M., Cho, Y. K. and Olson, D. L.: The Decentralization of Management Science and the Birth of Self-starters, *Journal of the Operational Research Society*, vol. 40, no. 4, 1989, p. 323

Lockett, G.: Applications of Mathematical Programming—Before, Now and After, *Journal of the Operational Research Society*, vol. 36, no. 5, 1985, p. 347

Pidd, M.: Assumptions and Methodologies in OR, *European Journal of Operational Research*, vol. 21, no. 1, 1985, p. 1

Raiszadeh, F. M. E. and Lingaraj, B. P.: Real-World OR/MS Applications in Journals, *Journal of the Operational Research Society*, vol. 37, no. 10, 1986, p. 937

Reisman, A.: Some Thoughts for Model Builders in the Management and Social Sciences, *Interfaces*, vol. 17, no. 5, 1987, p. 114

Riccio, L. J.: Management Science in New York's Department of Sanitation, *Interfaces*, vol. 14, no. 2, 1984, p. 1

Tait, J.: The Role of Values in Quantitative Decision-Making, *Journal of the Operational Research Society*, vol. 39, no. 7, 1988, p. 669

Ward, S. C.: Arguments for Constructively Simple Models, *Journal of the Operational Research Society*, vol. 40, no. 2, 1989, p. 141

PART A TRANSPORTATION AND ASSIGNMENT

Arsham, H. and Kahn, A. B.: A Simplex-type Algorithm for General Transportation Problems: An Alternative to Stepping-stone, *Journal of the Operational Research Society*, vol. 40, no. 6, 1989, p. 581

Currin, D. C.: Transportation Problems with Inadmissable Routes, *Journal of the Operational Research Society*, vol. 37, no. 4, 1986, p. 387

Dantzig, G. B.: Application of the Simplex Method to a Transportation Problem, in Koopmans, T. C. (ed.), *Activity Analysis of Production and Allocation*, Wiley, 1951

Dwyer, P. S.: A Solution to the Personnel Classification Problem with the Method of Optimal Regions, *Psychometrika*, vol. 19, March 1954, p. 11

Flood, M. M.: On the Hitchcock Distribution Problem, *Pacific Journal of Mathematics*, vol. 2, June 1953, p. 369

Ford, L. R. and Fulkerson, D. R.: Solving the Transportation Problem, *Management Science*, vol. 3, 1956, p. 24

Hitchcock, F. L.: The Distribution of a Product from Several Sources to Numerous Localities, *The Journal of Mathematical Physics*, vol. 20, August 1941, p. 224

Klingman, D. and Phillips, N. V.: Equitable Demand Adjustment for Infeasible Transportation Problems, *Journal of the Operational Research Society*, vol. 39, no. 8, 1988, p. 735

Klingman, D. and Russell, R.: Solving Constrained Transportation Problems, *Operations Research*, vol. 23, no. 1, 1975, p. 91

Koopmans, T. C.: Optimum Utilization of the Transportation System, *Econometrica*, vol. 17, July 1949, p. 136

Kuhn, H. W.: The Hungarian Method for the Assignment Problem, *Naval Research Logistics Quarterly*, vol. 2, 1955, p. 83

Ronen, D.: Perspectives on Practical Aspects of Truck Routing and Scheduling, *European Journal of Operational Research*, vol. 35, no. 2, 1988, p. 137

PART B LINEAR PROGRAMMING

Anderson, A. M. and Earle, M. D.: Diet Planning in the Third World by Linear and Goal Programming, *Journal of the Operational Research Society*, vol. 34, no. 1, 1983, p. 9

Avani, S.: A Linear Programming Approach to Air-Cleaner Design, *Operations Research*, vol. 22, March–April, 1974, p. 295

Avramovich, D., Cook, T. M., Langston, G. D. and Sutherland, F.: A Decision Support System for Fleet Management: A Linear Programming Approach, *Interfaces*, vol. 12, no. 3, 1982, p. 1

Balbirer, S. D. and Shaw, D.: An Application of Linear Programming to Bank Financial Planning, *Interfaces*, vol. 11, no. 5, 1981, p. 77

Bandyopadhyay, J. K.: A Resource Allocation Model for an Employability Planning System, *Interfaces*, vol. 10, no. 5, 1980, p. 53

Banker, R. D.: Estimating Most Productive Scale Size Using DEA, *European Journal of Operational Research*, vol. 17, 1984, p. 35

Baumol, W. J.: *Economic Theory and Operations Analysis*, 2nd edn, Prentice-Hall, 1965

Beale, E. M. L.: *Mathematical Programming in Practice*, Pitman, 1968

Beare, G. C.: Linear Programming in Air Defence Modelling, *Journal of the Operational Research Society*, vol. 38, no. 10, 1987, p. 899

Bhatnagar, S. C.: Implementing Linear Programming in a Textile Unit: Some Problems and a Solution, *Interfaces*, vol. 11, no. 2, 1981, p. 87

Boykin, R. F.: Opitmising Chemical Production at Monsanto, *Interfaces*, vol. 15, no. 1, 1985, p. 88

Brash, I.: Optimal Cargo Allocation on Board a Plane: A Sequential Linear Programming Model, *European Journal of Operational Research*, vol. 8, no. 2, 1981, p. 40

Butterworth, K.: Practical Application of Linear/Integer Programming in Agriculture, *Journal of the Operational Research Society*, vol. 36, no. 2, 1985, p. 99

Cabraal, R. A.: Production Planning in a Sri Lanka Coconut Mill Using Parametric Linear Programming, *Interfaces*, vol. 11, no. 3, 1981, p. 16

Charnes, A. and Cooper, W. W.: *An Introduction to Linear Programming*, Wiley, 1953

Charnes, A. and Cooper, W. W.: *Management Models and Industrial Applications of Linear Programming*, Wiley, 1961

Charnes, A., Cooper, W. W. and Rhodes, E.: Measuring the Efficiency of Decision Making Units, *European Journal of Operational Research*, vol. 2, 1978, p. 429

Copley, J. M. and Corbett, A. J.: The Minimisation of Capital Gains Tax Liabilities by Linear Programme, *Journal of the Operational Research Society*, vol. 39, no. 5, 1988, p. 347

Dantzig, G. B.: *Linear Programming and Extensions*, Princeton University Press, 1963

Darby-Dowman, K., Lucas, C., Mitra, G. and Yadegar, J.: Linear, Integer, Separable and Fuzzy Programming Problems: A Unified Approach, *Journal of the Operational Research Society*, vol. 39, no. 2, 1988, p. 161.

Dorfman, R. Samuelson, P. A. and Solow, R. M.: *Linear Programming and Economic Analysis*, McGraw-Hill, 1958

Edwards, J. R., Wagner, H. M. and Wood W. P.: Blue Bell Trims Its Inventory, *Interfaces*, vol. 15, no. 1, 1985, p. 34

Fokkens, B. and Puylaert, M.: A Linear Programming Model for Daily Harvesting Operations, *Journal of the Operational Research Society*, vol. 32, no. 7, 1981, p. 535

Gal, T.: *Postoptimality Analyses, Parametric Programming and Related Topics*, McGraw-Hill, 1979

Gass, S. I.: *An Illustrated Guide to Linear Programming*, McGraw-Hill, 1969

Golany, B.: An Interactive MOLP Procedure for the Extension of DEA to Effectiveness Analysis, *Journal of the Operational Research Society*, vol. 39, no. 8, 1988, p. 725

Greenwood, A. G. and Moore, L. J.: An Intertemporal Multi-goal Linear Programming Model for Optimising University Tuition and Fee Structures, *Journal of the Operational Research Society*, vol. 38, no. 7, 1987, p. 599

Haehling von Lanzenauer *et al.*: RRSP Flood: LP to the Rescue, *Interfaces*, vol. 17, no. 4, 1987, p. 27

Hay, D. A. and Dahl, P. N.: Strategic and Midterm Planning of Forest-to-product Flows, *Interfaces*, vol. 14, no. 5, 1984, p. 33

Hilal, S. S. and Erikson, W.: Matching Supplies to Save Lives: Linear Programming the Production of Heart Valves, *Interfaces*, vol. 11, no. 6, 1981, p. 48

Jack, W.: An Interactive, Graphical Approach to Linear Financial Models, *Journal of the Operational Research Society*, vol. 36, no. 5, 1985, p. 367

Jennergren, L. P. and Obel, B.: A Study in the Use of Linear Programming for School Planning in Odense, *Journal of the Operational Research Society*, vol. 31, no. 9, 1980, p. 791

Jordi, K. C. and Peddie, D.: A Wildlife Management Problem: A Case Study in Multiple-objective Linear Programming; *Journal of the Operational Research Society*, vol. 39, no. 11, Nov. 1988, p. 1011

Kolesar, P. J., Rider, K. L., Crabill, T. B. and Walker, W. E.: A Queuing–LP Approach to Scheduling Police Patrol Cars, *Operational Research*, vol. 23, no. 6, 1975, p. 1045

Might, R. J.: Decision Support for Aircraft and Munitions Procurement, *Interfaces*, vol. 17, no. 5, 1987, p. 55

Miller, H. E., Pierskella, W. P. and Roth, G. J.: Nurse Scheduling Using Mathematical Programming, *Operations Research*, vol. 24, no. 5, 1976, p. 857

Plane, D. R. and Hendrick, T. E.: Mathematical Programming and the Location of Fire Companies for the Denver Fire Department, *Operations Research*, vol. 25, no. 4, 1977, p. 563

Rumpf, D. L., Melachrinoides, E. and Rumpf T.: Improving Efficiency in a Forest Pest Control Spray Program, *Interfaces*, vol. 15, no. 5, 1985, p. 1

PART C ADVANCED MATHEMATICAL PROGRAMMING MODELS

Integer programming

Bean, J. C., Noon, C. E. and Salton, G. J.: Asset Divestiture at Hamart Development Company, *Interfaces*, vol. 17, no. 1, 1987, p. 48

Butterworth, K.: Practical Application of Linear/Integer Programming in Agriculture, *Journal of the Operational Research Society*, vol. 36, no. 2, 1985, p. 99

Benveniste, R.: An Integrated Plant Design and Scheduling Problem in the Food Industry, *Journal of the Operational Research Society*, vol. 37, no. 5, 1986, p. 453

Butterworth, K.: Practical Application of Linear/Integer Programming in Agriculture, *Journal of the Operational Research Society*, vol. 36, no. 2, 1985, p. 99

Choypeng, P., Puakpong, P. and Rosenthal, R. E.: Optimal Ship Routing and Personnel Assignment for Naval Recruitment in Thailand, *Interfaces*, vol. 16, no. 4, 1986, p. 47

Cooper, M. W.: A Survey of Methods for Pure Nonlinear Integer Programming, *Management Science*, vol. 27, no. 3, 1981, p. 353

Farley, A. A.: Mathematical Programming Models for Cutting-stock Problems in the Clothing Industry, *Journal of the Operational Research Society*, vol. 39, no. 1, Jan. 1988, p. 41

Keown, A. J. and Taylor, B. W. III: A Chance-Constrained Integer Goal Programming Model for Capital Budgeting in the Production Area, *Journal of the Operational Research Society*, vol. 31, no. 9, 1980, p. 579

Klingman, D. and Phillips, N.: Integer Programming for Optimal Phosphate-mining Strategies, *Journal of the Operational Research Society*, vol. 39, no. 9, Sept. 88, p. 805

Markland, R. E. and Nauss, R. M.: Improving Transit Check Clearing Operations at Maryland National Bank, *Interfaces*, vol. 13, no. 1, 1983, p. 1

Martin, C. H. and Lubin, S. L.: Optimization Modelling for Business Planning at Trumball Asphalt, *Interfaces*, vol. 15, no. 6, 1985, p. 66

Peiser, R. B. and Aridrus, S. G.: Phasing of Income-Producing Real Estate, *Interfaces*, vol. 13, no. 5, 1983, p. 1

Ruth, R. J.: A Mixed Integer Programming Model for Regional Planning of a Hospital Inpatient Service, *Management Science*, vol. 27, no. 5, 1981, p. 521

Scheider, D. P. and Kilpatrick, K. E.: An Optimum Manpower Utilisation Model for Health Maintenance Organisations, *Operations Research*, vol. 23, no. 5, 1975, p. 869

Wilson, J. M.: Integer Programming Approaches to Resource Allocation and Profit Budgeting, *Accounting and Business Research*, vol. 15, no. 57, 1984, p. 33

Goal programming

Aston, D. J.: Goal Programming and Intelligent Financial Simulation Models, *Accounting and Business Research*, vol. 16, no. 61, 1985, p. 3

Baker, J. R. and Fitzpatrick, K. E.: Determination of an Optimal Forecast Model for Ambulance Demand Using Goal Programming, *Journal of the Operational Research Society*, vol. 37, no. 11, 1986, p. 1047

Benjamin, C. O.: A Linear Goal Programming Model for Public Sector Project Selection, *Journal of the Operational Research Society*, vol. 36, no. 1, 1985, p. 13

Cook, W. D.: Goal Programming and Financial Planning Models for Highway Rehabilitation, *Journal of the Operational Research Society*, vol. 35, no. 3, 1984, p. 217

De, P. K., Acharya, D. and Sahn, K. C.: A Chance Constrained Goal Programming Model for Capital Budgeting, *Journal of the Operational Research Society*, vol. 33, no. 7, 1982, p. 635

Mingues, M. I., Remero, C. and Domingo, J.: Determining Optimum Fertilizer Combinations through Goal Progamming with Penalty Functions: An Application to Sugar Beet Production in Spain, *Journal of the Operational Research Society*, vol. 39, no. 1, Jan. 1988, p. 61

Lee, S. M. and Schiederjans, M. J.: A Multicriteria Assignment Problem: A Goal Programming Approach, *Interfaces*, vol. 13, no. 4, 1983, p. 75

Morey, R. C.: Managing the Armed Services' Delayed Entry Pools to Improve Productivity in Recruiting, *Interfaces*, vol. 15, no. 5, 1985, p. 81

Saatcioglu, O.: A Multi-attribute Assignment Goal Programming Model with Incentives, *Journal of the Operational Research Society*, vol. 38, no. 4, 1987, p. 361

Schiederjans, M. J., Kwak, N. K. and Helmer, M. C.: An Application of Goal Programming to Resolve a Site Location Problem, *Interfaces*, vol. 12, no. 3, 1982, p. 65
Sengupta, S.: Goal Programming Approach to a Type of Quality Control Problem, *Journal of the Operational Research Society*, vol. 32, no. 3, 1981, p. 207
Sutcliffe, C., Board, J. and Cheshire, P.: Goal Programming and Allocating Children to Secondary Schools in Reading, *Journal of the Operational Research Society*, vol. 35, no. 8, 1984, p. 719

Non-linear programming

Bracken, J. and McCormick, G. P.: *Selected Applications of Nonlinear Programming*, Wiley, 1968
Boot, J. C. G.: Notes on Quadratic Programming: The Kuhn–Tucker and Theil–Van de Panne Conditions, Degeneracy and Equality Constraints, *Management Science*, vol. 8, 1961, p. 85
Cooper, M. W.: A Survey of Methods for Pure Nonlinear Integer Programming, *Management Science*, vol. 27, no. 3, 1981, p. 353
Dorn, W. S.: Nonlinear Programming: A Survey, *Management Science*, vol. 9, 1963, p. 171
Gill, P. E., Murray, W., Saunders, M. A. and Wright, M. H.: Trends in Nonlinear Programming Software, *European Journal of Operational Research*, vol. 17, no. 2, 1984, p. 141
Guder, F.: An Iterative LP Algorithm for Quadratic Spatial Equilibria, *Journal of the Operational Research Society*, vol. 39, no. 12, 1988, p. 1147
Manos, B. D. and Kitsopanadis, G. I.: A Quadratic Programming Model for Farm Planning of a Region in Central Macedonia, *Interfaces*, vol. 16, no. 4, 1986, p. 2
Wolfe, P.: The Simplex Method for Quadratic Programming, *Econometrica*, vol. 27, no. 3, 1959

Dynamic programming

Abdul-Razaq, T. S. and Potts, C. N.: Dynamic Programming State–Space Relaxation for Single-machine Scheduling *Journal of the Operational Research Society*, vol. 39, no. 2, 1988, p. 141
Bellman, R. E.: *Dynamic Programming*, Princeton University Press, 1957
Bellman, R. E. and Dreyfus, S. E.: *Applied Dynamic Programming*, Princeton University Press, 1962
Clarke, S. R.: Dynamic Programming in Cricket-Optimal Scoring Rates, *Journal of the Operational Research Society*, vol. 39, no. 4, 1988, p. 331
Glen, J. J.: A Dynamic Programming Model for Pig Production, *Journal of the Operational Research Society*, vol. 34, no. 6, 1983, p. 511
Kennedy, J. O. S.: Approximately Optimal recovery of a Multicohort Fishery from Depleted Stocks and Excess Vessel Capacity, *Journal of the Operational Research Society*, vol. 40, no. 3, 1989, p. 231
Lack, G. N. T. *et al.*: The Search for a Second Sydney Airport: A Dynamic Programming Scheduling Model, *Journal of the Operational Research Society*, vol. 30, no. 3, 1979, p. 213
Moores, B.: Dynamic Programming in Transformer Design, *Journal of the Operational Research Society*, vol. 37, no. 10, 1986, p. 967
Sarker, B. R.: An Optimum Solution for One-Dimensional Slitting Problems: A Dynamic Programming Approach, *Journal of the Operational Research Society*, vol. 39, no. 8, 1988, p. 749

INDEX

Additive algorithm, 267
Additivity, assumption of, 214
Adjustable constraints, 233
All integer problems, 259
Alternate optima, 58, 81, 209
Artificial allocations, 68
Artificial variables, 152
Assignment models, 73
   applications of, 87
   solution of, 74
Assumptions:
   additivity, 214
   certainty, 217
   divisibility, 217
   linearity, 70, 214
   proportionality, 214
   single objectives, 218
   transportation models and, 70

Backtracking, 272
Balas additive algorithm, 267
Basic solution, 21, 140
Basic variables, 21, 140
Basis, 21
Bellman's principle of optimality, 326
Big M method, 54, 153
Binary:
   arithmetic, 267
   variables, 226
Binding constraints, 105
Blending problems, 122
Branch and bound method, 250

Budgeting problems, 128

Calculus, 299
   rules of, 302
Canonical form of the primal, 197
Capital budgeting problems, 128
Cargo loading problems, 330
Certainty, assumption of, 217
Complete enumeration, 328
Computer software, 7
Conditional logic, 231
Constrained optimization, 306
Constraint line, 97
Constraints:
   adjustable, 233
   conditional logic, 231
   cutting, 258
   discardable, 233
   equality, 20, 159
   hard, 281
   non-negativity, 20
   soft, 281
   threshold, 232
Cutting plane methods, 258

Decision making, 9
Decision rules, 349
Decision variables, 115
Degeneracy:
   in linear programming models, 211
   in sensitivity analysis, 212
   in transportation models, 67

INDEX

Derivative, 300
   and local/global optima, 303
   partial, 304
Destinations, 17
Deterministic models, 13
Deviational variables, 281
Diet problems, 122
Differential calculus, 299
Discardable constraints, 233
Distribution problems, 15
Divisibility, assumption of, 217
Dual, 194
   formulation of, 197
   and relationship with primal, 200
   variables, 200
Dummy activity, 45, 82
Dynamic programming, 323

Empty cells, 23
Enumeration methods, 267
Equality constraints, 20, 159

Fathoming, 254
Feasible solution:
   in assignment, 74
   in LP, 99
   in transportation, 22
Feasibility, 22
Feed mix problems, 122
Financial mix problems, 128
Fixed charge problems, 235
Flying doctor problems, 330
Formulation
   art of, 144
   assignment problems, 73
   linear programming problems, 93, 114
   transportation problems, 18
Free variables, 267

Global maximum/minimum, 298, 303
Goals, 283
Goal priorities, 283
Goal programming, 280
Goal simplex method, 288
Graphical solution, linear programming, 96

Hard constraints, 281
Heuristics, 13
Hungarian method, 74

Improvement index, 33
Infeasible problems, 207
Initial tableau, linear programming, 141
Integer linear programming, 223
Inventory problems, 116

Knapsack problems, 330, 339
Kuhn–Tucker conditions, 308

Labour scheduling problems, 119
Lagrange multipliers, 306
   calculus based solution and, 307
   interpretation of, 308
Least-cost method, 22
Linear programming:
   assumptions, 213
   duality, 194
   graphical solution, 96
   sensitivity analysis, 107
   simplex method, 138
Local maximum/minimum, 298, 303

Management science, 1
   methodology, 7
   process, 7
Marketing problems, 124
Mathematical models, 11
Mathematical programming, 2
Media selection problems, 124
Method of penalties, 153
Mixed integer problems, 228
Models:
   deterministic, 13
   stochastic, 13
   types of, 12
   use in decision making, 11
Modified distribution (MODI) method, 31
Multiple objectives, 280
Multiple optima, 58, 81, 209

Non-basic variables, 21
Non-binding constraints, 105
Non-linear constraints, 295
Non-linear function, linear approximation of, 315
Non-linear objective functions, 295
Non-linear optimization:
   constrained, 306
   Kuhn–Tucker conditions, 308
   Lagrange multipliers and, 306
   quadratic programming and, 312
Non-negativity constraints, 20

Objective function, 20
Occupied cells, 23
Operational research, 1
Opportunity costs:
   in assignment, 75
   in the dual, 203
   in LP, 107
   in transportation, 32

Optimality conditions in non-linear programming, 308
Order scheduling problems, 341

Partial derivatives, 304
Partial solutions, 270
Penalty values, 54
Piecewise linear approximation, 316
Pivot column, 150
Pivot element, 150
Pivot row, 150
Portfolio management problems, 128
Primal dual relationships, 200
Primal problem, 197
Production scheduling problems, 116
Prohibited and priority assignments, 83
Prohibited and priority routes, 53

Resource allocation problems, 116

Saddle point, 306
Sensitivity analysis:
   assignment and, 85
   graphical, 108
   Lagrange multipliers and, 306
   linear programming and, 168
   Simplex based, 168
   transportation and, 58
Separable functions, 320
Separable programming, 320
Shadow price, 196
Shortest route problems, 324
Simplex:
   formulation, 139
   method, 138
   method for goal programming, 288
   sensitivity analysis, 168
   tableau, 141
Slack variables, 139
Soft constraints, 281
State free problems, 338
Stepping stone method, 24
Stochastic models, 13, 343
Surplus variables, 151

Targets, 283
Threshold constraints, 232
Transportation problems:
   application of, 38
   balanced vs unbalanced, 43
   solution methods for, 24, 31
Tree search algorithms, 250
Two-phase method, 158

Unbalanced problems, transportation and, 43
Unbounded problems, 204
Unequal assignments, 81

Variables;
   artificial, 152
   basic, 21, 140
   binary, 226
   decision, 115
   deviational, 281
   dual, 200
   free, 267
   non-basic, 21
   slack, 139
   surplus, 151

Zero one variables, 226